THE COMPLEAT COPYWRITER

THE
COMPLEAT
COPYWRITER

A Comprehensive Guide to All Phases
of Advertising Communication

HANLEY NORINS

Vice President and Associate Creative Director
Young & Rubicam, Inc.

ROBERT E. KRIEGER PUBLISHING COMPANY
MALABAR, FLORIDA

Original Edition 1966
Reprint Edition 1980

Printed and Published by
ROBERT E. KRIEGER PUBLISHING COMPANY, INC.
KRIEGER DRIVE
MALABAR, FLORIDA 32950

Library of Congress Cataloging in Publication Data

Norins, Hanley.
    The compleat copywriter.

    Reprint of the edition published by McGraw-Hill, New York, in series: McGraw-Hill series in marketing and advertising.
    Bibliography: p.
    Includes index.
    1. Advertising copy.   I. Title.
[HF5825.N65 1980]   659.13'22   79-27107
ISBN 0-89874-117-3

To Marcy and Wendy, with love

PREFACE

This is a book of, by, and for copywriters—and for all those who have to deal with them.

Of course, I hope outsiders, especially college students who are interested in advertising, will also read these pages. They may discover why copywriting is such a fever in the blood—why it is so exciting that many of us can hardly wait to get to work in the morning.

When I started to write *The Compleat Copywriter,* I sent questionnaires to hundreds of professionals. I asked them, among other things, "What, specifically, would you like this book to accomplish?"

Almost to a man, the people inside advertising replied: "Let it be natural. Let it tell what copywriting is *really* like."

Here are two typical comments:

> The racks are full of advertising books by people who "remember when," and by people who want advertising to be an exact science. It would be refreshing to see a book that makes the business come alive. . . .

> The advertising books I have read don't really give any idea of what it is like to think of an idea, execute it, revise it, sell it, revise it again, produce it, and live with it. Each problem in advertising is unique, yet these books always try to make rules.

Well, *The Compleat Copywriter* is certainly not a rule book. It does reveal a lot of the methods I have learned in almost thirty years of writing and supervising copy. But above all, it tries, like a law casebook, to inspire by example, and to cultivate an *attitude* for writing copy of every kind.

What should this attitude be? It is impossible to sum it up in a few phrases. But as you read this book, you will begin to experience it. You will read about the attitudes of many people who are unknown to the public but who have written copy worth millions of dollars which has been read by millions of people. You will see how difficult copywriting can be, but how enjoyable too. If you are a newcomer, I hope you will come away with a healthy respect for this exacting craft. If you are already a seasoned copywriter, I hope you will gain some new insights.

Of course, *The Compleat Copywriter* can never be complete. First, because it covers too many phases for me to do justice to them all. And second, because advertising is the fastest-changing business there is. *Time* magazine called advertising "The Mammoth Mirror," and you know how fast the world it reflects is changing.

To me, that very change is what makes copywriting so fascinating. I am filled with awe and wonder at this dynamic era. None of that nostalgia for the good old days for me! I love change; and, as you will read in these pages, there could be no better attitude for a copywriter.

You will find a long list of acknowledgments at the end of the book. The list includes many of today's best and most successful creative people in advertising. Together, they form a kind of composite picture of the "compleat copywriter." With their help, I have tried to answer even the tallest order I received from my questionnaires. Here is what that request asked me to tell my readers about copywriting:

"Tell them the who, what, why, when, where, and, above all, the how of copywriting . . . and convince them that it is a proud and skillful and rewarding and enjoyable and demanding and an honorable profession."

Hanley Norins

CONTENTS

ix

PART **3**

The Future Campaign

Part 1

THE MESSAGE

1

THE COPYWRITER—
WHAT, WHO, HOW, AND WHY

What Is a Copywriter?

Was there ever a more crazy, mixed-up character to define?

The copywriter—to paraphrase Dickens in *A Tale of Two Cities*—is the best of writers, he is the worst of writers, he is a practical businessman, he is a temperamental artist, he is the bearer of benefits, he is the apostle of greed, he is an inspired craftsman, he's a frustrated hack.

Why all those contradictions?

Because the type of person the copywriter is depends on the situation.

It depends on whether he has written an ad like "The Penalty of Leadership" or "Spit is a Horrid Word."

It depends on whether his client is like H. F. Dunning, president of Scott Paper, who believes in selling products on quality and value "instead of trying to buy the customer's affection with gimmicks," or whether he is like the maker of Hadacol, who was merely after the fast buck.

It depends on whether the copywriter's bosses are sensitive to the way good copy is created—whether they provide an atmosphere where his ideas will thrive and encourage the irrational flights that precede pragmatic judgments.

But, most of all, it depends on the copywriter's own state of mind—his *weltanschauung.* Every time he goes digging for facts, every time his mind starts percolating with ideas, every time he sits down to the typewriter, every time he presents an idea to the people he works with or to his client, what he is and does depends on the sum total of his *attitude.*

Oscar Hammerstein II, writing about his craft, said, "This is the secret of the well-integrated musical play. It is not so much a method as a state of mind."

Here, then, is where we can find the clue to the best definition for a copywriter: by agreeing on the best state of mind he can have whenever he approaches *any* problem.

Let us see if we *can* agree.

How about the attitude that he is going to "sell" somebody something? For years now, advertising has been defined as "salesmanship in print." That thought is supposed to have been a revelation to advertising pioneer Albert D. Lasker when he had his famous meeting with copywriter John E. Kennedy in a Chicago saloon.

But the simple desire to sell is not the best definition when you consider all it leaves out. Of course the copywriter is a salesman. But what does that definition tell you about style and syntax? about his ability to visualize? about feeling for color, form, and balance? about the poetic imagination that can come up with a catchphrase that may motivate millions? What does it tell you about a good copywriter's ability to collaborate with artists, musicians, actors, and other creative people? Does it tell you that he and his collaborators during their careers may call on every kind of talent— talents far beyond the scope of a salesman?

Finally, does the definition "salesmanship in print," give you any advance confidence that the copywriter's work will be successful? Quite the contrary. That precise approach in the past created such semantic abortions as the school of "the hard sell," "legal puffery," and what George Gribbin, of the Young & Rubicam advertising agency, has called "hermaphroditic copy" (the kind that shouts so loudly that it creates the headache its product is designed to relieve). Today, we have to be more considerate of our audience or we will lose it.

How about defining the copywriter as a "persuader"? That seems reasonable enough when you consider the nature of his work. Nicholas Samstag made a distinction by entitling his book about our profession *Persuasion for Profit.* But don't most people anticipate some kind of profit if they want to win someone to their view? As the word "salesman" is too limiting, the word "persuader" is too broad.

For our part, after years and years of coping with this contradictory profession, the most useful attitude we have discovered is to feel that we are trying to "communicate" something to someone. *Really* to communicate, in the best sense of the dictionary definitions—"to give to someone as a partaker," "to impart knowledge," "to have interchange of thoughts," and "to have or form a connecting passage." (*The American College Dictionary*, Clarence L. Barnhart, ed.)

So the copywriter is a *communicator*.

Let us think of that definition in terms of how much easier it makes our job, and how much more successful we will be if we live by it. People don't *want* to be sold. They don't *want* to be persuaded. But they *do* want to have knowledge imparted to them, they *do* want to have an interchange of thoughts, they *do* want to make a connection.

Consider, also, how operational the definition "communicator" is when you use it to assess copy. If you ask "Will it sell? Will it persuade?" heaven only knows the answer. But if you ask "Does it tell people something they didn't know before?" it's easy to discover the answer. Suppose you have written an informative piece of copy and some client or colleague asks you to add "more urge to buy," or "more hard-selling copy." When you ask for specific information, he says, "We've got to make a stronger claim—try 'up to 45 percent better'; the words 'up to' give us a legal weasel." If, as we have assumed, the copy you have already written does communicate, then the addition of that so-called hard-selling copy could actually turn off the interchange. Weasel words might sound good to the seller, but they would not communicate to the buyer—because they would not be imparting knowledge.

Another beautiful quality of the term "communicator" is that it is open-ended. It encourages us to consider all forms of expression which might make a connection. One communicates with words, yes. But what about a look? a lift of an eyebrow? an intonation? a color? a shape? a mood? a certain smile? When he proudly wears this definition, the copywriter can, like Walt Whitman, "invite his soul."

Of course, there are lots and lots of communicators. The word applies to authors, playwrights, preachers, teachers, politicians, and to all of us who want to get along with our fellowmen. But when you stop to think of it, a copywriter can lay claim to the name "communicator" more intimately than any other person we know—and for three sound reasons.

Why Is the Copywriter the Communicator?

The first reason is that the copywriter has the toughest job of all communicators, bar none. Even outsiders, and detractors, are beginning to acknowledge this fact. "The advertisement," wrote Aldous Huxley, "is one of the most interesting and difficult of modern literary forms." Said etymologist Bergen Evans, "Next to poetry, the language is being used most intensely in advertising."

Our only quarrel with these authorities is that they did not go all the way and admit that copywriting is *the* most difficult and intense form of writing. Former copy chief Charles L. Whittier, in his book *Creative Advertising,* elaborated in this way:

> An author can specialize in one kind of writing—"whodunits," novels, short stories, or articles. A poet can restrict his writing to thoughts that both burn and scan. A playwright can concern himself exclusively with plot, execution, business, and dialogue. A newspaper reporter fulfills his responsibility by writing, in as interesting a way as possible, facts divorced from interpretation or opinion. But a top-level advertising writer must combine to a professional degree all of these abilities.

And even that is not all the difficulty. The copywriter has to communicate within tight restrictions of space and time. Playwrights have hours in which to present their story; novelists have many pages. Even a short story is a luxury compared with the abbreviated form of most ads, commercials, and billboards.

Difficulty enough? There is still more—the greatest burden of all: The copywriter seldom has a *voluntary* listener. The poet has his own devoted audience, though it may be a small one. The person who buys or borrows a book wants voluntarily to read it, even though he may find the going dull or difficult. Movie fans and playgoers are not captive audiences—they are in the mood to be captivated. The newspaper reporter has plenty of buying readers.

Let us go a step farther, to other forms of communication. The patient who asks the doctor for advice is all ears. The ambitious college student strains to be attentive to the professor. Even the politician, at election time, has an interested claque.

But the poor copywriter has not one single soul who, voluntarily and purposefully searches for his message. Of course, if someone who happens to be in the market to buy a car or a refrigerator comes across a magazine ad which catches his fancy, then he will voluntarily *become* an audience. But it never starts that way. The reader buys a magazine for the editorial content, the TV viewer tunes in for the programs. Unlike all other forms of communication, advertising has no ready-made audience.

Why *don't* we have a ready-made audience? Why don't people seek our expressions as they do those of other communicators? Perhaps it is because we have *not* defined ourselves as communicators. Perhaps they expect us to protest too much, because we *have* been only salesmen and persuaders. When the copywriter gets in the habit of trying to push people into buying a product or service, he adopts a kind of truculent attitude even though he may not be aware of it. What else do the phrases "urge to buy" and "call for action"—so popular in books on copywriting—imply? Maybe people expect us to grab their lapels and to try to *force* them to listen. So they get their backs up, they tune out their ears when the commercial comes on. Can we have been the sowers of our own discontent? Have we become frozen into the habit of the wrong state of mind?

Whatever the reasons, the copywriter has no voluntary audience. In fact, he usually faces an adversary whose attitude ranges from indifference to outright hostility. No wonder, more than anyone else, the copywriter has to be a communicator, with all that the word implies, to break through the mind barrier.

We said that there are three sound reasons why we have a special claim on the word communicator. The second reason is that we communicate on so many different levels, beyond the physical act of pounding a typewriter. The process of writing an ad or commercial takes only a small part of our time. The rest we spend communicating with many other people behind the scenes.

Take, for example, the sources the copywriter consults to learn the facts about the product, its competitors, and its consumers. Some copywriters receive their knowledge of a product secondhand. But to collect all the information they would like to have, copywriters communicate with development engineers, sales managers, advertising directors and their staffs. Each is a different audience, for each has his own job-oriented point of view.

Of course, those are just a few of the sources. Depending on the nature of the product or service, there is no end to the different kinds of audiences. The copywriter might communicate with doctors as he studies a drug product or with lawyers to solve the mysteries of Federal Trade Commission regulations. He might even consult an Indian chief (as in the case of an Ethyl *Magic Circle* ad about travel to an Indian reservation).

Doctor, lawyer, Indian chief—in each case, in order to communicate clearly, to make a connection, the copywriter has to know how to listen, question, and reply. He has to put himself in the other fellow's shoes. The better communicator he is in these areas, the more information he can draw on when he starts to conceive the ad.

But there are still more levels. One of the most important is communication with our co-workers. It is surprising how few textbooks on advertising discuss the technique of collaboration. A budding Thomas Wolfe needs only a typewriter or a pad and pencil before his words go to press. But the production of advertising is a complex cooperative enterprise. To be a successful copywriter, you have to be an entrepreneur too.

Consider the copywriter in the advertising agency. He is in constant touch with researchers, media, merchandising and account men—all working together for the fullest knowledge of the product, its purposes, and its market. In conceiving the message, he is in close contact with other creative specialists. In the case of a TV commercial, for example, he may be involved with as diverse people as the art director, producer, casting director, stylist, composer, lighting director, and the film editor, to name just a few. With all of this "audience," the copywriter has to communicate effectively if they are all going to contribute to the commercial and to make it a unified success.

The third reason why we feel that the copywriter should have a high priority claim on the title communicator is that his work is so thoroughly "experted." Not only does he have a difficult task of communicating, but he is heavily obliged to get results. Somebody is paying for the ad or commercial and wants assurance that it will be profitable. Often the investment in a copywriter's words makes them actually golden. For example, producing and broadcasting one sixty-second TV commercial can cost, at present, $50,000 or $60,000. Producing and placing a year's advertising campaign may cost $5 or $10 million. How can all the people involved feel confident that this expensive communication will prove profitable?

Here is where the most subtle, complex, and often frustrating communication comes into play. The agency copywriter has to make a connection with members of his product group, with people in the client's organization, with the researchers involved in pretesting the copy. What are the goals? Will the ideas and execution accomplish the goals? Many of these people have keen and inquiring minds. Each brings to this communication the training, needs, and value judgments of his own job. How can the copywriter communicate his way through *this* audience so the result will not be a hodgepodge and so the ad will be simple and meaningful to the consumer?

After the fact, after the ad has been written, the copywriter's work is judged by the hard demands of performance. The retail copywriter has to answer to the sales audit. The effectiveness of the mail-order writer is measured by coupon returns. Armies of learned researchers and audience juries keep tabs on the advertising agency writer. Was ever an author, poet, or reporter so rigidly required to get results?

For all these reasons, then, the copywriter is a *communicator*. This is our definition, our judge, counselor, and guide.

Who Is the Copywriter?

Claude Hopkins, one of the most famous copywriters, started to work as a country-school teacher.

John E. Kennedy began as a Royal Canadian Mountie.

J. K. Fraser, who conceived that frivolous advertising campaign, "Sapolio Town," studied to be an engineer.

Charley Feldman, who wrote one of the all-time great "house" ads (the Backbone ad for Young & Rubicam), first worked as a window trimmer.

David Ogilvy, in his book *Confessions of an Advertising Man,* tells how he spent 17 uncertain years as a chef, a door-to-door salesman, a social worker, and a research assistant to Dr. George H. Gallup, before he turned to copy.

What kind of education should copywriters have?

Successful copywriters have come to the industry after specializing in the social sciences, humanities, the liberal arts, journalism, marketing, and languages. But, as David McCall pointed out in a *Printers' Ink* article, many of the century's top advertising men never completed a formal education at all. He listed, among the dropouts from college, James Webb Young, Ray Rubicam, Rosser Reeves, Sid Ward, and Roy Whittier.

What about temperament? Will you be a better copywriter if you are neurotic or if you are well-balanced? David Ogilvy says that to accumulate a group of creative people, you need "a fairly high percentage of high-strung, brilliant, eccentric nonconformists." Agreed. But if you are not high-strung or eccentric, do not fear that you will be a failure. Top copywriter Norm Robbins is an island of calm; Stan Jones was the mildest of wordsmiths.

Who, then, is the copywriter? Can we find any generalities by which to identify him? Copy chiefs who have had long experience in interviewing, hiring, and training copywriters agree that they do have certain points of view in common. So we get back to the same method of identifying the copywriter as we used in defining him. He is a person who, through temperament, training, aptitude, and what have you, has a certain group of attitudes. For our purposes, we have summarized them into five qualities. There may be more; but we can promise that if you do not have these five qualities, in good measure, you cannot be the ideal copywriter.

The first quality is *curiosity.* Semanticist S. I. Hayakawa calls an idea "the verbalization of a cerebral itch." Copywriters are the itchiest people. The word "dilettante" is commonly used in a critical sense to describe someone who dips into too many subjects superficially. But just as the ideal copywriter should be diligent in his own field, he should be a supreme dilettante in all others.

This quality of curiosity, which the best copywriters have in common, is more than a coincidence. The wider ranging their interests, the more and better tools they have. This is because—as we shall discuss in Chap. 7 —the copywriter is forever dipping back into his past and finding new ways to connect old facts and happenings. "We think with our experience," writes Rudolph Flesch in *The Art Of Clear Thinking.* Insight, he stresses, is more than a blind flash of inspiration, and he reminds us of William James's famous comment, "A polyp would be a conceptual thinker if a feeling of 'Hollo! thingumbob again!' ever flitted through his mind."

How does the copywriter conceive ads like "To Peggy—for marrying me in the first place," ideas like the man in the Hathaway shirt, demonstrations like lifting a boiling egg with a sticky bandage? These all come from a creative mind connecting thingumbobs. So the more thingumbobs a copywriter has stored up in his mind, the more thoughts he will have to associate.

One of the pleasures of having such curiosity is that it gives you so much to do you can never be bored. When copy chief Sid Ward retired from the advertising agency business, one of his closest friends was asked, "What will Sid do? Won't he be restless?"

"You don't know Sid Ward," the friend replied. "He can make a day's adventure out of a walk to the rural post office an acre away. He'll examine every leaf of grass, listen to every bird. He'll find a lifetime of things to do in that one brief walk."

The second quality, a close corollary of the first, is *imagination.* "The basic characteristic of the creative mind," said agency head Earnest Elmo Calkins, "is one that is always open to inspiration."

"Open" is the key word in that statement. The copywriter tends to be more childlike, his mind like a clean slate, always ready to be written upon. He has a metaphorical bent, a talent for association—a mind that is forever seeing camels in clouds and "heaven in a grain of sand."

An article in the magazine *Changing Times* tells how to recognize a creative youngster: "Ordinary people trust hard facts; creative types are intuitive—they look beyond facts to what *might be.*" So it is with the copywriter. He lives in the world of "might be." A course for businessmen is not a dull chore to him; it is "a wonderful two years' trip at full pay." A cardiogram is not a technical chart; it is "a telegram from your heart." A car that is rejected from an assembly line is not just an example of quality control; it is "a lemon."

This writer, in his early youth, became fascinated with the concept of the macrocosm and the microcosm—the idea that the largest world, and the smallest world, and everything in between, are somehow interconnected. Such a belief can be the catalyst of imagination.

The third of the ideal copywriter's qualities is *empathy.* For those who work on national accounts, advertising to millions, empathy has to be all-embracing. Hopkins had it, in generous measure, but only for those he called the common people. He felt that he would fail if he tried to advertise for the Rolls-Royce, Tiffany, or Steinway pianos. "Those common people whom I know so well," he said, "became my future customers. When I talk to them, in print or in person, they recognize me as one of their kind."

Times have changed, and there are increasingly more sophisticated and better-educated consumers. Products, appeals, and audiences vary. But the copywriter, ideally, should empathize with everyone.

This is one of the hardest qualities to have and to cultivate. Many copywriters have curiosity and imagination, yet cannot sufficiently divorce *themselves* from the communication.

Former copy supervisor, Harry Hartwick, expressed this problem bluntly:

> Most copy is written in offices, by people (usually very young) who have no real picture or understanding of the people they are writing for. We talk a lot about getting out and studying the audience, but few of us ever do. So we sit in the office, surrounded only by people like ourselves, witty, sophisticated, educated. Human beings being what they are, I don't suppose there will ever be a cure for this. Copywriters are not going out into the field, are not going to think about who their audience is. They're going to sit at their typewriters and say, "What would be a clever way to do this?" They don't know the ugly houses in Gary, Indiana, the way the man on the street looks and talks in South Chicago, what problems the person has who sits down in front of a TV set in Keokuk, Iowa. The copywriter writes as though he has a captive audience, who will listen to every word. He doesn't stop to realize that people are walking around while half-listening, or busy with problems of their own, like the kids failing in school, the payments due on the furniture. The good copywriter has to have empathy; he has to imagine not only how the stuff is going to look going out over the TV, but how it will be received.

Hartwick paints a harsh picture of the average copywriter. But we are talking about the ideal example, and *he* is loaded with empathy for the whole family of man.

The fourth quality is *enthusiasm*—a high-keyed, almost tangible feeling that a good copywriter transmits. As Alex F. Osborn has pointed out in his book *Applied Imagination,* the generation of ideas often requires our enthusiasm to become almost irrational—"at least until verification shows that we have misfired." Judicial thinking, he says, is mostly negative. But the process of getting ideas calls for a positive attitude. "We have to be hopeful. We need enthusiasm. We have to encourage ourselves to the point of self-confidence. We have to beware of perfectionism lest it be abortive."

The word "enthusiasm" derives from the Greek *enthousiasmos,* and that started with the word *entheos,* literally meaning "full of the god," or inspired and possessed. This kind of absorption is a practical tool for the copywriter's craft. His god of the moment is the subject that absorbs him. It carries him along on a wave, pushes him so intensely into solving the problem that he has no time or inclination for negative thoughts that discourage free association. The wholehearted enthusiast can "stay loose." And it is in the nonstop, free-associative atmosphere that he gets his best ideas.

But enthusiasm has its usefulness, too, on all those other levels of communication we described. In fact-finding and collaboration, a copywriter's enthusiasm can be contagious and can work like a physical force.

Finally, in the finished product, the ad or commercial, the audience can feel enthusiasm the way they feel empathy. Words written in a white heat are often read with a warm glow. Honest enthusiasm—"corny," if you will —can make a connection far better than the most calculated, formulized "Now! New! Hurry-while-the-supply-lasts" kind of "action copy."

The fifth quality we have left for the last because it is the one that takes the longest to cultivate. It grows with the copywriter as he matures. This is *flexibility*. It is not to be mistaken for cowardice or compromise. It is not being indecisive but open-minded.

The problem of copy by committee is a very real one these days. The compleat copywriter is one who will fight for his convictions, if he is sure they are sound, and will know how to handle people so they will buy his convictions without constant hard feelings.

But the compleat copywriter also has the humility to be flexible. He is flexible in the true spirit of the scientist. "What we need," writes Rudolph Flesch, "is an attitude of distrust toward our own ideas. This is the scientific habit of thought: as soon as you have an idea, try to disprove it."

As we shall discuss in Chap. 7, the process of getting ideas takes two forms—first, completely uninhibited inspiration; second, the most objective evaluation. It is in this second stage that the ideal copywriter will be sweetly reasonable.

"Have convictions," says agency account supervisor Dave Cleary, "but don't be rigid. The wings on airplanes are built to 'give' so they won't snap. Copywriters, too, are supposed to be able to move successfully through a lot of turbulence."

These, then, are the five qualities—avid curiosity, vivid imagination, warm empathy, keen enthusiasm, and modest flexibility. A tall order for a paragon of people. But, mind you, we are talking about the compleat copywriter; and the more he has of these qualities, the more easily you can recognize him—as a successful communicator and a *most happy fella* to boot!

What Does the Copywriter Do?

We have already given you some inkling of what a copywriter does. He digs for facts, he works with his co-workers, he communicates about his communication, and finally he produces an advertisement.

But this book is called *The Compleat Copywriter* and there are many different kinds of copywriters and products. There are specialists in media —print copywriters, sales promotion writers, TV commercial writers, industrial copywriters, mail-order writers, and direct-mail specialists.

There are even specialists in particular products and services. Look through the classified sections in the newspapers and you will often see ads for "food copywriters," "copywriters with packaged goods experience," "automotive copywriters," etc.

Depending on the product and medium, the copywriter's work may vary greatly. A sales promotion writer may spend more time with premium and contest ideas than with the actual execution of an ad. A food copywriter may be her own home economist and do endless experiments over a hot stove. An industrial copywriter is often like an interpreter of a foreign language—translating technical material into imaginative ideas.

A television copywriter may do much of his "writing" over a Movieola, with a film editor, piecing together footage into the most effective continuity.

A mail-order copywriter may spend hours debating the reasons why one split-run headline outpulled another.

However specialized they are, all copywriters have certain problems and assignments in common. They all have to communicate information about products and services, hoping to interest and to influence their audience.

If the product is completely new, fills a need, has no competition, and requires repeat usage, the copywriter's job is easy; in fact, it could, in such a remote likelihood, be dispensed with completely. To the degree that the product has competition which is similarly priced, available, and desirable—to that degree is the copywriter's job more difficult and his ingenuity more taxed.

This latter case is the most common these days. As manufacturing and distribution methods become more efficient, the differences between competing products become less apparent. The copywriter's job gets harder and harder. If two products are alike, how can he make one more enticing? By dealing, as Hayakawa calls them, with "deceptive differentials"? This, though it may be done every day, is unethical and, in some cases, illegal. By writing positively about *his* product, without mentioning the competitors, but doing so more provocatively than *their* copywriters do? This is one way to freedom, success, and a clear conscience.

What else does the copywriter do?

Good advertising is measured by one agency in the following way: It has to reach the greatest possible number of prospects at the lowest possible cost with the best possible selling message. The key word in that definition is "reach." The advertiser and the copywriter have to select the best prospects and reach them with their message.

For example, if the product were a new golf club, the media selection might well be a sports magazine read by golfers. This would be a way of exposing a message to a selective audience. But the message would not necessarily *reach* them, since they might not be interested enough to read it. Therefore, the copywriter must find the most interesting information to impart, and he must present it in the most forceful manner. Suppose he is able to tell his readers that the new golf club will cut strokes from their game. (Isn't that the goal of every golfer?) If he says so in a provocative way, every one of his prospects may note and read the ad. Thus, he would be *reaching* the greatest number of prospects at the lowest possible cost.

On the other hand, if the copywriter's problem were to sell Life Savers, with no new story to tell and a mass market of every man, woman, and child, then his ingenuity is doubly taxed. He must simply communicate the fact that Life Savers are delicious and still cost only 5 cents. He must find a common denominator appealing to millions. The broader his audience and the more general his product appeal, the more the copywriter must use imagination to reach the greatest possible number of prospects at the lowest possible cost.

Generally speaking, as we have said, all copywriters try to communicate with people and to influence them. How do they do it?

How Does the Copywriter Communicate?

"The first rule for copywriters," says Dave Cleary, "is to be suspicious of rules. Rules have a way of turning into ruts."

This is why it is so difficult to write a book on copywriting and hope that it will be helpful. Of course, there are certain basics. Through the years, the rules in most textbooks have simply been paraphrases of one another.

Schwab says, "(1) Get attention. (2) Show people an advantage. (3) Prove it. (4) Persuade people to grasp this advantage. (5) Ask for Action."

Caples advises, "Give news, be specific, make your message clear, appeal to people's self-interest."

Whittier writes about "the five I's": (1) Idea. (2) Immediate Impact. (3) Incessant Interest. (4) Information. (5) Impulsion. He hastens to add that this test is only as useful as the judgment of the tester.

Finally, there is the copywriter's capsule course, "AIDA," which stands for Attention, Interest, Desire, and Action.

Most of these formulas were devised originally for print media, where there may be space and time for a headline to get attention and for body copy to hold the interest, arouse desire, and call for action. The principles can be good for all media, but there are cases, like billboards and short TV spots (I.D.'s), where these guides, simple as they are, are not followed. In fact, some of these basic rules have been broken with excellent effect. The salt ad "When it rains, it pours" did not call for action, yet somehow action was implicit in the claim. The clipper ship which adorned all Cutty Sark advertisements for years gave no information aside from a symbol of the name; yet sales for that Scotch kept growing steadily. "Modess because . . ." certainly attracted attention, but it broke every other rule in the book.

We can perhaps generalize that, for most successful communications, *clarity* and *interest* are vital ingredients. It is certainly imperative that the communicator be clear in his own mind what he wants to accomplish and that he himself should be interested in his subject.

"The communicator," said author Leo Rosten, "is the person who can make himself clear to himself first."

What is clarity?

"The degree to which there is communication," says Prof. Wendell Johnson, "depends precisely upon the degree to which the words represent the same thing for the receiver or reader that they do for the sender or writer. And the degree to which they do is an index of the clarity of the communication or written statement."

We will have something to say in Chap. 3 on how this statement applies to the Modess campaign. As Johnson points out, communication, in its most precise sense, is a two-way thing, a completed circuit. In a person-to-person situation, a customer can ask questions and a salesman can answer them. Together, they can reach an understanding. So it is an effective communication. Since the copywriter's audience is not present, he must play the role of both parties. True communication is a dialogue. You do not talk *at*, you communicate *with*. It does not matter that the copywriter does all the verbalizing. In his mind, the reader or viewer is filling in the rejoinders. If his audience can say, "that's bunk" or "it's unclear," the circuit is broken. If the audience can say, "I understand," "plausible," or "tell me more," the copywriter is on his way to a sale.

Interest is something else again. The copywriter communicates, not with an individual, but with a multitude. To seize and hold attention, he must interest his audience. But what might that interest be? Each individual in the audience is different. "Every man," says Johnson, "is his own most interested and affected listener." The copywriter must, in effect, speak with the voice and listen with the ear of his audience. He must be tuned to the vibrations of the multitude. He must find means of expression which are of common interest to all.

You may call this "mass psychology," "empathy," "para-psychology," but whatever it is, the copywriter must be born, trained, and dedicated to it.

What else does the competent copywriter do? In addition to his specialty, if he has one, in addition to attempting to meet some of the criteria above, here are just a few other considerations:

He seeks to involve his audience.

He strives for believability.

He inspires conviction.

He is aware of context.

He collects all the facts.

He conceives many ideas.

He selects the best idea and expresses it with the most appropriate technique.

He tries to communicate with "the whole man"—his five senses, his background, his experience.

He objectively assesses his work through constant copy research.

In the following pages, we shall try to present some of the aspects of this broad task in a tentative spirit of discussion, without hard-and-fast rules. The best way to learn is by doing. The most important asset for a copywriter is the desire to do. If these chapters can only help to provoke an attitude, a positive urge to be a good communicator, they will have accomplished their purpose.

Why Does He Do It?

Why, if the task is so difficult, does the copywriter do what he does?

Ask a number of copywriters and you will hear a number of answers, ranging from "the pay is good" to "I guess I'm a masochist." The pay *is* good. The few thousand American copywriters in advertising agencies now average $12 to $15 thousand a year salary. Some copywriters reach $50,000 and more.

But the main reason we do what we do is because we enjoy it. It is a tremendous challenge. Remember, we have said that the copywriter is the only communicator who has no voluntary audience. Imagine the reward to his ego, the feeling of satisfaction, when he does break through that wall of resistance!

Another attraction of copywriting is the opportunity to play. The word "play," in our Calvinistic heritage, may sound frivolous, but many respectable authorities have recognized its power. "Combinatory play," said Einstein, "seems to be the essential feature in productive thought." By combinatory play, he meant the playful combination of seemingly disconnected elements. This is one of the major clues to creativity and the theme of a relatively new science, synectics, on which we shall comment later.

This same kind of play was referred to by agency head Leo Burnett in a speech to a group of copywriters: "Creativity is the art of establishing new and meaningful relationships between previously unrelated things . . . which somehow present the product in a fresh new light."

The term "ad game" may be one of derision, but advertising is especially attractive to a creative person because it *is* so much like a game. You can recognize this atmosphere in the best ideas and copy. When copy "sings," you can tell that the writer has enjoyed himself.

We mentioned before how the copywriter can live, vicariously, in many different careers. Actually, this experience is not always vicarious. Some versatile copywriters, in the course of their activities, have been like Frank Demara, the great impostor, acting the roles of reporter, poet, lawyer, daredevil, scholar, traveler, scientist, artist. A few examples: Interviewing some of the foremost medical experts in the country for the carefully prepared and documented material that went into the health campaign for a life insurance company. Riding with stunt drivers to photograph tire demonstrations. Judging exotic recipes along with leading food editors. Traveling by plane, helicopter, submarine—every form of transportation in every part of the world—for "location shooting." Collaborating with stimulating "outside" artists, writers, photographers, and cinematographers. Working with talented and temperamental actors and movie stars. Delving into the intimate background and workings of all kinds of products and services—from the development and manufacture of automobiles and airplanes, to drugs, food, and finery.

The copywriter, with his inquiring mind and insatiable curiosity, can have access, during his career, to just about every field of modern progress. He can see the smoke and fire of the foundry and discover the mysteries of pure scientific research in the laboratory. Most important of all, he can go where the markets are and talk and live and experience the intensely interesting lives of other people.

The copywriter also does what he does because he enjoys the company he keeps. To him advertising people are stimulating to be with. Their conversation is never narrow, because they are the kind of people who have curiosity and broad interests. They are probably the least parochial of "ingroups." They are quick-witted and clever too, because their talents are perpetually honed by creative activity. When you have to spend most of your waking hours finding ways to break through human indifference and boredom, your mind becomes muscular and all your faculties more agile.

What's more, people in advertising are forever analyzing and coping with all kinds of consumers. So they are practiced in dealing with the motives and reactions of other human beings. It is hard to be a misanthrope and a successful copywriter too.

Here is another reason why the copywriter does what he does: all his creative activity, his knowledge of people, his active interest in the world around him—all these are intensified by an atmosphere of the most fierce competition. Advertising people are forever doing battle—battle for the understanding of the client, battle to win and keep an account, battle for the reader's attention, battle for the consumer's dollar.

The copywriter shares with his peers this high-pitched tension of daily war. They are all drawn together by the mutual bonds of combat. Certainly some become neurotic as a result. Most are more emotional, enthusiastic, and intense than people with more placid occupations. But it is these very qualities which make advertising people exciting to live and work with.

These are the many different reasons why the copywriter does what he does—why he is so dedicated to a profession which is often maligned and which is as demanding and rigorous as some stern, uncompromising sect. We have offered these reasons for the sake of those readers who may be outside the pale. But if you are a natural-born copywriter, you surely know why you do it. As Zero Mostel used to say—batting his eyes in a favorite comedy routine—"I'm doin' it 'cause I *wanna!*"

COMMUNICATION
AND OUR MASSIVE MISTAKE

Ady Ads

Advertising was born too old.

You can tell that someone is old—at least in spirit—when he talks in clichés. His mind has become structured. From the habit of saying and doing the same things, he has lost the ability to look at the world with the fresh viewpoint of youth.

William H. Whyte, Jr., in *Fortune* magazine, wrote about "The Language of Advertising." It is the language, he said, of " 'Quick, satisfying relief,' 'Yes!' 'No other,' 'Never before!' 'At last!' 'Rich, tangy, full-bodied, tree-fresh, firm-packed, sunshine-bright goodness'—a galaxy of superlatives and phrases so stylized that Americans know them by heart."

That article was written in September, 1952. Yet, more than a decade later we read the same fruity, overripe platitudes. An "amazing new" cold remedy promises "extra relief." A frozen juice is a "big flavor surprise." A cigarette offers "satisfying pleasure," while the pleasure you will get from a camera is "lasting." A remedy for psoriasis has the usual "fast-acting formula," a ham has "fabulous flavor." A beer "satisfies," a shampoo is "rich, instant-foaming," a soft drink is "fresh-tasting" and "thirst-quenching." And shaving accessories are "gifts for his majesty the American man" which offer "elegance in the royal manner."

19

Clichés are boring. When boredom begins, communication ceases. Yet we keep perpetuating this block to communication. Not just in words, but in pictures. Agency executive Sylvia Simmons demonstrates the sad situation by showing a montage of ads for cars, cigarettes, beer, cosmetics. The automobile ads run in schools: The "down at the dock" school, where all the cars are precisely planted beside yachts, launches, and oceangoing steamers. The "woodsy" school, where cars pose on the greensward, with woodeny models beside them. So it is with the other product categories. Beer ads run in shoals of toothy, ecstatic mannequins and addicts of outdoor sports. The cigarette ads look pretty much like the beer ads. Miss Simmons illustrates how the products' logotypes can be interchanged and be lost in the montage, so similar are the ads.

Why do we do it? What causes all our clichés? Carelessness. Laziness, of course. But the main reason why we perpetuate these platitudes in our copy, is that we think they work on their audience. When modern advertising got started, certain words and expressions seemed to be "trigger words." Textbooks, seeking to give aspiring copywriters easy formulas, invested the words "new," "improved," "now," "free," and so forth, with a magic all their own. They were supposed to arouse automatic reactions in that mass audience out there.

The trouble with our use of such words is that we mistake the shadow for the substance. The power was not in the adjectives but in what they modified. People responded to the word "new" because it was supposed to be connected with genuine news. To the extent that they found themselves cheated, to that degree did the word lose its effectiveness. Whyte says:

> Over the years a great number of the high-pulling headlines that made advertising history have contained the word "new." From this, many have deduced that the word "new" itself is a high-pulling word. . . . Is it? One of the reasons the great headlines scored was because they were advertising something that really was new. But the word "new" itself has little power independent of the context. When used to describe something not new or triflingly so—like a new picture on a cereal package—it has no punch; consistently, research has indicated that announcement type ads of the "new," or "revolutionary" kind trail the quieter merchandising ads in audience interest.

The same is true of the other clichés which have been endowed with magic power, including the typographic and illustrative ones. As Whyte points out:

> Those devices that stamp an ad as an ad—tint blocks, pyrotechnic changes of typeface, heavy areas of black ink—all tend to repel rather than command readership. The same is true of stereotyped illustrations.

As Gallup and Robinson have been demonstrating, the reader is so conditioned to seeing the bottle and glass in liquor ads, the pointing women in refrigerator ads, that brand identification is slight.

That "language of advertising" does *not* communicate. The reader is so conditioned that he is immune to it. All in all, Whyte found from the researchers that "ady" headlines were, in 1952, only 60 percent as effective as straight "consumer benefit" headlines. They, and all the other clichés of advertising, are probably far less effective today.

"Item by item," continues Whyte, "these testaments of consumer resistance are important enough, but it is only when we put them together that we begin to grasp their full implications. What they imply is nothing less than the falsity of one of the most prevalent concepts of American life: The Mass Audience."

The Massive Mistake of Appealing to "the Masses"

What is "the mass audience"? The social sciences, general semantics, and our own good sense should tell us that there is no such animal. Do you know any person who is the same as any other? Whose experience and perceptions are such that he will react to a given word or situation in precisely the same way as anyone else?

Would we treat anyone in person the way we treat him with our language of advertising? Would we run up to a friend and say *"Announcing a new, improved product that will give you quick, satisfying relief. Hurry! Try it now, while the supply lasts"*?

The language of advertising is especially decried by the experts in the meaning of language, including those familiar with the principles of general semantics. General semantics is concerned not just with words, but with all human symbolic functioning.

What is symbolic functioning? According to Professor of Anthropology Leslie A. White,

> The behavior of man is of two distinct kinds: symbolic and nonsymbolic. Man yawns, stretches, coughs, scratches himself, cries out in pain, shrinks with fear, bristles with anger, and so on. Nonsymbolic behavior of this sort is not peculiar to man; he shares it not only with other primates but with many other animal species as well. But man communicates with his fellows with articulate speech, uses amulets, confesses sins, makes laws, observes codes of etiquette, explains his dreams, classifies his relatives in designated categories, and so on. This behavior is unique; only man is capable of it; it is peculiar to man because it consists of, or is dependent on, the use of symbols.

Language, says White, only has significance because we arbitrarily say it has. "Let x equal 3 pounds of coal and it does equal 3 pounds of coal; let removal of the hat in a house of worship indicate respect and it becomes so. This creative faculty, that of freely, actively, and arbitrarily bestowing value upon things, is one of the most commonplace as well as *the* most important characteristic of man."

So here we are, we communicators, dealing with symbols arbitrarily imposed by men. It would be easy if everyone in our audience reacted to each symbol in the same way. But they don't. Each individual has his own collection of stuff. Without knowing each person intimately, it is impossible to predict precisely how he will react to the symbols we copywriters use. Semanticist S. I. Hayakawa writes:

> When we consider that each of us has different experience, different memories, different likes and dislikes, it is clear that all words evoke different responses in all of us. We may agree as to what the term "Mississippi River" stands for, but you and I recall different parts of the river; you and I have had different experiences with it; one of us has read more about it, while the other may recall chiefly tragic events connected with it. Hence your "Mississippi River" can never be identical with my "Mississippi River." The fact that we can communicate with each other about the "Mississippi River" often conceals the fact that we are talking about two different sets of memories and experiences.

We have said that the way to become a good communicator—i.e., copywriter—is to cultivate a certain state of mind. A vital part of that state of mind can be conditioned by the goal of general semantics: to be constantly *aware* of the differences in reactions to words and other forms of communication. If you are thus aware, you realize that we have been laboring under a massive mistake ever since advertising was born too old. "To transform millions of individuals into a mass," writes Prof. Martin Maloney of Northwestern University, "to endow them with group characteristics based on inferences or at best on a kind of group average, is to go beyond the scope of simple abstraction into the realm of fiction."

For years we copywriters have been dealing with just such fictions. We have been secure in the observation that certain words or symbols seemed to evince automatic responses from a great many people. Like witch doctors muttering incantations, we had only to say those words to win customers and influence people. This superstitious attitude has not taught us how to communicate. It has simply made us the victims of our own words.

"It is not the consumer who is in thrall," wrote Whyte in his searing article, "it is the manipulators—and to a great anonymous dope, the mathematical unit of the Mass Audience, who doesn't exist at all except in statistics."

The Many Moods of the Audience

Stuart Chase, in *The Tyranny of Words,* tells of an experiment in which twelve anonymous poems were sent to hundreds of students taking courses in literature at English and American colleges, with the request for detailed interpretations.

> One could not ask for a more somber example of communication failure. These students, presumably at the forefront of our cultural heritage, differed fantastically in their ideas of what the poems meant—as a whole, or phrase by phrase—and in their evaluations of them. The same poem was extravagantly praised and bitterly condemned. What confused the young people above all was that authors' *names* were omitted. How could they be expected to judge verse unless they knew who wrote it?

Advertising, which is written by anonymous authors and has no voluntary audience, is likely to receive even more contradictory interpretation —considering the prejudices as well as the varying backgrounds and personalities of the readers.

But the differences among readers are not the only confusing elements. Each individual is also reading at a quick moment in time, when his mood and circumstances will affect his reactions. What happened to him an instant, an hour, or a day before? What does he anticipate in the immediate or the far future? Every communication occurs in a constantly changing context. The semanticists are fond of quoting Heraclitus: "You can't step into the same river twice."

And that is not all the difficulty. We are trying to communicate not to a part of a person, but to all of him. "The act of perception is a whole act," writes Dr. J. Samuel Bois, Director of Education and Research at Viewpoints Institute, diagraming a *mental model.* "When you and I think, a great deal more than 'pure' thinking is going on within us and around us. Our past has much to do with our present thinking; our anticipated future influences it; our environment gives it a peculiar twist." When we communicate, we are trying to reach "the whole organism-in-a-particular-environment-at-a-particular-time."

This is one reason why we said in the preceding chapter that the copywriter is not just a writer. Too slavish an attention to words, in fact, can confuse the communication. Says John Blumenthal, a copy supervisor of the McCann-Erickson advertising agency:

> In the twelve years that I have been copywriting, mostly in television, I have been aware of the increasing *un*importance of words. When I first started, I would write the complete audio and then fill the video in. I would never leave it blank because I knew what I wanted the pictures to be like, but the video came second to me at that time. Today, the words

come second, if at all. I don't sit down and think of a visual sequence so much as I think about one single idea or impression.

One single idea or impression is another way of saying "concept," which means "a mental image of a thing formed by generalization from particulars." An idea, whether it is expressed by a painting that consists of pigment, color, and form, by a printed page that consists of type, words, and their arrangement, or by a film that consists of sound, color, and motion, is a generalization or composite. In the language of advertising, we are inclined to speak of "emotional copy" in contrast to rational or "reason-why copy." We categorize and analyze ads by components—large pictures versus small, long copy versus short, humorous versus serious, hard sell versus soft. But the audience is not so compartmentalized—one moment emotional, another rational. Nor do they break down the ads they read into components. Generally speaking, if they react, they react to our concepts.

Now then, if all people are different, and if they are unpredictably different in a given context and time, and if each person is many people in one, what kind of concepts can possibly communicate with all those individuals en masse?

Ways to Get Through

It is a bewildering situation, isn't it? The first natural reaction is to shrug our shoulders and to say, like the King of Siam, "Is a puzzlement."

But there *are* plenty of clues and precedents, and good communicators *are* connecting every day.

One way is to be intuitive and experienced enough to come up with common denominators. That is not to say common because they appeal to the least intelligence. You are not talking to a seven-year-old mentality when you keep your message simple. It makes sense to keep it simple, because advertisers are approaching an audience which is the most distracted and the least interested. And it makes sense to get down to basics which easily appeal to human beings. We all know what they are— interest in other people; desire to be loved, admired, and wanted; fear of ill health; fear of embarrassment; regard for the opposite sex, etc. Appeals to those emotions are perfectly reasonable, provided our appeals are based on genuine facts and rewards.

Common denominators have been used successfully with such headlines as:

DO YOU MAKE THESE MISTAKES IN ENGLISH?

HOW TO WIN FRIENDS AND INFLUENCE PEOPLE.

ALWAYS A BRIDESMAID, NEVER A BRIDE.

It is the appeal of that last headline which would strain credulity today and call down the wrath of the general semanticists. It is unlikely that it would prove operational. Though it might influence the naïve members of our audience, can we really promise marriage through the use of a bar of soap?

Another way to communicate with those many different individuals is to be specific. This guide, offered for years by the best textbooks and copy chiefs, is, in effect, the habit of deducing. The general semanticists use a method of "indexing" to remind us that "the word is not the thing," that we should try to differentiate as clearly as possible. Soap$_1$ is not soap$_2$; automobile$_1$ is not automobile$_2$; the tire which is designed to give you a soft ride is different from the tire designed for long wear; the advantages of synthetic fibers are different from those of natural wool. The more precise we are in our definition of a product, the more we can communicate to the individual, regardless of his collection of stuff. He can, if he wishes, verify and experience our statements. And, as we will discuss more fully in the next chapter, he can participate in the ad, drawing his own conclusions from our specific propositions.

This kind of specific writing is the opposite of the use of higher abstractions which are not referable to lower levels. Hayakawa points out that high-level abstractions have a bad reputation because they are so often used to confuse and befuddle people.

> A grab among competing powers for oil resources may be spoken of as "protecting the integrity of small nations." An unwillingness to pay social security taxes may be spoken of as "maintaining the system of free enterprise." Depriving the Negro of his vote in violation of the Constitution of the United States may be spoken of as "preserving states' rights." The consequence of this free, and often irresponsible, use of high-level abstractions in public controversy and special pleading is that a significant portion of the population has grown cynical about all abstractions.

Toward advertising, this cynicism is especially prevalent. Can we blame our audience when they are constantly exposed to such phrases? "For Those Who Prefer the Finest," says Quaker State Oil. "Only the Finest Is Stokely's Finest," says a food company. What is "the finest"? Is it verifiable? It would take a consumer a lifetime of carefully testing other products to "experience" those statements.

"Quality" is a favorite unspecific befuddler which has lost all meaning. Yet here are two car companies, in the same issue of a magazine, paying plenty of money to use these uncommunicative words: "Dad says don't settle for less than Quality Car Care at Ford Motor Company Dealers." "You Start with Quality! Stay with It! See your GM Dealer for the best kind of service."

The use of "borrowed interest" metaphors is a common way to say nothing expensively. "Working Partner!" is the headline for a picture of two baseball players completing a play. "You get him with Hyatt (roller bearings)" reads the subhead. A bank which promises to do a little *more* for you illustrates the point with a picture of an executive, his head protruding through a carnival target, as baseballs are thrown at him. "Like Sticking Our Neck Out," reads the copy, "to help you zero-in on your financial targets."

How unspecific, how vague can you be?

"Find the referent," wrote Rudolf Flesch many years ago. And he condemned advertising which could not answer his two cliché-deflating challenges: "Specify" and "So what?"

> "So what?" ads are perhaps more common than "Specify" ads. Advertisers love the supposed appeal of prestige, so we are told day in day out who uses what. Rita Hayworth uses Pan-Stik (So what?), Ava Gardner uses Lux (So what?), the Countess of Carnarvon uses Angel Face Make-Up (So what?), and Mrs. John A. Roosevelt, Mrs. George Jay Gould, Jr., Lady Bridgett Poulett, the Duchess de Richelieu, Miss Nancy duPont, and Mrs. Francis Grover Cleveland all use Pond's (So what?).
>
> "Specify" ads are all those that refer in general terms to the qualities or indirect effects of a product. Advertisers, for example, never specify why you should drink one whiskey rather than another. One is "America's mildest," another is "gentle in taste," a third has "good taste through the years," a fourth is "of the very finest flavor and quality," a fifth is "perfection in every glass," a sixth "has no substitute."

In contrast with the vague ads, here are some examples of headlines for General Electric products which do specify and therefore can communicate to many individuals, regardless of their differences:

> NOW GENERAL ELECTRIC REFRIGERATORS HAVE A ROLL-OUT FREEZER.
>
> GENERAL ELECTRIC'S TOAST-R-OVEN LETS YOU TOAST *OR* BAKE. (TOASTS THICK OR THIN SLICES: HANDLES BAKING JOBS, TOO).
>
> NEW 11" PERSONAL PORTABLE (TV SET) WEIGHS 12 LBS., COSTS $99.95.

Whether you find those three headlines aesthetically pleasing or not, they communicate because they are specific. They provide facts concrete enough to be verified, if someone wanted to take the trouble. And, incidentally, according to Starch scores of noting and reading, all three outpulled most of the competing ads in the magazines in which they appeared.

Finally, a way to communicate with individuals en masse is to be *inter-*

esting. This means to be original, and we come back to our statement at the beginning of this chapter—that clichés create boredom and block communication. Will a Camel smoker who is happy with his brand of cigarette really be *interested* in a message that tells him "Viceroy's got the taste that's right"? Will a Seagram's VO7 drinker, who's already quite sure about his choice of brands, be motivated by "Schenley . . . the life of your party"? Certainly we can tell them something more interesting than those flat promises.

"But," says the contentious copywriter, "almost any slogan, given enough repetition, is bound to get through."

Of course. But even George Washington Hill, the cigarette baron at whose door were laid many of the ills of advertising, began with a slogan which had a "twist," something different about it—enough to be interesting. Such slogans as "Nature in the raw is seldom mild" and "So round, so firm, so fully packed—so free and easy on the draw."

We copywriters should condition ourselves to be interesting. One way is to expose ourselves to interesting people, knowledge, and events. Creative director Dick Lord, of Warwick and Legler agency, gives this bibliography for copywriters:

1. Read Shakespeare—because he shows how effective language can be.
2. Read Hemingway—because he shows how simple it can be.
3. Read Strunk and White's *The Elements of Style*—because they show you the correct bricks with which to build.
4. Read magazines—because you should see what other ads look like and should know their environment.
5. See television, for the same reason.
6. See movies—because you can see what cameras can do.
7. Music—listen to all kinds.
8. Read poetry—because you can see what huge images and feelings can be expressed with very few words.
9. Go out and listen to people talk—eavesdrop, because this will give you an ear for dialogue and your writing won't sound artificial.
10. Live—do things, become involved in your world. The people you are writing to are a part of all that world.

Becoming an interesting person helps and finding something interesting about a product is crucial. Agency creative chief Charley Feldman says, "There are no dull ideas: there are only dull copywriters." The best copywriters know that every product is unique. There is a fallacious idea that certain classes of products do not have real differences—products like beer, cigarettes, and detergents.

This is not necessarily so. Olympia beer had a real difference in its water; Kent cigarettes were established by demonstration of their micro-nite filter; Cheer detergent had a blue-white fluorescer while its leading competitor had a yellow-white cast.

The most fascinating endeavor in the whole advertising activity is to find in each product that mysterious characteristic which sets it apart. Leo Burnett, head of the agency which bears his name, told how he learned a lesson from de Maupassant, describing his literary training under Flaubert in 1875:

> Talent is a matter of considering long and attentively what you want to express, so that you may discover an aspect of it that has never before been noticed or reported. Even the slightest thing contains a little that is unknown. We must find it. To describe a blazing fire or a tree in a plain, we must remain before that fire or that tree until they no longer resemble for us any other tree or any other fire.
>
> That is the way to become original.
>
> After repeating over and over again this truth, that there are not in the entire world two grains of sand, two flies, two hands or two noses that are absolutely the same, he (Flaubert) made me describe, in a few sentences, a being or an object in such a way as to particularize it clearly, to distinguish it from all the other beings or all the other objects of the same race or kind.

Why is originality so *interesting?* Perhaps the best way to understand that is to consider the world of an infant, which is completely original.

A baby, as anyone who is a parent or has read Gesell would agree, is the world's most interested person. Everything attracts his attention because to him everything is new.

It is when he acquires knowledge that the baby, in a manner of speaking, becomes less "interested." Knowledge takes the edge off his keen, pure, absolute interest. "The specialized semantics of established knowledge," says William J. J. Gordon, author of *Synectics,* "constitutes convention which make reality abstract and secondhand." The baby lives in the world of the firsthand—of the particular rather than the abstract. His is the real world, before parents and teachers have assigned labels and symbols to it.

This is why the baby is so interested. Everything he sees, hears, smells, feels is a communication. But it is operational. It is not something being *told* to him by someone. It is an event in his life. It is unanticipated. He is interested because *something new is happening to him.*

The baby is self-centered too. Nobody has yet told him about his place in society, about his need to cooperate, about sharing, tolerating, and turning the other cheek. This is another reason why his interest—whether it is caused by curiosity, fear, or need—is so concentrated. It is purely *his* interest. A stranger looms over the crib and the baby cries. He discovers a new, pleasant taste, and he demands more. He sees a bright, shiny object and shows interest by reaching out for it.

In each case, the baby is totally absorbed in his own subjective reactions. And each communication is getting results—it is inciting the baby to action.

We can learn a lot about interesting our adult audience by the way a baby is interested. Why does the grown-up go to movies, read newspapers, seek to be entertained? Can it be that he is seeking to recapture that fresh variety, the firsthand experience of his childhood? Isn't this the reason behind all his search for novelty? Why does he try to allay his anxieties with fresh cults and superstitions—to satisfy his wants with new acquisitions? Isn't all this a throwback to the baby's self-centered interest in his own fears and desires?

If it is, then the copywriter, as a communicator, can break through the boredom by denying the trite experience which causes it. He can communicate with the baby-grown-adult through fresh ways of expression.

William J. J. Gordon, in *Synectics* (the art of joining together different and apparently irrelevant elements) offers this guide for the creative solution of problems: (1) make the strange familiar; (2) make the familiar strange. "Human beings," he writes, "are heir to a legacy of frozen words and ways of perceiving which wrap their world in comfortable familiarity. This protective legacy must be disowned."

We copywriters, therefore, should find new ways to connect seemingly irrelevant elements so that our message has *never been heard before*. We should find ways to particularize so that our message is unique. We should not tell somebody something; we should interest him. Really to interest him our communication should be a new event in his life. It should interest him *because he is experiencing it for the first time*.

How Can We Create the Right State of Mind to Be Interesting?

"Every man is his own most interested listener."

To prepare ourselves to be interesting to someone else, we must first get rid of our own biases and become as naïve as an infant. That way, when we approach a product we have to advertise, we begin fresh, as though we had never been educated to it before. Leo Rosten asks, "What kinds of people know how to communicate? . . . I think they are people who have managed to retain their infantile *directness*, who have resisted the crippling effects of education."

To get into a product, we have to get out of ourselves. We have to become totally absorbed in our subject. Sooner or later, if we take Flaubert's advice, *the subject itself takes over*.

If this occurs, if the subject does become so engrossing as to dictate its own message—if at the same time it becomes so particularized as to be unique—then the audience must, like the baby, be interested in the communication, because it is truly new and unexpected.

Consider a few examples of advertising which illustrate the power of originality.

An ad which is now a classic took a familiar subject and made it strange by simply combining it with an incongruous and totally unexpected thought. This was the magazine ad for the Volkswagen car which illustrated a perfectly normal automobile above the headline "Lemon."

The subject of the ad was the rather hackneyed subject of quality control. That a company would so boldly advertise one of its products as a reject and express it in such a sharp metaphorical way was an outstanding example of *interest*.

A newspaper ad on a more serious subject seized its readers' attention with an original approach that was as shocking as a slap. The subject was a series of articles in the *New York Herald Tribune* on the political problem of integration. The headline interested the reader with words which, at that time, he was totally unaccustomed to hear: "Shut Up White Man, and Listen."

A magazine ad illustrated a reversible blanket. One might simply have said that you can use the blanket on either side. A more interesting headline was, "This new Fieldcrest blanket lets you change your mind."

An ad for a car which people ordinarily think is expensive (the Rolls-Royce) featured this wily headline, "This car was conceived as a protest against extravagance."

All such examples have the same knack in common—that of giving a twist to the ordinary—of placing well-known words out of phase, so the audience has a fresh experience.

Of course ads which are *naturally* original are those which tell genuine news. They make the strange familiar. For example, "General Electric Introduces P-7, the Oven that Cleans Itself Electrically." This has been one of the best-read ads of the sixties. The copywriter's task was easy because he had an intrinsically exciting product which spoke for itself.

Finding common denominators, being specific, being original (on the subject), and telling genuine news—these are some of the ways to get through. They are ways to communicate. And let us always remember—*communication,* not just advertising, is our business.

3

THE ACTIVE POWER
OF INVOLVEMENT

The Principle of Participation

If this book could have only one chapter, this would be it.

To the degree that the person who is being communicated to is involved in your message—to that extent, and only to that extent, are you getting your message across.

But there is a mistake in that last paragraph. We said that we communicate something *to* someone, but we don't. Not if we want to make a connection. We communicate *with*. "The communicator," said Leo Rosten, "is motivated by the desire to make contact." And how can you make contact with somebody else, outside your skin, unless he becomes involved? You have to converse *with* him, you have to plunge him into your subject. You have to engage his mind.

Participation is the most essential element in all forms of communication. We know it well in literature and drama. We read fiction and get caught up in the narrative. When a novel is absorbing, we are there, we are in it—oblivious to everything else. Parents can observe the intensity of that participation when a child becomes absorbed in a book. "Come to the table!" they call. Even a loud shout falls on deaf ears. That boy is far, far away from the dinner table. He is with Jim Hawkins, crouching in the apple barrel, listening to the pirates plotting on the deck. He *is* Jim Hawkins.

How vitally playgoers can get engrossed in a play. If it is completely absorbing, if the actors are communicating their roles, the viewers are not really viewers—they are part of the cast. Somerset Maugham said it well when he was criticizing a drama critic: "He does not see the play they see" [speaking of the audience] "because he has not, as they have, acted in it." The audience participates. They are acting the play.

The success of the movies—how patently clear that it all comes from the principle of participation. The people are taken out of themselves. As they enter the movie house and the lights go down, they are participating in the pictures. The best Hollywood producers know well how to communicate; they involve the viewers in a living experience. And the more those viewers are engrossed, the bigger the box office.

"I want to cause the audience to emote," said Alfred Hitchcock. "To do that, one must throw himself into the picture completely. . . . Often, you see, when a character is doing wrong, the audience still wants him to succeed. That only works if they are totally involved with the picture and the character."

What about spectator sports? Here the principle of participation is especially strong. Go to a baseball game and feel the pulse of the crowd during a crucial play. Thousands of people, as one man, strain forward as the pitch is made. They are the batter. They see with his eyes. They connect with his bat. They run with him, they strain round the bases, they win with him as he crosses the plate. This is empathy. It is the imaginative projection of one's own consciousness into that of another person. It is a thrilling manifestation of our humanity. It is also the basic clue to the writing of effective copy.

A true proposition, say the logicians, must be related to experience. When someone reads your words, he may observe them, he may remember them by rote, yet they may not communicate a thing. Why not? Because he is not *experiencing* them. He is not involved in their meaning. "You can define words," says Hayakawa, "but their ultimate meaning is 'an event within someone's system.'"

An event within someone's system. An event. That is a meaningful concept. It cuts across all the lines and defines the purpose of all forms of communication. Take education, for example. For centuries parents and educators have been debating the problems and solutions of the teaching method. But all would agree that a child can be better educated if he *wants* to learn. Author and teacher Steuart Britt points out that things learned and understood are better retained than things learned by rote. If a child is voluntarily seeking knowledge, then he is really learning, because he is participating in the knowledge.

So that, we repeat, is the key to the copywriter's communication. If we can *involve* our audience, we are not talking *to* them—we are communicating *with* them.

"Reciprocity is important to human meaning." And "communication is a means of sharing perceptions."

The special word there is "sharing." The copywriter perceives the product and the message he has to deliver about it. But, like a messenger, he may deliver the message, the recipient may receive it, and the communication may end there. The receiver must share in the perception. He must become involved.

Ways to Involve the Audience

We have spoken, in the last chapter, about the problems of communicating with people in the mass, with individuals you do not know personally. We have stressed the fact that each individual in that audience, which often consists of millions, has his own collection of stuff with which he perceives your message. That message, therefore, can be open to millions of different interpretations, according to the character and background of the reader. We can't possibly know precisely how each one of those millions of people will construe our message.

How, then, can we communicate effectively with such a mass of unpredictable reactions?

Here the principle of participation is all-important. It is what the copywriter leaves *unsaid* that completes the connection. The reader or viewer becomes, in a sense, an active copywriter himself. If he is truly involved, our message is an event in his life—his event—and *he* completes the communication.

This is the method used in "nondirective guidance," where a teacher or psychiatrist, instead of preaching solutions, will encourage the subject to realize them himself. Professor John T. Lanzetta, in a speech entitled "Changing Men's Minds," expressed it this way:

> If you were interested . . . in changing someone's attitude toward a political issue it turns out to be fairly effective to put him in the position of giving a talk—say he is "pro"—stressing the "con" position. There should be no implication that you are trying to change or trying to convince the individual of the contrary position. Simply ask him to present the "con" position . . . to marshall the evidence and to role-play. Rather interestingly, in the process of role-playing he proves to be quite an effective propagandist; he convinces himself more than he does anyone else. Now this, of course, can be used in a wide variety of ways. If you want people to change their attitudes toward a particular practice, you might not try to convince them or force them, but simply set up a situation in which

role-playing of this new procedure takes place. Maybe in the process of playing the new role, change can be effected. We are all familiar with the phenomenon of the union steward who gets promoted to foreman of the plant. Inside of six months his attitudes have gradually shifted more and more toward agreement with those of management and less and less with the union position. In effect, this amounts to putting a man in a position in which he plays a new role.

Professor of marketing John Aberle gives another practical example of nondirective guidance:

> The National Association of Manufacturers has been roundly damned by educators for being completely unsophisticated in attempts to convey a philosophy—their own notion of the American way of life. However, they have been most effective in communicating their notions through a program entitled "Junior Achievement." In this program youngsters supervised by an adult will form a corporation, sell stock, use the money to manufacture a product, sell the product, and after a year dissolve the corporation after paying dividends if any profits have been earned. I personally know of no better way in which to communicate the theory of capitalism.

Role-playing is another way of saying "involvement," for in the situations mentioned above—the involvement with the novel, the play, the movie, the baseball game, the plant, and the corporation—in each case the audience was playing a role.

Now how does this work with an ad? There are many ways to encourage involvement. The use of questions involves the reader. "Do You Make These Mistakes in English?" "Who Else Wants a Screen Star Figure?" The copywriter is actively involving the reader. How much less effective those headlines would have been if they had read, "Here are some mistakes some people make in English" and "These people wanted a screen star figure."

"How to" is a popular, almost foolproof device, assuming that the reader is interested in the subject. "Win friends and influence people" would have been a completed, closed injunction. But "How to win friends and influence people" invited the reader to participate in the ad.

Another powerful way to involve the reader is to leave a provocative message deliberately open-ended. This, of course, is what every interrogative does—for asking a question presupposes an answer. The reader participates by providing the answer. But beyond simple interrogatives, there are many ways to encourage our audience to complete the open end. One astute method is to give a report without personal editorializing. As Hayakawa points out,

> Often . . . a report with accurately stated facts is more affective in result than outright and explicit judgments. By bringing the report down

to even lower levels of abstraction—describing the blood on the victim's face and torn clothing, the torn ligaments hanging out of the remaining stump of his arm, and so on—one can make it even more affective. Instead of telling the reader, "It was a ghastly accident!" we can make the reader say it for himself. The reader is, so to speak, made to participate in the communicative act by being left to draw his own conclusions. We are more likely to be convinced by such descriptive and factual writing than by a series of explicit judgments, because the writer does not ask us to take his word for it that the accident was "ghastly." Such a conclusion becomes, in a sense, our own discovery rather than his.

All sampling and demonstrations of a product are attempts to involve the audience. Hopkins recognized this potent fact many years ago when he wrote: "The way to sell goods is to sell them. The way to do that is to sample and demonstrate, and the more attractive you can make your demonstration, the better it will be for you."

Obviously, if we can give our prospect a sample of our product and induce him to try it, we are achieving the ultimate in participation. Then it is up to the product to sell itself. But in the case of a demonstration in an ad or commercial, we are involving the viewer by encouraging him to watch the product in action. If we could be as absorbing with our demonstration as the baseball player is with his crucial play, we could be sure that our audience would be with and of the action.

Take the demonstration of the egg and the BAND-AID plastic strip which lifted the egg from boiling water to prove its stickiness. In a way, the audience, too, was lifting the egg. This kind of demonstration is even more effective when the audience is told that it is "live," rather than on film. Then they are involved with the suspenseful feeling that the demonstration may not succeed. Live TV commercials in the old days, when the refrigerator door would not open and the garbage disposal refused to work, far from undermining the on-camera presenter, won the audience's sympathy and loyalty.

Another way to encourage participation is to tell a story. "Short stories are short," writes Alex Osborn, author of *Applied Imagination*, "because they leave so much to imagination." This is a form of the open-ended communication. If we can involve our audience to the extent that they are using *their* imagination to embroider our story, we have caught them. *They* become copywriters; they are involved.

Of course, the reason why all the copybooks hammer away at the importance of appealing to the self-interest and of offering a consumer benefit, is to invite participation. Certainly, if someone is suffering from an ailment and an ad promises him relief, he will participate in the communication—though he might not believe it. Those people in our audience who are pinpointed by a particular appeal are very likely to participate regardless of the technique. The trick is to involve the greatest number of listeners, regardless of the context and their immediate readiness for the message.

One of the strongest of all methods for involving our audience is to trigger the deepest wellsprings of their emotions. Participants at the baseball game are even more deeply involved if they are tied up with the player—if he and his team are the underdogs, if he is overcoming some physical difficulty, or if he is strongly liked or disliked. There are many ways to appeal to our audience emotionally, but it is usually more effective to appeal to elemental emotions than to rational opinions. One pretty good way to assess whether your ad will involve the reader emotionally is to ask yourself, "Would it involve me?"

Some Pertinent Examples of Involvement

The copywriter who involves his audience in a reciprocal action is effectively communicating. Let us look at some examples which speak for themselves.

"Modess because. . . ." Here is a campaign which has run successfully for many years. The dots are there for the reader to complete the sentence. How she is participating, no one knows. It all depends on the reader. Perhaps, in her mind, she says something like this: "That is a picture of a beautiful woman in an elegant gown—a woman so poised, so lovely, so confident, I would like to be like her. The advertiser is talking about a product which is deeply personal to me. He does not embarrass me in public by spelling out what the product is or its characteristics. The ad means that this product will help me to be poised, self-confident, and at ease."

Or—that may not be what she thinks at all. Only the reader could tell you and she might not be able or wish to express her thoughts. But the important thing is the connection. In this case, she has not been *told* about the product; she has participated in its unspoken meaning.

In direct contrast is the famous ad for a brokerage house, "What everybody ought to know . . . about this Stock and Bond Business." That ad contained about five or six thousand words of copy. But every word of the copy was factual and operational. There were no affective words or connotations, no editorializing.

Again, like the two-word Modess ad, this long-copy ad appealed to the reader's intelligence. It implied, "If you are interested in stocks and bonds, you will read this long, informative copy and draw your own conclusions. We are not trying to bludgeon you into buying anything; we are only seeking to inform you." From the moment the reader started to read the ad he was a complete participator. *He* was doing the interpreting, *he* was making the judgments.

"If You Can Find a Better Bourbon, Buy It." Here is a slogan which has appeared in ads and on billboards, with little other copy, for many years. It helped Ancient Age whiskey to rise to first place among six-year-old bourbons. The message is open-ended. The reader is complimented and involved. He may say to himself, "They mean that they have a bourbon so good they can afford to dare me to find one that is better." He is participating in the completion of the idea.

"Whaddaya want in your milkshake—two eggs or one?" This well-known example of soda-fountain psychology was an instance of participation advertising. The audience participated by choosing an alternative.

A short-copy ad from the Cigar Institute of America shows a closeup of a woman's face and one tear rolling down her cheek. No cigars, no men, no smoke. Just the caption, "A good cigar is as great a comfort to a man as a good cry is to a woman."

What a provocative idea, and how it involves the male reader! He completes the thought, "Men don't cry, but they need an outlet for their emotions." He probably mulls over the idea too—pictures himself smoking a cigar, thinks of the outlet of chomping on the end of it, savors the maleness of the situation.

And, of course, women are also involved in that ad. It probably helps to overcome their prejudice toward cigars. They feel a sympathy for those poor grown-up boys who are never allowed to cry. It's a small enough concession to let them smoke their cigars, repulsive though they may be.

In a similar vein is an ad for After Six tuxedos. In the foreground, we see the picture of a husband—not a handsome, wooden model, but an "ordinary Joe," with a large nose and a craggy face—happily wearing his formal garb. In the background is his wife, under a hair dryer, surrounded by finery. The copy reads, "For the big party your wife will buy a new gown, shoes, stockings, lingerie, lipstick, nail polish, hairdo, earrings, stole, perfume, gloves, even eyelashes. . . . You deserve one After Six tuxedo."

That delightful ad shouts for participation. Every male in the audience feels a sympathetic tremor. He is involved in the war between the sexes. He empathizes with the poor guy who always pays and pays. ("You're damned right he deserves one lousy tuxedo. Wives won't admit it, but how often do we give ourselves a break?")

So it goes. Here is an enticing ad, in an editorial style, with the one-word headline, "Jamaica," and a cool picture of a white house in a forest of green trees. The small caption below the picture invites participation: "Under cover of darkness, the town's lonely bachelors climbed to this secluded inn on Blue Mountain. And it wasn't for dinner." This caption, with its suggestion of intrigue, and promise of a story, pulls you into the body copy. And the first sentence there makes you want to read more: "Blue Mountain Inn has led a wicked, wicked life. For years, she was the queen of Kingston's bordellos."

Want to read more? Here is the rest of the copy:

> Can you imagine a more beautiful location? A thousand feet up a mist-touched mountain, on the banks of a crystal stream, with its own water-falls, and surrounded by giant tree ferns, climbing vines, flaming wild flowers and gorgeously plumed tropical birds.
>
> No wonder there were mumblings of discontent among certain segments of the population when the lady was rehabilitated into an elegant inn. (Even though she's reformed, she's lost none of her appeal. Jamaicans still climb there. But, now, for dinner.)
>
> In this once-scandalous great stone house, you can now order Chateau-briand and Mouton Rothschild, '47. These days, a plump bed costs you $10, including breakfast. On another mountain, four miles from Kingston, is Casa Monte, of a style best described as neo-Italian-Jamaican. $6.50 buys you a room with a view so fantastic, visitors have been known to cap their bottles of Jamaican rum—just so they wouldn't miss anything.
>
> At the other extreme of the island is a hotel room (if you can call something that's 50' × 35' a "room") that's at the other extreme of price. It's the Honeymoon Suite at the Jamaica Inn in Ocho Rios. $100 a day for two, including your own private outdoor swimming pool. At that price, you may want to leave here under cover of darkness.
>
> For more information about formerly wicked inns, $6.50 views and $100 a day suites, see your travel agent or Jamaica Tourist Board, Dept. 1A, 630 Fifth Ave., N.Y.C.

Now, wasn't that rewarding? And didn't it give you ideas about going to Jamaica? Notice, by the way, how specific the copy became. This ad is not only participatory—it's operational as well.

We mentioned the use of questions. Of course they must be provocative. Not like the ad for the Brand Names Foundation which asks the question "Who Took the Gloom out of Grooming?" and elicits the answer, "I couldn't care less." Who said you were gloomy about grooming? Why should you want to participate? And if you did, you would probably feel cheated because the answer doesn't tell you anything about grooming, but simply about the advantages of brand names. On the other hand, consider the question Metrecal asks, "Is This the Day You Really Do Something about Your Weight?" This interrogative speaks to the heart of everyone who has a weight problem. How often each one has wanted to do something and procrastinated. This ad involves the reader with a question and, if he answers "yes," rewards him with a weight chart in which he can further participate—scanning the columns for his height and desirable weight, checking the information against the facts he knows so well.

A strikingly simple ad, which practically reaches out to involve the reader, shows a picture of a girl pressing two fingers over each eye. The copy reads, "Try this for 5 minutes. Then imagine what it would be like . . . forever. You have only one pair of eyes. When was the last time you had them examined? Better Vision Institute." If the readers don't actually perform this demonstration, we'll bet a good number of them do so in their mind's eye.

Involvement through storytelling is achieved in many ways. Here is a picture of a boy with a jam-covered face and the copy, "Don't you dare wipe that jelly off your face with my expensive paper napkins, Sidney! The *Zee paper napkins* are good enough! What do you think I am—made of money!" The reader, in a few instants, tells his own story and completes the unfinished thought which is implied by the picture and caption —"Zee paper napkins are inexpensive."

An ad for Excedrin shows a candid photo of Mrs. Patricia Barry, Yorktown Heights, N.Y. The copy reads, "With four small boys, I can't cater to a headache. I need something that'll give me the same effect as if I'd taken two aspirin and a long nap. That's why Excedrin is so good for me." This is a testimonial ad, to be sure. But it tells a believable story and may involve the reader in any of a number of ways. Perhaps the reader is a housewife who has only one child, yet she can contribute to the ad, saying, "Don't I know it! And I've only got one!" The phrase "I can't cater to a headache" can involve every reader who is ever busy and has a headache. Contained in this brief story are many other stories each reader can embroider, according to his own makeup and experience.

This ad for Excedrin brings us to another genre which is the ultimate in participation advertising—the use of the candid camera and candid microphone. Mishandled, this technique can be less effective than almost any other form. Executed with scrupulous honesty, it can have untold power. Most Americans are familiar with what Allen Funt has done with this involving technique. He uses hidden cameras to catch people "in the act of being themselves."

People are interested in other people. But why? Probably because we are all quite lonely. We are born alone and we die alone, and in between there is this longing to touch the lives of other human beings, to participate, to become involved, to get out of ourselves. Maybe it is to bolster our own egos by seeing that other people are like us—insecure, awkward at times, even inferior to ourselves. Maybe it is tied up with love and sex and all sorts of Freudian overtones. We don't presume to be wise enough to know all the reasons, but the fact is, people do want to be involved with one another, and it is the root and bedrock of communication.

Communicators, as we have said, can involve their audiences with provocative questions and vivid storytelling. But the relatively new technique of showing people as they *really* are can have power beyond all secondhand reports.

The naturalistic painting of the Renaissance was a form of the candid genre. But photography was the greatest leap forward. And the publication of *Life* magazine, in the late thirties, epitomized the force of photojournalism. We have seen, in *Life* and other magazines which soon cropped up, a kind of truth in still photography which Edward Steichen describes as "The Exact Instant" and Cartier Bresson calls "The Precise Moment." This is the communication of the height of an action, of an emotion, which has the ring of absolute veracity. People are seized and recorded at moments when they are not aware of themselves or of the consequences. They *are* themselves, and we can eavesdrop on them.

The tape recorder has made possible the most authentic playback of the way we speak. It is an appalling revelation, in fact, when we first study verbatims, to see how tongue-tied, repetitious, syncopated, and redundant our speech actually is. Here, for example, are some remarks, taken from the author's conversation with one of the experts in the candid technique, Bob Drew. You would find it hard to understand these sentences anyway, since they are taken out of the context of several days' conversation about Drew's methods. They are included here only to magnify the difference between actual speech and that which is composed and written. Notice how drastically this taped reproduction differs from the formalized speech of literature. In this case it is barely intelligible:

DREW: There, they captured people at the precise moment, uh—anda, anda, anda, printed them on a page, on a magazine page to capture the whole ten million absorbed readers every week, y'know, and so forth.

NORINS: So, uh, this Penne, and-a, uh, is not a cameraman, and this, then, Hope is not a sound recorder, uh, and she's not a reporter, and he's not a-uh, uh, a-uh, a photographer, uh—nor is she a writer, y'know. What they are, when they're creating this film, is that—everything at once—right?

DREW: They're—they have to be one person, so to speak. They have to be writer, producer, cameraman, sound recorder. Uh, uh, they have to be plot-uh, plotter. Uh, they have to uh, uh—and they have to be—and then we get the—y'know

NORINS: human relationship

DREW: human relationship—they've gotta be psychologists. They've got to uh, uh, be so'n-so'n-so'n-so. All right. Now these other people, these actors, and actresses, are people who, like Hope and Penne, are so absorbed in what they're doing and what they're trying to create—in what they're living—that they aren't—they aren't actors and actresses in a film. They're people of uh—oh, gee, this is terrible (two or three unintelligible words, which Norins covers with exclamation)

NORINS: Well, keep it up! It's a line a thought . . .

One reason why those written words look so peculiar is because they are only a small part of the communication. Along with the actual words are facial expressions, gestures, tones of voice, shared and unshared meanings between the speakers. The semanticists refer to these forms of communication which are, strictly speaking, nonverbal as "metacommunication." This is a relatively untapped field for study, rich in possibilities. Film, videotape, and the tape recorder can reproduce *all* those levels of the complex tapestry of communication which are going on at one and the same time.

The biggest revolution, now occurring in communication, is the development of mobile and miniaturized equipment which can reveal people precisely as they are, where they are, as it happens. Possibly the most dramatic reproduction of life in our century was the on-camera shooting of Lee Harvey Oswald following the assassination of President John F. Kennedy. Millions of television viewers watched in horrified fascination as a play far beyond all fictional dimension, occurred before their eyes and ears. This was the ultimate in participation, for it was altogether authentic.

The development of this new form of communication is, we believe, of the most historic importance. In politics and journalism, it can have crucial significance.

What will happen when film equipment is so miniaturized as to make privacy difficult, if not impossible? Will we, to protect ourselves, have to settle for some form of thought control? Will the equipment prove as potentially dangerous and beneficial as atomic power?

Such questions are outside the purview of this book on advertising. But the advances of these new forms of communication can be made largely through the investment of the advertisers. Their commercial use, though it be less significant, is certainly germane to this chapter on involvement.

The testimonial campaign was one of the first clichés in the language of advertising. It worked until it became altogether unbelievable and, like the dinosaur, disappeared. Recent television commercials which use the candid technique, are reviving the testimonial, but in a new, vigorous way. For one thing, the candid camera, unless film is carefully edited, can ruthlessly reveal the truth. There are manners of voice and expression which immediately tell whether a subject is prompted and coached or truly authentic. Here, for example, are side-by-side scripts of two commercials for Cheer detergent—the one rehearsed and fictionalized, the other reproduced by the hidden camera.

Hidden Camera Commercial— *at a Florida Laundromat*	*Staged Commercial—Dramatized* *Story in a Supermarket*
WOMAN: Mostly by the white things. NARRATOR (*voice-over*): This is Mrs. Clyde Speed. We asked her to	CHEER BOX (*speaking*): Over this way. WOMAN: What? Who called?

make the Cheer Eye Witness Test and tell us which stack of laundry looked better.

WOMAN: I believe this pile looks better.

INTERVIEWER (*on camera*): This one looks better over here . . . Would y' mind telling me why?

WOMAN: I had these things . . . they had very bad stains and the little boy was wearin' them around' the floor . . . and . . . ah . . . although it had gotten 'em out pretty well there, y'see . . . this was very . . . ah . . . very much cleaner.

INTERVIEWER: Really got it cleaner . . . Mrs. Speed, somewhere under here are identifying cards . . .

WOMAN (*nervous laugh*): Ah . . . ?

INTERVIEWER (*showing identifying cards*): And that tells you that this was done in New Blue Cheer, and the one over here, which was not—ah—quite what you were looking for—was done in another brand.

WOMAN: Well, *isn't* that something!

BOX: It's me. Cheer

WOMAN: But—

BOX: That's right. Take me. (*She takes the package*) Ah, that's better. Now, let me show you how to get your clothes really white.

WOMAN: How?

BOX: Look on the package . . . exclusive blue magic whitener. You see, only Cheer has it. That's why Cheer gives a really different kind of white—a deeper, fresher white. (*Later, at home, as woman inspects wash*)

BOX: Now, look.

WOMAN: Why, compared to my last wash, I can see the difference.

BOX: Sure. And when white clothes are that white you know your colored things are perfect too.

WOMAN: You're right.

BOX (*to audience*): Why don't you choose me. Switch to Cheer. If you're like most women, we bet you'll say—

BOX AND WOMAN, IN UNISON: Cheer washes so white you can see the difference.

You can see a difference in the printed form in which those words appear here. There is an even greater difference when you see and hear the film and add the dimensions of metacommunication. In the candid-camera version, a lift of an eyebrow, the shrug of a shoulder, can have a world of meaning, and can make the difference between involving the viewer and having her think, "Oh, that's just another commercial" or "that person was rehearsed to say what she said."

Since the candid-camera Cheer commercials appeared, there have been many successful campaigns which have further developed the use of authentic, unrehearsed testimonials. These include campaigns for Excedrin, Ban deodorant, Sanka coffee. Like all "schools" of advertising, the technique has also become structured and has been overdone to the point where the viewer is bored and, therefore, fails to participate.

But the uses of miniaturized and mobile equipment, to communicate the real life of human beings, has just begun, has barely been tapped. How often have many of us—especially when we were young—dreamed of being invisible, of getting into the lives, under the skin of other people? Haven't you ever thought, "What is it *really* like to be somebody else?" Through these new technological advances, we can finally find out. We *will* be able to participate in the lives of others, exactly as they live them.

If this book could only have one chapter, we said at the beginning, this would be it. It is a chapter that is being written every day, by communicators everywhere. It is the chapter that began with the early steles of the Egyptians, expanded mightily with Gutenberg's printing press, leaped forward when Edison recorded sound, reached a profound expression with the arrival of cinematography, and is now, in the jet age, bursting with new and astounding discoveries. We have hardly begun to communicate, and the more we do, the more we find ourselves involved with one another.

A DOZEN WAYS
TO WIN CONVICTION

The word "believability" has been applied to all kinds of advertising which are in no way believable (such as the so-called "slice of life" commercials). And the phrase "call for action" has been translated by the language of advertising into "Now!" "Hurry!" and "While the Supply Lasts!" We promised that we would offer no magic formulas and would not try to map some royal road to successful copywriting; but surely it is possible to pin down some principles of communication which make for true believability and real conviction. In this chapter we discuss twelve—seven to do with believability and five toward assuring the sale.

Seven Keys to Confidence

One way we can achieve believability and win the consumer's confidence is to search for the intrinsic drama in our subject. Every product, as we have already emphasized, deserves its own identity. Otherwise, why would the world be "so full of a number of things"? Flaubert was right. There is inherent drama in every single subject; we only have to find it.

It is easy to find that drama when the subject is naturally newsworthy. When a product is developed to fill a genuine need, it dictates its own communication. No one had to elaborate when the electric light was invented; it lit up itself. Just so, it is easy to communicate about the new General Electric oven which automatically cleans itself. Those claims are believable because the reader knows that he has only to see the products in action to test their validity.

Here is an ad that pictures an 8-lb. Sony television set. It is a Japanese import. The set is shown atop an attaché case. The headline says what you see: "As portable as your attaché case." The product has so much inherent drama that even its somewhat tortuous sentences are engrossing:

> SONY Micro-TV with UHF convertor for *total television reception*. . . . For the man on the move, SONY Micro-TV with UHF is as natural as an attaché case, and weighs little more. Perfect for the office or conference room the 8-lb Television of the Future goes along easily on plane or train to keep you constantly abreast of world developments and with its UHF convertor you can enjoy Channels 14 to 83 for the full range of television broadcasting. Weekends, the 25-transistor Micro-TV goes home with you, to be used about the house on AC, anywhere outdoors on its own rechargeable battery pack, and even in an auto or boat, with 12v power, Micro-TV is made for close-up watching, with all controls right at hand, and no obtrusive scanning lines to mar the clean, beautifully sharp picture on the new SONY-designed 70° picture tube. Exclusive SONY "Synchro-Noise Suppressor" circuitry permits operation in electrically "noisy" environments such as near fluorescent lights and motors. Built-in telescoping antenna for maximum signal. $189.95. UHF convertor $49.95. Rechargeable battery pack, luggage carrying case and auto accessory pack extra.

That copy is believable because the product is unique. It is loaded with benefits. Here is one case where you could even use that usually unbelievable word "miraculous."

The difficulty comes, of course, when a product is less obviously distinctive. There is no profit in devising a uniqueness which is out of proportion or unsupportable. For example, here is an ad for a soft drink, 7-Up, which asks the audience: "Need alley-oop?" The subhead then promises, "It's yours with this *quick, fresh lift!*" The ad goes on to promise "brand new energy . . . in just 2 to 6 minutes" and "new sparkle for your spirit."

Surely there is something else one can say that is truly inherent to this product. What do they mean by "brand new energy in 2 to 6 minutes"? Is that true? Will 7-Up really deliver that promise? And what is this "new sparkle for your spirit"? Sounds interesting, if only they would specify.

"Oh, but this is merely reminder copy," someone may answer.

"Reminder of what?"

"Of the name '7-Up'."

"Then why don't they simply show the name the way they blow up the Seagram's 7 Crown? At least the name is distinctive."

But the main reason this ad is unbelievable is not because it is unspecific but because it promises too much. Coca-Cola offered "The Pause
that Refreshes"—which is reasonable enough for a soft, carbonated drink.
Alley-oop and sparkle for the spirit might better be attributed to a
medicinal product or to psychedelic drugs!

Intrinsic drama does not have to be flamboyant. It should be what the
nature of the product requires. The copywriter who came up with the
slogan "The Good Maxwell" probably saw, in his mind's eye, a sturdy,
dependable car and chose, for his communication, that confident but
quiet assumption.

Finding the inherent drama of a product enables the copywriter to
forget himself. And this makes for believability because there is no so-
called "style" or "borrowed interest" between audience and subject.
Said William Strunk, "Place yourself in the background. Write in a way
that draws the reader's attention to the sense and substance of the writing,
rather than to the mood and temper of the author." This means "the sense
and substance of the *product*," not one iota of meaning or illustration
outside it.

"The greatest thing to be achieved in advertising . . . is believability,"
says Leo Burnett, "and nothing is more believable than the product
itself."

A second key to winning the confidence of our audience is to be concrete. People feel uneasy and at sea when we're vague. They have nothing
to grab on to. Facts are the handholds for climbing that steep cliff of
communication.

That's why the Avis rental car advertising has been so outstanding in
the 1960s. Their larger competitor, Hertz, said, vaguely, "When you've
got to be *sure,* be sure it's Hertz." But Avis told the public that because
they were in second place, they had to try harder. Therefore, they promised, they would keep their cars cleaner, you would not find cigarette
butts in the ashtrays, the gas tanks would always be full, etc. Concrete
promises, not vague ones about "surety."

Consider two ads for two typewriters. One reads as follows:

> The typing requirements of modern management vary widely even
> within a single company; Underwood meets this challenge with the most
> complete line of typewriters available from a single source, designed to
> fulfill every typing requirement from the board chairman's correspondence
> to the mailroom's labels. Each Underwood typewriter is intended for
> specific applications; to each of these it brings speed, ease of operation
> and dependability.

The other tells you:

> The new IBM Selectric is no ordinary typewriter! It has no typebars,

no moving paper carriage. Instead, a selective printing element skims across the page, typing out characters faster than the eye can see. And it can be changed in seconds to adapt type styles to many applications. The new IBM Selectric Typewriter is the result of 15 years of research—developed and engineered to meet the demand for faster business communications.

Of those two ads, which was the more concrete, the more explicit? Which, then, was the more believable?

The third key to winning confidence is for the product to live up to its claims once it has been bought. Does the copywriter have any control over this factor? Certainly, because he can refuse to write claims which cannot be lived up to.

Dave Garroway, one of television's most popular personalities, gave a speech for the 4A's (American Association of Advertising Agencies) entitled "How to Get People to Believe You":

> When you say this car will save you up to 40 percent on gas mileage, it means nothing to the public. And I think the public is becoming more and more aware of this. "Up to 40 percent" means nothing. Perhaps you lose 10 percent. It means you cannot save more than 40 percent, but it doesn't imply that you will save anything. So I try very hard to keep weasels out of commercials—things that don't quite say something, but imply something else.
>
> *The limits of a product are very real.* No one thing will do everything well, even in a small group of things. So I make a point of studying the product as best I can—the product engineering, the nature of the product, how it is used, where it is used, by whom it is used. So when I speak about it, I will have some idea of who I am talking to, and be able to relate to them. You don't talk about a Cadillac car as you do about a piece of pie.

But weasel words and mere omission of facts are not the worst crimes of unbelievable copy. One of the biggest debates is over the use of what some critics call "deceptive differentials." Rosser Reeves and S. I. Hayakawa got into the thick of that one when the latter criticized Reeves's book, *Reality in Advertising:*

> Reeves cites with vast admiration, as models for other advertising men to emulate, phenomenally successful campaigns employing what are clearly "deceptive differentials" according to his own definition—and admission! Here are his examples of "great" campaigns along with his own comment on their "truth": "Our Bottles Are Washed with Live Steam" ("His client protested that every other brewery did the same"); "It's Toasted" ("So, indeed, is every other cigarette"); "Gets Rid of Film on Teeth" ("So, indeed, does every other toothpaste"); "Stops Halitosis" ("Dozens of other mouth-washes stop halitosis"); "Stops B.O." ("All soaps stop body odor") (pp. 55–57).

Where does this leave the author's assertion that "the better product, advertised equally, will win in the long run"? His own evidence indicates an entirely different conclusion, namely, that, given a number of similar products, the one that is advertised with the most ingeniously contrived deceptive differential will clobber all others in the marketplace. And the 180,000,000 consumers policing this operation at the check-out counter do nothing of the kind, because enough of them are led to believe that the bottles of one brewery are "washed with live steam," and that others' bottles are not. (This is known in the industry as "truth in advertising.") I am reminded of the famous lines from William Blake: "A truth that's told with bad intent/Beats all the lies you can invent."

Replied Rosser Reeves:

If a manufacturer's bottles are washed with live steam, and this is important to the public, why should not the manufacturer so state in his advertisement? If a manufacturer heat-treats his tobacco so that harsh irritants are removed (which is true, and important to any smoker), why should he not advertise this fact? If a manufacturer has a mouthwash which stops bad breath, why should he not proclaim it—even if his competitors do not do so?

Does the fact that some competing product may also have these same qualities, in itself make these claims "minuscule," or "deceptive," or "exaggerated," or "fake claims"?

I do not think so.

This debate—about the right of an advertiser to stress a benefit which is true of other products, but has not been said by them—could go on 'til doomsday with no conclusion. But whether or not the use of these so-called "deceptive differentials" is ethical is not the point we want to make here. The point is that a person influenced by a deceptive differential to switch from one product to another may be disappointed when he finds that the product is no better because of its claim. The bottle may have been washed in live steam, but there is no distinctive difference he can detect when he drinks the beer. If the beer was, in fact, heavier, lighter, more or less carbonated, with a longer-lasting head, etc., and the claim had been made, it could have lived up to its promise.

Someone may say that a person often rationalizes qualities into a product he has bought and that if you tell him it is such and so, you can make him believe it, whether it is or not. This may sometimes be possible, but isn't the result more predictable, with a greater number of people, if you tell them the inherent truth and difference to begin with?

In the long run, if a product does *not* live up to its promise, and it is a product that requires repeat purchases, the advertising will actually hasten the product's demise. Even if it does not require repeat purchase, the negative word of mouth can bury the product—as in the well-known case of the Edsel. "Good Ads Hasten Bad Products' Death," read the headline of an *Ad Age* story. But they are not "good ads" if they make promises the product cannot deliver. Perhaps the Edsel might have been more successful if the ads had recognized the ugliness of the car. They might have referred to its "horsecollar hood," as another company's ads recognized the fact that their car looked like a bug.

Claude Hopkins refers to a much earlier experience with hyperbolic automobile advertising: "The car was a fizzle. Its engineers had skimped in every detail. The very success of the advertising, with the car that was offered, led to destruction. We played too high a note for the car we had to sell. The bad reputation was so widely spread that recovery proved impossible. That formed another lesson in advertising."

Hopkins may have learned his lesson, but those who came after him had not learned theirs. We suppose that many who read *these* words will go on making the same foolish mistake; for the language of advertising somehow condones the untruths.

But the consumer does not. "The customer is relentless," says Burnett, "when he catches a product in a lie." And little by little, like drops of water on a stone, lies and half-truths will wear away the entire trust of the public. "I respect faith," said a pundit, "but doubt is what gets you an education." The people are becoming more educated and the copywriters are going to *have* to tell the truth or fail to communicate.

The fourth key to confidence is, very simply, to demonstrate the product. We referred before to this relatively easy method and will come back to it over and over throughout this book. Yet we can predict that many so-called copywriters will continue to avoid the obvious. Why? Perhaps because demonstration does not always seem to be artistic. Or because they get into the habit of having to *persuade* their audience. "No argument in the world," said Hopkins, "can ever compare with one dramatic demonstration." He tells how he learned his trade from the street peddlers. "They never tried to sell things without demonstration. They showed in some dramatic way what the product they sold would do. It is amazing how many advertisers know less than those men about salesmanship."

Demonstrations will be believable if the audience feels quite sure they have not been rigged. Unfortunately, so many have been deceiving— especially on television—that our reservoir of credulity has, again, run low. This makes it even more necessary to let the product dictate its own demonstration. And the simpler the better.

A good and consistent demonstration campaign is the one which has been running for years for the Zippo cigarette lighter. Each ad shows a black-and-white photograph of an actual lighter which has undergone some extraordinary usage. The owner of the lighter is identified. Here are some typical headlines:

> THIS ZIPPO WEATHERED THE HURRICANE OF 1938.
> IT STILL WORKS TODAY.
>
> THIS ZIPPO TOURED THE NEW YORK WORLD'S FAIR OF 1939.
> IT STILL WORKS TODAY.
>
> THIS ZIPPO CRASH-LANDED AT BOUGAINVILLE IN 1944.
> IT STILL WORKS TODAY.
>
> THIS ZIPPO WAS SHIPWRECKED IN 1950.
> IT STILL WORKS TODAY.

The believable payoff to each of these ads for Zippo is this italicized subhead:

"If any Zippo ever fails to work, we'll fix it free."

No weasel words in that campaign. Just powerful demonstration and the art of plain talk.

Another neat demonstration is the one for Volkswagen (we keep returning to this admirable campaign) which shows a picture of the car without fenders: "See?" says the headline, "No springs." Then the copy demonstrates the idea:

> VWs have torsion bars instead of springs. They run horizontally between the wheels. This is how they work. Take a 3-foot steel ruler. Hold one end in each hand and twist. Let one end go. It bounces right back to shape, without going boing, boing, boing. The same thing happens when you drive a VW over a bump. You sit and wait for the next bounce, only it never comes. The Volkswagen has separate torsion bars on all 4 wheels. So each wheel feels its own separate way over the road (and spends more time in touch with the road). You get a firm, solid ride, with exceptionally accurate control. Torsion bars alone aren't unique. Nor is 4-wheel independent suspension. But the combination of both systems is extremely rare. You can count all the sedans that have it on one finger.

Television has given us copywriters our best chance to demonstrate products in action. But we have failed more often than we have succeeded in using the enormous power of the TV tube to win confidence. Often its technical limitations required some kind of weaseling to duplicate reality —the use of shaving cream for cake frosting, the use of blue shirts to resemble white. The viewers became skeptical, and copywriters, hard-pressed to find believable demonstrations, took the easier route of claim without proof.

Still, the great TV demonstrations go on. And invariably the good ones are simple. Two good examples of the sixties are the slow-motion demonstration of the suction of the Rubbermaid bathmat and the "egg test" with a Chevrolet truck. In the latter case, one free-swinging basket of eggs is attached to the hub of a wheel and another to the truck's chassis. As the truck travels, the wheel's eggs are thrown out and break, while those in the other basket remain unharmed—thanks to the truck's even suspension. This demonstration is shown in slow-motion too, which adds to the believability, as the viewer has plenty of time to study and understand the action.

The possibilities of demonstrating most present products have hardly been tapped. We shall have more to say on the subject, especially in Chap. 11, on television copy.

The fifth key to confidence is the relentless pursuit of reality in advertising. As we said before, people in actuality speak quite differently from the way they do in fiction. They constantly repeat words, speak in unfinished phrases and sentences, interpolate stammers and expletives. Imbalances like these give natural conversation a homely ease. The same is true of the way people act, look, and write. The less self-conscious, the more believable. When you are completely absorbed in writing a letter to a close friend, you express yourself easily, without being stilted. Communication which is free of artifice may not be artistic but it gets through.

But the language of advertising has become artifice to the nth degree. A couple in evening dress walk down a city street pulling a child's wagon. "If they're out of imported O.F.C., I'm going on the wagon," reads the headline. A smiling smoker with a swollen lip and a black eye tells his audience, "Us Tareyton smokers would rather fight than switch!" A gaggle of cheerleaders, holding up hands wearing wrist watches are shown above the headline "Rah! Rah! Rah! Sis boom Bulova! (375 strong)".

The silly school goes on. Homburg-hatted stereotypes, posed in the financial district with six Hoover vacuum cleaners, illustrate the headline "How to clean up on Wall Street." A fashion model, in one of those ungainly contortions only the fashion ads can affect, is seen with a bear, a llama, and a pony to illustrate a Borg fabric two-piece dress: "Everybody's wearing the furry dress this year." Another awkward young lady is shown attired in a bedspread: "Dramatic enough to wear."

Everywhere, the stiff, posed, retouched, slick, wooden, unreal models make advertising a cult of unbelievability. Sure, some of them, by attracting attention, help to sell products, but at what expense and for how long?

Creative director Jim Nelson's memorable 4A's speech ("My Son, the Creative Director," 1963) tore into the lot of them by satirically presenting "his family" as seen in the unreal ads. He showed his wife dressed in a bedspread, lying on silver lamé pillows, wearing dozens of powder puffs on her head, "saying a little prayer of thanksgiving after one of her products helped her do the dishes," and wearing a huge hat in her bathtub. He showed his dog carrying a television set and a can of dogfood, his children eating pizza and pancakes with the packages carefully posed on the table.

Jim then hammered his point home by comparing the phony ads with the editorial pictures in some of the magazines: "They're real. Real, honest-to-goodness, living, breathing people, like you and me," he said, and he continued:

> In a recent issue of *Holiday* I read that someone asked Maggi Brown, a red-haired English model who is turning into an actress, why so few models ever make the grade in films. She said, "They don't look like people."
>
> Amen, Maggi Brown. Models don't look like people. They don't look like me, and they don't look like you, and they don't look like the people who shop at my supermarket, or ride my bus, or sell me a cup of coffee in the morning, or teach my kids, or fix my car, or pass me on the highway in their Cadillacs and Plymouths and VW's . . .
>
> You show me a human being, and I'll show you a person who considers himself an expert when it comes to judging people. We in the advertising business especially, I think, pride ourselves on our powers of observation, our perceptiveness, our acute sensitivities. We throw up enormous barricades to try to keep our offices free of phony account executives, phony copywriters, phony media directors. And while our mighty cannon are trained on the front door, the Family Phonus Balonus—Ma, Pa, and the kids—waltz in through the executive washroom and get not into our offices —but into our product.

Amen, Jim Nelson.

Another copywriter, good and true, Stan Burkoff, gets his licks in on the phonus balonus with these words:

> If I were sitting in my living room extolling the virtues of my new car to a friend, I can't imagine my referring to it as "spirited," a "wildcat," or the possessor of "dynamic thrust." The words would flop awkwardly off my lips. I'm sure any friend of mine would look at me as if I were a seven dollar bill. At least one of his eyebrows would raise at my choice of words. Worse, he'd think I was stupid to have overlooked the really meaningful virtues of the car. Because I am sensitive to raised eyebrows, I'd probably tell him, instead, that I found the car smooth on the road, peppy on the getaway, and it only cost me $7.24 when I drove it from Toronto to the Yukon.
>
> These are meaningful claims in a face-to-face conversation. Why in the living name of heaven do so many copywriters put so many things on paper that would curdle their milk if they said them aloud?
>
> Rule: I think a copywriter should try to persuade through his typewriter the way he'd try to persuade in conversation. He should clarify the subject matter quickly. He should state his product's benefit quickly. He should

try to use conversational language. And his claims should be meaningful. They should add up to a real, not a phony, reason to buy.

Need we give more examples? Just for fun, here is one outside the field of advertising—a caption for a *New Yorker* cartoon which shows a prize-fighter being coached by his second: "When the bell rings, come out fighting. Land a couple of lefts to the jaw in rapid succession, back off, dance around a bit, then come in suddenly with a right hook to the ear, then a left, then a right, clinch, back off and feint with a left, feint again, then come in with a right jab to the body and then a left to the body, clinch, back off and dance around for a bit again, then suddenly come in with a long left uppercut. . . ."

The point? We all, we communicators, get the hackney habit. We're the cliché-makers. We imitate one another. Like clowns, we leap and cavort to call attention to ourselves, instead of to our subject.

Instead of to our subject.

It's time we cultivated awareness that we aren't getting through and started writing for real!

Now that we have got *that* off our chest, we can continue with the sixth key to confidence: Understatement. As we said in Chap. 3, elements left out can encourage participation. Communication is a two-way thing and the art of understatement can help to involve our audience. What's more, in the context of the braggadocio around it, an understated ad can stand out by contrast.

For example, such is the TV commercial for Johnson & Johnson. It shows a little girl running down a long expanse of beach, with a hurt expression on her face. No announcer or words accompany her, just the sound of music. At the end of sixty seconds, she holds a cut finger toward the camera and says "Mommy." The voice-over says, simply, "Kiss it—with Johnson and Johnson."

Such is the headline for an ad for Chivas Regal whiskey, in which three sizes of the bottle are depicted, plus a filled shot glass: "Why risk $8.90? Or $4.65? Or even $2.95? Order a glass in your local bar. Be sure to resist any offer of soda, water or ice. Your first sip of Chivas Regal should be undiluted."

Contrast this kind of understated advertising with boastful communiqués like these: "The World Agrees On 'Gilbey's Please.'" (Who says so?) "Anything to declare? . . . Only our genius." (Copy for an MG car ad.) "Suddenly everybody's serving Hiram Walker's Cordials On-the-Rocks." (Oh yeah?) "My mother said, 'I like aluminum baby food caps because they're pure and friendly to food.'" (Like hell she did!)

The power of understatement is neglected by most advertisers because they are close to their products and enthusiastic about them. They feel that if *they* love their factory, and show it in all its glory, all the world should be interested. Said Claude Hopkins, "They desire to exploit their accomplishments, just as I do. But they represent the seller's side. I must represent the consumer."

We copywriters are a boastful breed. "We are professional enthusiasts and therefore readers tend to discount our claims," says Victor O. Schwab, mail-order expert.

How much more reason, if we are cultivating an attitude, not to let our enthusiasm color our claims.

There may be many more keys to confidence in your pocket but there is one more that deserves special consideration.

That is the *golden rule.*

However we make rules and break rules, however we cultivate awareness, the best communication comes, above all, from the attitude of consideration for others. We can throw all the rest of our guides out the window, if only, when we sit down to write, we are considerate of our audience.

Five Steps Toward Making a Sale

We may follow all the precepts we have outlined, and achieve utter believability, yet may not clinch the sale.

Believability alone does not make for conviction. For example, you might believe that a man is sincere when he says he's a Democrat, but that alone could not make you stop being a Republican. You might believe an advertiser when he tells you his beer bottles are washed in live steam, but you might also react with a "so what?"

Here, then, for discussion, are some practices which can help add to believability that power of conviction which gets action.

First is the conviction that comes from believing you are getting a good deal. Everyone likes to find a bargain; every buyer wants to get value for his money; and everyone has wants which can be satisfied by the best bidder. "When we make an offer one cannot reasonably refuse," said Hopkins, "it's pretty sure to gain acceptance. . . . I have always taken chances on the other fellow. I have analyzed my proposition until I made sure that he had the best of the bargain. Then I had something people could not well neglect."

This principle is easily applied when you can offer a genuine benefit—one that is competitively superior—and particularly one that is new. For example, practically everyone who has had a tape recorder knows that to thread the tape on the pickup reel is a nuisance. Some people are "all thumbs" and the tape keeps coming unwound. At least to that audience this news from the 3M Company must have been irresistible when it first appeared: "New! a Tape Reel that Threads Itself! (even in the dark!)"

Here is an offer "one cannot reasonably refuse": "*Sears announces color TV your kids can tune as easily as black and white.*" Here is one most housewives could not well neglect: "*Mini-Basket washes all the things you now wash by hand.*" And Lady Esquire has a good proposition for fashion-conscious women: "Now change your shoe color . . . as easily as you change your nail color!"

Irresistible values need not always come from new product developments. With ingenuity, we can communicate intriguing new uses for old products. Jell-O, whose dominant share of the market reached a point of diminishing returns, came up with dozens of attractive recipes and food combinations which gave new luster to the product. Campbell Soup is forever refurbishing its offers. The "soup and sandwich" campaign provided plenty of novelty. Here is an ad that shows four easy, mouth-watering meals:

> Men's favorite: Campbell's Soup
> . . . with extras they like
> Ham chunks in Campbell's Cheddar Cheese Soup
> Tiny meatballs in Campbell's Minestrone Soup
> Crisp bacon bits in Campbell's Green Pea Soup
> Frankfurter slices in Campbell's Bean with Bacon Soup

Whether the offer is the benefit of a new product or a new use for an old one, obviously it should be a benefit. Yet many advertisers spend millions of dollars trying to sell their products through borrowed interest which offers nothing. Here is an ad for instant tea which illustrates a tennis player and says "*Fast Serve!* And the winner every time." There is nothing generous about this offer. All instant teas can be served quickly. Here is another ad which forces the reader to study long, negative copy in order to discover the benefit of the product: "*6 common traps in carpet-buying*" is the headline, and the subheads read:

> 1. The buying-by-fiber trap.
> 2. The buying-by-price trap.
> 3. The buying-only-by-looks trap.
> 4. The buying-by-hearsay trap.
> 5. The buying-from-an-unknown-dealer trap.
> 6. The buying-without-knowing-who-made-it trap.

That kind of copy borrows its interest from what is *wrong* with its competitors. As was amusingly explained by a "B.C." cartoon by Johnny Hart: "To form an advertising campaign," says one of his caveman characters, "first you analyze the product. . . . Then you play up its good points."

"What if it ain't got any?" asks the second caveman.

"Then you play down your competitors' good points," says the first. Communicating successfully is really quite simple if we have something to say. Harry Hartwick gets right to the nub of it:

> If I were a client, and spent, say, 6 million dollars a year on advertising, I would subtract 1 million each year to *improve my product*. There's nothing like a better product. Otherwise advertising increasingly becomes hot air, puffery, nothing about nothing. Down underneath, is the product good? If I spent that million on improving my product, I would do several valuable things: Make it possible for the copywriter and agency to do more striking, memorable ads; build a better all-over image for myself as a business; and hold customers. This last is important. When I write a commercial for an aspirin, a certain number of people exist out there as a possible market. My commercial will sweep some of them up for our side. But if the product doesn't live up to my claims in the ad, they will leave us. And then we have ruined that part of the market for further, later exploitation in the future. Clients, by having poor products that at first sell people by clever ads and then lose them by poor products, are destroying the available prospects in great bunches every day. More prospects keep entering the market, of course. But this business of selling people and then letting them get unsold is wasteful and builds cynicism in the public. Soon we will have a market that is tough, irritable, hard to sell, and disgusted—more and more skeptical of advertising because it doesn't deliver what it says it will in terms of excellent products.

Excellent products: how easy they make this trade of ours. Hartwick goes on:

> Build your advertising around a great, thrilling *thought* or *idea* about the product. Not around a technique. Sure, the technique is fine as an addition, a striking way of putting the idea across, but the idea is the big thing. I have read thousands of research playbacks from respondents, but almost never did any of them ever mention the technique, even in connection with very clever commercials. They usually remarked: "They said that this soap would not curdle in cold water," "A man said that these razor blades were made by the same people who make swords for the King of England," etc. It's the idea that grabs people deep. The way of presenting it all too often gets most of the copywriter's thought and attention. . . . I'm not knocking technique, far from it. But if some client will let me say that his aspirin will kill any headache in 6 seconds on a stopwatch, I will be willing to have an announcer just stand in front of the camera and *read* it to the audience—and I will sell more of the product than a commercial which is very brilliantly presented but doesn't have this beautiful idea, only a mediocre idea.

A second step toward making a sale is to appeal to both "the head and the heart" of our audience. Too often we get into debates about the relative merits of "reason-why" versus "emotional" copy. Surely none of us thinks or reacts this way—separating the one from the other.

"We believe what we want to believe," says Victor O. Schwab and he maintains that the original source of conviction is emotion.

On the other hand, he says, "emotion and reason work together. . . . The more strongly and effectively the emotional appeal is presented, the more fully and readily will your proof material be accepted and believed."

The emotional appeal of the Cadillac car was long a built-in asset. It was a strong status symbol. But the advertiser, to help overcome his prospect's feeling of guilt, stressed the essential economy of the car due to its high trade-in value. Thus, the reader could rationally indulge his emotion.

Similar was the appeal of the Rolls Royce headline: "This car was conceived as a protest against extravagance."

A neat parlay of head and heart is the way Allstate refers to its health insurance as "sick pay." Another is the way P&O-Orient Lines rationalize the emotional appeal of a sea voyage: "Why not run away to sea—and actually save money? It costs you less a day to see faraway ports and exotic places on one of these great ocean liners than you'd pay in a resort hotel."

One way to communicate emotion to our readers is to be emotional ourselves. Not necessarily in the style of our copy, but in the conviction we feel about it. This gets back to the contention that it's difficult for us to communicate effectively if we don't believe in what we are saying.

Some semanticists and most men of religion believe in "the self-fulfilling prophecy"—in the ability to make things happen because you have faith that they will. We have all seen how a speaker with intense conviction can lift and carry his audience along with him. His language has an almost physical force. Their emotion reflects the emotion he communicates.

How can we work up enthusiasm? Certainly not for a poor product. Or for a specious benefit. We have to dig into the subject, to search for its inherent drama and be moved by it. How can we expect to win conviction if we are not convinced?

A third step to conviction is to communicate something that can be acted upon. "Words *mean* insofar as they *act*," says Stuart Chase. "The true meaning of a term is what a man does with it." He tells how primitive people, close to nature, assign names chiefly to the things they *use:*

> Walking with a native in a New Guinea forest, Malinowski would find his attention arrested by a strange plant. On being asked its name, the native would shrug his shoulders and say, "Oh, that's just 'bush.' " A bird with no function in the larder is merely "flying animal." Malinowski found a general tendency to isolate and name that which stands in some specific connection, traditional or useful, to man and to bundle the rest into limbo.

Similarly, I remember the names of those trees and plants which were useful to me as a boy on camping expeditions, or useful in making implements for games. The other flora I learn dutifully from time to time, and soon forget.

The scientific method, Chase points out, is concerned with how things *do* happen, not how they *ought* to happen. Since the more scientifically we write copy the more sure we can feel of results, it makes sense to seek this kind of conviction. The test of this method is whether "another man can perform the operation and check the concept." Here are some examples of good operational copy:

An ad for Comet cleanser:

Does your sink need Comet, the deep-cleaning cleanser? Try this test and see.

1. Try marking the side of your sink with a pencil. You'll find it's almost impossible. The protective porcelain glaze is too smooth.

2. Now try marking the bottom—the "deep stain" zone. It's easy, because the protective glaze is worn away from constant usage. This rougher, worn surface lets stains go deep to hide beyond the reach of your sponge.

3. The best way to remove these deep stains is Comet's deep-cleaning action. Here's why: When you rub a stain with Comet, you're not only cleaning the surface, you're cleaning deep. Comet goes down and gets out the deepest stains because it contains Chlorinol—best cleaning, bleaching, and disinfecting agent in any cleanser.

4. Comet gets the "deep stain" zone, and your whole sink, sparkling clean and white. You'll find even the deepest, toughest food stains are completely gone. The darkest aluminum potmarks are removed (the pencil mark is cleaned away, too). So, before you put that pencil away, why not use it to write "Comet" on your shopping list?

Deep-cleaning Comet gets out stains better than any other leading cleanser.

An ad for Scripto pencil, with appropriate pictures over each caption:

(pic) Because the tip of an ordinary ball pen is straight
(pic) you have to hold the pen more or less upright
(pic) so your hand tends to tire when you write a lot.
(pic) Because Scripto Tilt-Tip has an angled point
(pic) the pen leans back at a more comfortable angle
(pic) so your hand stays relaxed instead of cramping.
It's as simple as that.

An ad for Betty Crocker Noodles Almondine:

Simmer celery, onion and a plump young chicken to make broth. Stir in flour, butter, milk, green pepper. Pour over cooked noodles. Blanket with almonds and bake. Making time: 3 hours. *Or* make Betty Crocker Noodles Almondine in 15 minutes—a great new dinner idea!

Those three examples above are operational because you can do something about what they say. In contrast, here's how copy supervisor Ed Reich describes "my least effective campaign":

> I can relate a campaign with which I was concerned in England. The foreign branch of an American maker of toothpaste wanted commercials for Lebanon, Syria, Egypt and Turkey supporting the introduction of their product. First, they insisted that the copy policy follow the U.S. pattern . . . that the toothpaste would last between brushings . . . in spite of agency warning that less than five per cent of the population even owned toothbrushes. Then, through some office politics, the agency creative recommendations were ignored in favor of a TV commercial producer's suggestions, which showed sailors from a British warship anchored in "typical Near Eastern City Harbor," landing and consorting with gay, unveiled, unchaperoned women . . . who select the sailor whose teeth are not crawling with wee buggies. Unbelievably the commercials were produced and shown in the intended markets despite pleas from the agency. Finally, a protest, lodged through diplomatic channels from the British ambassador in Beirut, closed the incident.

Fourth step to a sale is the plain art of thoroughness. This does not necessarily mean long copy, but it does mean careful preparation to arrive at the best copy, short or long. This is especially true of a "high ticket" item. The person who is going to invest in the purchase deserves to be thoroughly sold.

And "thoroughly selling" is good discipline for good copy. It certainly can do no harm to act as if the ad itself should clinch the sale, not to fall back on the time-honored assumption that advertising won't sell. It can do no harm either, to assume the most difficult audience. "Doubt makes demands," says Schwab:

> Doubt . . . impels the copy man to take the first giant step toward better copy—by making him more demanding about his own work. It brings him to a fuller realization that the more completely his advertisement—on its own—sells the reader, the nearer and quicker it will get that reader to the sales counter. And this realization can lead to the kind of critical analysis that is typical of a more hard-boiled attitude toward advertising. Here, for example, are just a few of the challenges presented by such analysis:
> Brand Switching—Is my ad convincing enough to make people insist, I want that product and no other?
> Poor Dealer-Distribution—Is my advertising persuasive enough to create the insistent consumer demand that would automatically increase distribution?
> Weak Dealer-Cooperation—How can a retailer be anything but lukewarm about the product if this copy of mine does not produce an active demand at his own counter?
> Incapable Salesmanship at the Counter—Can I shift more of the selling burden to the shoulders of my copy, a factor which I control?

Unfavorable Price Comparison—If so, then the advertising I write must contain more reason why to help offset this competitive disadvantage.

Thorough copy, especially for an audience interested in an immediate purchase, commands respect. The look, sound, and feel of the message presage the character of the product. They say that thoroughness went into its manufacture, that it is so intrinsically interesting as to invite discussion. Thorough copy can be dull, but not if, as we keep preaching, the product is interesting and does the writing. Witness this long-copy example, thoroughly quoted so it will demonstrate for itself:

THE EXTRAVAGANCE OF RITVA PUOTILA

An unlikely story that happens to be true
about a Finnish beauty, an American businessman,
some colored damasks, and an impossible task that was
finally accomplished after 3200 tries.

She was naive. Anyone with any experience at all could have told Ritva Puotila that what she wanted to do was impossible. After all, people had been weaving linen damask for over eight hundred years. And, if it were possible to weave it with colored warp threads, surely, in all that time, someone would have done it.

But she didn't ask anyone with any experience at all. She had something fixed firmly in her mind. And this young Finnish beauty didn't yet know enough to doubt that she could do it.

She loved the silkiness, and the shimmer, and the good solid feel of the double-damask table linens that she lived with every day. (They'd never gone out of style in Finland, as they had in the United States.) But she was bored to tears with the slim pickings: nothing but white on white or occasionally a washed out pink, or a watered down yellow. She longed to give them some of the throb, and passion, and juice, and wildness that she put into her handwoven rya rugs (one of which, The Zeus, had taken a Gold Medal at the '60 Triennale Di Milano).

Enter American businessman, smiling.

It was these rya rugs which had gotten Ritva involved with the American businessman in the first place. A few years before, he had come to Helsinki looking for six ryas for his home in Great Neck, New York. He had spent two days in one shop looking at the work of fifteen Finnish rya weavers. By the time he was finished, he had culled out six designs. Surprisingly, they all turned out to be the work of one person. (Who else but Ritva Puotila.) And, even more surprisingly, they were her first commercial assignment.

He asked to meet her.

Now it happened that, at this time, the American businessman was sponsoring an all-Scandinavia design competition to find someone fresh and exciting to do the first collection of table linens for Dansk Designs.

At their very first meeting, he persuaded Ritva to enter this competition. And, though she had absolutely no experience with table linens, and knew very little about machine production, she won. And he hired her.

Right from the start, Ritva broke all the rules.

Typically, she did 38 napkin colors which harmonized with, accented, heightened, dramatized, fought against—but never matched—her cloths and mats. There were no nice, safe, preassembled sets. You had a chance to stick your chin out, depend on your own good eye, and make your own personal statement. She designed that whole first Finnish Accent collection on the heretical assumption that America was full of people with galloping imaginations and strong independent tastes. She was right. As the sales figures are still proving.

Meanwhile, back at the damask.

As we said before, Ritva was naively unaware of the impossibility of weaving strongly-colored damask. So was the American businessman—so he gave her the go ahead. Thus began The Extravagance of Ritva Puotila.

To get the kind of colors Ritva wanted, she had to dye both the woof and the warp threads. (It was the interplay between warp threads of one color and woof threads of another that was to give her damasks their throb, and passion, and juice, and wildness.) For wan pastels, only the woof threads had to be dyed. What Ritva didn't know was that the moment you dyed the warp threads, you weakened them just enough so that at least a few of them were likely to pop under the yank of the damask loom. And, if just one warp thread per hundred thousand pops, it automatically stops the whole loom cold. And stop it did.

For six months, all sorts of experts tinkered with thread weights, loom tensions and dyeing methods—while Ritva kept prodding. And that other naive optimist, the American businessman, kept paying. Finally the impossible problem was solved. Now they went on to the really difficult one.

Not only did Ritva insist upon throbbing, passionate, juicy, wild colors. She also insisted that they throb differently on each side of her cloths. Each side had to have a character all its own.

One, for example, was to look candlelit on one side, and moonlit on the other. She wove it. The moonlit side looked leaden. The candlelit side turned out to be merely dun. So she wove it again. And again. And again —ad infinitum—until she got it. (Each time varying the dyes, or the thread mix, or both.) And she was just as stubborn about her pointillist red and blue cloth. And the mat that was to flip from morning sun to evening sun.

3200 expensive trial weaves later, Ritva finally got her fourteen color combinations to work. And if you like her throbbing, passionate, juicy, wild damasks as much as we do, Ritva will live happily ever after. And the American businessman will live happily ever after. And, incidentally, Ritva's damasks will live happily ever after, too. (They get even silkier and more shimmering with every wash.)

Epilogue: in spite of Ritva's extravagance, you can buy these damasks without being too extravagant. The mats, which come in seven different reversible combinations of throbbing, passionate, juicy, wild colors, are four for $11.00. Napkins come in nine such reversible combinations, and are four for $10.00. And a 60-by-90 inch tablecloth comes in four combinations, and is just $34.95.

If you've read this far, you must be almost as stubborn as Ritva. So perhaps you're just as insistent as she, that the things you live with be perfect all the way through. There are 493 such things in the catalogue of the Dansk "Top-of-the-Table" collection. Write for it to: Dansk Designs, Inc., Dept. RP, Great Neck, New York.

Thorough copy does not have to be lengthy, but even a short message may have infinitely complex elements contributing to its success.

Instant Maxwell House was successfully launched with a copy message of 20 words ("Amazing coffee discovery . . . Not a powder, not a grind, but millions of tiny 'flavor buds' of 100% pure coffee.") Thoroughness went far beyond the words themselves. The thoroughness was in the strategy that led to those words and in the coordinated campaign that made them meaningful.

A fifth step toward a successful sale is the age-old rule of repetition. But this rule has been so abused by all of us, we hesitate to bring it up. Repetition *ad nauseam*. Repetition of meaningless phrases which are supposed to mesmerize an exhausted listener into an automatic response. Repetition without taste, consideration, or conviction.

After years of that kind of communication, many advertisers felt a revulsion and the pendulum swung the other way—toward constantly new campaigns and ideas, so that many products have no consistent claim or personality.

What we are looking for, given all the assets of drama, concreteness, reality, interest, etc., is an idea which invites rereading or lends itself to endless variations—to reiteration without stagnation. An idea which will not grow stale with the "reservoir of 'partly-sold' customers" who are familiar with our message but have not yet bought. An idea which, at the same time, will be fresh and provocative to the new audience constantly coming into our market.

Once found, the idea is pure gold. "If you're lucky enough to write a good advertisement," says agency head David Ogilvy, "repeat it until it stops pulling." And he cites the classic, Sherwin Cody's ad about English.

"Never give up a campaign just because you have grown tired of it," he says; "housewives don't see your advertisements as often as you do."

Campbell Soup is one of the few companies which could run an ad in the September, 1963, issue of the *Saturday Evening Post*, which reprinted an ad run 42 years before, and have the two show a family resemblance. Volkswagen runs an ad illustrating its car and a bottle of Coca Cola,

"Two Shapes Known the World Over." That ad illustrates how the continuity of a trademark builds familiarity.

Leo Burnett says,

> Too many advertisers are disappointed with the results of a 13-week splash. None of us can underestimate the glacierlike power of friendly familiarity. The simple fact is that the better people know you, the better they will like you and the more likely they will be to accept your proposition.
>
> I have learned that news is news for longer than most clients think it is; that the public doesn't know a new fiscal year is started; that change of pace has ruined many a good campaign which was just getting into its stride; that many a smart and conscientious agency has been charged with laziness when it has come back with what is called "the same old stuff."
>
> I have learned that a good ad often deserves repetition, and frequently does a better job the second or third time than it did the first time around.

David Ogilvy forcefully agrees:

> What a miracle it is when a manufacturer manages to sustain a coherent style in his advertising over a period of years! Think of all the forces that work to change it. The advertising managers come and go. The copywriters come and go. Even the agencies come and go.
>
> It takes uncommon guts to stick to one style in the face of all the pressures to "come up with something new" every six months. It is tragically easy to be stampeded into change. But golden rewards await the advertiser who has the brains to create a coherent image, and the stability to stick with it over a long period. As examples, I cite Campbell Soup, Ivory Soap, Esso, Betty Crocker, and Guinness Stout (in England). The men who have been responsible for the advertising of these hardy perennials have understood that every advertisement, every radio program, every TV commercial is not a one-time shot, but a long-term investment in the total personality of their brands. They have presented a consistent image to the world, and grown rich in the process.

Ogilvy agrees, Burnett agrees, ask half a hundred other skilled copywriters and they will all agree. Continuity is important, consistency is important, familiarity is vital. Yet we all honor the principle in the breach. Why do we do it? Pressures from others to change, yes. But also, because of our own pride, doubt, and desire for novelty. Surely there is a way to be consistent and still stay fresh and imaginative.

These, then, are the seven keys to confidence:

1. Find the intrinsic drama.
2. Be specific.
3. Make sure the subject can live up to its claims.
4. Demonstrate the product.

5. Strive for reality.
6. Understate.
7. Practice the golden rule.

And here are the five steps toward making a sale:

1. Make a generous offer.
2. Appeal to both head and heart.
3. Be operational
4. Be thorough.
5. Be rationally (and tastefully) repetitive.

Doubtless you can provide your own checklist which is more broad or more simplified.

The important goal is that they should all lead to conviction. "The consciously entertained product of learning," writes Prof. John R. Kirk, "is *belief*. It does not . . . incite us to immediate action, but 'puts us into such a condition that we shall behave in some certain way, when the occasion arises.'"

For every ad, commercial, and campaign, there are two kinds of audiences: those who may do something about the message later, and those who may do something about it now. Copy which communicates to both audiences produces lasting conviction.

CONTEXT

Where Copy Strategy Comes From

If you could write a newspaper ad, to appear tomorrow, about an ingenious new kind of umbrella, and if you could be sure that tomorrow it would rain, you could expect that ad to be effective.

If you could create a television commercial that would be seen in three-dimensional color, while all other television commercials were in two-dimensional black and white, you could expect your commercial to be noticed and talked about.

If you could write a magazine ad about the first low-priced helicopter that could be carried on a man's back, you could be pretty sure of an audience.

The point is that *context* is important. Important? It's as crucial to you, as a communicator, as gravity is to you as a human being. (But come to think of it, gravity too is only a context, for when you are a space copywriter you will have to learn to write without it!)

What kind of contexts must you contend with? An infinite number. Psychologist Samuel Bois defines context as "the field of forces" in a situation, which he divides into environment, individual perceptions, group formations, and communication patterns.

Thinking in advertising terms, we should be aware of such contexts as the following: competition; time and seasonality; media; distribution, price and trade relations; the changing market, with its complex audience; people's habits, shared views, and prejudices.

Remember that the ideal copywriter is a mirror, a chameleon, a sounding board. He is so aware, so sensitive to the situation, that whatever his copy strategy may be, it reflects all the contexts relating to it.

A Brief Catalogue of Contexts

Let us first consider how copy strategy is affected by the context of its competition—by the facts about other similar products with which it is connected in the public's mind.

We copywriters have to be keenly aware of how our product stacks up with our competitor's products. What is its primary purpose compared with theirs? Why did its manufacturer develop it in the first place, and what is its history and future potential relative to theirs?

Suppose our product is a household cleanser, like Spic & Span, in a powder form. Along comes a liquid cleanser like Lestoil, and starts gobbling up the market. Lestoil does so well that the other manufacturers, including the makers of Spic & Span, introduce liquid cleansers, such as Mr. Clean and Handy Andy. Poor Spic & Span, in context with these new, glamorous products, seems to be old-fashioned and out of step. It begins to lose its share of the market. The brand men responsible for Spic & Span's sales, plus the copywriters and their fellow strategists at the agency, all search for a solution for the slipping brand within the context of the new competitive picture. They find it in that very concentrated, powdery consistency of Spic & Span which had seemed to be all negative and in the very nature of the liquids which had seemed to be all positive. Liquid cleaners, they discover, are fine when taken directly from the bottle and used for small spots. But when they are diluted in water, for the larger areas, they do not have as much cleaning power as concentrated, powdery Spic & Span has. A new copy strategy is written. The advertisers decide to concentrate their attack on one specific context in the household cleaning a woman does. Spic & Span, they say, is "The Big Job Cleaner." The brand's share-of-market immediately starts climbing.

A similar situation is the context of Clorox bleach. Clorox is a relatively strong disinfectant stain remover. Detergents are the big sellers. But Clorox, in this competitive context, runs ads featuring dirty little boys and girls who have *really* rubbed the grime into their clothes. "Clorox gets out dirt detergents leave in!" says the headline and the copy reads "Detergents alone can't wash out ground-in body dirt. You need the added power of Clorox bleach. Moral: *Don't ask detergents to do a Clorox job!*"

Dynel was a new synthetic kind of fiber which could be used to make women's coats resembling different kinds of fur. The competitive context was the built-in respect women have for "the real thing" and their long association with animal furs. The advertiser ran a series of ads featuring haughty models with handsome coats and the proud line, "It's not fake anything. It's real Dynel."

Excedrin and Compōz were two new remedies in a competitive context of aspirin, Bufferin, Anacin and many other analgesics. Excedrin was formulated and advertised as "The extra-strength pain reliever—tablet for tablet 50% stronger than aspirin for relief of headache pain." Compōz was advertised for *its* own segment of the market: "Headache, take aspirin; tension, take Compōz" . . . "Compōz does for tension, what aspirin does for headache." Both products won immediate success, because their copy was aware of context and they carved their own exclusive new niches.

Manufacturers Trust, a bank indistinguishable in the context of dozens of other New York banks, gained immediate attention with clever "non-ady" animated commercials. (They have since been emulated, but at that time the approach was brand new.) They followed these attention-getters by offering fashionable checkbooks, in various colorful designs and materials. The commercial featuring those checkbooks had, as its spokeswoman, a beautiful Negro entertainer, Diahann Carroll. Casting of Miss Carroll, some years before the Civil Rights campaign made integration in commercials commonplace, was also a context of unusual interest.

All successful new products, or products which effectively advertise innovations, are taking advantage of their competitive context: Chase & Sanborn, the first *dated* coffee; Tender Leaf Tea, the first to use teabags; Blue Bonnet Margarine, the first with a "squeeze bag" when margarine, by law, had to be artificially colored by the consumer; Boron premium gas, the first to claim that "it cleans your carburetor while you drive"; Winston, the cigarette which dramatized most forcefully the fact that it had good taste as well as filtering ("Tastes good, like a cigarette should").

Yet, in contrast with the copywriting which has recognized the need to stand out in the competitive context, we have the age-old sameness of the language of advertising. Here, for example, are the headlines of six different cigarette ads, all of which have hackneyed illustrations:

> Viceroy's got the taste that's right!
>
> Hungry for flavor? Tareyton's got it!
>
> Taste the delicious difference—only in new Montclair!
>
> When a cigarette means a lot . . . get lots more from L & M.
>
> Camel—every inch a real smoke.
>
> Tastes great because the tobaccos are!

Competitive context covers a wide range of considerations, and we copywriters, if we are thorough, will consider them all before rushing into print. For example, here is a checklist which creative director Dermott McCarthy presented for the General Foods advertisers:

> The competitive climate calls for a lot of knowledge about competing brands and all that competes for the prospect's interest and attention.
>
> 1. *Direct competition:* Whether the product is a cereal, a dog food, or a beverage, there is a great deal to know and learn about all other brands that compete directly with it. About the products themselves, their advertising, product image, distribution. About their strengths and weaknesses and the attitudes of their users. The current strategy for Gaines-burgers reflects facts learned about the appeals of canned and dry dog foods.
>
> 2. *Indirect competition:* This requires knowledge of other products that fill similar needs but are not exactly like your product. Orange juice is Tang's competitor—not some other brand of instant breakfast drink. Competition for Postum came from Sanka, not from another cereal beverage.
>
> Other indirect competition may include quite different products and services that compete for the consumer's dollars. This applies more often to fields other than the food field—when a family makes do with an old car, for instance, in order to take a trip to Europe or buy a new house.
>
> 3. *Competition for consumer attention:* All other advertising competes for consumer attention. So does the editorial material in the magazine in which your ad appears . . . so does the programming on the network or the opposite network compete for attention with your commercial. Current events—the World Series or Christmas may be competing with your advertising at certain times.

The second category of contexts we mentioned was "time and seasonality."

Consider the context of the season. We imagined the case of the umbrella. More predictable was the copy for Ballantine's beer with the catchy theme song "Hey, get your cold beer!" Beer sales go up in the summer. It took no great prescience for the copywriter to know there would be hot days during the summer. Americans like their beer cold. And when the weather is hot, they like to quench their thirst with ice-cold liquids. "Hey, get your cold beer!" was a natural in that seasonal context. So obvious, indeed, it seemed strange that no beer had stressed the point so effectively before. But that is the case with all good copy. You know it's good when it is so simple that everyone automatically asks, "Why didn't someone think of that before?"

The context of time—or timing—is one of the most common considerations. "Showmanship," said a producer, "is knowing what the public wants before it knows it wants it." Often an inventor—or a copywriter— can be ahead of his times, as Alex F. Osborn points out in the cases of the gyroscope and pneumatic tires:

He (Léon Foucault) worked this out (his gyroscope) in 1852 to demonstrate the rotation of the earth. Thus its only use at that time was to prove something already known. On the other hand, when Elmer Sperry worked out his gyrocompass, there was an urgent need for it on airplanes, as well as on modern ocean liners.

When Robert Thompson thought up pneumatic tires in 1845, there were no motor vehicles. But when, in 1888, John Boyd Dunlop brought out an improvement on Thompson's creation, Dunlop's new air-filled tire fitted a need that was just starting to snowball—automobiles were on their way.

Here are some examples of good copy, in the context of time.

An ad for White Owl cigars entitled "What a man should know when he switches to cigar smoking." The ad was informative and specific, with subheads like these:

The correct way to light a cigar.
You don't have to inhale to enjoy a cigar.
How to add to your cigar smoking pleasure.
What shape of cigar to start with.
Why smoke a White Owl Miniature?
Extra enjoyment in the fraternity of cigar smokers.

Copywriter Jack Reynolds describes the circumstance that made this ad so timely:

The ad ran on the Monday morning following the U.S. Surgeon General's report condemning cigarette smoking and giving a clean bill of health to cigar smoking. This was the first informative ad run by a cigar maker on the joys of cigar smoking and the only ad run by any cigar manufacturer following the health bombshell. The ad was quoted in Bob Considine's nationally syndicated column, reprinted in a *Business Week* editorial, quoted extensively in a *Wall Street Journal* front-page article, and mentioned in the Reuters news dispatch to London. Meanwhile, back at the cigar stand, the phones were ringing from distributors, salesmen and competitors complimenting the ad for its timing, tone and execution. Orders were booked in such volume that the problem now has become "how will we be able to make enough cigars?"

That Sears, Roebuck ad mentioned before, which featured a new kind of TV set appeared at a time when color TV, after years of slow sales, came into its own and many more TV programs were broadcast in color: "Sears announces color TV your kids can tune as easily as black and white."

Bert and Harry, the two animated characters who appeared on TV for Piel's Beer, were the brainchildren of a copywriter and art director who felt the context of the times—i.e., a revulsion, especially in New York, where Piel's was sold, against the pompousness of most beer advertising. The copy was satirical. The advertiser, in effect, joked about himself, and for a year or two the public responded mightily.

Greyhound Bus recognized the context of overcrowded highways, the danger of legalized high speed, and the increasing inconvenience of motoring. Their new slogan: "It's such a comfort to take the bus and leave the driving to us."

Kaiser Steel, at a time when many civic groups in California were up in arms over the size and ugliness of new freeway construction, ran several newspaper ads about the lightness and beauty of steel over concrete. A few years before or after, the ads might have received scant attention. In their context, they drew response so intense that Kaiser had to stop the campaign to devote time to servicing the inquirers.

"Blow some my way" was a cigarette ad, featuring a woman, which appeared at a time when women's suffrage led to new daring. "A Hog Can Cross the Country without Changing Trains—But You Can't" struck a public nerve when railroad travel was at its height.

Timing is crucially important. But how do you recognize the time, appreciate the right time?

The solution goes back to the determination to steep ourselves in our subject and all the field of forces that can affect it. If we know them well enough, they will not only tell us what to do but when to do it.

Now let us consider the context of the media in which the communication will appear. Day by day, in every way, media have become more competitive. The competition among advertisers in any one magazine is intense. But the competitive context is even stiffer from the editorial content (who *wants* to read the advertisements?). Often-repeated statistics include the fact that the average person reads only four ads in a magazine, devotes only 14 hours to reading ads in newspapers during a year, is exposed to half a billion advertising messages. That's *some* context in which to write copy.

What can we do about it? One way is to be compatible with the context of the media in which our messages appear. When advertising was first accepted for the *Reader's Digest,* some advertisers used the same informative, storytelling technique of the editorial context. This worked fine until everyone began to do it and many advertisers cheated the reader by pulling him into a dull, meretricious ad. Then readers probably became suspicious of *all* the imitators.

But we can be compatible without being slavishly imitative. Recently, there has been a trend toward more selective media-buying. An ad in the *New Yorker* or the *Saturday Review* usually deserves a different tone of voice from one in *Life* or *Look*. Certainly sports fans who read *Sports Illustrated* would be interested in an ad which had something really useful to say about their special interest, at the very time they are concentrating on the subject.

But another way to take advantage of the context of media is by being deliberately *in*compatible—in order to stand out by contrast. For example, the CBS network ran a picture of its distinctive trademark, the big eye, in the midst of an all-type page of classified ads. Goodyear tires dominated an issue of *Harper's Bazaar* with pictures of delicate fashion models astride those usually mundane black rubber doughnuts.

Innovations which have taken advantage of media context include the first comic strip ad, the first full-color ads in newspapers with the quality of magazine reproduction, inserts and gatefolds and "pop-ups" in magazines, television commercials without words and radio commercials that stressed color. These, and many more, were techniques which enabled their messages to stand out in the context of their media. But all the other principles on which these chapters are based—interest, believability, involvement, conviction—all these can make your messages more effective in media context, if you keep yourself constantly *aware.*

What about the context of distribution? Sometimes a product has the problem—as in the case of the variety of new products developed by the Alberto-Culver company—of shelf-space lagging behind popular demand. Their advertising won the consumers, but they could not keep enough "facings" on the dealers' shelves. One obvious way for the copywriter to help solve such a problem is to tell the *consumer* about it. ("If you can't find the product on the shelf, demand it!")

Another example of distribution context was the case of Kaiser aluminum foil, which, being a latecomer in the market, lagged in distribution behind Alcoa and Reynolds. A brief "blitz" campaign was launched, using the most shocking kind of copy, originated by Stan Freberg. An animated oil salesman named Clark Smathers took his message to the public, in zany commercials that were "crazy like a fox." He demanded, in tongue-in-cheek fashion, that the grocers of America give equal shelf space to Kaiser Foil. "That's the American way," cried Smathers, hitting the grocer on the head with a mallet, as a toy band wildly played patriotic music.

We mentioned the context of price. What does the copywriter say if the product he writes about is higher or lower priced than its competition? Is it worth a higher price, and why? Will a lower price cheapen its reputation? One obvious way to offset the high-price problem is to tell its advantages more forcefully. Another is to preselect your audience and speak only to them. Copywriter Leo Burnett quotes this letter by Earle C. Howard to an automobile salesman, which long ago exemplified one answer to this problem of price context:

> Of course there will always be men who say, "Your price is too high"; "What discount will you give?"
> Some men go through life wearing "guaranteed all wool" suits marked

down to $11.98 (half cotton); hats "just as good as Knox" (no style to start with and which fade in two weeks to a sickly green); shoes "as good as Johnson & Murphy," marked down to $3.15 (paper soles); and watches in their pockets that can't tell the truth, $7.50. Some men go through life continuously uncomfortable, continuously wrong, continuously at a disadvantage, because they don't want quality—they aren't quality men. A Cadillac salesman hasn't time to fool with them.

There are, on the other hand, thousands of men who know what quality means; who know the mental ease and satisfaction which always accompanies quality. Many of these men can afford a Cadillac. These are our prospects. Depending on the quality and aggressiveness of Cadillac salesmanship, from 30 to 50% of these men in your territory will become Cadillac owners within three years or less.

What about the context of a lower price? One interesting way to capitalize on that situation is what was done for Hunt's Catsup. Instead of shouting the fact that Hunt's cost less, they traded themselves up—running advertising with the look and feel of a premium product. The customer was doubly pleased to find at the store that Hunt's actually cost less. Another approach is to capitalize on the *reason* for the low price, as did Robert Hall Clothes with their "low overhead" story.

We copywriters can never overlook the context of our product's status with the trade; for advertising can be totally effective with its audience and way off base with the men and women who still sell the public face to face. This is why copy should be thoroughly merchandised to the trade, and why you cannot divorce mass communication from personal salesmanship.

There is no point in writing copy that says "see our friendly dealer" if the dealer is unfriendly or "stop at the sign of service" if most of those gas stations are unattractive and their operators only concerned with pumping gas.

One effective idea has been for companies to *force* their personal representatives to live up to their advertising—as in the case of Texaco's "We promise" campaign and the Avis "We try harder" campaign.

Next comes the context of the changing market, with its complex audience. If we cultivate the everlasting attitude of the ideal copywriter, we must be always young and flexible. For the one truth about time is change. The city-dwellers move to the suburbs. The suburbs become megalopoles. Rural areas become mechanized. The teeming shopping district of the past, in the heart of the city, has lost the crowd to the superstore in the suburb. Supersonic jets are coming fast and international advertising grows twice as fast as domestic. "To market, to market, to buy a fat pig"—we can't find the market, it's getting too big!

But geographical markets are only part of the context. As people change physically and economically, they change in their needs and desires. The copywriter must be sensitive to social context—with his intuition, plus thorough, fact-finding research. For example, at this writing, the fastest growing market, quantitatively, is the youth market. Then, too, we have to consider that women in America are becoming more numerous than men, more wealthy and more influential. There is, of course, the increase in longevity which affects the market among the aged. All of these contexts have critical bearing on the form and content of the copywriter's message. "You aren't advertising to a standing army," says copywriter David Ogilvy, "you are advertising to a moving parade."

The context of the changing market emphasizes the need to treat each copy problem on its own without trying to codify rules from past advertising that appeared in different contexts. A browse through Julian Watkins' "100 Greatest Advertisements" is a nostalgic experience, but if we are clear-eyed we know that many of them are out of date today. "They Laughed When I Sat Down At the Piano" (Steinway) might sound cornball. "99 and 44/100% Pure" (Ivory soap) might be unbelievable. "Within The Curve Of A Woman's Arm," which was so daring that it deserved long copy, would get scant reading now. And "Somewhere West of Laramie"—"really, daddy, that's *too much!*"

Those ads would have the wrong context in tone. Phoebe Snow and "His Master's Voice" wouldn't square with today's technology. And movie star testimonials of the past, which had so much power, would now be passé to a public which is more sophisticated about movie stars and their endorsements.

The one sure prediction we can make about context is that the copy *we* write today will be just as dated to copywriters who come after us. This is why copywriting is a great profession for somebody who is a restless soul, who is youthful in spirit and wide-eyed with expectation.

The final item in our brief catalogue of contexts is people. Who are they at that "quick moment of time" when they are exposed to our ad? We already insisted that they are individuals and that we must treat them accordingly. But in the context of our times, we can find certain habits, shared views, and prejudices which they have in common and which copy can trigger.

Here are some examples:

The introduction of the Mustang played to a mood quite common to the people of 1964. Youth was in the news, restless, and reckless. American economy was booming. Young marrieds, with much disposable income, were leisure conscious, travel conscious, style conscious. It was a year of the swingers. Car racing, skiing, golf were on the rise. The Olympics were in the air. And here was a stick-shift, bucket-seat, Walter Mitty dream of a sports car at a popular price. The copy strategy was made to order. The campaign couldn't miss.

Diet-Rite Cola was a typical low-calorie product that rode the crest of a widespread feeling. The desire for physical fitness was in the air. The Kennedy family had left its mark on American mores—a need for excellence, a look of breeding and class. There had been a swing, for years, to light products—light beers and liquors, lightweight fabrics, a light cigarette. Pepsi had led the parade "for those who think young." Now people could drink the same good-tasting, lighthearted drink, but without the calories.

The context in which the Miss Clairol ads appeared ("Does she . . . or doesn't she?") was ripe for their strategy. Just a few years before, dyeing the hair was only for "cheap women." Now, with the improvement in those products (and the adroit change of the category to "hair coloring") that campaign was "right on target."

The context of people's views and habits seems constantly to change for the better. For one thing, more people are better educated. Higher wages and shorter work days make for more leisure—more leisure for more culture and broader interests. And all this makes for better communication, better copywriting.

This, then, is a brief catalogue of copy contexts. We have to be aware of all of them when we sit down to write. Most good copywriters try to be aware. Yet communication by context is still, and always will be, an inexact science. For how can anyone predict the many, many contexts tomorrow, next month, or next year?

Nobody can—no computer, no plans board, no research panel, no advertiser.

You have to be clairvoyant.

Supporting the Strategy

Copy strategy is a sometime thing. Sometimes we arrive at the strategy by long and rational study of all the contexts. Sometimes we have an inspiration so irresistible that we rationalize the strategy to suit the idea. In either case, we are sometimes right and sometimes wrong—the strategy may be right and the execution wrong, or vice versa.

Courage and vigor often have been able to defeat the most brilliant, reasonable strategists. John Caples cites how Napoleon succeeded by giving full rein to his horse, never looking to the rear, and how Willie Hoppe, the billiards expert, kept beating his opponents, because he was playing billiards, while they were playing Hoppe. Sheer momentum and confidence can make a campaign succeed even when the strategy seems wrong. The ideal, of course, is to have the right strategy, the right execution, and the courage and vigor to put across both.

We have already, throughout this chapter, cited examples where the copy strategy took fullest advantage of its surrounding context. The Spic

& Span strategy was a prime example. So were the strategies of the White Owl, Clorox, and Excedrin campaigns. Here are a few more examples which have already proved their success.

Bufferin, when it was first introduced, faced the context of overwhelming consumer acceptance of aspirin. Like the dwarf who can see farther than a giant when he is standing on the giant's shoulders, Bufferin succeeded through its competitor's popularity.

The Nash Rambler made its success in the context of the big, high-powered cars of Detroit. Its copy strategy was plain and simple—to fill a need for a compact, economy car. Acting like Jack the giant killer didn't hurt either.

The "institutional" magazine ads of Sears, Roebuck and Co. were designed to enhance the quality image of a chain store already accepted for low price. But these ads also operate in the context of discount houses attracting Sears' customers, department stores fighting for their lives, retail specialists for all sorts of items Sears sells, and local stores which may be closer to the consumer.

Those are all campaigns whose strategy reflected their contexts. How they were determined is a context in itself. Sooner or later it became a matter of someone making a judgment and being decisive. The common element in all those examples was this: whoever made the decision never looked to the rear. He put his full force behind the strategy and stayed with it; the ads were planned in a context of courage.

We copywriters, as we said in Chap. 1, are forever doing battle. Like all of the language of advertising, the term "copy strategy" has become sterile. Seldom, in our stuffy meetings, does it have the sound of a call to arms. But the true copy strategy should come from the gut. It should come from a copywriter acutely aware of his subject, familiar with all the facts in their context, *feeling* the right strategy, and then wholeheartedly fighting for it.

6

FACT-FINDING CAN BE FUN

Digging for facts can be every bit as exciting as using them—if we keep that state of mind, that special attitude we are so constantly prescribing. It is a wide-open attitude, or perhaps we should say wide-eyed—so that almost every fact you explore is a possibility.

There are a thousand ways to dig for facts, and they are often found in the unlikeliest places. The copywriter, if he has an intense curiosity, will not simply sit in his office and read the reports and interviews the other people bring him. But even quietly poring over books and reports can give you that heightened pulsebeat of discovery. Somewhere buried in the fine print may be the germ of a tremendous idea.

Fact-finding from Reports and Verbatims

Take the case of the headache remedy, Bufferin. It began as a minor new product for a limited market. Some people—less than 20 percent— are sensitive to plain aspirin, and Bufferin, with a combination of antacids added, was developed to oblige that small but potentially profitable group. The copywriter, searching for information, was poring over a long medical report containing statistics on levels of salicylate in the bloodstream.

Sounds pretty dull, doesn't it? Not on your life! Considering the eventual payoff, that copywriter was like a miner prospecting for gold.

Buried in the fine print, he discovered pay dirt. According to one statistical chart, salicylate—the pain-relieving ingredient of plain aspirin—got into the bloodstream faster when combined with Bufferin's ingredients, than it did with just plain aspirin.

How much faster? The mathematics were checked out, further laboratory tests were initiated, and from that time-consuming hunt came the copy claim, "Bufferin Acts Twice as Fast as Aspirin to Relieve Pain." A product which had been developed for only 20 percent of the market all at once had a powerful appeal for 100 percent, and a famous sales success was born.

Sitting on the desk of another copywriter were three or four fat books entitled *Depth Interviews*. It was motivation research, about half a million words—verbatim interviews with women about laundry soaps and detergents. The research department had sent interviewers into fifty housewives' homes, armed with tape recorders. The interviews were not intended to be statistical findings. The women were encouraged to talk freely, for as long as an hour, so their comments would not be what *they* would expect the interviewer to expect, but what they really believed.

On that occasion, the housewives were asked such questions as "What do you think of soap and detergent advertising?" "What do these soap claims mean to you (selection of claims)?" "Do you like to wash clothes?"

The interviewers could not have been more welcome. Those women had been exposed too long to the language of advertising. It was like the storming of the Bastille. They really let go. Soap and detergent advertising was all the same. It was unbelievable. Soap claims were insulting to a person's intelligence. White—clean—it's all the same. Who likes to wash clothes? But the *result*—*that* can be enjoyable.

The beauty of the comments was not that they were totally new or unexpected, but that they were natural and sincere and, above all, that they were *verbatim*—in the person's own words, unrehearsed and spontaneous. The copywriter, after reading hundreds of pages of such verbatim reports, got a feel for those poor consumers. While they all differed in the manner of their expression, certain common attitudes emerged. And they confirmed what the copywriter had felt for a long time, in his own "secret knowing."

In this case, the copywriter and researcher who had studied the interviews pieced them together into a montage—an audio tape recording, which was presented at a major meeting with the advertiser's staff. They had all received copies of the interviews, and presumably many had also read and studied them. But the authenticity and naturalness of the tape recordings drove home the points as no reading of them could do. The advertisers sat for an hour in a crowded conference room and heard themselves criticized, questioned, pleaded with, and pilloried. They *listened* to what the consumers had to say. Then, with a unanimity seldom achieved by a committee meeting, they made decisions. From that initial meeting emerged a new kind of detergent advertising campaign—the so-called "eye-witness" campaign for Cheer, in which hidden cameras were used to witness women's reactions to wash.

The cases of Cheer and Bufferin are examples of tracking down facts from reports. Even more exciting are the times when the copywriter goes "on location" to find them.

Fact-finding from Personal Interviews

You can find plenty of usable facts from secondhand reports. But most good copywriters feel more confident when they get out of the ivory tower and do the interviewing themselves.

The knack of interviewing can be as much a part of your trade as the ability to put words together. You not only have to have a nose for news, but you have to be able to draw people out, to keep stubbornly following one line of questioning without antagonizing. And you have to be a "quick study" when you scent some random clue in the conversation. Good ideas don't always happen dramatically; they can be buried in the mine of murky conversation.

Take the case of the author interviewing a tire engineer to get an idea for a TV commercial about aviation tires. In this case, the interviewer had a somewhat antagonistic audience. You will often find that scientists are suspicious of "admen" who come ferreting out facts that might be twisted or misconstrued to mislead the public.

One way to communicate with that audience was to convince him that the copywriter had the same passion for veracity that he had. Another was to admit ignorance and patiently to ask him to keep translating into layman's language. A third was to show a complete absorption and interest in his work, to ask him to talk all around it, and to proceed at his own pace.

Some writers have "total recall" and only need a few trigger words to bring back the whole interview. This writer, on the other hand, has acquired a lifelong habit of taking word-for-word notes of every interview, in a speedwriting of his own. In more recent years, the tape recorder has supplemented the notebook. But in either case, those tools have to be made so unobtrusive that the person interviewed will not feel "on stage." The secret is an almost hypnotic trick—to keep his eyes fixed on yours and to show him such undivided attention that he becomes engrossed in his subject and concentrates on answering the questions put to him. After a brief warmup, he forgets the notebook or the tape recorder, his possible prejudice toward the outsider, and even, at times, the identity of the questioner himself. People like to talk about what interests them most; the knack is to get them warmed up and going.

To get back to the case of the aviation tires. This was a typically modest development engineer. He resisted, for at least an hour, answering any question with a positive assertion that *his* company's tires were different or better or, for that matter, interesting to a television audience. But he did, in answer to many questions, get warmed up on the subject of cord angles, plies, tread thickness, rubber compounds, etc. He answered questions about high-speed testing, about over- and under-inflation, about the scope and variety of aviation tires. And each time, he would say, "but your audience wouldn't be interested in that," or "of course, most good tire makers do exactly the same thing."

Somewhere in the course of this long, seemingly unrewarding interview, the engineer let drop a curious irrelevance. It was said so softly and passed over so quickly that the copywriter only half heard it.

He had to pause and ask the engineer to repeat himself: "What was that? Will you repeat that? When those tires take off from the aircraft carrier . . . ?"

"I said, of course, when the catapult releases the plane, the centrifugal force is so great that the tires, for a split-second, are a hundred percent deflated. You see . . ."

"A what percent deflated?"

"Well, in a manner of speaking, a hundred percent deflated. You see, the force is so great, they are pushed down so violently on the deck . . ."

From that chance, almost inaudible remark buried in the midst of an hour's conversation the copywriter found his gold nugget: an intriguing lead for a commercial which began, "Imagine a tire that has to be built so strong that it can actually run, for a split second, one hundred percent flat. . . ."

"*Will you repeat that?*" This is a key query for the successful interviewer, which this writer learned from the master, Allen Funt. To Funt, who for so many years produced "Candid Mike" and "Candid Camera," the art of questioning is second nature. He has noticed that people, speaking normally, repeat phrases and expressions a great number of times. So they are seldom surprised when asked by an interviewer to repeat themselves. He tells how, when he wishes to shoot plenty of film of one particular sequence, to allow for ease of editing later, he can ask a person to repeat a remark over and over again.

"What did you say?" Funt will ask. "Oh, come now, I don't believe you. Will you repeat that? You really mean it? Say that again. . . . Say that again. . . . Say that again." When you are a reporter, it is a good practice to encourage your subject to keep repeating himself, until you have thoroughly clarified and simplified his comments.

The example of the aviation tires was an isolated remark in the midst of much unusable material. Often a copywriter will find an embarrassment of riches. As he delves for information, his imaginative mind will project itself into dozens of different creative directions. As in the process of looking for ideas, we are best advised not to try to rationalize, assess, and reject the material as we are collecting it. We should take it in helter-skelter and absorb and evaluate it later. Even so, as he interviews, the copywriter is practicing his craft, thinking of creative ideas which may lead the interview down one path and another. Here, for example, are notes from an interview about the production of beer. In parentheses, along with some of the comments, we have inserted the kind of "instant ideas" a copywriter might be having, along with his questions and answers:

BREWER: If you put a bottle of beer on your shelf for a year and tasted it, the chances are you wouldn't like it.

COPYWRITER: Why not?

BREWER: Well, there are certain reactions that occur, a breakdown of certain proteins and you get a bad flavor.

(*Copywriter's thoughts:* "Could we educate the public that beer should be fresh—date the cans—talk about beer the way we talk about fresh bread—guarantee it will be taken off the shelves if it isn't?")

COPYWRITER: Do you have any different kind of barley from your competitors?

BREWER: They buy the same types. There are certain approved malting barley varieties and we buy the same varieties. However, each company uses different blends in processing.

COPYWRITER: They have names?

BREWER: Yes . . .

COPYWRITER: What are they called?

BREWER: Kindred, Traill, Moncalm, and Parkland. And then there have been some new varieties, Trophy and Larker, approved for brewing purposes.

(*Copywriter's thoughts:* "Must look into that—some of those names might be provocative or different. Maybe they could concentrate on one special variety for us to dramatize—or we could play up the color or taste or characteristics of one or two . . . or a blend. 'The beer with a blend of barleys,' not a bad slogan. Would different blends affect the flavor? The color of the beer? That name 'Kindred' might give rise to some phrase like 'kindred soul' (ugh!). Maybe 'The Soul of Beer.' ")

COPYWRITER: Well now, the higher the figure on the pH, what would that mean in terms of beer?

BREWER: The higher the figure the more alkaline it would be. Beers are usually on the tart or slightly acid side. A very narrow range too. It might be a pH of around 4 to 4.5.

COPYWRITER: What does acid mean, sour?

BREWER: Slight acidity, yes.

COPYWRITER: The more acid it is the more you feel a tartness, a sourness. So you say the more pH the less tartness?

BREWER: Yes, but then you have to watch for an alkalinity taste.

(*Copywriter's thoughts:* "Wonder if there's anything in 'not too bitter, not too sweet' or just the opposite—should they make their beer the sweet one or the tart one, like 'just a hint of mint,' the beer with a gentle bite or nip or tender touch on the tongue????")

COPYWRITER: Is there anything besides aesthetics that's important about a head?

BREWER: No, I would say primarily aesthetics—to me, that's important. It does foam—in other words. A lot of people drink beer without foam. They intentionally pour their beer so there is no foam after they fill their glass. But for us in the brewing industry, our whole tradition is in favor of foam.

(*Copywriter's thoughts:* " 'If we can hold our head while all about us' . . . 'Our beer keeps its head' . . . 'Head and shoulders above the others' . . . 'Do you like old-fashioned foam?' Maybe we feature guys with handlebar moustaches —handlebar foam—foam you can wrap your lips around . . . Foam, Home, Roam, Dome, Comb. . . .")

But interviewing the men who make the beer gives the copywriter only part of the facts. From his feel for the beer in the brewery, he wants to get a feel for beer at the store. How and why do people buy beer in general and one brand in particular? Armed with a tape recorder, he goes to the marketplace. He stops consumers, fixes them with his glittering eye, and asks all sorts of seemingly irrelevant questions.

COPYWRITER: Why is it that you selected Olympia just now instead of another among the many other brands here?

CONSUMER: Well, I like the bottles better.

COPYWRITER: Why is that? What is the difference between the bottles?

CONSUMER: I don't know, I just like them better than cans.

COPYWRITER: What has this brand got over any other brand, besides the bottles that you just mentioned. Any other reason you buy it?

CONSUMER: No.

COPYWRITER: Would you usually choose a light beer then, because Oly is considered a light beer rather than a heavy?

CONSUMER: Now, that's something I never understood, the difference between a light beer and a heavy beer. There are so many different types out that I go for taste more than anything.

COPYWRITER: Would you buy a fresh brewed, that is a beer that might have a date on the can indicating how long it had been aged?

CONSUMER: Well, they never put out a fresh-brewed beer anyway. They let it age for a few months anyway . . . a few months before they put it on the market.

COPYWRITER: In other words you would assume that it was fresh anyway if it were out on the counter of the store. Can you tell me the ingredients of beer?

CONSUMER: No, I don't know much about that.

COPYWRITER: Would the aroma of the beer make any difference to you?

CONSUMER: That's the reason. Some beers are too sour, and I don't like that either.

COPYWRITER: Does the aroma have anything to do with your likes or dislikes of the beer or brand?

CONSUMER: No, I don't think it does.

COPYWRITER: Or the color of the beer?

CONSUMER: I think the light color is more desirable.

COPYWRITER: Do you like a long-lasting head on a glass of beer?

CONSUMER: Yes, I believe I do. When you used to get beer, they'd sell it to you in a bucket and it had to be creamy on the top of it and it had to stay there for a long time. It doesn't stay on beer now, hardly any brand.

COPYWRITER: Do you prefer a light or a full-bodied beer?

CONSUMER: Well, as a matter of fact, to be honest with you, during the past seven or eight years, the only beer that I have ever drank is Oly and Miller's. I have deviated once in a while when we were over at some other people's homes or something like that—we have whatever they have—but in regards to a full-bodied beer what I would say is a full-bodied beer is one of these imports such as Löwenbrau, or something like that.

No one of those questions and answers, in itself, will produce worthwhile creative ideas. But the copywriter is gestating. He is absorbing facts from a variety of different directions. Somehow, somewhere, the jigsaw puzzle may suddenly be assembled.

And so it goes. We dig for facts by reading up on them, getting out and going places, questioning, questioning, questioning. We go "all around the subject"—the "serendipity" route.

Experiments with the Product

Another exciting way we get our facts is by doing. Sometimes, to find the inherent interest of a product, we have to play with it, handle it, eye it, examine it, use it in a hundred different ways, many for which it was never intended. Those who make the product can tell us just so much. Often they themselves are too close to their brainchild to discover the elusive clue to selling it.

Several copywriters, for example, spent months of experimenting, to find a series of meaningful claims and demonstrations for Kaiser aluminum foil. This foil had a unique quilted pattern, embossed into the foil as it was rolled. Originally, the pattern had been designed not only for aesthetic reasons, but because the manner of its embossing gave the metal extra tensile strength. Now, after long experience in many uses of the foil, the "home economist" copywriter, Jane Worthington, felt that there were side benefits to the quilted pattern. Her hunch told her that the hundreds of tiny quilts, with their ridges and valleys, would have an effect on the cooking of various kinds of food.

In a spirit of serendipity (thinking in all different directions, hoping for that lucky inspiration), she and her colleagues went into the kitchen and began to cook. Packets containing individual vegetables—peas, corn, broccoli. Packets with a mixture of meats and vegetables. Packets with different cuts of meat. Various baked dishes. Would the quilts help to prevent sticking? An experiment with the stickiest kind of pastry— caramel rolls—indicated that they would. One experiment with tender tiny peas had the writers hopping. The peas cooked in plain foil came out shriveled and dry compared with the peas in quilted foil. But in the next experiment, under the same conditions, the phenomenon failed to repeat itself. Both sets of peas were big and robust. A dead end.

How about the different ways of wrapping the food? Drugstore wraps. The copywriters' own ingenious folds. Loose wraps and tight. They tried dozens of experiments, some faintly encouraging, most dashingly bad.

After these relatively amateur attempts, the writers and their clients approached the experimental kitchens of an independent magazine and those of outside home economists to pursue some of their faint glimmers and copy approaches on a more scientifically controlled basis.

Somewhere along the line the head of the home economics department of a large university let drop the fact that, when she used plain foil to pot-roast meat or to roast turkey, she always crinkled the foil to give the juices some kind of surface on which "to get a grip"—otherwise the moisture might all roll down to the bottom of the wrap. From the independent magazine came word that condensation forming inside the wrap might, through the outside heat in the oven, rise and fall with a kind of "basting action," helping to keep the meat moist.

More experiments were held. More substantiation. Careful records were kept. All types of ingenious trials were made.

From the first free-wheeling experiments and the more scientific ones which grew out of them came an interesting new advertising campaign: "Quilted Kaiser foil 'does the basting for you.'" From the experiments made with all different types and grades of meat later arose a campaign encouraging consumers to cook "bargain cuts" of meat in quilted Kaiser foil, to enable them to "cook in their own rich juices" and to taste more juicy and tender than with the open-roasting method.

Here is another example of a copywriter experimenting with the product —a new General Electric portable TV set. Bob Higbee, the writer, not only demonstrated the product, but also appeared in the ad. Here are the headline and captions of the ad, which were accompanied by news-type photos:

GENERAL ELECTRIC BIG-SCREEN PORTABLE
PULLED IN A SHARP PICTURE FROM 62½ MILES AWAY

1. 6 A.M.—Midtown Manhattan. We loaded a General Electric Big-Screen Portable into a car. After a preliminary test, we set off through the

Lincoln Tunnel. Object: To see how far away we could go from TV stations and still get a sharp picture.

2. Noon—Old Bridge, N.J. We carried the set (easily—it weighs only 30 lbs.) into a diner, plugged it in. It got a brilliant picture. As the diner owner remarked, a big picture. She's right. It's 155 square inches big. Distance: 32 air miles from N.Y.

3. 4 P.M.—Mantoloking, N.J. In the police station, the Big-Screen pulled in N.Y.—51 miles away. More amazing, the police chief noted, we did it with "horns" (his term for the built-in antenna).

4. 4:30 P.M.—Mantoloking, N.J. The police sergeant let us try out set on his roof antenna in his apartment above the station. It fought his console to a stand-off, 62½ miles from Philadelphia.

5. Next day—Bear Mountain Park, N.Y. At the Inn, the General Electric Big-Screen did nobly. It's easy to take on a trip—light and trim . . . its Slim Silhouette cabinet is 15 inches deep. From N.Y.: 31 miles.

6. Third day—Easton, Conn. New York came in sharp and clear from 51 air miles out. How? Because the tetrode tuner packs even greater picture power than before.

7. 6 P.M.—Lenox, Mass. High in the Berkshires. We hooked up to a rotating roof antenna at Cranwell School, run by the Jesuit Fathers. New York came in as well as it does on their console—from 119 miles out! This portable works wherever a console will.

And here is the writer's explanation:

At the time this ad appeared, portable television was still in the experimental stage.

People liked the idea, but naturally wondered whether the little job could perform as well as the leviathans they were used to.

I figured it would be a good idea to take the set out and prove it. I took a photographer along with me, and we produced the ad as we went along.

The ad performed top of its category in Starch, and the General Electric people pulled in a lot of mail, two of which letters complained that G. E. now seemed to be under the Roman church. The portable had been proved once and for all.

This kind of pursuit is both fact-finding and creative. You have to be persistent, too, and not allow a few blind alleys to stop the pursuit. Once, when this writer had the inspiration to shave the fuzz off a peach with a Remington shaver—to demonstrate its clean, gentle shave—his first experiments failed. No fuzz would fall. He was about to abandon the idea when it was discovered that the particular batch of peaches he had been shaving had been carefully defuzzed before delivery to the store.

So far we have been talking about digging for facts in order to find a creative direction. Often, when the direction is already established, the digging just begins. Here, for example, are some verbatims from a copywriter's interviews for a whole new direction in paint advertising. The idea was to advertise a new line of interior paints with a fashion approach similar to that used for cosmetics and clothing. Paints in the past had always been sold as hardware items. The writers, and other members of their team (art director, stylist, etc.) went to the experts (the editors of a leading beauty magazine) for reactions to this new marketing approach:

INTERVIEWER: The reason why we came to you was that we got an idea about house paints that comes closer to your area than it does to the decorating area. The colors that you see in front of you and the layouts and copy that I've asked you to look at are part of a whole new theory we have about promoting paint. It probably looks to you more like a cosmetic ad, doesn't it, than a paint ad?

EDITOR: Yes, it does, and I think probably for that reason it looks very exciting to me. I think the colors in themselves—many of them are actually—well, certainly three of them, the blue, the turquoise blue and the deeper blue— and the raspberry, would you call that?—are shades that look very good to us in the fashion magazines for fall ready-to-wear.

INTERVIEWER: We had thought so. You could tell us a great deal about color as it applies to the cosmetic field. The paint people are also in the color business but have never identified themselves as closely with it as the cosmetic houses. I wonder if you could tell us a bit about color from a business point of view as it applies to cosmetics.

EDITOR: I think the main point that the large cosmetic houses have achieved is that they have been able to impress upon the American woman that every Spring and every Fall she has to completely retrain her eye toward color, both in fashion and in makeup. I think where she might have had only one lipstick in her wardrobe 10 years ago—and that would be a nice true clear red, which she felt would coordinate with anything in her wardrobe—she now wouldn't be caught dead without three lipsticks—a clear red, a pink tone red, and perhaps a coral tone red. And I think how she blends these, or wears one over the other, or changes to a deeper intensity for evening is all something that the manufacturer himself, through his own advertising, has trained her to expect and need.

ASSISTANT EDITOR: Don't you think that the American woman has lost a lot of her self-consciousness about colors?

EDITOR: Yes, absolutely. I think for instance now, she'll wear, on a city street in the middle of winter, a bright orange coat, and she'll know that she has to have a lipstick somewhere in that shade range to look becoming. By the same token she's been trained, through the manufacturer in his advertising and in promotion, to realize that all makeup and fashion color interrelate. The hair-coloring field, which is so phenomenally successful right now, is related to your complexion. You can't change your hair color unless you change your complexion shade accordingly, or if you have a certain complexion you know you may only go to a certain range of hair shades. You key your fashion shades to your dress shade, and I think this idea, where you would then key your room colors to your own fashion concept would be great.

INTERVIEWER: Now do you think the concept that the ready-to-wear industries and the cosmetic industry and several other industries have used in relation to each other could be applied to the paint business?

EDITOR: Yes, I do and I think the more concrete direction you could give the women as to feeling secure in selecting a given shade or combining shades better, the more help you'd be to her.

INTERVIEWER: Well they'll have to be educated in much the same way they were in makeup.

EDITOR: Exactly.

Facts from that interview were not only helpful in developing advertising, but the tape recordings were used in validating the approach to the client.

What Facts Should We Know?

Again, we repeat, there is no formula. Through our own ingenuity, and through the fact-finding convenience of computers, there is no possible fact pertinent to a product that we cannot discover. Can we know too much? It used to be said that copywriters could know too much about a subject—that they would lose their fresh objectivity if they became as familiar with a product as are the specialists who produce it.

There may be some validity to that notion. Certainly if a copywriter becomes pedantic about his subject, it will be difficult for him to communicate clearly with the consumer who is relatively ignorant about it.

But, in most cases, there need be no fear this will happen, however thorough the copywriter may be in his quest. For one thing, deadlines to produce advertising are usually so tight that copywriters would never have enough time to become pedantic on any given subject. For another thing, the copywriter usually sweeps the product with a broader radar than its creators do. Dermott McCarthy lists the following characteristics one should know about a product:

1. *Physical characteristics*
    a. Its form, price, packaging, sizes, etc.
    b. What is it made from? How is it made?
    c. Color, flavor, shape.
    (Is it a brand-new form of dog food, like Gaines-burgers? Cheer's blue color was of major advertising importance.)
2. *Functional characteristics*
    a. What is it used for? What might it be used for?
    b. What problems does it solve? How well?
    c. What emotional needs does it satisfy?

  d. How often is it used? When? Where?
  (The nutritional problem solved by Borden's Life-Line is a rational thing;
  the appetite appeal of Lady Borden Cherry Vanilla ice cream is a more
  emotional matter.)
 3. *"Personal" characteristics*
  a. Is it a new product like Excedrin?
   Well established like Jell-O?
  b. Is it a leader? A runner up?
  c. What is its personality—how is it seen?
   Modern, or old-fashioned as Postum?
   Masculine or feminine?
   Quick-and-easy or worth the effort?
   Pure pleasure or serious problem-solver?
 4. *More*
  Study it. Find something new and interesting about it. There is no
  such thing as a *dull product.*

McCarthy, in his talk from which the above extract was taken, then quotes copy from the following Young & Rubicam house ad, which simply depicts a nail with callouts of all the characteristics one might notice about it:

  (*Illustration of nail*)
  You'd expect to pay a nickel for such a nail
  (*Callouts:*) 1. This tempered-steel nail will penetrate *poured* concrete.
      2. Notice the lengthwise fluting on the shaft: it prevents split-
       ting, whether you are driving into concrete or wood.
      3. The fluting gives the nail a screw-like grip. It won't pull
       out.
      4. The head will not split off. See how it is shaped to counter-
       sink itself on the final blow of the hammer.
      5. Good as it is, you can buy a pound of these nails for 49¢.
       There are approximately 100 in a pound.
 Moral: There is no such thing as a dull product.
    Only dull approaches to interesting products.
    What's your problem?

Another reason why the copywriter cannot know too much about a product is that he usually approaches it from a standing start. The specialists who make it have usually spent a lifetime in their particular specialty. The copywriter is a dilettante about the product. And because he has to translate what he has learned to other dilettantes, he is forever simplifying what he has learned in terms everyone can understand.

Finally, as we have said before, the facts we look for, the facts we find, and the facts we interpret, should all be usable. Each person who comes fresh to our message should be able to "perform the operation and check the concept." Our facts should *not* be, like Robert Paul Smith's facts of childhood (in *Where did you go? Out. What did you do? Nothing.*):

> Facts, facts, facts. If you cut yourself in the web of skin between your thumb and forefinger, you die. That's it. No ifs or buts. Cut. Die. Let's get on to other things. If you eat sugar lumps, you get worms. If you cut a worm in half, he don't feel a thing, and you get two worms. Grasshoppers spit tobacco. Step on a crack, break your mother's back.

Those are superstitious facts, passed on from one generation to another. The copywriter's facts are supposed to contribute to the essence and reality of what he has to communicate. That is why he, and he alone, must collect them—firsthand.

7

HOW DO WE GET IDEAS?

Ideas are the coin of the copywriter's realm. We know how we get them, but it is difficult to articulate. Because the minute you start to analyze the process of getting ideas—the minute you start to get formal about it—you are denying the spirit of the act itself. People who are creative (and everyone is creative, but we are talking about those who make their living at it, day in and day out) are probably a little ashamed to tell the truth. We know, in our secret knowing, that the best ways we get ideas are childlike, irrational, and—in our solemn society—seemingly frivolous.

So we give formal names to the process, like "creativity" and "ideation." Students like Alex Osborn, Harold Rugg, and James Webb Young, who have attempted to codify the process, agree that it *is* a process, with certain definable stages. Osborn once wrote:

> Those who have studied and practiced creativity realize that its process is necessarily a stop-and-go, catch-as-catch-can operation—one which can never be exact enough to rate as scientific. The most that can honestly be said is that it usually includes some or all of these phases:
> 1. Orientation: Pointing up the problem.
> 2. Preparation: Gathering pertinent data.
> 3. Analysis: Breaking down the relevant material.
> 4. Ideation: Piling up alternatives by way of ideas.

5. Incubation: Letting up, to invite illumination.
6. Synthesis: Putting the pieces together.
7. Evaluation: Judging the resultant ideas.

Harold Rugg gave his summary in a somewhat different order, but in similar terms:

> These are the conditions . . . that favor the act of discovery: the quiet mind of relaxed concentration, prolonged conscious preparation, pertinent and ordered storage in the nonconscious mind, a perceptive and alert observer, the stimulation of curious aids to concentration, the disciplinary effect of the form of the medium and finally the compelling and passionate drive. But one mood pervades them all—the mood of quiet intuitive concentration.

We do not want to be quite so formal in this chapter—to go step by step through the phases of "ideation," in an attempt to provide some sort of formula for getting ideas. Again, we insist, copywriters need no formulas, but only an attitude, a stance, a state of mind. To help cultivate such an attitude, let us just browse through some of the notions about how ideas are born.

Stating the Problem

"A problem well stated is half-solved," said Dewey. And every idea we have as copywriters, like the ideas inventors have, is designed to solve a problem. True, some of the best ideas we have happen by accident and lead us to the solution of a problem different from the one we started with. So it was, Osborn tells us, with Kettering and his men, who set out to increase the mileage of gasoline and wound up discovering an antiknock compound. And with the Corning Glass people, who wanted to make globes stronger for railroad lanterns and succeeded in marketing Pyrex for millions.

But we have to start somewhere. We have to have *some* narrow discipline, before we start broadening out. Why? Because the basic process of getting ideas is association, and a man with imagination could start associating and go on forever. If we start with a given problem we can have a point of reference to keep coming back to. If some lucky accident forces us later to restate the problem, well and good. We must not be rigid—as some advertisers have been when an exciting inspiration has failed to fit a prestated strategy. But we have to start somewhere, and stating the problem is a good place to start.

Stating the problem is a quite rational, hardheaded procedure. Usually it is done with a copy strategy. Someone, or a group, assembles all the facts, studies them, gets more facts, studies them, analyzes the facts, debates the facts, juggles the facts, and states the problem. Maybe the problem is "to convince the public that this tire will give more mileage." Yet the tire may have been developed to give more blowout protection or more traction. Sometimes the statement of a problem would be simple if we went back to the source of the product itself. Why was it created in the first place?

The arrival of today's high-speed computers makes some problem-solving easier. But it does not help at all in problem-stating. "Cast up mechanization's total account," writes Rugg, "the machine can 'solve' any problem the data of which have been built into it. It can answer a question but it cannot ask it. It can 'think' logically, but not creatively."

The first thing we have to do, in order to start thinking creatively, is to ask the question that will start the rush of ideas. How do we communicate the facts about this year's car, an electric shaver, an old product like Jell-O, a new product like an electric toothbrush? We consider all the contexts, we weigh all the facts, and then somebody, God help us, states the problem. Getting the ideas, let us admit, is fun. Because it is irrational, because it is game-playing, because it is the heart and soul of the men with imagination. Stating the problem—that is hard, cold, mind-sapping work. It is a source of endless argument. It is often the bottleneck in our business.

But we have got to put up with it, because we have to start somewhere. "It is only from the concept and the planning," says Burnett, "that real advertising gets its conviction and its breath of life."

It is better to spend weeks and months arguing, researching, fact-finding, and debating to reach agreement on what the problem is than to start hastily getting ideas when there is no way to judge them (i.e., "Will they solve the problem?").

In the course of writing this book, we have asked many copywriters how they got their best ideas. All, to a man, credit the art of free association. This irrational flow of ideas leads eventually to a rational judgment, but most agree that they begin best with a rational statement of the problem. "There are only a couple of things I do consciously," says associate creative director Charley Sweeney. "First I *try* to figure out what it is that I'm trying to say. The one hard core of the promise. . . . That's a matter of judgment, fact-finding, and knowing what the big area of promise is. After I settle on that, I then try to get the best execution of it that I can. Keep the pencil moving until you've not only done it well, you've done it the best you can."

One way to state the problem is to start with that "big area of promise." And this often means starting with the *ideal* and working toward it. Just as an inventor says to himself "Wouldn't it be wonderful if . . . ?", so the advertiser can say, "Wouldn't it be wonderful if every housewife would be interested in the meals she can make with my food product? if every motorist would be influenced to buy my gas because it will clean his engine? if every homeowner would use Drāno to clean the drains, Cheer to whiten the clothes, Beautyrest mattresses for a healthier sleep?"

The big trouble comes from advertisers who insist on an ideal promise without an ideal benefit. The perfect combination begins when the manufacturer works toward the ideal benefit in developing his product. Then the copywriter can work toward the ideal in expressing that benefit.

Once stating the problem is out of the way, a good copywriter is like an unleashed locomotive: he goes hurtling down the track of ideas as fast as his vaulting mind can take him. And that is *fast*.

Free Association

Notice that undisciplined first sentence in the last paragraph. It would horrify a good English teacher because it has at least two mixed metaphors. It speaks of "an unleashed locomotive." That makes you picture both a locomotive train and a dog. One does not ordinarily "leash" a locomotive. The phrase "his vaulting mind" evokes a picture of an athlete vaulting. The mind may not actually "vault," but we attribute this action to it metaphorically because it suggests what may be an apt picture for an active mind.

A metaphor is "a figure of speech in which a term or phrase is applied to something which is not literally applicable, in order to suggest a resemblance, as 'A mighty fortress is our God.'" The word "metaphor" comes from the Greek "*metaphora*" which stood for "a transfer."

The point of all this is that we are constantly transferring one idea, or thought, to another by the creative process of interconnecting previously disconnected elements. And it is the act of association which is the root of getting ideas. William J. J. Gordon, who wrote that stimulating book *Synectics*, which we mentioned earlier, says, "Contemporary theory about language holds that language is essentially metaphorical in its nature and development." In other words, every sentence we speak or write is a combination of what we might call mixed metaphors. This squares with what we said earlier—that "the word is not the thing." To communicate with words, we are constantly stringing together symbols which are not *literally* applicable, but rather metaphorical.

Now, let us discuss the exciting exercise of getting ideas, and how it applies to copywriting. Let us go back to that unleashed locomotive of a copywriter, whose vaulting mind goes hurtling down the track of ideas. As we said before, all of our correspondents agreed that they get their ideas by the process of association. Here is our philosophy: The world is one and the world contains infinite elements. Everything is dissimilar and everything is interconnected. You can put your world together in an infinite number of combinations. The creative mind—the mind with a "vaulting" imagination—given a stated problem, can immediately begin to associate hundreds and thousands and millions of symbols that may lead to an ideal solution.

Hundreds and thousands and millions. Maybe trillions. These thrilling minds of ours can easily cope with such vast quantities of symbols. Considering the brain only as a mechanical entity, it has many times more potential than even the fastest electronic counterpart. One illustration of this potential is the fact that our minds, when we are asleep and in the mood to think without external pressures, work incredibly fast. "What magic our imaginations must possess," says Osborn, "when, in two seconds, we can dream the equivalent of 2,000 words!"

Here is how this applies to getting ideas. We start associating. We free-associate as fast as we possibly can. The key word in that last sentence is "free." We free ourselves of all preconceptions and inhibitions. We go all around the subject and put down every thought, every word, every image it calls to mind, no matter how irrelevant it may seem. This is purposely an irrational process; if we accept that fact and stop trying to fight it, we will save ourselves endless grief. In this initial creative exercise, our associations must come as quickly as possible. We have to let them proliferate and in some way capture them as they do. To capture them is difficult, because writing is slow. The mind moves faster than the typewriter and we have to capture our best thoughts on the wing.

Some writers, especially in a "gangup" (sometimes called "groupthink" and "brainstorming"), capture their fast-winging associations by tape-recording everything spoken. But the many associations are not always said aloud. Another way to capture them fast is to use a mental and physical shorthand, with which you document everything possible. H. G. Wells, in writing *The Shape of Things To Come*, kept a notebook by his bed and captured his best thoughts between sleeping and waking. However we do it, we must try to freeze every fleeting inspiration.

This makes sense, if only because of the laws of chance. In problem-solving, the more solutions we have to choose from, the more chances we have to find the idea. "Quantity, quantity, and more *quantity!*" says Osborn. "This should be the order of the day when building up hypotheses. 'As in navigation, the more sights we take, the more likely we are to hit port.' That is the analogy used by naval officer John Caples. The principle of the machine-gun is another parallel."

Notice, in that paragraph, the different metaphors the author uses to drive home his point. This is a good way, in an operational sense, to communicate, because it gives the reader some precedent, in other experience, to prove the principle. Many sights in navigation, the reader will agree, and many shots in machine-gunning have worked successfully in arriving at a solution; therefore, indeed, it would make sense to let the mind range and find lots of solutions to his particular problem. Osborn goes on, to cite Alfred North Whitehead, on "the wisdom of copious ideation":

> We need to entertain every prospect of novelty, every chance that could result in new combinations, and subject them to the most impartial scrutiny. For the probability is that nine hundred and ninety-nine of them will come to nothing, either because they are worthless in themselves or because we shall not know how to elicit their value; but we had better entertain them all, however skeptically, for the *thousandth* idea may be the one that will change the world.

Now, to get down to particulars, let us consider how the spirit of free association works in the practice of copywriting. Charley Sweeney describes the informal atmosphere in which he and his collaborators came up with "a big idea":

> Several months ago when we started some work on Birds Eye in New York, there were a number of ideas boarded but we didn't feel that we really had it. Time was short. So we had lunch sent in to Art Harris's office and several of us went in there and shut the door with the idea of not coming out until we got something. We talked and talked and ate and, as we talked, we decided that nothing we had up to that point was good enough. Art happened to have an empty plate right beside his drawing board. He picked up the plate and said: "Look. Here's what we're trying to say. This part of the plate—the vegetable part—is dull and uninteresting. The other part of the plate gets all the attention. How can we dramatize the fact that the vegetable part of the plate isn't exciting enough compared to the rest of the plate?" Holding the plate like this helped. Tony Isidore stared at it and came up with a line: "Why should vegetables be The Quiet Corner of your plate?" With that we were off on a pretty exciting bunch of commercials. When we sold the client on the idea, we actually brought a plate with us and had the vegetable part sawed off and then glued back on. We brought the plate to White Plains and, in the meeting, broke off the vegetable third and turned it over to show the legend "Quiet Corner." There were a lot of execution problems after that and, as I understand, there still is a lot of discussion about them. But everybody felt that the Quiet Corner concept was a good one. That was a lunch and sandwich meeting idea.

The story Charley tells is a fairly typical example of the way we copywriters work. It is not portentous. It does not seem a scholarly, orderly method of getting important ideas. You can picture the gang, their feet on the desks, idly swapping ideas, with some asides for a joke or gossip or a discussion of a movie somebody had seen. But, given the stated problem, any and every chance remark might be that lucky accident—the association which lights the spark.

In the scope of time, we think that more important discoveries must have been made more formally. But we will bet that all creative people —whether they be scientists, artists, or copywriters—know in their hearts that irrational *free* association is the secret of their success.

Is "irrational" a dirty word? Does *this* symbol evoke associations of beatniks, wild-eyed radicals, people who "shoot off at the mouth" without thinking? If so, it is understandable, because "irrational" means "without sound judgment" and without the faculty of reason. It places us with the animals, whereas being rational, capable of judgment, is the highest form of human intellect.

But let us forget our prejudice and agree that the process of *getting ideas,* long before the act of judgment, should be deliberately irrational. Says Gordon, "Insofar as the mind can permit the specific creative problem to oscillate in and out of consciousness, there is practically no observation, perception, idea, or generality which is not potentially useful to a solution."

Do you still feel a little uneasy about the whole notion? Does it sound too undisciplined? Well, let us look to some of the best creative brains in history, who have acquired the respectability of performance:

"Combinatory play," said Einstein, "seems to be the essential feature in productive thought."

"I require," said Stendhal, "three or four cubic feet of new ideas per day, as a steamboat requires coal."

"The process of research," said Kettering, "is to pull the problem apart into its different elements, a great many of which you already know about. When you get it pulled apart, you can work on the things you don't know about."

"The things you don't know about": these are irrational things. That is, you cannot have any sound judgment about them *yet*. All you can do, at the beginning, is explore them, in a spirit of wide-eyed expectancy. The judgment comes later.

Remember, we mentioned Osborn's and Rugg's codification for the creative process; how the former referred to the period of "incubation" and the latter to "the quiet mind of relaxed concentration." In both cases, the creator is free—free of the hard, narrowing confines of judgment.

"The root of that noun (incubation)," says Osborn, "is a verb meaning 'to lie down'; thus it carries a connotation of purposive relaxation."

The Practical Purpose of Play

Relaxation is also a corollary of the word "play," to which Einstein referred. And this is why the creative process is so intensely appealing to those of us who "never grew up." We said that people who are creative are probably a little ashamed to tell the truth. It seems frivolous for grown men to be playing games all day, and to be paid for it. But why, if this *is* the way great ideas are born, if it is the *best* way, if it has plenty of precedent in the work of the scientists, artists, and writers who have achieved such human progress, should we not openly recognize the fact and glory in it? The way to get the best ideas is to *let* our minds roam, to play the association game, to have fun.

Dick Lord, asked to give guides for successful copywriting, began with this one:

> *Stay loose.* I think that's important for any guy who wants to be a copywriter. "Stay loose" means you should respect tradition, but not wear it like a corset. It means you shouldn't let your typewriter get between you and the people you're talking to. Many times, there's a rigid formality that sets in when a guy sits down to write the same thought he has just said so well outside his office. I call it getting a glass arm. The very act of typing or setting it down on paper often steals all the heart and emotion out of the message.

The best example of "staying loose," as we mentioned in Chap. 2, is the activity of a child at play. Because he has fewer precedents, he can achieve naturally that easy state which we always have to cajole ourselves into. But this does not mean that the child's play is not constructive. Says Gordon,

> A child digs a tunnel in the sand and supports the tunnel wall with leaves and sticks. He makes a waterfall by detouring a rivulet. He improvises toy boats out of pine cones and sails them down the stream. It is child's play, but it indicates a primitive sensitivity to volume displacement, gravity, and hydraulic flow. It is also form-making, involving inventive solutions to small technical problems. It is also illusionary. A world-which-is-not is created in which pine cones are boats and a rivulet is the Congo.

In looking for ideas, we are looking for "a world-which-is-not"—a new combination of old elements. And all of the attitudes the experts tell us are ripe for creating are found in child's-play.

Think how it is when we adults are relaxing and allow ourselves to play games. We get together with a group of congenial friends for a party. Sometimes, when we have had a few drinks and are not concerned with formality, we start a game like charades, twenty questions, or "the association game." Nobody is concerned that what he says is for publication. The game is an end in itself and the group is enjoying itself.

What happens? They "stay loose." And flights of wonderful fancies are wasted on the air in useless frivolity.

But the process by which we incubate ideas from which one will be later chosen, refined, polished, and used to communicate multimillion-dollar messages, is exactly the same as that enjoyable, easy-going party.

Take the association game. The rules are simple. One player goes out of the room and the others think of some person, living or dead, who is known to all the players. When the first player returns, he is to ask "association questions" as fast as he can think of them and each person questioned must answer "the first thing that comes into his head." This is a crucial rule of the game—that you must answer spontaneously.

The questions go something like this: "What kind of bird does this person remind you of?" "What kind of music does this person remind you of?" "What color?" "What emotion—love, hate, awe, fear?" "What kind of literature?" "What kind of tree?" "What mode of transportation does this person remind you of?"

The questioner may ask different questions of each of the group, or the same question of several people. He may, in the latter case, get entirely different answers—the colors may range from black to white, the music from jazz to classical, the transportation from plane to dogsled—all according to the "collection of stuff" of the person being questioned and how he or she views the subject. Yet, eventually, if the game is played honestly, if a broad enough range of questions is asked and enough spontaneous answers are given, a picture emerges and the questioner guesses the mystery person and wins the game.

This game illustrates how seemingly irrelevant and often contradictory answers will eventually piece together into a relevant whole and solve a problem. It illustrates the advantage of the ability to range freely, continually oscillating in search of unity from multiplicity.

But, above all, the game illustrates the advantage of being absorbed, at ease, and spontaneous—staying loose and enjoying your work. The word "work," to naturally creative people, is interchangeable with the word "play." Said our friend Hopkins,

> The love of work can be cultivated, just like the love of play. The terms are interchangeable. What others call work I call play, and vice versa. We do best what we like best. If that is chasing a polo ball, one will probably excel in that. If it means checkmating competitors, or getting a home run in something worthwhile, he will excel in that. So it means a great deal when a young man can come to regard his life work as the most fascinating game he knows.

And now, listen to how this attitude of play worked in the cases of three copywriters, who conceived three successful campaigns. Each gives an example of getting ideas by association. In addition, notice their playful mood:

> I can clearly recollect the thought sequence involved in the evolution of the Jell-O "Chinese Baby" commercial, probably the most notorious single spot I personally have been connected with.

Jell-O is a joy for creative people to work on and has always seemed to bring out bright, ingenious thinking from those who got involved in it. I suppose it's because it is absolutely unique—plus the fact that it tastes good, looks pretty, wiggles, is healthful, low in calories and just plain fun. The uniqueness has usually led people who are preparing ads for it to think in fresh directions to reflect the freshness of Jell-O's true image.

No particular plan was in my mind when this idea came to me, but I *was* casting about for clever and attractive ways to say that Jell-O is unique and that it's fun. I think most creative people have had experiences where a sudden flash revealed a more or less complete idea. Mine was for a print ad, and it was a picture idea—a color photograph of a little Chinese baby sitting in a high chair, a dish of Jello in front of him. The baby had chopsticks in his hands, and he was crying with frustration. The headline, reflecting a campaign we were considering, was to be, "There's nothing quite like Jell-O."

I told my copy supervisor about my idea, and suggested it to the art director. The supervisor, who shall be nameless, chuckled, but didn't take the idea seriously. The a.d. thought it had something and wanted to do a layout—but this idea didn't fit with other things we were doing, and time was short before the Big Meeting, and it never got done.

The idea rested in my mind (along with all my other truly *great* ideas, all of which have been deemed impractical) until we were asked to do push work on Jell-O TV. I submitted the idea again as a TV idea as one of several suggestions. This time, it was to be live film photography with a real baby, a sort of Candid Camera treatment of the little Chinese baby trying to eat a dish of Jell-O, accompanied only by music and sound—no copy. The supervisor, this time Mac' Rainbolt, thought two things: it should have copy, and it should be animation. I hadn't thought of either, but gave it a try.

I suppose since the idea had been kicking around in my head for awhile the copy was easy to write: I had it completed in less than ten minutes. As far as I can recall, Mac' didn't change a word of it, nor did the client.

—BILL LACEY

The Daily News was being marketed under the line, "Reads Faster and Livelier." Well, if you think about that line you can come up with some wild visuals. We did. We showed people so engrossed in the newspaper that they were spilling cream on the table instead of in their coffee, conductors were punching commuters' ties instead of tickets, etc. So successful was this simple, quick translation of a selling line that the posters themselves carried no line. It was all visual and so much better that the line was dropped.

—DICK LORD

We needed a new television campaign for Prell Concentrate Shampoo. To me, shampooing was a sensual experience, that is, it numbed the senses after awhile, especially a luxurious long shampoo, which you'd like to be given. I got the idea of the combination of slow-motion photography simulating the sensuality (especially with closed eyes—you think of that as sensual, or at least I did here—a woman with closed eyes slowly shampooing) against a very fast Afro-Cuban music track. The juxtaposition of the two created a sensual experience. . . .

Usually you don't know where an idea comes from. But in this case, I remember being given a shampoo in a barber's chair that was so great it made me feel fantastically relaxed. Massage of the scalp slowly takes the tension away. I got this idea from my own personal experience.

—MAURY FLANTZMAN

Another example of playful serendipity is shown on the following page of doodles by art director Jack Sidebotham.

In this case, Jack was not solving a problem. He was sitting in a long, administrative meeting, extemporizing as he listened and spoke. He was perfectly alert to the full sense of the meeting, but his subconscious, "stay loose" mind was pleasantly extemporizing. Doodling is what free association is all about. It was with just such doodles, in a sense, that Jack, and his collaborator, Ed Graham, conceived the famous "Bert and Harry" television campaign.

Judy Blumenthal, who won the Advertising Writers Association Gold Key for her copy on Berlitz language lessons, tells how a doodle ends up in an ad. The final copy read as follows: "*When in Rome* can you chatter, flatter, question, quip and quibble, captivate, cajole, extol, rattle on and prattle on *as the Romans do?* Enroll at Berlitz, and if you have no ear for languages we'll lend you ours."

Judy's doodle started with a sketch of a face and the line, "So you don't have an ear for languages." "This doodle," she wrote, "ended up as the last line of the ad 'When in Rome.' I think I worked backwards from 'don't have an ear for languages,' to 'if you have no ear for languages we'll lend you ours,' . . . to 'When in Rome.' "

Here is an example, taken verbatim from a tape recording, of a copywriter, copy supervisor, and account executive, enjoying themselves at the first revelation of a new campaign idea. The campaign was to be for the Wine Advisory Board, and the problem had been clearly stated—how to broaden the appeal of California wines to the vast majority of families who are not knowledgeable about wine while, at the same time, retaining the franchise already existing with wine connoisseurs. Many facts had been studied, many ideas discussed, and eventually, as in the association game, a happy conjunction of elements led to one idea that seemed *right:* Why not start a controversy; the wine snobs versus the nonconformists? Here were a few comments, as the group started to explore the idea. (As usual, with these verbatims, you will find it difficult to understand the full meaning of the conversation, without seeing the expressions, or knowing

Reproduced by permission of Jack Sidebotham, Creative Director, C. J. LaRoche & Co., Inc.

the connectives that went before. We reproduce the conversation simply to illustrate the spirit of the activity.)

COPYWRITER: Suppose you have each one of these guys, take Doberman for example, he might say "Me, I like to serve white wine with steak," you know, and you take each one of these taboos—the rituals that surround wine serving, glasses chilled, what have you, and you have each one of these guys doing it the opposite from what the rules say.

SUPERVISOR: I think it's a great idea.

ACCOUNT EXECUTIVE: You could say something in the headline like "Revolutionary breakthrough—Doberman serves red wine with fish—he's an anarchist, you know."

COPYWRITER: What, red wine with fish!

SUPERVISOR: Wonderful.

ACCOUNT EXECUTIVE: I could see a whole campaign with one stet headline— Snobs Hate Doberman. Wine snobs hate Art Carney and he's doing something that's wrong, and this is why, but what the heck, he's having fun.

SUPERVISOR: Children, be happy. Keep going.

(*Several days later*)

SUPERVISOR: This way too we can identify all of these people, then we can get off into areas where we just use familiar faces that people don't know the names of, we don't expect them to and we . . .

ACCOUNT EXECUTIVE: Yeah, but the fine part about it, we'll use the name they're popular for or their first name. Like maybe you're using Maurice Chevalier and you say wine snobs hate Maury.

COPYWRITER: I think you can have a lot of fun with it, I really do. We can have a kit but it could be a nonconformist kit that tells you the kinds of wines that are available—use any that you happen to like—just try them. I like my sherry cold out of the jelly jar . . .

SUPERVISOR: In the morning . . .

COPYWRITER: Tie-in with Skippy Peanut Butter with your glasses . . .

ACCOUNT EXECUTIVE: Why don't I sit down and start—I'll write out all the various taboos that I can think of and we'll see how we can twist them around and keep them clever and funny, and yet keep them a little classy too.

COPYWRITER: I serve all my wine in one glass—this is the same kind of glass.

Later, many weeks later, after the idea had been thoroughly chewed over, some of those chance thoughts were refined. That last sentence, for example, an inspiration picked out of the air, became the basis of a historically successful premium offer—a set of all-purpose wine glasses, offered in advertisements, with coupons, for $2.50.

Play certainly has a practical purpose. Play and enthusiasm and sheer love of the creative exercise.

"Work is love made visible," said Gibran.

What a delightful way to make a living!

Working Alone and Together

No rules; we keep saying "break the rules." And there are no rules for whether you should get ideas alone or in collaboration.

We copywriters tend, in our "bull sessions," to speak in black-and-white ways. After all, we are professional enthusiasts, and probably the majority of us are in some way neurotic. So we make sweeping generalities about the best way to get ideas and to write great ads.

One of the favorite debates, in which we are most heated and emphatic, is the one about "making ads by committee." In an advertising agency, a meeting of the product group will be called. "This is the problem," says the account executive. "How can we solve it?"

The most articulate members of the group proceed to deliver themselves of a few thousand well-chosen words, while the shy and overfed members resemble the Dormouse and have to be prodded into wakeful assent. Sometimes nothing is accomplished and the group files out with a vague feeling of having looked foolish. Later, perhaps, the account executive or the traffic man rushes into the smallest office of the lowliest copywriter and screams desperately, "We've passed our closing date and the client is furious. We're going to lose the account. *Do* something."

Then the lowliest copywriter cranks a piece of copy paper into his typewriter, stares at its blank surface for some time, and with a great sigh that means "I told you so" and "they'll never learn," starts bashing away at the keys.

Nevertheless, we can get ideas by committee (or rather, we prefer to say, by collaboration). Many of the best ones have been found that way. The problem, again, lies with the attitude, the state of mind.

Actually, in a way we are talking about the same thing, whether it is getting ideas alone or ensemble. The group gangup is an attempt to reproduce en masse the imaginative workings of an individual's mind. The individual, when he looks for ideas, has a sort of group discussion going on in his mind. When we think, we hold a kind of dialogue with ourselves. Maybe that is what they mean when they say that psychotics are "hearing voices." As we call up associations, our experience, our memory, our free imagination, ghosts of a million people, are holding a colloquy. Just for fun, try illustrating that fact by writing, for five minutes, a nonstop, free-association essay on any subject that pops into your head. Again, as in the association game, do not pause for an instant to be analytical. Let the words fall as they may. Then, afterwards, analyze the unstructured piece you have written. Where did those thoughts come from? From many, many sources of memory and experience. From a process of synectics—"the joining together of different and apparently irrelevant elements." From a kind of "brainstorming"—a gangup of disparate ideas.

This is how ideas are born, and who cares whether they are born by one mind, by two, or in a group. They are created and you should enjoy creating them. If you are stimulated, excited, natural, in a white heat of creativity, you are *bound* to come up with fresh ideas—ideas that ring true because they were begotten spontaneously, in a spirit of joy and affection. "The thing created is loved before it exists," said Chesterton. Every creation is an act of love.

That feeling of love, of sheer joy in the game of getting ideas, can be felt like a warm glow when a compatible group of creative people are working together. Says Carlyle, "The spark of thought, generated in a solitary mind, awakens listeners in another mind." If you have never participated in the glow of such a "gangup," you have an exciting emotional experience still coming to you. It is contagious fever. As the group relaxes and the ideas come fast, the individuals in the group are reaching out with their minds to one another. There is a tight community of interest, for all are concentrated on the same problem.

Here are some verbatims from such a group session of some eight or nine writers and artists. Again, there are as many meanings in the words left out, the facial expressions, the laughter, the relationships of the individuals, as there are in what you actually read here. The problem, in this case, was to come up with the "big idea" for a new advertising account the agency had just acquired—the Lamb Council. Much fact-finding had preceded this meeting, and they had discovered a multiplicity of problems in the sale of lamb. This meat was served less regularly than beef, ham, and pork; consumers knew little about the various cuts and uses of lamb; many consumers were prejudiced by their experiences during the war overseas, when they lived on a diet of tough mutton; consumers considered lamb relatively expensive even though many cuts are less expensive than those of beef. These were just a few of the findings, and the general problem stated, as a result, was "How can we overcome apathy about lamb?"

For this gangup, a long piece of wrapping paper was tacked on the bulletin board. As the group sang out ideas, one of the art directors scribbled them, with a Magic Marker, on the paper. It was soon filled with a huge list, complete with the artist's doodles and humorous asides, and the paper was later used as a checklist from which to associate more and better ideas, and with which to associate compatible ideas. Notice, in these alternating comments, how each thought triggers another one, in a kind of rhythmic pattern: (Phrases in parentheses are the editor's notations. Speakers are not identified, but each new paragraph indicates a change of speaker.)

"This is a Beefeater." (*Jed dressed as a Beefeater.*) "Lambeater. Lambeater." (This idea was a satire on the Beefeater Gin campaign.)
"It's the old lamb-lighter." (*Singing*)

"Packaging lamb chops with other meats to make a mixed grill."

(Ideas like this, and the following, were designed to show the variety of lamb uses.)

"I came out with an easy Saturday night supper—chops and chips. Simple and simply delicious. Good, and good for you. Nutritious and full of vitamins and minerals."

"Lamb and eggs—lamb and eggs—that's nice."

"Chops and chips."

"Chops and franks—shanks and franks." (*Big laugh*)

"Lamb 'n yams—Lamb 'n limas or lamb shanks would be a pretty good dish."

"Lamb 'n yams for Easter, Thanksgiving, Christmas. The best thing to have would be lamb 'n yams."

"And then there's the idea of patty cakes for youngsters—with a ground lamb. Would you call them lamb pattie cakes?"

"No, no."

"Pattie cakes and potato pops." (*Big laugh*)

"Pattie cakes and potato chips." (*Singing and laughing*)

"Sirlamb steak?"

"Good, good."

"Lambasting—lambrosia. What is lambasting?"

"I don't know. . . ."

"Baste lamb with a sauce or barbecue lamb. That's good."

"Lambrosia—lambasting—lambrosia. This is more the gourmet type. We will have this campaign whipped by the end of the day."

"Lamb-bake."

"Wonderful."

"Old-fashioned lamb-bake." (*Singing*)

"This was a real nice lamb-bake, and we all had a real good time."

"Can we have lamb chowder? (*More laughter*) You can make a lamb stew, you can make it with . . . then you can call it lamb chowder."

"Maybe there is something in lamb slang that could be a theme. You could have a lamb roast and call it grand slamb."

"Never mind the categories." (*Instructions to art director making list*)

"Lamb shanks are midget legs. What would you call them?"

"Lamb lollipops. They are tiny legs."

"Can we call them leglets or lamb leglets or lamb lollipops or drum sticks?"

"We have a name for them. Individual legs of lamb they call them."

"To each his own leg of lamb. You take the shank and it looks like a miniature leg of lamb and you have your own personal leg of lamb. It's a little bitty thing. To each his own leg of lamb. If you can think of a song—a cute way to say it. Eat a leg of lamb. Write it like one word—eatalegalamb!"

"Lamashanta."

"Put that down, what is it?"

"That's scotch broth."

"OK, lamashanta broth." (*Instructions to art director*)

"Good, good. What's that expression—Lambi-pie?"

"Sugar lamb?"

(*Writer exercising her vocal chords again*) "Chops 'n chips . . . Chops 'n chips . . . tra-la-la . . . tra-la-la . . ."

"Where do we go from here?"

"The shank of the evening."

"Wonderful."

"What I want to do with you, Lou, is one of our radio commercials that when it ends you say 'shanks' and I say 'you're welcome.' " (*More laughter*)

"Can we say lamb from the land of milk and honey?"

"This is a calorie thing, where you set up this big dish of mashed potatoes, green peas, sauce and you have lamb riblets and you label all the calories in this dish and you say so much in the potatoes, so much in this, so much in that. We can make a low-calorie story on some of the lowest cuts. Whatever's the lowest. Well, whatever the lean part like a leg, or the lean part of chops."

"OK, what's next?"

"We have a lot of ideas here we were batting about yesterday and they are sort of noncategorizable."

"OK, put down noncategorizable."

(*Typist comment:* "Can you use easier-to-spell words?")

"A barren of lamb. It's a cut of lamb called a barren of lamb. It's the most wonderful thing you can put on the table."

"What about Columbus discovered lamb and it turns out his name is Joe Columbus."

"What about—'lamb ho'?"

"Alright put it down. Joe Columbus discovers lamb."

"Another thing—we had a lot of ideas for shopping, like making Thursday lamb day. . . ."

"Yeh, put down a lamb day, we've talked about that before."

"Quit beefing and eat lamb. Don't be chicken eat Lamb. There is something fishy going on—eat lamb. Don't duck the issue."

(*Singing*)

"Anything ham can do lamb can do better.

Lamb can do anything better than ham.

It can make a lamb shank.

It can make a pot roast. . . ."

"Put up there lamb speaks many languages."

"You could change languages and have many commercials."

"How about a flaming dish *flambé*?"

"Alakazam . . ."

"Alaka*lamb*!"

"Jane said that all these new spices are great for basting lamb. What about giving away free spices?"

"Put down tie-ins and let's get some of those."

"I have one thing here lamb stamps like green stamps. You can get lamb stamps."

"Some kind of contest where maybe you win a freezer full of lamb."

"Put that up for promotions."

"One idea is taking lamb and putting it in very strange situations. Like you can have an elevator door open where there is a fellow eating a lamb chop and there are a lot of people looking at him. Or a fellow is walking down the street, eating a lamb chop."

"We haven't touched on the unique flavor of lamb. We were going to make an asset out of a debit. Some people object to what they call strong flavor of lamb, what we call the unique flavor of lamb. And I wonder if this might be something to think about. The unique flavor of lamb."

"There is nothing like a lamb." (*Singing again*)

"Now eggs will never be the same. Now franks will never be the same."

"Limas love lamb. You love lamb."

"Here's something different—lamb and limas."

"You don't even need to say here's something different. You just use a question mark. You've got a beautiful photograph of lamb and yams. Then you just say, lamb and *yams?* All of these have question marks. Lamb and *yams?* Lamb and *franks?*"

"Maybe that's it. Maybe the question makes them notice the difference."

(*The group has been searching for one overall theme.*)

"We have been looking for a line and the question itself makes the difference. Lamb and *eggs?* I think we have it. The question is a wonderful device, anyway. Lamb and *limas?* Whoever heard of that?"

Frivolous as all the above may seem, a surprising number of the spontaneous ideas were later used in an informative newspaper and radio campaign. Above all, the gangup served to lubricate the minds and get them going.

Since we are trying to reach "unity from multiplicity," the more experience and sources for association we have, the better. That is why, as we mentioned in Chap. 1, the copywriter should be an inquisitive person. In a gangup, an aggregate of inquisitive people simply compounds the possibilities. But we individuals, when we are getting ideas by ourselves, are drawing on the same sort of wellsprings as the group draws on. That is why Dick Lord's advice is so pertinent: "Be hep. Know what's going on around you in the world and all the little worlds within it. I've never met a good copywriter who was a dull person."

Possible disadvantages of getting ideas in a group stem from atmosphere and the character of the participants. Gordon, in *Synectics,* emphasizes over and over the need for a skilled and sensitive group leader, who can, on the one hand, encourage the group to stay on the track of the problem and, on the other, discourage any inhibiting argument. If there is one person in the group, especially a dominating type, who insists on being narrow, the whole purpose is negated. "The attitude of mind which rigidly carves out established intentions precludes learning, except in the narrowest of ways, because according to this attitude accidents and all orders of irrelevance must be rejected as foreign."

When we are getting ideas alone, we need the same kind of discipline for freedom we had with the group. As we associate freely, keep connecting ideas, we must concentrate hard on the object with which we are connecting, while at the same time we are suspending judgment about the metaphors we dream up. Creative director Stan Burkoff illustrates how one thinks around a given object:

> The thought process is something like this. Let's say you're selling a plain brass door knob. Most normal people would say, "What can you say about a plain brass door knob?" And that's when the copywriter and the art director have to stand back and re-examine brass door knobs in the light of their relationships to doors, to people, to little kids reaching up to turn them, to safety, to ease of grasping, to their conformity to the grip, to the light they reflect, to their feel, to their function as coat hangers, back scratchers, sign holders, and even to the dandy job they do holding strings which are tied to the loose teeth of six-year-olds.

But in this business of ours, we doubt whether any successful copywriter ever does, as a rule, get his ideas alone. The most common, and essential, collaboration is that between a copywriter and an art director. For the ideas we conceive are seldom wholly verbal or, for that matter, rarely all visual. And, as we shall discuss in the next chapter, our ideas are not only verbal and visual. Depending on the medium, music and sounds can be vitally important, and they deserve close collaboration with the music and sound experts. Sometimes an individual can hear, see, and express the whole message out of his one mind; but usually we hobble ourselves if we fail to collaborate with everyone worth drawing upon.

Working together, besides increasing the range of ideas and the enjoyment of the situation, is a good way to keep ideas going. Wrote Oscar Hammerstein, of his work with Richard Rodgers:

> One of the most helpful features of these periods of collaboration is the quick reaction you can get from your collaborator which helps you throw out bad ideas quickly and sustains your confidence in good ideas so that you go ahead. I remember particularly one afternoon when Dick and I were working on the score of the motion picture, State Fair. As the story opens, the young girl is unhappy. She is not in love with anybody. She is going to a state fair with her family, but is not looking forward to it. She has the blues. She doesn't know why. It occurred to me that her feeling was very much like spring fever. It then occurred to me, very unhappily, that all state fairs are held in the autumn, September or early October. Then, wanting desperately to write a song about spring fever, I toyed with the notion of having her say, in effect, "It's autumn, but I have spring fever so 'it might as well be spring.'" Rather half-heartedly I threw the idea at Dick. He jumped up excitedly and said, 'That's it.' And from then on, that was it. All my doubts were gone. I had a partner behind me.

Collaboration is good. And getting ideas alone, in a euphoric atmosphere of self-indulgence, is good. The point, again, is not to make rules and to say this way or that way is best, but to work out your own systems and to be free and easy in those pleasant periods of creativity. Creative director Pete Peabody, expressing *his* way of working, seems to express it well for us all:

> Here's how I make advertising: I try to get a firm idea of the thing the piece of advertising is meant to put into the minds of people. This is often the hardest part of the whole job. I also try to find out all there is to know about the product, paying particular attention to the things that make it different from its competition and the things that make it better. If they are both the same thing, I'm lucky, because I have facts for my copy and the best copy is facts. Facts touched with a distinctive style and taste, but facts.
>
> Then I start to think about the product and everything I've ever heard of that is connected with it. Free association. That's just the beginning. . . . As for the rest of it, I have to say that frankly I'm not even sure of how I go about it myself; at least I'm not sure how to put it into words. And even if I could be coherent about it, probably nobody would care anyway. Because one person's patterns of working are hardly ever comfortable for another.
>
> Anyway, to go on, somewhere in the mess that gurgles up there ought to be a combination of words and pictures that is reasonably new, and fairly fascinating to observe. Because it's going to have to be more fascinating than its surroundings or it's a waste of money to run it. If I go dry, I get sad, but stop and do something else. At the beginning, I didn't used to do this. I'd slave away until I got something I liked, getting tireder and tireder all the time. I didn't really have the confidence to loosen up and forget about it. I figured that if it didn't come at the first crack, it never would. Invariably, the next morning, I'd wake up with a better idea. I finally realized that relaxing doesn't mean shutting off your mind. Now, I find myself going back to the problem no matter what I'm doing or where I am: at dinner, in the bathroom, at the movies, anywhere. Because it's fun solving problems. I guess also a sort of built-in feeling of responsibility to get the job done helps; you know, the feeling of having something sitting on your neck like a lead weight until you get it done. . . .
>
> When I get the ideas I pick the one *I* like the best . . . and that's it. Actually, there is no bolt from the blue involved. It's a set pattern of work, a craft or trade just like anybody else's. And it takes off from a mental exercise just about everybody else uses. However, I formulated this pattern for myself. . . .
>
> That's a point that is important. When I first got into the business, I worked with a smart guy named Herb Fox at Cunningham and Walsh. We are still very close, and so I know it's not going to hurt our friendship for me to say he is also a most inarticulate man. He mumbles. But he can

think up pure advertising ideas better than anybody I've ever met. I didn't even know what an advertising idea was at that time, but I had a hot poker in me to be original and do stuff that would make people fascinated, amazed, sold, think I was clever, and so on. And I loved pictures and words.

One of the two best things that ever happened to me in this business was Fox. His stuff made me jealous. But luckily he could hardly say a clear sentence. He couldn't have told me how he did it even if I had subdued my pride and asked him. What I did was study his end results and figure backwards in my own mind how I would have arrived at them myself. I evolved an orderly pattern. And since it was my own pattern, for better or worse, it had a trace of one person's individuality and style in it. If Fox had been able to tell me his way, then that would have been his way, not mine; and therefore an artificial method for me to employ.

So, falling into the traditional trap of using one's own experience as a point from which to generalize, I would say that I think you can't teach this trade completely and probably shouldn't. But you can inspire and let the individual brain take over from there.

8

STYLE AND THE FIVE SENSES

Style, like everything else we talk about in this book, is determined by the copywriter's state of mind.

But we've said that copywriting is a tough profession, and nowhere is it tougher than in the matter of style. The biggest difference between literary style and copywriting style is that the author's personality *should* come through in the former, and that, in the latter, it *should not.*

"Style *is* the writer," wrote Strunk and White, authors of the famous little book, *The Elements of Style,* "and therefore what a man is, rather than what he knows, will at last determine his style."

But what *is* the copywriter as he approaches his product? Is he sophisticated or naïve, soft-spoken or outspoken, flippant or serious? It is the product, not the writer, that must decide.

"Creative writing is communication through revelation," says Strunk, "—it is the Self escaping into the open. No writer long remains incognito."

But it is the function of the copywriter to *be* incognito. He, and the ad manager, and the art director, and the production man—they must all, somehow, submerge their egos to the ego of the product itself. The product has its own personality, separate entirely from that of the copywriter. Somehow, the copywriter must "become" the product.

"Style not only reveals the spirit of the man, it reveals his identity, as surely as would his fingerprints," writes Strunk.

So says the master on style, but the fingerprints of the copywriter who too often reveals himself can smudge the image of the product he is communicating about.

This is the hardest lesson for any new copywriter to learn. And too often, rebelling against the need for anonymity, he will cite famous copywriters whose ads had a "house look" because their individual styles came through. Ogilvy, Burnett, Bernbach, Hopkins, he will tell you—all had distinctive, personal styles.

This is possibly true, but it may be that their styles, if they proved successful for certain products, were so because they happened to be compatible with those products. Or, through the rugged power of their styles, they may seize and hold a reader's attention, *despite* the fact that the style *is* incompatible with the product.

But it should not be incompatible, and it need not be, if our attitude is one of submission to, and identification with, the subject.

The following are two pieces of magazine ad copy written in Great Britain—the first addressed to male readers, the second to female readers. Notice how dissimilar are the styles:

Example 1

TWO CAME TO BRITAIN . . .
how far did they get for $30?

J.J. hired a car. Just for a couple of days. Cost $8.40 down, plus 10 cents a mile.

It was a very *small* car. Un-American. With strange shift gears and right-hand drive. And the English roads didn't help much, either! Narrow things, most of them . . . all meandering and quaint. His progress was solemn.

Still, he eventually made it to Stratford-upon-Avon. And back. A modest 220 miles all told. And his $30 was up!

T.T. spent his $30 before he left home. He spent them with his travel agent . . . on ThriftRail Coupons. And when he got to Britain, he traded his ThriftRails for train tickets. That way, he saved a lot of money. . . .

And did he travel in style! Sitting back in armchair comfort, in an airy compartment with plenty of room . . . watching through picture windows as the green hills and hedgerows slipped by. He could even get all his meals en route—sound British fare at low charges. Like being in a traveling hotel!

So his travel was fast . . . and relaxing. Left him with plenty of time and *energy* for sightseeing. He really got around in Britain. And all for $30.

$30 worth of ThriftRail Coupons will buy *you* up to 1,000 miles of rail

travel in Britain . . . a big saving on normal fares. ($45 books available, too.) But remember, you can only buy ThriftRails *in the States*. So have a chat with your travel agent about it.

Be seeing you.

British Rail—International Inc.

Example 2

PINK FOR IMPACT!

Undress into something sensational

Shrug away the day and slip into a dream-world—on a drifting cloud of rose-tinted nylon. Soft . . . cool . . . pink—perfectly feminine . . . it soon has you feeling your own pretty self again. In the mood for the sweetest dreams!

Miss Wolsey's gown-and-negligee set is exquisitely styled on Grecian lines—especially delectable in fragile Dawn Pink. Gown 63/–, negligee 95/–. For your nearest stockist, write to Wolsey Limited, King Street, Leicester.

wolsey
vanity fair

Those two examples had rather dissimilar styles. Yet they were both written by the same copywriter (Toni Bird).

Once you are reconciled to the fact that in the case of copywriting the style is not the man but the product—or, rather, once you revel in that fact, and enjoy it, there are practical ways to improve your style, other than by merely becoming a medium.

For example, every ad, every piece of copy, must have a shape, and the shape can be formed in the copywriter's mind as structurally as the poet conceives a sonnet. A sonnet has 14 lines, which might seem a too-rigid discipline, yet thousands of sonnets have been written with no other resemblance to one another. The copywriter will have space or time requirements to which he must accommodate the shape of his message. But the shape, ideally, would emerge inevitably its own.

How do you figure what shape to use? It is impossible to define a way. But you do steep yourself in your subject. You try to be totally aware of its purpose and target. And, if you are successful, the shape will emerge.

Here, for example, is a headline for an ad for Oroweat Bread, which somehow has an inevitable shape:

It toasts up
solid and
chewy . . . yet
it crunches
and it is
fragrant.

The copywriter might have written, "This bread makes good toast." But he was well aware of the nature of bread and toast. He wanted to say that the bread would remain "solid," but solid alone would evoke a heavy image. "Chewy," yes, but "solid" and "chewy" alone could not express the gestalt of good toast; by all means "it crunches" must be added. And how could one evoke the full pleasure of bread and toast without some reference to its fragrance? All in all, the headline came out, inevitably, its full, toasty, completed shape.

Within every given ad or commercial, there are certain aids to style which we may accept as common. For example, one form keeps emerging, whatever unit of a composition we are considering—whether it be a paragraph, a sentence, or a clause, or an entire chapter, story, piece of copy, or play. This is what one of our early professors, David Cheney, referred to as "The 2-1-3 System"—2 referring to "stronger," 1 to "strong" and 3 to "strongest." That is, the stronger words would come at the beginning of a clause, sentence, or paragraph, those which are merely "strong" in the middle, and the "strongest" at the end.

Take, for example, this seven-word sentence: "The end of all life is death." "The end" we consider stronger words than "of all life," and "is death" are the most powerful words in the sentence. If the sentence had been arranged as "Death is the end of all life," it would, to some extent, have been less effective. Why is this so? Perhaps because language is merely the symbolic expression of physical facts. "Death" is the most terminal fact in that sentence, and when the word comes at the end, it can strike you like the physical force of a fist.

Consider the intonations with which we communicate orally. If you analyze the natural rise and fall of your voice, you will find that each complete expression tends to assume the "2-1-3" positions.

Thinking of style with regard to the smallest units, our individual words, we know that verbs and nouns have more natural power than adjectives and adverbs. Nouns and verbs are the foundations, basic and concrete; adverbs and adjectives are the filigrees and appendages we use to decorate the structure. Nouns and verbs give to good writing its toughness and color. Experts have contrasted writings which have proved historically effective and ineffective—Lincoln's Gettysburg Address versus Everett's;

the Bible versus the Congressional Record; Churchill's speeches versus the average ads in *Life*—and in all cases, the ineffective prose has been overloaded with additives.

Another useful style habit, especially in communicating about products, is to be idiomatic. Not self-consciously so, but in the spirit of "being natural." A good habit is to remind oneself constantly, "How would I tell a friend?" Many successful copywriters deliberately sit down, after all the fact-finding and incubating, and bash off a letter to a close friend, telling him about the product. Because he is a friend, the writer has no need to be self-conscious or to strive for effect. He has no need to acquaint his reader with the *writer*, but only with *the subject*. And so the subject emerges pure and without borrowed interest, and behold, we have written effective copy. How about those idiomatic words we used? They are idiomatic because they emerged *naturally* into the idiom. The best style, the teachers keep telling us, is to affect no style at all—to be *natural*. If to be natural is to be idiomatic, more power to us.

So much for style. The "style" we have been referring to, mainly, has to do with words. But communication is not, essentially, words. In fact, words are an artificial form of communication—symbols attached to the actual communication, which is the thing itself. If we are striving to cultivate a state of mind which will cause us to be natural—which will communicate the thing, according to its nature—we must work with far more than word style. We must work with the whole spectrum—all the senses through which the communication is made.

The World of the Senses

The world of the senses is multivalued, and to be keenly aware of all the senses is to enter a fresh life of communication.

As copywriters, we tend to confine ourselves to the importance of words —particularly of the written word. But deep stirrings are going on in far more powerful modes of communication, and we have to wake up or we will find ourselves obsolete.

The Tyranny of Words, Stuart Chase entitles his book. And students of communication soon learn that, as psychologist Irving A. Taylor has said, "words can easily conceal rather than reveal information." Hayakawa refers to "the screen of language."

Words can conceal because, as we have said before, they mean different things to different people. And because they so vitally affect our thoughts and actions they can cause one person to do or not to do the very opposite of another. They produce violently affective reactions too, as in the case of the words "Negro," "Republican," "Nazi," and certain four-letter expletives. They are often completely impossible to interpret, as in the case of people who speak different languages. Communicators give as an example of the difficulty of translation the confusion the word "democracy" causes in the dissimilar minds of the members of the United Nations.

In the study of language, linguists also recognize that words differ widely according to whether they are written or spoken. "Noises made with the face," writes Chase, "antedated 'scratches made with the fist'" and he points out the differences in the way words are mouthed. "An advertising man in his cubicle on Madison Avenue," he says, "may christen a new breakfast food 'crunchy, vitamin-packed THRUB', but he cannot call it 'DLUB,' not in English he can't. If he tried to name it NFPK, a common sound in other tongues, he would undoubtedly be fired. Again, English permits no words to begin with NG, but Eskimo is full of them."

Stuart Chase, and many other thoughtful students of words, stress these differences because they want us to be aware. They are inspired by the "metalinguistics" of Benjamin Lee Whorf, who predicted that beyond language there are "further planes still, the full import of which may some day stagger us."

"Metalinguistics," writes Chase, "is the top rung of communication study; it throws the longest shadow. It may be doing for language what relativity did for physics. Furthermore, it is based on linguistic relativity. Metalinguists ask: How does a given language shape the thought of the speaker and his view of nature and the world? How does the structure of English, say, differ from that of Maya, and what are the comparative effects on speakers of the two?"

Now, with metalinguistics in mind, and being *aware* that, even with people who speak the same language, there are vast differences of interpretation, we can see that other forms of communication beyond language are important. As we simplify our manner of communication, we become more intelligible to more people. Sign language antedated both noises and scratches, and good pantomimists can often make themselves more profoundly understood than the most verbal orators.

So for this chapter, at least, let us think not only about verbal communication, but all kinds of nonverbal ways as well. This is an exciting field for exploration because, among other things, it plays right to the principle of involvement. The simpler the communication, the more it calls on your audience to participate, to embroider, to fill in the unseen and unspoken, according to their "collection of stuff."

Let us think about the senses. We tend to compartmentalize our forms of communication—to study speech separately from sight. But in actual experience, we communicate, and are communicated to, with all our senses operating at once. Some are more acutely engaged at one time than another. But the most successful communication unites all forces.

It does not matter, either, whether just one sense *seems* to be engaged.

Our imaginations fill in the others. This is called metaphorical thinking
So powerful is this form of communication that even Helen Keller, bereft
of most senses, could fill them in. Her "initial awareness of words was
. . . relational, involving temperature and motion rather than use; and
thus, in a rudimentary sense, it was metaphorical rather than utilitarian."
When you *hear* a foghorn, does it not evoke *pictures* in your mind—pictures of the pilot peering from the bridge, the ship feeling its way through
the gray-white? You can practically *smell* the tangy scent of the sea and
feel the wet touch of the air and *taste* the salty iodine air.

Such images are evoked by an ad for tourists by the Bahamas Development Board. A photograph shows a girl swimming in exquisitely clear
water. The reader can feel the water and the sun, smell the soft, languor-
ous scent of the tropics. Have you ever looked at an array of food—or simply read a menu—and savored the selection? Your mouth can water for a
taste of fruit one moment and the next turn its attention to the feeling of
ice cream. This is participation on a nonverbal level that can be every bit
as effective as simply the word "fruit." By the same token, appetizing use
of words can evoke marvelous nonverbal pictures.

What about the ability of a piece of music to engage all your senses?
Everybody knows how a mood can come rushing back, in all its variety,
through the association of a song.

Colors, of course, have a power beyond words, to communicate worlds
of emotion. A tablet named "Compōz," designed to relieve tension, was
advertised, appropriately, with a subdued background of blue and grey.
"Good Coffee is like friendship," said the Pan-American Coffee Bureau,
"rich and warm and strong." The colors for that series of ads were rich,
warm colors—orange, gold, amber. The famous all-white campaign for
Gulf Premium Oil was designed to stress the cleanliness of the product
and of the Gulf service stations. And a news item mentioned that the
Youngstown Sheet & Tile Company switched from brown shipping boxes
for its wire coils to white ones. The white boxes, said the item, "seem to
have a psychological effect on truckers—so they handle the packages more
carefully on the way to the customers."

Psychologist Taylor predicts that future creativity will stress shapes
and textures more than words and he tells how he used shape symbols
to convey ideas and emotions. He told, in a speech, how he studied the
reactions of large groups of people to his nonverbal forms:

> I was very interested in how far I could develop non-verbalese. I asked
> large groups of subjects in Missouri, Texas and New York to give me the
> emphatic associations to various emotions in terms of the color, the texture,
> the shape, the size, the weight, the material, the body and other design
> components that might be important. Then an industrial designer inter-
> preted these associations, very much as the conductor interprets the notes
> of a composer. . . .

Using this approach I was able to develop dials and knobs for airplanes and cars that would say, without words, "Turn me slowly, I'm dangerous." It is possible to design any object with varying degrees of communicational precision—typewriters, cars, etc. Cookies could be designed to say, "Eat me quickly."

Anything that can be said verbally can be said better non-verbally.

Artists, of course, have used such symbolic shapes and colors to evoke responses since time immemorial. We may think them too subtle and non-objective, but whether we know it or not, we are constantly affected by them—our emotions are stirred to love, fear, joy, and depression according to the shapes and colors we see every day.

Consider the traffic signs, for example: red and green lights, symbols for "curve ahead," railroad crossing, etc. Consider the affect of a hand raised, palm forward; if it is a policeman's hand, it means "stop," if it is a Nazi's hand, it means "heil," if it is an Indian's hand, it means "peace." Such graphic symbols can be read fast and, in their utter simplicity, can evoke powerful responses.

Yet we are so inundated by words that our attention is more often distracted from the nonverbal. The point, again, is to cultivate an *attitude*. And awareness of the power of "symbology" is essential for the complete communicator. A copywriter with such an attitude, will collaborate more fully with art director, photographer, music and film producer, or with the production man who can affect so strongly the nonverbal overtones of an ad by the typography. These specialists in the various senses will collaborate so closely, it will be impossible, when someone sees the message, to know where one's function left off and another's began.

Another form of nonverbal expression, called phatic communication, is the way facial expressions, gestures, and tone of voice can affect meaning. Every good actor knows that you can say "Hello" with dozens of different inflections, to connote hate, love, fear, awe, indifference, or what have you. The lift of an eyebrow can have a world of meaning. And all different forms of action, even without words, can communicate. This is why the subtleties of TV commercial direction, of casting, of voice inflection can be so important. Notice how Hooper White, a film director with a keen sense for the nonverbal, describes commercials. His phrases are "visual," rather than "verbal":

Of a Chevrolet commercial—"One 60-second running, swooping, arc-ing, unforgettable shot from a helicopter."

Of the action in a Chemstrand Cumuloft rug commercial—"Shot from rug-level . . . the editing yanks you through the rug's day of being danced on, sprawled on, spilled on, crawled on."

Of the visual strength of a Sprite commercial—"Graphics are the open sesame, carefully planned disarray—Sprite in a crystal bowl, shot from overhead with a translucent, base-lit table top."

But such visual, nonverbal subtleties do not apply only to commercials. "One of the strongest incentives to attention is movement," writes Schwab of print advertising. We can see such strong nonverbal overtones in a photograph for a Metrecal (diet aid) ad. It shows an overweight man running for a bus. "Is this the day you really do something about your weight?" reads the headline. Without any further copy, we can feel the man's exertion, feel breathless ourselves, our hearts pumping, our lungs out of breath.

The copywriter of today and tomorrow must live, work, and practice a sense of graphics. He does not have to be an art director to be sensitive to the power of a picture. Two ads for the same product boldly illustrate the strength of the verbal and the nonverbal. One is an ad for Crepe de Chine perfume which uses 100 words to tell its sensual story:

> (*Illustration:* Beautiful girl, in a slip, lying on a bed, applying Crepe de Chine to her wrist.)
>
> WEAR CREPE DE CHINE AT 80 THROBS A MINUTE
> Don't just throw it on
> Use your heart.
> Put a little Crepe de Chine wherever the skin is thinnest and you can feel your pulse.
> The same spot the doctor holds your wrist.
> Your hairline at the temples.
> The base of your throat, the nape of the neck. The inside of your elbows. The back of your knees.
> And with each throb of your heart . . . a little Crepe de Chine pulses out in circles. Subtly.
> You ought to try it. Like so.
> And rush your way up to 90 throbs.

The other "service" ad consists of nine pictures, without any copy, illustrating the pulse points at which perfume is applied. First picture: girl's hand removing stopper from Crepe de Chine bottle. Second, closeup of hand touching stopper to earlobe. Third, closeup, touching stopper to wrist. Fourth, inside arm. Fifth, behind knee. Sixth, between breasts. Seventh, to the base of the throat. Eighth, to the nape of the neck. And ninth, on the forehead.

This writer, for one, found the nonverbal version the more fascinating of the two. Certainly it involved the reader. Here is how Herb Green, the copywriter, described the evolution of his graphic idea:

> I remember the day because it was so violent. I was in the A.D.'s office with a finished piece of copy for the "Pulse Point" ad. I read it to him (a good piece of copy should be read to an A.D. so they get spoiled by it!) and when I finished and he applauded I simply and quietly tore it up and told him the copy didn't say one more thing than the pictures. It was

redundant. But entirely. He got quite furious. I had thought he would love the whole thing. An ad with no copy. Just pictures. The argument was so bad that the entire agency took sides. Strangely enough all the writers were for no copy. All A.D.'s for copy. Account execs split and most of the secretaries were for no copy. So the compromise was to present both versions to the client. Strangely enough the client was once a very fine writer and that's why the ad has no copy.

An ad for Yardley Black Label After Shave used the lever of association to involve all of the reader's senses. It showed a picture of the open Yardley bottle, along with a smoking pipe, a soft leather glove, and a snifter of brandy: "Four great masculine fragrances," read the headline. "One of them is brand new."

A human being, if he is alive, has five senses. Some work more acutely than others, depending on the individual. But depending on the communicator, all can be roused to greater activity. If the senses are invoked, you have the best answer to the problem of communication—an involved audience.

9

COPY RESEARCH—OR
HOW TO LIVE WITH THE INEVITABLE

Predicting the Unpredictable

The advertiser asks for something different, exciting, a campaign that will make his product stand out from all others, a provocative idea, an inspiration.

The copywriter follows all the steps we have described to get the big idea. He studies all he can about the product, its market and competition. He goes all around the subject in a spirit of free association. Ideas arrive like salmon rushing to spawn. Then comes the incubation period. He mulls over all the ideas. He is restless, uncertain.

And suddenly, the flash of inspiration! He has it. The one ideal, beautifully right idea—one that has never existed before. He *knows* it is right. He *feels* it. Whit Hobbs, creative head of the Benton & Bowles Agency, called that illumination the "boiing" system. Something went "boiing" and, lo and behold, the idea was born. This writer uses the "hackles" method. When the hackles on the back of his neck start to prickle, he recognizes that he is getting the ideal solution.

Another way most people recognize inspiration is when it seems "such a simple solution." Everyone says, wonderingly, "Why didn't somebody think of that before?"

This kind of intuitive inspiration is the lifeblood of our business. It is what makes all the sweat and tears worthwhile. It is what creative people since the beginning of time have had in common that makes them creative—the ability, based on conditioned insight, to invent something unique, or a unique combination of somethings, which wins instant response from those who are exposed to it.

Now, let us suppose, in the case of our fictitious copywriter, that the exciting idea he has conceived *is* a breakthrough. The advertiser asked for something unique and he got it. It is so shiningly right that it speaks for itself. "If you have to explain how great an ad is, it isn't," said creative director Fred Manley to an audience of copywriters. Everyone recognized what he meant. When you get a real inspiration, you do not have to labor the point. Other copywriters just naturally think, "I wish I had thought of it." The idea takes over.

And yet, when the unique idea the advertiser asked for is presented to him in the cold light of day, he says, "How can I be *sure* it will work? Give me some guarantee of its power. Go out and research it."

Now the trouble begins. Maybe the advertiser had the same initial reaction everybody else had. In his secret knowing, he may well, for a while, have been sure that the inspiration was right. (The best test he has is to think of how miserable he would be if his toughest competitor had the idea.) But he has bosses and stockholders and a board of directors to consider. Usually, if he is a major advertiser, he has to invest millions of their dollars in this tenuous thing, an idea. With some other investments, he can be fairly sure in advance. For example, if he invests money in more manpower, he can be reasonably sure of more production. But in the never-never world of ideas, he has only that initial judgment to guide him. And after the first boing, soberness sets in.

So he turns to research. And research, in the case of an idea that is completely new, can squeeze the lifeblood out of the inspiration. As research approaches it dispassionately, it can gradually cease to be actively passionate. If the idea *is* truly new, if it has never existed before, it is difficult to predict how effective it will be. "In our quest for reliable information," writes Walter Weir, author of *On the Writing of Advertising,* "we must face at least one inescapable fact . . . that we cannot send our researchers into the future." Researchers are analytical; to be so, they must weigh all hypotheses in the light of past facts. But it is wrong, says Weir, "to assume that because we have accumulated facts we necessarily have a reliable guide to the future when actually what we have gathered is . . . only a fairly accurate estimate of the past."

So we have this contradiction. The advertiser asks for something excitingly new. The copywriter comes up with it. If it is really new, it cannot be researched in the light of past experience—because it *has* no past experience. But the advertiser has to be reassured by research. Result: many an exciting new idea never gets used. Or, if it is used, it will often become a shadow of itself between the inspiration and the execution. It will have acquired accretions of things which *are* researchable—i.e., the safe, the already-tried. It will be executed with a big, single picture (because one big picture works generally better than many), with a short headline (because short headlines are more readable), with an illustration that includes a dog and a baby (because they are sure-fire), with a logo of a certain size and copy of a certain length—in short, according to researchable, verifiable facts, rather than what is naturally right for the idea.

"A lot of advertising today," says Leo Burnett, "is being analyzed, engineered, researched and nit-picked within an inch of its life. . . . The result is a lot of expensive advertising that is irrefutably rational but hopelessly dull."

Does this mean that we should not do copy research? *Certainly not.* But it does mean that we should research only what we *can* research. Too many exciting new campaigns have been killed because fearful men refused to rely on their judgments and insisted on measuring the immeasurable. They used research as a creative crutch. They settled for statistics which they knew, in their hearts, were invalid, so they could give themselves the air of authenticity.

"The first user of any novel method of advertising," wrote Prof. George Burton Hotchkiss, author of *Advertising Copy*, "gains far greater value than is open to any imitator." But to be an innovator takes courage—the courage of conviction. Most advertisers today want to be innovators without risk.

A Confusion of Research Methods

Lucas and Britt point out, in their book *Measuring Advertising Effectiveness,*

> Sometimes research has been looked upon as a substitute for judgment. Research itself, of course, requires a good deal of judgment. It requires judgment to decide when to test, where to test, what to test, how to test, and how to use the results. . . . All these decisions must be made if the research practitioner is to aid the advertising practitioner in making still more important decisions. At times these important decisions can be little more than guesses, and the real challenge for the researcher is to provide facts which will reduce guesswork to a minimum.

The key word in that statement is the word "facts." For if we are using research to reduce guesswork, we are looking for those findings which are irrefutable. Russell H. Colley, author of *Defining Advertising Goals for*

. *Measured Advertising Results,* stressed that research can only be an aid to judgment, not a substitute for it. "Some advertising decisions must be based 90% on judgment or intuition (another way of saying the stored-up knowledge of a lifetime). Other decisions may be based 90% on fact, 10% on judgment." The trouble is that, while many people can agree instinctively on what is a really inspired idea, few can agree on what kind of research provides reliable facts about it.

It all depends on who your researcher is. It is much easier to find writers in agreement on good copy than to find researchers agreed on valid research. Says Alfred Politz, himself an eminent researcher, in *Measuring Advertising Effectiveness:*

> If someone thinks that the ability of advertising to attract attention is directly related to its effectiveness, he will then, of course, measure the attention-getting ability and consider the results to be a measure of advertising effectiveness. If someone thinks the fact that an advertising phrase is remembered signifies effectiveness, he will use memory measurements as a criterion of performance. If someone believes that advertising has to give pleasure and be liked, he may then subject the pleasantness or the aesthetic values to measurement and will interpret a positive result as proof of the effectiveness of the advertising. In each case the researcher calls upon an implicit assumption about the mechanisms by which advertising achieves its effect.

One way to get around those contradictions is to find your facts after the fact—i.e., after the advertising has appeared and something has happened or failed to happen. "The proof of art is in the response." This is research which, like the use of verifiable copy, is operational. That is, it tests an idea by seeing whether it works or does not work.

That is one reason why mail-order advertising has always been a favorite tool of research. You can get a fast and practical answer to the pulling power of one headline over another, one layout over another. Few advertisers use the mail-order type of ad any more, except those who do sell by mail. But it might be a good idea to tailor-make such ads for the sole purpose of testing copy ideas which can later be used in more general advertising.

Another way to test advertising by how it works is to run it in test markets. It is extremely hard to isolate the effects of the advertising from many other factors—the climate, environment, competitive advertising, local events, the pricing and distribution of your product and those of your competitors, the media mix and amount of your competitors' advertising. But at least, with scientific controls, you can approach conditions similar to those for the national advertising campaign and get some measure of its possible effectiveness. This is the kind of research that has been conducted by the *Milwaukee Journal,* where matched samples

of newspaper readers and TV viewers have been separately advertised
to, over long periods, and the results continuously measured.

We can measure certain aspects of the advertising, in its natural environment, and make alterations and improvements while the campaign
goes along. (This is done, for example, by quantitative measurements of
the noting and reading of magazine ads.) People are questioned as to how
keenly they noticed an ad and how carefully they read it. They are
sometimes asked whether the ad made them feel more like buying and
other probing questions.

The best-known method, as to readership, is the Starch report on national magazine and newspaper advertising. But even in this nose-count-
ing post-testing method, there is division on who has the right system.

The major advantage of the Starch method is that it has been used
with the greatest consistency for the most number of years. Therefore,
there is a large body of benchmarks. It falls short of measuring effectiveness, though, for it tells you mainly what percentage of the readers
noticed and read your ad. Certainly that is useful research, because your
ad cannot accomplish any objective if nobody sees it. But an ad for an
automobile featuring a two page picture of a nude woman might get
100 percent noting and still fail to be effective in selling a car.

(Starch) scores can tell us which of two executions of an idea will get
more attention, but they cannot tell us what the idea should be. Nor, for
that matter, can they give us the judgment to know which of those two
ads will produce more sales. It is possible to get very low noting and
read-most scores with highly effective ads. For example, ads which carefully select their audience, such as the long-copy ads for the Famous
Artists' School, may get low read-most scores, but those who do read
them are avidly interested.

The same is true of the quantitative research done with television commercials—such methods as the telephone surveys run by the Burke and
Gallup & Robinson organizations. People in various parts of the country
are telephoned after seeing television programs, asked to identify the
shows they watched and what they remembered about the commercials.
Some systems use "immediate-after" recall, others call the day after, when
there has been time for the respondents to have forgotten. The scores,
therefore, vary, but they are all intended to measure how well the commercials communicated what they set out to say. How effective the
message will be in promoting sales deponent sayeth not.

Some advertising agencies and research organizations have devised
ways to pretest advertising. But to the extent that they are removed from
the actual context in which they will appear, to that degree they are
suspect. And these methods, and the opinions about them, are so divergent
that, if you wanted to be impartial, you could have an infinite combination of measures before you ever considered results. Here are some of the

techniques: paired comparisons, in which people are shown different ads and questioned about their preferences; the shuffle-card test, in which people are given stacks of cards with copy phrases on them, and asked to arrange them in order of preference; the checkerboard test, in which words or phrases are listed in boxes and people check off their likes and dislikes; the layout test, in which respondents are shown contrasting layouts, in rough or finished form, interrupted by other ads of a dissimilar product, and then asked what they recall about the first ads; the aided usage method, in which unlabeled samples of the same product, purporting to be different products, are placed in the home, together with copy that refers to their respective benefits—after a certain length of time, the product which has had more consumption indicates which copy is the more effective.

Then there are various laboratory tests, which keep being publicized and which survive according to the enthusiasm and salesmanship of their champions. The tachistoscope enables slides of ads to be shown in quick flashes, to measure how fast they get recognition, what elements are dominant, and how well people remember them. Pupil dilation is a measure of how forcefully advertising impinges on the eyeball. Galvanic skin response measures the reaction of that part of the body.

New methods of pretesting come and go, and no doubt, as you read these words, a "foolproof" method is being touted, which is not mentioned in this chapter. At the moment, the most popular systems appear to be the Gallup & Robinson magazine for pretesting print ads and the Schwerin audience jury for pretesting commercials.

The G & R magazine, *Impact*, is published about once a month and placed in a number of homes. After a while, interviewers return to the homes and question the readers. The magazine is spiral-bound and has little editorial material. It is a primitive imitation of an actual magazine, but the purpose of the research is to compare the findings of one ad with another, and the researchers claim consistency between the scores in the test magazine and those of some of the same ads which they later test after they appear in actual magazines. Again, this kind of pretesting, like Starch scores, cannot predict effectiveness, although the findings do include "feel more like buying" scores.

One of the most useful findings from this method is the verbatim transcript of the respondents' remarks. Here, outside the sterility of the scores, are the actual comments real, live people made about the ads. The copywriter, whose talents derive from his feeling and understanding for people, can read verbatims with a psychologically attuned mind.

This does not mean that he accepts what people have said as the gospel. There is a big difference between what people say and what they do. Furthermore, people commenting on ads are in the position of being judges, rather than consumers. But the copywriter, over many readings and with practical experience, can get a "feel" for the respondents and their reactions to his ads. He can detect insincerity. In the nuances of what they say and leave unsaid, he can gauge how well he has communicated. It is *he* who must study the verbatims. No outside source, no statistician can interpret them for him. This is all part of getting the feel of his product and finding out how well he has communicated it. The best way to learn is to listen. As a copywriter reads the verbatims, he becomes a listener. Listening to many different people, reacting to the questions researchers ask them, the copywriter can feel whether he is on the right track or not.

Let us take, as an example, research done in conjunction with Goodyear's Communications Research Department on the copy approach for the Goodyear Double Eagle tire with the LifeGuard Safety Spare. This was the campaign with the theme, "When there's no man around . . . Goodyear should be." An ad was prepared for pretesting and placed, along with two other tire ads, in one issue of the Gallup & Robinson pretest magazine. This was a triple split run of the magazine. Three different groups of people were asked to comment about the three different tire ads.

In this case, all three ads were ingenious and original, and all, to some extent, followed the communication tenets we have discussed in this book so far. The statistical scores on all three ads were relatively close. But the verbatims for the "No Man Around" ad, to a reader psychologically attuned, strongly favored that approach. Contrast the following remarks and see if you do not agree . . .

Typical Verbatims about "No Man Around" Ad:

It had a picture of a girl standing in the rain. She had a flat tire. I thought, "I could see my wife out on a lonely stretch of road with a flat."

The tire is actually two tires in one. It wouldn't leave you stranded in the middle of nowhere. . . . I think every man can see his wife in the same situation.

The ad said something about the safety guard inside the tire. . . . I thought the woman looked miserable out there in the wilderness. . . . My interest was increased, because it was more of a report than an advertisement.

I thought about the many times I've worried about my wife when she took the car at night.

Typical Verbatims about Other Two Ads:

There was a tire, just a smooth tire. The ad said, "She tried to run me down at 20,000 miles." . . . I thought that it was catchy.

I learned from the ad that it (the tire) could take quite a bit of abuse. . . . I thought that as an attention-getter, the ad was so much better than the run-of-the-mill tire ads.

The ad pictured a great big tire that covered the whole page. . . . I vaguely recall some reference to the mileage. . . . I thought the ad was very striking.

The ad said, "Does your wife run around?" It told a little story about running around on Goodyear tires, and this tire went 26,000. . . . I thought it was a clever story and ad in general.

Note that all the remarks quoted were favorable to the ads. But this was not the important finding. In areas of interest, believability, and context, all three ads may have been equally effective. But the verbatims indicated that the "No Man Around" ad involved the reader to a greater degree. A reader, seeing any ad in a favorable light, might use such hackneyed and expected phrases as "I thought it was catchy," "an attention-getter," "striking," etc. In such cases, the reader, who is not a skillful advertiser, is nevertheless responding in his own terms of judgment. He is becoming an "ad expert"—a critic. And remember what Maugham said about critics, that they cannot see the play the audience sees because they have not acted in it.

From the verbatims on the "No Man Around" ad, the copywriter could see that the readers were "acting in" the situation. They were part of it, and therefore it was communicating with the most effectiveness.

The copy research methods we have discussed so far are, by and large, quantitative measures. That is, the G & R *Impact* magazine, except for the verbatims, measures the quantity of the people to whom the ad communicated the message, not whether the message was the right one to communicate. That is what the Starch measurements do, and the various kinds of telephone surveys about TV commercials. If you want to communicate the fact that your bread is fresh, and pretesting by one of these methods shows that your message has come through like a blockbuster, you are still not sure that your competitor's message, about vitamin enrichment, will not be a more motivating idea.

Attempting to find the true motivation behind people's buying habits, advertisers some years ago borrowed the methods of psychologists and delved into "motivation research" (M.R.).

"Where does the phrase 'motivation research' come from?" writes Steuart Henderson Britt, in *The Spenders*. "Actually the term is a misnomer. The phrase 'motivation research' refers to what are called 'projective techniques,' which are used by clinical psychologists. . . . These methods are used to discover as much as possible about a person's characteristic modes of behavior, by presenting him with rather vague or ambiguous stimuli. The theory is that the individual who is being interviewed or tested will in various ways *project* his own personality traits into a situation, and that by examining the resultant data the psychologist can discover something about the individual's personality traits which that person might not reveal through direct questioning."

Motivation research techniques include such methods as the *thematic apperception test,* in which the respondent is shown a drawing of people and asked to tell a story about them; the *sentence-completion* method, in which he finishes a group of incomplete sentences which may give clues to his motivation; the *word association test;* depth interviews; and group interviews.

Britt cites, as examples of successful M.R.: The discovery, by the makers of Ry-Krisp crackers, that their copy approach of offering a reducing food was limiting their appeal—they decided to advertise Ry-Krisp as a cocktail cracker and for snacks instead. The discovery by the Tea Council that the slogan "Tired? Nervous? Try Tea" was emphasizing a negative (that tea was for sick, nervous people), resulting in a change to "Drink it hefty, hot, and hearty!" The discovery by the makers of Wesson Oil's Snowdrift that the swirl on the top of the shortening evoked images of purity and fluffiness, causing them to feature the swirl on the package label.

With motivation research, as with most other advertising measurements, contradictions arise according to who does the research and who makes the analysis. *Fortune* magazine, said Britt, reported that Drs. Ernest Dichter and Burleigh Gardner were hired separately to analyze consumer attitudes toward the advertising of Dial soap and that they came out with completely contradictory findings. "Obviously contradictions of this kind, as they get known in the business world, result in considerable skepticism about motivation research. But it is not too surprising to have different interpretations and recommendations from two different M.R. practitioners. Don't you sometimes find different interpretations about what's ailing you from two different M.D.s?"

Setting motivation research aside, there is one kind of qualitative research which is reassuringly pragmatic and therefore popular. This is the method of the Schwerin Research Corp., which pretests TV commercials. They do this with a simulation of television viewing, consisting of a live audience in a company-operated theatre.

The Schwerin method has a language all its own, which often determines the life or death of an advertising idea. It involves "Pre-Choice" scores, "Post-Choice" scores, "Product Field Norm" and "Relative Competitive Preference." What all this signifies is that the people are asked what products, in a given category, they prefer *before* they see the commercials and what products they prefer *after*. The motivation for their response is that they may win a prize, consisting of one of those products, through a lucky number drawing. If, after viewing a commercial, they have indicated a "Change of Preference," this is supposed to be a prediction of how they will react to the commercial when they see it on their TV screen at home.

The Schwerin method has devout adherents and violent critics. One major advertiser—Leonard Lavin of the Alberto-Culver Company—claims that there has been a great correlation between commercials which received high scores in Schwerin tests and successful sales results. His method of using Schwerin is more exhaustive and expensive than most. After reviewing all possible creative approaches, he tests as many as 10 or more different rough commercials to find one motivating concept. Then he refines that concept with more finished commercials and tests them as well. Finally, he runs the winning commercial on the air, with minor variations, in a saturated, concentrated campaign. Lavin maintains that the combination of trial and error, plus judgment in the market-research phase, plus judicious and heavy buying of TV time, is highly effective. The phenomenal growth of his company does not disprove his belief.

On the other hand, there are successful advertisers to whom the Schwerin method is anathema. Many sophisticated advertisers prefer quantitative measures which simply reveal how well advertising communicates. They consider Schwerin jury predictions of effectiveness too artificial to be scientific.

One of the biggest problems with the Schwerin method is that busy executives tend to use the change of preference results as an oversimplified scoring method. Few test as many rough and finished commercials as Lavin does. And if one commercial receives a 9 rather than its predecessor's 13, it is summarily killed. Since finished TV commercials may cost up to $20,000 to produce, frequent mortality due to low Schwerin scores would be too costly. The solution to this problem, they decide, is to test rough, unfinished commercials—often merely a series of still photographs following an artist's story board. The researchers claim that the roughness of most commercials does not appreciably affect the scores. But the critics of the method consider this one more unscientific variable.

And the variables are legion—the mood and composition of the audience, the carnival spirit, which encourages the people in the theatre to talk to one another and, conceivably, to influence the choice of prizes. One of the most criticized variables is the fact that different products have higher or lower "going-in" scores of preference, depending on their reputation outside the theatre. That is, a highly reputed product, with a high initial score, can obviously gain less change of preference than one which is totally unknown, and starts from a base of 0. While this difference is supposed to be factored into the outcoming score, that answer does not satisfy the critics.

Finally, the most serious criticism is the fact that the Schwerin jury operates outside the context of reality—the actual conditions that affect a consumer buying a product. As a captive audience in the theatre, the jurors may watch and be influenced by a commercial which they might ignore in their homes. For example, one of the first rules in writing TV commercials is to have an intriguing opening, to seize the viewers' attention. Some commercials have won high scores from Schwerin despite dull openings because a captive audience is more liable to watch everything. Furthermore, a consumer may be influenced to buy through many repeated impressions of an advertising campaign which, initially, might have scored poorly in one exposure on Schwerin. His choice, when he pays deliberately for a product, may be quite different from the choice he makes in a theatre when he is playing a lottery game.

Quantitative research, qualitative research, nose counting, mind probing of the unconscious and subconscious, simulations of television viewing: all these, and many, many more are the copy-research methods which confuse that conscientious advertiser who asks, "How can I be *sure?*"

It is no wonder that many advertisers, after dallying with one or another of the alluring research mistresses, turn back with relief to the comfortable marriage of creative intuition and seasoned judgment.

Being Creative about Copy Research

What is research anyway? It is "a diligent and systematic inquiry or investigation into a subject in order to discover facts or principles." We are doing research, as described in Chap. 6, when we investigate all kinds of facts regarding our product and market. We are doing research, too, as described in Chap. 7, when our free, uninhibited minds investigate every possible idea associated with our subject.

But when it comes to copy research, to the pretesting and posttesting of advertising ideas, we too often tighten up and start keeping score. We test a commercial with an audience jury, or one or two executions of an idea with a dummy magazine. Then we wait many days, sometimes weeks and months, for the dogmatic scores, and agree that we have failed or succeeded. This is not the scientific way. "In the exact sciences," says Politz, "the viewpoint has been accepted for hundreds of years that research and experiments involve the testing of hypotheses." These hypotheses, or hunches, are expected, as a matter of course, to lead into endless blind alleys before a fact or a principle is discovered.

Bob Mayer, associate research director of Young & Rubicam, Inc., gives a candid talk to agency personnel and clients entitled, "Into the Forest of Copy Research." He tells how anything that affects human beings in the marketplace can be rightly called copy research, including finding out the relative position of competitors and attitudes toward them. He tells how going to plays and reading novels—anything that helps writers to understand humanity, through vicarious experience and acquired insights—are forms of research. And he frankly declares that he and his colleagues are suspicious of any one research answer for any problem.

"I have been in the area (of copy research) a good many years," says Mayer. "The more I know about it, the larger the question marks become." This is because, he continues, there are so many areas to explore and so many different kinds of measures. The three main areas in which copy research can help are in the developmental stages (to stimulate new ideas in copy), in the testing of alternative individual ads, and in the area of testing an entire campaign. Constructing a "sequential model" of how advertising works, Mayer lists six steps it takes in order to be effective: (1) attention, (2) comprehension, (3) believability, (4) intention to purchase, (5) actual purchase, and (6) repurchase (which, he says, is the real measure of profitability).

Charting the measuring methods, both in his agency and from outside services, Mayer demonstrates all the variables which can affect the meaning of a given test result in any of the sequential steps. On the following pages are three typical charts (Audience Studies, Inc. is a system of TV commercial testing somewhat similar to the Schwerin jury).

As you can see from those charts, each research method has different variables. Calculating the number of relevant criteria which could affect a decision, given the many methods and variables, Mayer comes up with a conservative figure of 480,000, each of which purports to measure the performance of a single ad or commercial.

When you consider that staggering number of variables, you wonder how anyone can fairly make a decision based on copy research. One answer was that given by Colley—that only specific, measurable objectives be stated and researched (e.g., that the awareness of a brand should increase by such-and-such a percentage). Colley did not feel, however, that advertisers could go beyond the measurement of attention, comprehension, and believability, into the areas of intent to buy, purchase, and repurchase. It was when advertisers insisted that they must measure those areas that a research method like the Schwerin audience jury (which claims to predict sales intent) became popular.

One creative answer which more copywriters and researchers, in collaboration, are trying to use is the assumption that copy research should parallel the thought process involved in copywriting. "Research must be *integrated* into the process of creating advertising," said Britt, in an address before the Advertising Research Foundation; and he called for empirical research methods, never relying on any one pat answer. This is precisely how our creative minds operate.

The main fault of today's copy research is that it is too slow to parallel

BURKE IV

Type of Exposure	Measurement Unit	Performance Criteria
√ Absolutely normal	√ Open End	**ATTENTION**
Forced to the medium	Multiple Choice	Ad as a whole
Forced to series of ads	Dichotomous	Specific elements of ad
Forced to single ad	Semantic Scales	√ Association with
Forced to only parts of an ad	Machine	advertiser
		COMPREHENSION
Time Lapse	*Target Group*	√ Playback of one or more
		sales points
None	Brand Users	√ Playback of individual
√ 1–5 hours	Product Category Users	sales points
12–24 hours	Prospects	Playback of concepts
More than 24 hours	Total Audience	Interpretation or meaning
Indefinite	√ Commercial Audience	of ad
		Specific vs. generic
Response Cue	*Interview Situation*	playback
		BELIEF
Recognition	Personal Interview	Statement of belief or
Masked recognition	√ Telephone	disbelief
Unaided	Direct Mail	Image change
Media cue	Panel	Image comparison
Situation cue		
√ Brand cue	√ Individual Interview	**ATTITUDE**
√ Product cue	Group Interview	FMLB
		Favor toward product
		Buying preference
Sample Distribution	*Sample Size*	change
		REPORTED SALES
√ Local	Less than 50	
Regional	To 100	**LOYALTY**
National	√ 100–500	BFQ
	300+	
Quota		**IMPORTANCE**
Block		Differentiation
√ Probability		uniqueness
		SALIENCY
		Top-of-mind awareness
		LIKEABILITY
		Favor toward ad

AUDIENCE STUDIES, INC.

Type of Exposure	Measurement Unit	Performance Criteria
Absolutely normal	√ Open End	ATTENTION
Forced to the medium	√ Multiple Choice	√ Ad as a whole
√ Forced to series of ads	Dichotomous	√ Specific elements of ad
Forced to single ad	√ Semantic Scales	√ Association with
Forced to only parts of	Machine	advertiser
an ad		
		COMPREHENSION
		Playback of one or more
Time Lapse	Target Group	sales points
√ None	Brand Users	√ Playback of individual
1–5 hours	Product Category Users	sales points
12–24 hours	Prospects	Playback of concepts
More than 24 hours	√ Total Audience	Interpretation or
Indefinite	Commercial Audience	meaning of ad
		Specific vs. generic
		playback
Response Cue	Interview Situation	
Recognition	Personal Interview	BELIEF
Masked recognition	Telephone	Statement of belief or
√ Unaided	Direct Mail	disbelief
Media cue	Panel	Image change
Situation cue		√ Image comparison
Brand cue	Individual Interview	ATTITUDE
Product cue	√ Group Interview	FMLB
		Favor toward product
		√ Buying preference
Sample Distribution	Sample Size	change
√ Local	Less than 50	REPORTED SALES
Regional	To 100	
National	√ 100–300	LOYALTY
√ Quota	300+	BFQ
Block		IMPORTANCE
Probability		Differentiation
		uniqueness
		SALIENCY
		Top-of-mind awareness
		LIKEABILITY
		√ Favor toward ad

GALLUP & ROBINSON PRINT

Type of Exposure	Measurement Unit	Performance Criteria
√ Absolutely normal	√ Open End	**ATTENTION**
Forced to the medium	Multiple Choice	Ad as a whole
Forced to series of ads	Dichotomous	Specific elements of ad
Forced to single ad	Semantic Scales	√ Association with
Forced to only parts of	Machine	advertiser
an ad		
		COMPREHENSION
		√ Playback of one or more
Time Lapse	*Target Group*	sales points
		√ Playback of individual
None	Brand Users	sales points
1–5 hours	Product Category Users	Playback of concepts
12–24 hours	Prospects	Interpretation or
√ More than 24 hours	√ Total Audience	meaning of ad
Indefinite	Commercial Audience	Specific vs. generic
		playback
Response Cue	*Interview Situation*	
		BELIEF
Recognition	√ Personal Interview	Statement of belief or
Masked recognition	Telephone	disbelief
Unaided	Direct Mail	Image change
Media cue	Panel	Image comparison
Situation cue		
√ Brand cue	√ Individual Interview	**ATTITUDE**
Product cue	Group Interview	FMLB
		√ Favor toward product
		Buying preference
Sample Distribution	*Sample Size*	change
Local	Less than 50	**REPORTED SALES**
Regional	To 100	
√ National	√ 100–300	**LOYALTY**
	300+	BFQ
√ Quota		
Block		**IMPORTANCE**
Probability		Differentiation
		uniqueness
		SALIENCY
		Top-of-mind awareness
		LIKEABILITY
		Favor toward ad

our thought process and, therefore, to enable us to explore the endless blind alleys. The copywriter can amass pounds of facts about the product, the medium, and the market, in a very short time (with electronic data processing, his sources are even more readily available). Then, with his imaginative mind, he can quickly free-associate hundreds of ideas.

But when the advertiser says, "How can I be *sure?*" rigor mortis sets in. Depending on the tastes of the researchers, the ingrained habits of the company, the fearful desire for statistics (any statistics, so long as they will get us off that long limb of having to make a personal judgment), some one method of measuring is chosen. Then everybody sits back and waits for the scores.)

It will take a lot of time and money and will require many intricate experiments before copywriters can use multiple measures the way their minds accept and reject multiple ideas. But this is the wave of the future for copy research. If fact-finding and idea-getting are themselves a form of research, and if they are done in a spirit of serendipity—of going all around the subject to find the elusive fact and idea that may click—then why should not copy research be of the same nature? We copywriters could be doing consumer research at the same time as we are conceiving ideas—trying out phrases, copy appeals, rough layouts, and storyboards on the very audience whose verbatims we now study long afterwards.

Can you imagine a research chemist operating without hunches—without himself trying this and that combination of ingredients before he lights on the right formula? Why should not the copywriter himself use all the tools of copy research more frequently and more broadly—whether they be the tachistoscope, the audience jury, paired comparisons, or M.R.? Of course, the copywriter must be aided by the specialists in those research methods—just as he is aided by the film producer, the typographer, the artist, and the photographer in their fields. But he should be constantly implementing the copy research himself, because only he can ask the questions, as he conceives the ideas. "Too frequently," says Politz, "the attempt is made to separate the 'analytical' mind from the 'creative' mind. . . . The main function of research must be to help to create something." As the copywriter presents his creative hunches to a live audience and listens and senses reactions, his ideas can feed and grow on their response. As he compares the quantitative answers with the qualitative probings, he can fit the findings together, the way you solve a jigsaw puzzle. Through the use of many different methods, as checks and balances on one another, major areas of good and poor communication can be found. The more measurements we have, the more we can reduce the variables and the chances for accidentally high or low scores. Just as in the association game we described in the last chapter, a solution will gradually emerge, even though some of the pieces seem contradictory.

Bob Mayer comments frankly on this new, broad method of copy research:

> The answer is not always as obvious when using multiple measures as it is when using a single measurement dimension. Martin Mayer (no relation, incidentally) wrote a 1965 ARF report called "The Intelligent Man's Guide to Sales Measures of Advertising." He makes this point:

" 'Certainty,' Justice Holmes once wrote, 'is generally an illusion; and repose is not the destiny of man.'

"Though brave things sometimes get said at meetings, the researcher, however mathematical his techniques, is not in the business of providing certainty. Decisions still have to be made, and often the information provided by research makes the decision process more rather than less difficult."

Research which uses multiple measures is not always easy to use and it may make decision-making a more difficult process, but it also will provide a higher percentage of right judgments.

The copywriter, of course, cannot accomplish this kind of empirical research by himself. The advertiser we described earlier who asks "How can we be *sure?*" has to be taking the creative approach to copy research too. Together, they will use combinations of research methods. When they find discrepancies, they will not select one method over another, but will proceed to further checks and balances, always looking for areas of coincidence. This may require testing the same ad or commercial in countless different ways. It may require more research at the beginning and far fewer ads at the end. But those fewer ads will be worth repeating, so the empirical approach will not have been extravagant.

In any case, the purpose of this kind of research would be to further the power of creative intuition, not to deny it. It would be research to improve advertising, not to score it. It would not be research that would attempt to predict the future, but would adjust dynamically to the ever-changing present.

10

COMMUNICATING
ABOUT THE COMMUNICATION

The Copywriter's Desperate Condition

Many copywriters lead lives of quiet desperation. They can feel happy and secure at their typewriters—and in collaboration with kindred souls like the art director and the film producer. But then their copy goes "out there," and it gets cut to ribbons.

The account executive says it is not hard-selling enough. The merchandising man asks why a cents-off coupon cannot be included. The research department does a survey and reveals that 42 out of 50 women questioned were confused by the headline. The advertising director complains that the copy is "too cute" and the layout is arty. The sales manager wants the product shown twice as big. The president of the company says whatever the experts want is okay by him, so long as the name of the company is three times as large and the trademark is mortised into the main illustration.

Often the copywriter's best polished prose never gets as far as those inquisitors. His boss or the copy chief has already performed the operation, perhaps having automatically blue-penciled the first paragraph, covered the margins with question marks, and returned the copy with a savage "Rewrite! rewrite!"

Or, worse than that, the copy chief has, regretfully, rewritten the offending sections himself, or written an entirely new piece of copy. Or, wanting to see more versions, he has given a duplicate assignment to another writer. Often our suffering copywriter is never told what happened to *his* deathless prose, until he sees an entirely different ad, in proof form, and somebody else gets the credit.

What other tortures can the copywriter endure? One common gauntlet he has to run is to have his copy revised by committee. Perhaps his boss calls in the other copywriters and artists and they have a jolly gangup. Everyone suggests alternative headlines and pictures. Some of the ideas are too good to lose, so it is decided to submit three different versions of the ad to the product group or to the clients. When this is done, the copywriter may then undergo a strappado of a more fiendish nature. The inquisition judges all three ads to be superior. The verdict is for the offending copywriter, who started the crime in the first place, to go back to his office and, somehow, to create one combination ad out of the three.

Probably the worst punishment a copywriter endures—akin to the Chinese water torture—is to write, write, write, write, write . . . and never to see his copy in print. This can go on, literally, for many months. The author, in fact, wrote and supervised 146 different commercials for one client, during a period of less than a year, and saw only three produced. It would be theoretically possible, with the current insistence on copy pretesting, for a writer to work full-time on experimental copy which would never score high enough to appear in public. If that happened, he might leave the occupation, screaming; but it would probably be a long time before he did because copywriters, like a democracy, can stand a lot of ruin.

A Cure for the Copywriter's Condition

One way for these problems to disappear, and for the copywriter to be everlastingly happy, would be for someone on high to give *him* the absolute power of decision. He is the expert in his field, this benefactor would say, just as the merchandising man, and the sales manager, are experts in theirs. Let whatever the copywriter writes be gospel.

Besides the fact that there never will be such a benefactor, his edict would not work. For an ad, as we have said before, is more than the mere writing of words. It is a totality which can include a copy strategy, a company policy, a connection with other parts of a campaign, plus merchandising to the trade and stockholders. Because those other people are intimately concerned with the ad's meaning and purpose, they cannot be completely divorced from its execution.

The only alternative, then, is to cultivate an attitude which will reduce the pain. And the attitude harks back to what we said in Chap. 1, about the real meaning of the word communicator. The copywriter is not just a writer. He is a communicator on all levels, no less in the area of conferring with his bosses, colleagues, and clients than in the actual performance of writing copy. As a matter of fact, if you were to judge his work by the actual time consumed, his job description should have more emphasis on the former than on the latter. If the truth were told, probably most copywriters spend more than half of their time conferring.

Now, if we consider that the copy chief, the account executive, the researchers, the ad manager, the sales manager, and the president of the company are all part of the copywriter's *audience*—that he has to communicate with them before he can communicate with the readers of ads and viewers of commercials—then the whole nature of his frustration takes another perspective. It is no different, in its way, from the difficulties we willingly admit we have, in getting through to those masses of people to whom we are directing our advertisements. It should, in fact, be less difficult than connecting with the unseen masses, for the people with whom we work have faces and names and personalities we know. Since all our conferences and research are dedicated to trying to identify our audiences more intimately, how much easier it should be to communicate with *these* people, who have already been identified.

This, then, is our attitude when it comes to communicating about the communication. We are going to approach these colleagues and clients of ours just as we approach our readers, listeners, and viewers. Adopting this attitude, we can use the same principles with them as we use in communicating about products: the principle of being interesting, of trying to *involve* them, of showing the inherent drama of our product (the copy we are presenting), of being explicit, of convincing them that our subject will live up to its claims, of demonstrating, of appealing to both the head and the heart, of being thorough, tastefully repetitive, etc.

Let us see how this new state of mind actually works in practice.

How to Administer the Cure

One of the best experiences a copywriter can have is to work for an advertising agency handling a Procter & Gamble account. P&G, one of the world's largest advertisers, employs many agencies and advertises scores of different consumer products, including packaged goods, comparatively low-priced, in such categories as soaps and detergents, foods and drugs. Within each category, the products are competing with one another. So a copywriter, working for one agency on one of these products, and competing against all the other P&G agencies and products, is really on his mettle.

Because the stakes are high, the judgments are severe. To maintain the greatest quality control over the creative output of their agencies, Procter & Gamble maintains a large advertising staff of its own. Most key positions in the agency have their opposites at P&G. So there are copy and production supervisors, representing the client and attempting objectively to pass on the advertising turned out by the agency.

Many copywriters find working on a P&G product more frustrating than on most other accounts. And there has long been a feeling in the trade that, because the standards are so rigorous, no radically different or daring advertising can get through P&G—only advertising which is relatively "safe."

This may or may not be true, but in this writer's experience, the presentation of copy to the experts at P&G has been a stimulating challenge. Their minds are sharp and analytical, their experience, through vast advertising resources, is so broad that it is never enough simply to present an idea. One must have already anticipated all its pros and cons, must have had the ingenuity and thoroughness to find ways to validate the idea, and must be ready with answers to any number of probing questions. This is like a chess game—subtle, complex, and bracing to a mind with the energy to dig deep.

How does the copywriter anticipate the answers? In the same way, as we described in the preceding chapters, that he conceived the copy in the first place. He found all the facts possible. In a free spirit, he explored all possible creative directions. Then, bearing in mind all the contexts—the nature of the market, the competitive situation, the media and the extent of the budget—he weighed each direction against the other. When he is asked why he is presenting a certain creative approach, and when alternatives are suggested, he is ready with answers. All the thoughts and criticisms his interrogators may muster he can answer, because he has been down that road before.

This is true not only when big issues are being discussed, but also when his questioners get down to the fine points of the copy. Every element of the ad or the commercial has a function, and the copywriter has found a way to articulate that function.

It often requires the same kind of ingenuity to express an argument *for* a communication as it does to conceive the communication itself. For example, how do you explain, to someone who is not naturally a poet, the poetical values of a particular slogan? Somehow, you have to be able to demonstrate the value of rhythm, of alliteration, of mnemonics.

Perhaps you can do it by citing precedents—other slogans that illustrate, by their nature, what yours is trying to do. Or you can write alternatives to yours, and have your questioner recite them aloud and try to remember them and compare them with the slogan you are trying to sell. In order to do that, you must anticipate this very question. You must be imaginative and thorough enough to be ready for it.

The principle of involvement is every bit as important in this communication as in your ad. The way of selling an idea to a client "by making him think he thought of it" is not as cynical as it may sound. Just as you can involve your audience in an ad by leaving something unspoken, which their minds automatically fill in, just so it can be a way of demonstrating to your client how valid your idea is. And it is, of course, a psychologically sound approach to communicating with him—as Professor Lanzetta illustrated in his talk on role-playing.

We spoke earlier of "making a connection" with your audience by being interesting (i.e., original), by making the strange familiar and the familiar strange. This is another way of suggesting showmanship in the way you present your copy.

Showmanship can be many things. It can be a whisper as well as a shout. It can be razzle-dazzle or it can be the ultimate in restraint. And the kind of showmanship you use depends entirely on the audience. An agency, making a solicitation for a new account, may win it through sky-writing, closed-circuit TV, elephants and dancing girls. Or, as Ben Duffy is supposed to have done when he won the Lucky Strike account for BBD&O, they may win it with a few words written on the back of a matchbook cover.

This knowing your audience, and catering to it, is not sycophancy—any more than is consideration for the reader of your ad. For example, one client who has seen countless TV storyboards for years still might not understand them. He might have the kind of literal mind that has to see the pictures moving before he can judge the commercial. So it is a matter of consideration and, in the long run, an economy to present all new television ideas to him already filmed. On the other hand, another client might be insulted if he were shown new ideas in so finished a form. In fact, he might fancy himself such a quick study that he might not even want to see storyboards—but only to hear, and to debate, the basic idea of the commercial.

We said that being interesting involves showmanship, and there is no question that originality is just as appealing to this audience—your colleagues and clients—as to the audience reading your ad. Stanley Arnold, a sales promoter, has had enviable success through doing the unexpected in a flamboyant way. Once, in order to punch across a point to a prospect, he strode to the window, opened the shade and exclaimed "That's a horse of a different color!" In the field outside, carefully stationed there beforehand, was a horse dyed a bright blue.

That kind of approach, however, might be considered gauche by a different audience. An impressive presenter, agency executive Bill Howard, used to keep his audience attentive by speaking so softly that they had to strain to hear him.

We mentioned the advantages of communicating with this audience by being explicit. That requires the same kind of diligence with which you put essential facts into an ad. For example, one writer presenting a woman's campaign to an automotive client who had never advertised expressly to women, knew she could not simply present the advertising. Nor would it have been enough for the writer, because she was a woman, to say, "Take my word for it—this is a good idea." Instead, she presented the campaign with specific facts, as well as with showmanship. Her presentation began with a human and entertaining touch—the playing of the popular song "There is nothing like a dame!" She followed that up with the following (accompanied by appropriate slides): "That was to remind you that there are women out there. Millions of them. Matter of fact, by 1980 there will be 5 million more women than men. Right now there are approximately 62 million women of driving age. Twenty-five million women are wage earners. These women earn $50 billion annually. Women control 65 percent of the savings accounts. . . ." Her presentation proceeded through more pertinent statistics, and built up to the reasons why this particular client should approach this market. Then she was ready to show how and why her copy theme would be right for the market.

Just as in making claims in ads, we must never communicate to a client an idea which cannot live up to our claims. The more original a copy idea is, the more difficult it may be to execute. Say, for example, that we are presenting a "blue sky" idea like running a special sample of a product inserted into a newspaper. With showmanship and enthusiasm, we describe the potential payoff of the idea. We are explicit, spelling out the method and the cost relative to the possible returns. But if we are not yet certain that we can bring it off, to live up to our principles of communication we must frankly tell our audience the truth—"The gamble is great, but the possible results are greater."

"Demonstrate the product" we said in Chap. 4, as a guide to conviction. And how do we demonstrate the validity of our copy to this audience? Well, take the example of that tough copy chief we described earlier. Enter the copywriter, knowing, through experience, the nature of this beast. Does he wait for the copy chief to strike out the first paragraph? He has already done so. Does he wait for the question marks and the injunction to rewrite? He has already written plenty of versions, and he has them ready to show, if need be. Perhaps, anticipating that the copy chief might call a gangup, he has already shown his copy to some other objective person—another copywriter or an art director—and can demonstrate the fact that he has been dispassionate and has already collaborated. We all should realize that, whenever we get a new idea, we love it because it is our brainchild. Therefore we know that we are *not* dispassionate. We must have a copy chief or collaborators we can respect.

Another way to demonstrate our copy is not to wait for the research department's horseback research, but to do some of our own. We go out, with a tape recorder, discussing our ideas with consumers, to see if they will "play back" some of the things we think are good about the copy. Then we see that tough copy chief, or the inquisitors on the product group, and we play them the recorded demonstration of the rightness of our ideas.

We said, in Chap. 4, that to win conviction, we should practice the golden rule. As copywriters, we like to have our colleagues and clients respect us for knowing more about our craft than they do. But the fact is that they will, inevitably, contribute to the final result, even if it is to OK the ad as is. That OK, in the case of an advertising manager, for example, may be an act of some courage, for enormous investments are often riding on the scraps of paper we write. Practicing the golden rule toward this audience means understanding *his* need—the need for ammunition to help him make costly decisions, the need to give him validation to communicate to *his* colleagues and clients.

If we agree that this is the attitude we must take to communicate about the communication, that it is just another corollary to the work we do at the typewriter, then we have nothing to complain about if our copy never does appear. For it will not have appeared because we have been unable to communicate with the first audience; and that being the case, chances are that we might not have connected with the second.

The Media for Communicating with One Another

We use every imaginable audio and visual aid to communicate with the consumer. And since getting our message across to him means first getting it over to our "inside audience," why not use all our skill and imagination to do that superbly well too?

In Part 2 we shall discuss the various modes of communication that go with the various media. In communicating with our colleagues and clients, we use all kinds of media too. One is the medium of the memo. Memos run from short to long, formal to informal. But when we think of them with this very special attitude—that they are addressed to people who are audiences, en route to the larger audience of our magazine ad or TV commercial—do they not seem remarkably bad?

David Ogilvy, speaking about our structured language, bewails the marketing plans that come out of agencies. "Some of them are written in a business lingo which makes me squirm—percentagewise, importantly, mitigate against, maximize, and so on. . . . American businessmen are not taught that it is a sin to *bore* your fellow creatures."

Surely it is possible, when we have to write memos and marketing plans, to write them without self-consciousness. The easiest way is to write as though we were writing an informal letter to a friend. Just as an actor singles out one person in the audience to play to, we are able to do that with our memos—and, again, it is easy to connect, because we can identify the people at the other end.

Of course, we write many too many memos and make too many telephone calls to be really communicating. Somebody once pointed out that business firms were more efficient before they had phones and typewriters and a fast postal system. At that time, communicating took so long that they wanted to make every letter count. So they thought first about what they were going to say, wrote few letters, and made those as clear and meaningful as possible. Imagine, if we had sent a memo off then to some business colleague in another city—a memo that enclosed a clipping and simply said "F.Y.I." (for your information). A week or two later comes the reply: "What do you want me to do about it?" If we wanted him to do something about it, we should have said so in the first place and specified what we wanted him to do.

But the most horrendous hindrance to communication is the business conference. If there are more than three people in a room, we tend to go on stage. Being on stage, we would not want to say anything that would make us look or sound radical or silly. So we often wind up saying nothing in a highly pretentious way.

We suppose the business conference is a necessary evil. When there are many people involved in doing a job and they all have to be informed, one has to call a meeting—otherwise we would have to write still more and longer memos. However, the anatomy of a meeting is always the same —one person does most of the talking. Knowing that this is so, why not streamline the meetings in the following way: (1) Have the people responsible for each facet of whatever has to be done organize their thoughts thoroughly, either in their heads or on paper. (2) Have the person who is going to do most of the talking meet separately with the individuals (individuals are less liable to be on stage), and digest their thoughts, which *they* have already so thoughtfully digested. (3) Hold a lightning-fast meeting of the entire group, at which time the ringleader should act like the decisive leader he always fancied himself to be, outlining the digested thoughts of the individuals, giving assignments and deadlines, making sure everybody understands, and dismissing the group at once to do their respective jobs.

If we follow this method, we may well reduce our communications with one another to such an extent that we will have time to create better ads and commercials.

So far, we have been speaking of the secondhand media, of memos and meetings. But the most important medium of all—the one we are unable to use with the public at large—is word of mouth. "Get down to the units," said Claude Hopkins, but in a literal sense, we cannot communicate directly with individuals when we are dealing with mass media. In communicating about the communication, with our colleagues and clients, we *can* talk man to man. How fortunate we are to have this privilege. Yet how seldom do we use it. Certainly, we make and attend presentations at which we all speak and hear many words. But we are, by and large, on stage then. How often do we sit down quietly, person to person, and communicate about our mutual problems? Note, we said *communicate*, in the sense of "to give to someone as a partaker," "to impart knowledge," "to have an interchange of thoughts," and "to have or form a connecting passage." How often do we attempt to impart knowledge, reasonably, as to why it is difficult to combine three different ads, why the company trademark should not be mortised into the picture? And how often do we accept an interchange of thoughts, listening to that other point of view and trying to understand it?

Perhaps, using this medium more often—the medium of person to person word of mouth—copywriters can reduce, and eventually eliminate all the self-consciousness. If they could do that, they would stop leading lives of quiet desperation. They would see more and more of their ads in print—ads that would satisfy them because they would have been created in a reasonable way.

They would, in other words, have formed a connecting passage.

Part 2

THE MEDIA

11

THE FAST, FAST MEDIUM

The Ripe World of TV

A copywriter entering the world of television is like a child turned loose in a candy store. He has a surfeit of goodies. Sight, sound, motion, and the increasing use of color. Animation, stop motion, freeze frames, and skip frames. The use of opticals, like wipes and dissolves, with which he can signal, without words, the passage of space and time. Sound effects and music, with which he can turn on moods and memories. Personalities, pacing, lighting, and intonation—he has an inexhaustible well of wizardry.

And yet it is the same old problem as when G. B. Shaw was told about the technological miracle of the international cable ("What are they going to *say?*" he asked). Crowded into the precious prime time between 7:30 and 11 each night, jammed with greater frequency into the programs during the day, are some of the most hackneyed, loud, tasteless, uncommunicative ad messages ever conceived. They cost a fortune. At this writing, production of a one-minute commercial may cost from $5,000 to $50,000. Average cost for time and talent per network commercial minute can run from $3,500 to about $9;000 in the daytime, $35,000 to $50,000 during prime viewing hours, depending on the season of the year. The advertiser may appear on a show or film that has taken many months to produce. As many as 75 million viewers may, at one time, be watching.

149

(Imagine—more people watched one night's television production of "Hamlet" than its total audience for the preceding 350 years!)

And yet those lifeless, weary commercials go on. The unhappy housewife holds an incredible dialogue with the offstage voice of an unnatural announcer. The pompous presenter, holding the package of cigarettes at a carefully directed angle, says the same old words in the same old unctuous way. And all around the breaks in the entertainment—often several in a row, butting on one another—come screaming and squawking, hollering and hammering, the same old strident calls to action we heard on that one-dimensional radio and saw in that black-and-white newspaper.

What can we do about it?

Again, the answer is in the copywriter's *attitude*. Television has been so powerful a medium, especially in its years of novelty, that if a sponsor spent enough money, and repeated his commercials enough times, even the uninformative, inconsiderate commercials helped to sell products. The incredible power of the medium is further emphasized when you consider that these messages are compressed into such a fleeting period, that they are competing with one another and with the program for which the viewer tuned in, that they are trying to capture that same implacable enemy we described—the person who does not want, voluntarily, to watch advertising.

This inherent power of television gave copywriters a license to be lazy and imitative. But if it worked so well for the banal, bad commercials, think of what it can achieve for copywriters who have a more ambitious attitude, for those who are determined to pursue the objectives we discussed earlier (clarity, interest, involvement), for those who respect their subject, their audience, and their craft.

Conceiving the Commercial

As with every other new medium, the unfamiliar writer gets bogged down at first in learning the lingo. He is more apt to worry about dissolving, panning and dollying than about the essence of the message. He finds it hard to separate technique from content, especially since there is so much technique to call on.

When we cut through all the verbiage, we get back to the good old truth that the way to write ads effectively for television (just as it is for magazine ads or for skywriting) is to let the subject dictate. Suppose, for example, that the subject is a potato chip that wants to say it is fresh or an electric shaver that wants to say that it can shave close, yet be gentle. Or suppose it is a bandage whose main copy point is that it will stay stuck or a car whose main advantage is that it will hold many more people than other cars.

In all of these cases, the subject eventually dictated its own commercial concept. The writer, forgetting technique for the moment, and letting himself be absorbed in the potato chip—in the very essence of potato chippiness—had one of those oh-so-obvious inspirations: that the epitome of freshness, in a potato chip, is crispness. Then the power of association took over. What says crispness? Snap, crunch, crack—sound! What could better demonstrate crispness than the *sound* of a potato chip being crunched by a chewer? Lo and behold, an idea is born: "Laura Scudder, the Noisiest Potato Chips in the World!"

Now, thinks the writer, what technique can we use to show this phenomenon on television? Through the power of association, noisiness makes him think of quietness. Quietness, serenity, peace: how about a little old lady, in a serene Victorian setting? She dips her hand into a bag of Laura Scudder's potato chips, puts one in her mouth—and all hell breaks loose! The house shakes, the pictures fall down. The noise has caused a positive earthquake!

Thus we have an entertaining commercial and, at the same time, a beautifully simple demonstration of the main point we want to communicate—freshness.

Notice, that in all that process, we have not mentioned dollying, panning, or any of the lingo of the television technique. Nor was there any discussion about copying some other TV idea for some other potato chip. To conceive the idea, we simply let the subject take over.

What of the electric shaver? How did it dictate its message? Again, through the process of free association, it led its writer inevitably to his inspiration. He thought of every symbol that he might associate with shaving—smooth, rough, beard, cheek, hair, whisker, bristle, fuzz, rub, stroke, etc. At the same time, he was thinking of the shaver's advantage—that it would shave close, yet be gentle. Each of those symbols evoked other symbols, and the word "fuzz" called up the word "peach." The pencil then wrote, "shave the fuzz off a peach." Connecting "close and gentle" with "shave the fuzz off a peach" gave birth to another simple, compelling TV demonstration.

What about the sticky bandage? It told the writer to think of an unsticky surface. He saw an egg, a marvelously smooth invention, and conceived a simple demonstration of the bandage stickily removing an egg from boiling water.

As for the car that would hold a lot of people, that was of course the Volkswagen bus, and that demonstration was quite simple—an entire high school band, complete with instruments, emerged, one after the other, from the innards of that spacious box, and one more unforgettable TV demonstration was created.

The words "demonstration" and "simple" have been repeated in all four of the cases above, because those words are the keys to effective television commercials. As we have said earlier, the best communication is operational—i.e., the communicator can see for himself what is being communicated; it is not a secondhand report.

"Television," wrote Arnold Toynbee, "is the nearest thing to meeting physically face to face. It is, in fact, a passable substitute for it." By the same token, the TV commercial, through which most of the senses can be reached, is the next best thing to the actual experience of sampling a product. If it moves, if it has form and shape and color and dimension, it can be shown on television. Only smell and touch are missing, and no doubt some miracle worker will soon find a way to transmit those senses too.

So the first thing to do, if we want to communicate about a tangible product, is to figure how best we can demonstrate it.

To demonstrate is "to make something evident"; it is the proving of something conclusively, by arguments, reasoning, or evidence. When television commercials first burst onto the scene, it was common for the announcer to say "Here's proof" and "This demonstration proves conclusively." After a while, through repetition of the word "proof," combined with a rash of rigged demonstrations which were gradually investigated and ruled off the air, the public became bored and skeptical of even the most honest demonstrations. This is why, each year, as television grows older and the viewer more sophisticated, we are hard pressed to find demonstrations which are at once so forceful and believable that they no longer require the stentorian cliché "Here's proof."

The goal, nevertheless, is to prove our claim—to demonstrate it. If we consider that television is the next best thing to sampling the product, then we might also think of all TV commercials, no matter what their technique, as a form of demonstration.

Our first task, of course, is to find a viable claim, which should derive from the product's main purpose. It may be expressed in words ("Winston Tastes Good like a Cigarette Should . . ." "Windex Gets Glass So Clean It Seems to Disappear"), or it may be implicit in the demonstration (as in the Johnson & Johnson Baby Powder commercials, where the product's softness is stressed most powerfully by the obvious demonstration of a mother's hands powdering a baby).

The claim, or concept, should then dictate its execution. In the case of the Volkswagen and the shaver, the demonstration of the claim is self-evident. But subjects which are less tangible like beverages, life insurance, and headache remedies, are more difficult to demonstrate.

We may use analogies, enactments, and testimonials to prove our point. Pepsi-Cola's television campaign, based on the slogan "For Those Who Think Young," expressed the effervescence and freshness of the drink through music, models, and situations which were compatible with the claim. The actual taste of the beverage was impossible to depict, but appetizing, mouth-watering shots were designed to involve the viewer. All of those devices were, in effect, a "demonstration" of the product in action.

Food demonstrations on television suffered, for many years, in contrast with full-color magazine illustrations. Still, even in black and white, Kraft's famous commercials, simply concentrating on tight closeups of the demonstration of a recipe, had potent appetite appeal. Here the motions of making the meal involved and interested the viewer. Now, with color television come of age, we can add to those already powerful methods the sensual appeal of natural food colors.

What about the use of phantasy and humor? They, too, are a form of demonstration, if they succeed in "making something evident." The trouble with many such techniques is that the phantasy and humor have too little to do with the subject. They use borrowed interest to entertain the viewer, who enjoys the commercial but forgets the message. On the other hand, as in the case of the Laura Scudder commercial, even the most fantastic humor can be completely relevant.

A TV commercial is an entity, and it should be conceived that way. It should begin as an idea, or concept, with a central theme, and the video and audio should contribute naturally to that theme. Of course, the opening of a commercial does have some similarity to the headline of a print ad. The TV audience, like the magazine reader, is not automatically interested, so the opening must seize and hold the attention. But too many new TV writers tend to concentrate on the opening, which often consists of borrowed interest, and then afterwards fill in the "dull stuff"—the "sell" and the "sacred cows" about the product—like an embarrassing long tail on a very brief dog.

One way to think of the commercial as a whole is to be able to sum it up, in your mind, in one sentence—just as you do with a billboard. The discipline of writing for the confined space of one sentence requires you to strip away all the nonessentials and to get to the heart of the subject.

A letter from a television supervisor of a large advertiser cited this need for "single, simple, dramatized ideas":

> For many years, all of us in commercial production have been reminding one another that great commericals are usually simple, unified, relevant, and deal with a single idea in highly visual terms.
>
> Lately, however, we have been struck by the communicative power of *dramatizing* a "single, simple idea." We started collecting commercials of this type and finally, after much winnowing and sifting, came up with a reel of ten spots which we feel exemplify "single, simple, dramatized ideas."

Because we found it helpful to set up criteria for evaluating the ideas, here is the way we have defined a dramatized idea:

We believe we have dramatized a copy idea when we create a situation or a sequence of pictures that lead inevitably to the single conclusion we want the viewer to reach about our product; when the desired copy idea is literally built into the situation and the events illustrated; when a viewer's recall of a commercial can lead to almost *no other conclusion* than the desired one.

The commercials selected were described as follows:

The idea of:	*is dramatized by:*
1. Anyone can make good copies with a Xerox	Showing a chimpanzee making a standard office copy
2. Crisco ends piecrust failure	Showing a little girl baking a father-pleasing pie
3. Johns-Manville Seal-O-Matic shingles seal themselves down to resist wind	Demonstrating how J-M and competitive shingles stand up to the prop wash of a DC-6
4. Lilt Speed Bath is absolutely mess-less to use	Showing a woman giving herself a permanent *in an expensive gown*
5. Volkswagen Buses are uniquely roomy	Showing an entire band—with instruments—getting out of a Volkswagen Bus
6. Remington Electric Shavers shave tough beards close without skin irritation	Shaving a peach and a brush
7. Lava is the only soap especially made to clean hands	Showing a uniquely tough hand-cleaning job
8. Instant Maxwell House is loaded with flavor	Showing a "cup-and-a-half" of coffee
9. Ivory Liquid gives women younger-looking hands	Showing a woman whose hands look indistinguishably as young as her daughter's
10. Goodyear Snow Tires pull through any snow	Showing the problems and inconveniences of being stuck in snow

Once you conceive the single, simple concept of a commercial, and after you free-associate and arrive at the ideal technique to express it, the commercial should begin as it needs to begin and should march to its inevitable conclusion. Of course, that seldom happens, entirely, when the writer sits down to write. As all professional TV writers know, ideas and executions of commercials usually go through many permutations in the process of production—usually more than in print advertising, where the actual production of type and engraving are of less concern to the writer. The TV commercial is a deeply collaborative effort. Creative refinements may constantly be needed during the preproduction and production meetings, the filming of the video, and the recording of audio. Editing the film itself can be part of the "writing" process, for the way scenes are juxtaposed affects their meanings.

It should be emphasized that the TV writer is a new breed of communicator—a hydra-headed character, with heads labeled "art director," "film director," "casting director," "music and sound effects director," and usually more heads besides. It is seldom that any one person does all these jobs—though the trend is toward a synthesis of the positions, and many art directors are now becoming "writers," as TV gets more graphic and less verbal. For the purpose of this book, we are calling our TV commercial creator a "copywriter." If he actually has only one head, he must communicate and collaborate so closely with those colleagues that the commercial emerges as though it came from one source.

Such collaboration requires the most clear and delicate communication. And this is why the actual articulating of "I see" and "I hear" is so crucial.

Writing the Commercial

This is the nub of it: You are *seeing* and *hearing*. That is why the script is designed in two columns, one headed "I see" (video), the other "I hear" (audio). The tendency, with new writers, is to write one column, and then to fill in the other to coincide. But that is not the way we do "see" and "hear." We enjoy both senses together.

Of course, you cannot physically write both columns simultaneously, but you do *think* them at once. Why not put down the hieroglyphics to follow your thought?

This writer finds the actual process of moving from video to audio an enjoyable kind of rhythmic counterpoint. The two are rather like the hands of a pianist, playing different chords but, through long practice, controlled by a concurrent double message in his brain.

The TV writer should put down, in the most precise terms, *exactly* what he sees and hears in his mind. Writing clear video instructions is a fine art. Grades ought to be given for limpid video prose, though it will never be seen or heard by the public. Good video directions should be so clear and complete that a child, or a client completely unfamiliar with television, could easily translate them into the very same pictures you see in your mind. The art director, even if you were not present, could draw the same pictures, exactly as you see them. The film producer, director, and cameraman, planning their shots, could follow your directions even without a storyboard. Some writers who work in close conjunction with their teammates may not bother to spell out such precise directions. The members of the team articulate the idea as they collaborate, and the video is written, for the record, after the fact. But this is a slipshod method. We all know how difficult it is to communicate so clearly that even the closest friends can play back exactly what we said. Those video instructions should be the unambiguous evidence of what you have in your mind.

To illustrate the precision with which TV instructions are written, let us take the trouble to track through an award-winning, sales-producing commercial for Rubbermaid. The essence of the idea was to demonstrate the suction of a bathtub mat. The claim was that the Rubbermaid Bathtub Mat had "the grip that will not slip." The subject dictated a simple demonstration which marched to its inevitable conclusion. Here is how the copywriter said "I see" and "I hear":

VIDEO

1. *Open on: Very tight closeup of Rubbermaid Bathtub mat being pulled up with great pressure. It very reluctantly "gives in" to the pressure.*

Visualize those precise directions. He says "very tight closeup" because he wants to intrigue and involve the viewer with the action of the suction cups on the bottom of the bathtub mat. He says "great pressure" and "very reluctantly" because he wants to demonstrate the tremendous grip of the suction cups. This kind of dramatic visual is really "hard sell." Now here is what the copywriter hears in his mind as he sees that picture:

AUDIO

1. *Sound: Suction cups releasing dramatically and stubbornly, up three seconds and under for—*
ANNOUNCER: *You are listening to the new sound of safety.*

Notice how the writer uses the word "stubbornly" to instruct the producer and sound engineer to synchronize the sound of the suction precisely as the picture reveals it. Here is the ideal marriage of sight and sound to produce a double wallop. Note, also, how the writer specifies "three seconds" of the sound effect before the announcer speaks. He has heard, in his own mind's ear, three beats of a baton, not one or two or four, to capture his audience and to pull them into what follows. Then he sums up, in one sentence, the whole story of what is to follow—"You are listening to the sound of safety."

Ed Barnes, an agency account supervisor who taught many a copywriter his exacting craft, used to insist that a TV commercial follow the injunction of the country preacher: "Tell 'em what you're gonna tell 'em. Then tell 'em. Then tell 'em what you told 'em." This is *one* formula this chapter will prescribe, although this too will certainly have its exceptions. A TV commercial, unlike a magazine ad, cannot be lingered over. It flashes by the viewer, at the rate of 24 still pictures a second (in a one-minute commercial, 1,440 stills), and once they are gone, his mind is off on another tangent. So it makes sense to repeat the summary of our message several times, to underscore the idea, as it were. This repetition need not be insistent or in poor taste (as was the much-criticized commercial for Anacin, with its reiterated words "Fast! Fast! Fast!"). The repetition, in fact, might not even be verbal; you may simply use a visual device (a kind of "trigger for the memory") which recurs through the span of a commercial. In this sixty-second Rubbermaid commercial, the words "sound of safety" are repeated twice—once at the beginning and once near the end —and the sound effect of the suction cups is a leitmotiv which occurs only twice but takes about thirty seconds.

Now, to continue our exercise in the writing of "I see" and "I hear":

VIDEO

2. *Slow pull out to reveal full shot of mat being pulled up in tub.*

Notice, by the way, how specifically the words "slow pull out" and "full shot" instruct the producer. If the video had instructed the producer to "cut" to this scene, the writer would have lost the effect he saw in his mind. He wanted to continue to involve the viewer in the action of the suction cups, yet he wanted to display the entire product, so the viewer could now see what it was—a bathtub mat. Also, the "slow pull out" would be keyed to the audio, which exactly matches the action:

AUDIO

2. . . . the grip that will not slip!

Here is a fine point about TV writing that cannot be overemphasized: *the audio should match the video.* It is peculiar how many copywriters rebel against this injunction. Often one sees a title, on a TV screen, such as "The Grip that Will Not Slip" while hearing the announcer speak some such words as, "This bathtub mat is guaranteed not to slip." How does the viewer's attention cope with the incompatible audio and video? To some degree, however slight, his attention is distracted. How many dollars—if the commercial cost $10,000 to produce—were wasted by that seemingly minor error? We may never know, but the combined power of the fleeting sounds and pictures were somewhat diminished. So part of our $10,000 was wasted. How much more insurance we would have had if the idea had been expressed "in synch" and then reexpressed later, in exactly the same words and pictures, to enable it to cling to the mind of its elusive audience.

Just to belabor this point a little longer, here is an example of the power of distraction: Suppose you were looking at some sight—say, the lifting of a teacup—and you heard an irrelevant sound at the same time— say, the sound of a foghorn. That sound might trigger your mind to a ship at sea, the smell of salt air, and the feel of a boat's motion. Certainly it would not contribute, at that precise moment, to your awareness of the teacup. This is why the audio should match the video—they should contribute to the awareness of each other.

Scene 3, in our spell-out of how a copywriter writes for TV:

VIDEO	AUDIO
3. *Zoom up animated title:* "Rubbermaid," *in synch with announcer's voice.*	The dependable holding power of the all-new Rubbermaid Safti-Grip Bathtub Mat!

Notice how the writer instructs the producer to have the name of the product visually punctuated. By zooming up an animated title, the name, which it is most important to register, gains visual impact. At the same time, the writer instructs the producer to have the audio exactly match the video. Notice that the word "Rubbermaid" appears in the middle of the sentence. If the writer had written the sentence with the product name at the beginning, it would not have matched the video—i.e., the announcer's speaking of the word "Rubbermaid" would have been heard in advance of the full impact of the zooming visual.

Next, we come to Scene 4, in which our TV copywriter describes the *reason why* what he has shown and said are true:

VIDEO	AUDIO
4. *Ripple dissolve to: Tight close-up of underside of mat showing cups gripping. Our shot is taken looking up through glass surface. Possible sudsy water effect for realism.*	Over six hundred gripping suction cups offer maximum protection against slips and slides.

These words are very interesting. A "dissolve" denotes a passage of time or space and this will require a so-called "optical," for which the film producer must estimate extra cost. The words "ripple dissolve" are to indicate that the writer sees, in his mind, a watery effect which emphasizes the locale of his bathtub mat and anticipates the scene which is about to follow. The specification, to see the underside of the mat and, at the same time, to be literally in the water, is going to require a special prop—i.e., the location or construction of a glass bathtub. And the "sudsy water effect" is to emphasize the main sales point—that soapy water can be slippery and dangerous, while those six hundred suction cups will grip tightly and be safe.

The audio, of course, matches the video. We see many suction cups and the announcer specifies their number. Nothing abstract or vague about this commercial. The copy is operational. The viewer can see the facts for himself, and if he were to go to the store to buy the bathtub mat, he could count the cups and check the commercial's veracity.

VIDEO	AUDIO
5. *Cut to: Closeup of small child bathing in tub. Having a good time.*	*Sound: Natural bath effects mingled with child's happy sounds splashing in tub. (Sneak music in background)*

The directions for Scene 5 introduce a human reason why the sound of safety is important, and the feeling of authenticity is explained with the audio instructions "*natural* bath effects." This informs the producer that he is to record real sound effects, not to simulate them. "Sneaking" the music in makes certain that it will be unobtrusive, to underscore the human scene but not to distract from it.

We will not take the time here to track through the following scenes (6 through 16). In all of them, the writer continues to write video clearly, with concrete, operational directions. From the demonstration of the child, sitting safely on the bathtub mat—introduced, in addition, to show the textured top of the mat and to illustrate its comfort—the commercial moves to a scene of a man in a shower, to illustrate safe footing. Finally, there is a reprise of Scenes 1 to 3, exactly as they occurred. Their precise repetition is important, for they are the "touch of singularity" which David Ogilvy calls "a burr . . . that will stick in the viewer's mind."

Does the commercial end with its singular demonstration? In this case, there is one postscript—a scene referring to the cleanability of the mat and its availability in a variety of colors. Plus a "call to action"—i.e., "Don't fall! Bathe with safety on a Rubbermaid Bathtub Mat!" The Rubbermaid logo is shown, in the clear, with the prices "$2.49—3.98" added.

Were those final scenes necessary? One could quarrel with the scene showing the variety of colors. While this copy point was no doubt important, there is always a debate as to how many points should be introduced into a commercial. Should those precious seconds have been devoted, rather, to a continuance of the hypnotic demonstration? This writer would probably have pleaded for more of the same. The last scenes, however, of the logo and price, were essential. For in every commercial, considering its cost and brevity, the name registration of the product cannot be underplayed. And specifying price (especially in this case, where the powerful demonstration points up that the price is reasonable) helps to complete the communication.

This, then, is a demonstration of the clear writing of TV copy. From it the commercial can be produced. But, as we indicated before, television commercials are created in every phase of the production as well as in the writing—and in ways that can vitally affect their meaning. Let us look at a few examples.

Magnifying the "I See" and "I Hear"

Because it is a medium so rich in the appeal to the senses, TV can be all-video or all-audio, with infinite degrees of shading in between. This is why the art director, the producer, and the sound expert must be as one man with the copywriter if he is not handling all these jobs by himself.

Take, for example, the extraordinary visual effects of the Chevrolet commercials, which won so many awards for years and were, in the beginning of the sixties, the most noted automotive commercials on the air. Kensinger Jones, creative director of the Campbell-Ewald Company, describes the purpose of the commercials and then the visual tour de force behind two of them:

> All of these commercials have important elements in common. Each presents the car in a unique way visually. This attracts attention when the commercial is seen and makes for memorability and conversation long after viewing. Each commercial gains additional interest by arousing curiosity as to how it was done, in the sense of actual production. In connection with this, there is also the plus of a spirit of daring on the part of Chevrolet. This spirit of daring, which suggests Chevrolet leadership, has to do not only with production ingenuity and hazard but also with the thought itself in each commercial. A final point in common to all these commercials is that the visual stunts are related to acceptable, sensible thoughts. They are not, in other words, merely stunts for the sake of stunts.

> "CHEVROLET VISITS VENICE"—1963 CHEVROLET IMPALA CONVERTIBLE
> The goal here was multiple: to relate Chevrolet's modern beauty to the historic beauty of Venice, to allow the glamour and romance of Venice to "rub off" on the Chevrolet, and to attract attention to the car by showing it in a highly unlikely setting.
> Trick shots can be fascinating, but seldom more fascinating than the real thing. It would have been easy to matte a moving car over scenes of the Grand Canal. It also would have looked like a trick shot instead of a car driving on water. So at the outset we decided not to matte car over

water. The basic production hurdle in producing this commercial was the design and construction of a raft upon which to float the car—not as simple as it sounds.

Note the specifications:

Must safely support a 3,000 lb. automobile in choppy water

Must be self-propelled in water

Must be operated from the driver's seat

Wheels must turn to give illusion of driving on water, and

Must be portable—for construction in the U.S. and shipment to Venice

Leading naval architects had estimated that the raft would cost at least $15,000 to build and could not guarantee it would stay afloat. The raft as finally constructed actually cost a fraction of this estimate. But most important—the raft worked. It was a driveable, steerable, portable wheel turnable gimcrack thing that looked like it belonged on Mars; the product of the imagination and skilled hands of Bill Frick who has been working with Campbell-Ewald production department for several years, solving difficult automotive cinemagraphic problems. It was Frick who worked out the lift problem on the Pinnacle commercial. He also worked, designed and built a lift mechanism for some Firestone commercials wherein the car, wheels and all, lifts off the road and floats 8 feet above the earth while driving into the next county. With the car in place on the Grand Canal, several devices were used to give the illusion of swift movement—not the least of which was to keep the camera moving past the car. By moving the camera past a big foreground with the moving car in the background, a strong pace was maintained.

The "logic" of the fantasy is derived from the fact that Venetian boat traffic behaves very much like regular street traffic and also from the fact that Venice is known as a fabulous blend of fantasy and reality. These points are established in the narration and in scenes like those around the traffic light on the Grand Canal. To keep the obvious fantasy from taking itself too seriously, there are several touches of light, good humor, the most noticeable being the vignettes where Venetians look at the car and exclaim in Italian, while English subtitles appear on the screen. (This is, after all, a "foreign film.")

"PINNACLE"—1964 CHEVROLET IMPALA

The goal here was to present the 1964 Chevrolet in a hard-to-ignore situation and to stress the sales leadership point that "Chevrolet stands alone."

Imagine, if you can, a pin the head of which is the dimension of a baseball infield. Castle Rock, near Moab, Utah, is such a pin. 6,000 feet above sea level, the summit of Castle Rock is a weather-scarred moonscape—accessible only by helicopter or rope and piton. Temperatures of over 100 degrees make thin air thinner and flying hazardous. Heat from the sun-baked desert floor churns 35 m.p.h. gusts and up-drifts around the spire.

The problem of placing a 3,000 lb. car on the pinnacle with a copter whose capacity was 1,000 lbs. was accomplished by disassembling the car in sections weighing less than 1,000 lbs. and then re-assembling the car in sections on the summit. This alone took two days—not done without some difficulty. On one return trip an empty pallet used to haul parts was jettisoned from 2,000 feet because winds had swung it dangerously close to the copter rotors.

A lighter, more maneuverable helicopter equipped with a camera mounted on an anti-vibration device was used for the actual filming which could take place only in the relative calm of the early morning hours. The camera copter would stay aloft for only fifteen minutes, then return to base camp for fuel, the lighter fuel load providing much needed maneuverability and emergency power. The fuel stops were also an opportunity for director and cameraman to review each take and plan every shot, mindful of the editing of all the shots into a meaningful sequence. Planning each shot was the heart of the problem.

The attractive girl, sitting alone on the convertible, atop the towering peak, arouses a combination of awe, admiration and—with some viewers—sympathy (with a resultant urge to come to the rescue). The result is emotional involvement, in addition to agreement that Chevrolet really does stand alone. The closing scenes, in which the camera goes away from the girl and the car, creates a viewer desire to see more of the car . . . in a more conventional and accessible location (for example, a Chevrolet showroom).

The Chevrolet commercials, while they utilized music, were most memorable for their visual audacity. One of the most striking features of the nonverbal TV commercials for the Goodyear Tire & Rubber Company, which appeared at the same time, was the sweep and drive of their music tracks. These were composed by Bob Thompson, already a top arranger and conductor outside the commercial field. To illustrate how creative is the audio art, beyond the copywriter's verbal instructions, here is a verbatim from Norm Toback, who was in charge of producing the commercials and of utilizing Thompson's special talents. Toback is not only a film producer, but also a Juilliard-schooled musician; and this knowledge, as you will see, was especially valuable. The commercial being discussed was one entitled "Tufsyn Torture," in which a car ran over rocks and railroad ties, and leaped off ramps, to demonstrate the durability of Goodyear tires made with Tufsyn rubber.

> We had established a musical theme for Goodyear that was just 58 seconds long. We were then trying to figure out how to cut the torture test footage to that musical idea.
>
> I sat down with Thompson and we physically wrote out, on a score, the melodic and rhythmic figures that were necessary to the theme, but allowing ourselves a considerable amount of room to improvise.
>
> We then made a click track, using, by virtue of our experience, a faster click than we had used before. A click track is simply a time measurement

in frames of film. We use this, rather than working in seconds, since we're dealing with film, which is in synch. We simply make a sound, let's say every 10 frames. You can calibrate in seconds, but for our purposes, working at the Movieola, it's much easier to listen to a thing going by that clicks at every 10 frames or so (that's two clicks to a measure, which would be a normal cut time for some pop, up-tempo kind of music, which our theme is).

Well, I know by looking at the score that every two clicks that I hear is a bar of music. I can sing the melody against it as I'm looking at the pictures, or create a rhythmic figure with my mouth or in my mind, while I'm hearing those clicks go by, so I have a pretty good idea as to how those pictures would work. . . . In other words, I had a visual guide. I can read music, so I knew what portion of the theme occurred where, and consequently could plan—for instance, there was one phrase that was particularly lyrical, so I planned a lyrical shot for that phrase (that's the one shot that we used several times, of the car in Arrowhead going all the way around a very long curve, you remember, so it had the same sort of sweep as the music had).

We cut the film to the click track by number. Each click was numbered —let's say, from 1 to 137. And I laid it out on a piece of paper—like, when we were going to do the rock sequence, this many clicks . . . the next sequence, the railroad ties, this many clicks. . . . We then go to the jump, and the jump would extend for this many clicks. Then we started to cut the film.

We didn't record the music till the film was cut, because we knew, within the discipline we set ourselves, that we had certain freedom. For instance, I left Joe (Joe Morrisey, the film cutter) saying, "I'd like you to extend the jump as long as possible. . . . I figure we can go for this many measures of music." . . . And Joe, being the cutter he is, sat there and figured he should take it for two bars more. And so what we did is, we worked backwards. We reduced—we built a different situation in front of it to accomodate those extra two bars. . . .

Finally, Bob came back, after we had our rough cut to the click track, and he physically started to score the actual percussion sounds he was going to use against the pictures. But in the interim, he has been, like, halfway there, by knowing how many bars, approximately, he had for each shot. . . .

As I say, this is not the only way to do it. In this particular case, having 15,000 feet of the torture footage, and knowing basically what we had, we just decided to work that way. Since there were no words, and the music was so important, I wanted it to be as musically sound as possible. Now, Bob is so brilliant as a composer that you can give him phrases that have no logic musically and he invents a way to write a track which gives it logic. I've seen him save spots of ours that we were in dire trouble with. . . . But in this case, we had the opportunity to work in a musically more logical fashion, so we did.

Trend Setters and Trend Followers

> It's the most exciting thing you could do, after all the *visual* is gonna be so goddamned exciting. Just a little dot way up in the screen and you just hear this (*imitating faint sound of car*). The distance will squeeze the sound of the engine down to just a thin buzz. The car moves into the corner, you hear just a brrr. The car gets closer, it comes down into the corner, the title goes off the screen, the car begins to drift, drifts right up at the camera, he's coming right at you, he's gonna run right over you and all you hear is this (*car imitation*) and the camera swishes right by with him so you get a blur as he goes by and we cut right behind him and he's moving anywhere between 140, 145, up to 175 miles an hour, and the camera is right there, right behind him. You see his helmet, you see his hands on the wheel, you build up the pitch of the sound as the car approaches. You just barely hear it, just a (*imitation*) and then as he gets up close this thing is a deafening roar. The minute you get this blur as he's right on top of you then we cut to this shot where you literally jump right into the car.

This quotation was from a tape-recording of a TV art director, Paul Frahm, describing a new "breakthrough" idea. The commercial was about the use of aluminum in cars. It would be the first time in American TV commercials that a camera would be mounted behind a racecar driver and the viewer would experience the driver's sensation of speed.

In no medium is the need for originality so pressing as in TV. "The value of an advertising idea is in inverse ratio to the number of times it has been used." Nowhere as in TV is that statement so true. For TV is "a gigantic furnace." It burns up ideas, in programming and advertising, as fast as they are produced. This is another reason why it is impossible to establish rules for commercial writing. Most rules this book might express would be obsolete by the time you read these words.

TV is the fast medium in a jet-propelled world. Speed is its keynote: the speed of its need for new material, the speed of the flickering film on the tube, the speed at which the viewer's mind must be captured, and the speed with which he can forget what he has just seen.

Then, too, there is the speed with which imitators make the most original ideas passé. Trends in TV are constantly starting. Plagiarism is the norm. You have to be self-regenerating, to forget today's commercial the minute it is "in the can" and move on to tomorrow's trend setting.

How do you begin a trend? Again, it is the communicator's *attitude* that counts. He must think of his subject, think all around it, think of his problem, think of that central *idea,* and say to himself, "How can I express this idea in a way that has *never been seen before?"*

Films of cars at a racetrack have usually been disappointing. Shot from the side, at an angle, in long shots, even overhead, the cars never seem to be going very fast. They become distorted, foreshortened; optical illusions make them actually seem to be stalling. It would take a special expensive rig to climb into the cockpit with the driver. Regulations, in actual races, would prevent it (in one such instance, a rig had flown off a car and caused a pileup). But for commercial purposes, it could be done, and it was.

There are few technical problems that today's ingenious cameramen, producers, and optical labs cannot solve. You have to convince yourself and your clients that it is worth the doing.

One state of mind is to think of the ideal. "Wouldn't it be ideal if . . ." and you take off from there. "Wouldn't it be ideal," thought the team of Graham and Sidebotham, "if just one sponsor of a TV commercial would satirize himself and admit that selling products is not as important as life and death?" Dreaming of the ideal, this writer and artist conceived the idea of an animated series of commercials featuring the brothers "Bert and Harry" for Piel's Beer. At the precise moment those characters appeared, TV commercials were relatively new, and there was a surfeit of hard-selling, "here's proof," stand-up announcers on the air. Bert and Harry —the former a plump, enthusiastic salesman, and the latter his tall, diffident straight man—hit the airwaves with enormous impact. Viewers formed Bert and Harry fan clubs. Somehow, though they were animated, Bert and Harry came alive, and millions of people knew them as friends.

But the joke wore thin. Sales of the beer soared for the first year, leveled off in the second, then declined in the third. In the interim, the imitators rushed in, and the air was filled with characters satirizing their own products.

A breakthrough in the use of voices in TV commercials were the tapes of Tony Schwartz, a candid-microphone expert, who for years had wandered the streets of New York, recording authentic sounds. In a commercial for J & J Baby Powder—now listed as a "classic" by the American Commercial Film Festival—Tony managed to record a little boy's voice speaking lines written by copywriter Bill Schnurr, yet with a natural, unrehearsed quality (try to picture the spontaneous sound as you read this):

AUDIO

Sound: Doorbell
LITTLE BOY'S VOICE (*voice-over*): Hey, hear y' got a new baby.
MOTHER (*vo*): That's right, Vernon.
BOY: Like to see 'er!

MOTHER: All right, come on. Here's
the baby.

BOY (giggling): Huh. Baby's got a
bald head.

MOTHER: Well, right now, yes . . .

BOY: What's that stuff?

MOTHER: Johnson's Baby Powder. I
put it on her after her bath so she
doesn't get chapped or chafed.

BOY: Put Johnson's on her bald head
too?

MOTHER: I put it all over her, Vernon. 'Cause it's the softest baby
powder in the world, and babies
are the softest people in the world.

BOY: Got any other babies?

MOTHER: No, she's the first . . .

BOY: Hmmm. . . . Too bad y' had
to get a bald-headed one. . . .

MUSIC

ANNOUNCER (*vo*): Fragile. . . . Handle
with Johnson's.

The use of candid sounds and pictures on TV, however, was a breakthrough with a far longer life than the animated satire. This is because real
life has endless variety, believability and involvement.

Some of the early uses of candid film commercials were those for Cheer
detergent, Remington shavers, and Excedrin headache remedy. The first
two used hidden cameras. In the case of Excedrin, users were interviewed
without guile, but the interviewers and film editors were so skillful, and
those interviewed were so absorbed in their subject, that there was no
self-consciousness revealed on the screen.

The use of reality in TV advertising, as in TV programming, has barely
been tapped. And social critics, like Arnold Toynbee and Margaret Mead,
have pleaded for the reality of a return to live TV, where the viewer
knows that what he watches is happening at the same time as he sees it.
This is a subtle, but important distinction. When film is used, today's
sophisticated TV viewer knows it. Film is a chemical medium while TV is
an electronic one. With film, there can be a lack of gray scale variations,
occasional spots from dirt on the film, and muffled sound or vertical
streaks. The viewer also knows, when he recognizes film, that there has
been time for editing after the fact. The potency of live TV stems from
that most important word in communication—involvement. Even videotape, which is an electronic medium, does not have the veracity of live TV.

In live TV, when the commercial announcer might make a mistake, when the demonstration provides the immediate suspense that it may possibly fail, the viewer is involved more intensely than when he knows the outcome has been preplanned.

Breakthroughs in TV commercials include ingenious combinations of sensual appeals which only this miraculous medium can allow. Music and sound effects have been used with staggering effect to create moods and nuances which eliminating the audio would instantly destroy. We have already mentioned the sound of the noisy potato chips. The whole idea depended on sound. Just so, a famous animated commercial for the Bank of America (BankAmericard) showed a conductor leading an orchestra in a frenetic symphony while loud, postery words filled the screen. Without the tempestuous music, the idea would have been puny.

Humor, too, can be used to break through the apathy and indifference of the TV viewer. But this is perhaps the trickiest technique, because many viewers, like many individuals we know, do not have a well-honed sense of humor. We can take inspiration from some of the most popular humorists of the movies, such as the Marx brothers, whose humor was outlandishly broad enough to satisfy the less cultivated customer, yet had overtones for even the most sophisticated. A successful humorous commercial was the one for Purolator Oil Filters. A beautiful girl parks with a libidinous escort in a lover's lane, and gets out and under the car to examine what is wrong with it. She emerges, triumphant, covered with grease from a filthy oil filter, having replaced it with a Purolator. She then proceeds, grease and all, to the more expected activity of a lover's lane. The incongruity of a gorgeously feminine mechanic involved the viewer from beginning to end.

By the same token, the recent series of nonverbal commercials for Goodyear tires gained extra power by their viewer involvement. In these commercials, there was no announcer at all. Only titles and pictures were used, and these were edited to the exact rhythm of an exciting musical score. Like Bert and Harry, these commercials were refreshingly original to audiences who had suffered from a steady dose of announcers. Viewers wrote the company appreciative letters like the following:

> You are to be complimented on your TV commercial showing your snow tires. What a relief to see an intelligent way of showing what your product can do.

> This won't be the first letter you receive commenting on your latest "snow tire" TV commercial. However, I feel compelled to write. I've never thanked anyone for telling me to buy their product but I do thank you now. It's truly a great pleasure to see a commercial without some an-

nouncer blasting in your ear, telling you how good a product is. A company with such progressive insight to sacrifice this "blasting" one gets must be very sure of its product.

> May I congratulate you on your television commercial, "Go Go Goodyear." I am not usually, consciously at any rate, unduly influenced by advertisements, but it is a pleasure, for once, to be pleasantly informed on a product, rather than irritated and patronized by the sponsor.

Sometimes it is necessary to use great restraint when attempting a breakthrough. The emulators who copied those nonverbal commercials usually used some announcement or dialogue. But the essence of the first nonverbal commercials was that they featured not *one* word of a speaking voice. Their power was magnified by their unexpected restraint.

It is not essential to use totally new techniques to conceive TV commercial breakthroughs. You can "make the strange familiar and the familiar strange" within the context of a given product category. It was a provocative twist to demonstrate the strength of Kleenex tissues by showing trumpeter Harry James playing a tune with a Kleenex capping his trumpet. Demonstrating the principle of a Sarong girdle by the simple expedient of a girl draping herself with a towel was different and descriptive. The visual pun of showing a cup and a half of coffee was highly memorable because of its phantasy and its contrast with other coffee commercials which described coffee beans, flavor, aroma, etc., in more conventional terms. A chimpanzee does not ordinarily operate a Xerox copying machine, but what better twist to illustrate its simplicity?

"Twist" is a good word to describe how the copywriter conceives television breakthroughs. He first thinks of the obvious and then, with a deft turn of mind, twists it out of phase to attract the attention.

But no matter how many degrees the copywriter twists, he is always relevant to his subject. To our knowledge, no TV campaign based on borrowed interest has been consistently successful. "Arouse quick related interest" is the first principle preached by the researchers of thousands of commercials. They are four good words to remember every time you approach a commercial: "A.Q.R.I."—*Arouse . . . Quick . . . Related . . . Interest.* Good seeds for the cultivation of the right state of mind for this fast, fast medium.

The Challenges of Future TV

Who knows what changes are ahead for this incredible medium! No doubt new uses of color and some such development as 3D will affect the way we write and produce commercials for TV. But the most predictable change and challenge is probably the state of the medium as affected by new stations and the Federal Communications Commission. With UHF stations licensed and encouraged, it is likely that television will go the same way as radio did—multiplying in outlets, number of programs, local appeals.

Already, at this writing, CATV (cable TV) enables many towns and cities to receive programs from dozens of stations, instead of from the usual two or three. At the moment, pay TV is in suspense, following its legislative defeat in California. But this writer, for one, predicts that pay TV, in our competitive society, is inevitable. When it comes, it will increase the competition. Commercial TV, to survive, will have to offer the viewer more and more varied programming. Very possibly, the pay TV stations, as did *The Reader's Digest*, will accept advertising.

The full use of International Television, through COMSAT, and other satellite systems will, again, broaden the market, the programs, and the challenges to communicators. In our society, where automation is making for more leisure and more cultural activities, and where the have-not countries are clamoring for the gains of our prosperity, educational TV may become more powerful and solvent.

Shopping services in the home, through TV, home videotape systems, multiple TV set ownership in each given home, portable, miniaturized TV sets—all of these eventualities are bound to require more communication in terms of quantity.

And this may prove to be the making of the fast, fast medium. For with more quantity may come more informality, more naturalness, more live commercials. As Peter Ustinov wrote in the *Atlantic*, "Television. I don't find it at all fascinating at the time. It's really the medium of intimacy. . . . You are in fact really talking, or revealing yourself, to one person. If you talk to that *single* person as though he were eleven million, he will turn the set off. . . ."

12

THE MEDIUM OF CONFIDENCE

Why Magazines Are So Vigorously Alive

Competition is a wonderful thing. Whether it is caused by greed, ambition, or simply personal pride, it is one of the biggest reasons for our technological progress. It is the reason why products keep getting better, competing to fill more needs, to win the consumer's dollars. It is the reason why standards of living throughout the world are bound to keep rising.

Nowhere can you find a more classic example of the influence of competition than in the rise and perpetuation of magazines.

Television, you would think, with its extra dimensions and its infinite potential to communicate, would have set magazines way back, as a medium. Of course, it made some magazines groggy and hastened the demise of a few; but, in 1963, when *Barron's* reported about a TV program—one devoted to a discussion of "The Crisis in American Magazines" —it told how the moderator, Prof. Eric Goldman, had been confounded by the panelists. He had taunted them, said the report, with being part of a horse-and-buggy industry, destined to disappear from the American scene. "The five (panelists) really demolished Prof. Goldman. Mr. Mich pointed out that magazines had their best year in history, both in advertising revenues and in copies sold, and Mr. Fischer was able to prove that they are growing in influence."

In general, magazines have had, and will continue to have, some tough times, with the rise of other media. Every year, according to the context of the times and their inability to compete, some magazines disappear, as have *Flair*, *'47*, *Collier's*, and *Coronet*.

But the stimulation of competition from TV and other media has made many magazines stronger than ever. They have had to strengthen their editorial appeals to hold and win readers. They have come up with new printing, production, and distribution advances to attract advertisers. They have competed successfully against other media, even the young monster, TV, by filling the needs the other media cannot provide.

One of those needs is for the confidence and respect of the audience. And no medium, to date, has that confidence as securely as magazines. For one reason, people take pride in the personal medium of their choice. As soon as they part with their good money to subscribe to a magazine, they are committed to believe in their own good judgment. Free TV can never inspire such confidence, nor can radio. And newspapers, while people may be proud of their choice, are transient each day. A magazine remains intimately around the home. It is dipped into at leisure, it wins pass-along readers, and, in proportion to its integrity and the personalized nature of its contents, it can inspire considerable conviction in its owner.

This has become more and more true of the, so-called, specialized magazines, and they range from those with intense appeal for minorities— everything from *Harper's* and *The Saturday Review* to *Ramparts* and *The Commonweal*—to magazines of special informational appeal, such as *Hot Rod*, *National Geographic*, and such business and industrial magazines as the thirty-odd published by McGraw-Hill. Most have small, but extremely selective circulations which are valuable to advertisers. *The New Yorker* has achieved almost a half-million and *Sports Illustrated* more than a million, but their readers are still specialized. *The New Yorker* has become so respected a medium for its "in" readers that it carries more pages of advertising than any other magazine, including the biggest mass circulation ones like *Life*, *Look*, and *The Reader's Digest*.

The rise of the specialized magazines, incidentally, is an encouraging solution to "our massive mistake." They require more thoughtful copy to communicate to people with special interests. Columnist John Crosby, writing in the *New York Herald Tribune*, attributed a sociological trend to the healthy growth of these magazines:

> I harbor the suspicion and the hope that we are on the threshold, if not already inside, the century of the uncommon man. . . . Today it's the mass man and the mass thing that is in trouble. The mass magazines are in terrible trouble, floundering around to find a formula to satisfy a mass man who seems to be not as responsive to formulas as he once

was. Meanwhile, the quality magazines—*The New Yorker, Harper's, The Saturday Review*—are coining profits.

Another reason magazines win so much respect is the same reason books do. The reader is not compelled, as Leo Rosten has pointed out, "to surrender to another's tempo," as he is in the case of television, radio, or movies.

Of course, the leisure we have to read magazines today is only relative. We live in an accelerated atmosphere of communication. Even if we learn to read faster than our forebears, how much time can we possibly devote to how many magazines, to how many stories and articles, when we are bombarded with so many other activities and messages? Why did *The Reader's Digest*, with its capsule material, and *Life* and *Look*, with their fast photojournalism, win so many readers? They were competitively savvy. They filled a need, in the context of their time. This, too, is why some of the women's magazines, led by *McCall's*, laced their content with serious nonfiction; they reacted to competition and filled a gap which other media, at that time, failed to provide.

Considering the greater respect and attention magazines can attract, we find them capitalizing on their greatest asset: the ability to provide services to the reader. Services include "How to —" and "What to —" and "Why to —" for the most avid minds. Readers of *Sunset Magazine* can find every operational service they could possibly require for living in the West—for the garden, home, kitchen, and hobbies. Readers of *Vogue* and *Harper's Bazaar* get all the latest news of fashion, *Holiday* readers learn all about travel, *Popular Science* and the fast-prospering *Scientific American* supply the endless information about our new technologies.

In more and more prospering magazines we find the most popular service of them all—new and better ways to prepare food.

To meet competition and to make their services more appealing, magazines are bursting with new ideas and excitement. Color processes that can make food look more delicious virtually leap off the page. Inserts and swatches, gatefolds, foldouts, popups, and, most recently, three-dimensional printing—all of these techniques add to magazines' appeal.

The magazines also keep finding ways to reach more people faster with the most current news and services, so their circulations can keep increasing. *Life*, for example, at this writing, prints in a half-dozen different parts of the country simultaneously. Their presses roll at thousands of feet a minute, with electronic monitors making delicate adjustments so the thirty-two-page forms can take six colors on each side, in perfect register. With incredible speed, they print different versions for regional editions, for test market areas. Thousands of copies of the magazine are addressed every minute, so they can be rushed into mounds of mailbags and on to planes, trains, and trucks to speed that magazine's weekly services to its millions of readers.

Spurred on by the competition of other media, magazines will probably achieve the same speed and fidelity of reproduction for their international editions. And these will bring new challenges and a new competitive climate.

The modern magazine is barely a hundred years old. It started most vigorously with *McClure's;* the idea behind this magazine was militant reform and exposure ("The Shame of the Cities," "The Railroads on Trial"). Later came a new, intimate friend, *The Saturday Evening Post,* with its superb fiction and influential editorial opinion. (It is interesting that most of the top American authors in this century won their first audiences in such magazines as the *Post.*) *The Reader's Digest* was another striking idea. And *Good Housekeeping* started, and kept going, a powerful franchise of reader confidence by testing and endorsing products with its guaranty seal. Henry Luce's *Time* style and *Life* photojournalism were trend-setting ideas. *The New Yorker,* proudly proclaiming that it was not for the old lady in Dubuque and "the plain reader be damned," built such a reputation that it could refuse $500,000 worth of advertising a year and charge advertisers a stiff $7.46 per thousand readers. Publisher Herbert Mayes and art director Otto Storch made *McCall's* in the fifties a graphic delight. Today *TV Guide* has been coming up. *Look,* through controversial articles and technical breakthroughs, has been outselling *Life.* The magazines with the fastest rate of growth, at this writing, are the specialized ones—for the eggheads, the well-heeled, and the increasing college-educated population.

But sure as the competition will get hotter, what we say about *these* magazines will be outdated tomorrow. Herbert Mayes, speaking of the future of magazines, predicted facsimile transmission into the home, magazines being sold in combination with paperback books and newspapers, astonishing developments in the use of paper, in magazine covers, in the enclosure of merchandise samples, more small magazines, to "explore new territory and challenge old concepts." And he also foresaw the mass magazines getting more masses—with circulations of 20 and 25 million.

Whatever happens, the successful magazines will be those with new and better ideas. And those are the magazines in which our work—the new and better ideas of the copywriter (and his art director partner)—is bound to continue to thrive.

Attitudes for Using This Medium

Again, we repeat, there are no rules, only the cultivation of a state of mind. How should we copywriters approach magazines? Why, with the same attitudes with which *they* approach the public. How, as we have implied in the foregoing, do magazines survive and prosper? By coming up with new and better ideas, by giving more service, by offering more enjoyment, more enlightenment, more provocative words, more evocative pictures.

Ady ads are not the answer. Whyte, in his *Fortune* article that debunked the whole cult of the masses, also cited research to show that non-ady ads get 60 percent more attention in magazines than the commercial cliehés. A browse through the editorial content of the successful magazines reveals the intriguing, fresh ways *they* communicate.

From *The Reader's Digest:*

> *Are Cars as Good as They Used to Be?*
> Here are the most common complaints—and some illuminating answers, obtained from a behind-the-scenes tour of the major automobile plants.

How many automobile ads have you seen with as interesting and candid a headline and subhead? Most of them sound like these:

> Engineered better . . . backed better than any car in its class.
> New name, new size, new style, new comfort.
> The world's most copied car.

Bragging headlines, cliché headlines. Which story would you be more likely to read—one of those or the one in *The Reader's Digest?*

From *Time:*

> *Cutting Calories*
> The affluent life in the U.S. of the 1960's is also the sweet life, the fat life and the soft life—or so the top U.S. experts have decided. Last week they announced that if the average American male wants to stay lean and healthy, he should cut 300 calories out of his daily diet and his wife should cut 200 from hers.

Isn't that story in the "medicine" section expressed more colorfully and informatively than most of the patent medicine advertising of the fast! fast! fast! variety?

From *Look:*

> *He Keeps An Eye On 2,300 Girls*
> Thomas Corwin Mendenhall II, B.A., Ph.D., B. Litt. (Oxon.) is a historian who sports loud jackets, whacks together boats in his basement and pilots with a flair the largest independent women's college in the nation.

Isn't that a more interesting lead to a story than you usually see in an "institutional" ad? Note its idiomatic conversational style. Most ady institutional ads are written in stuffed-shirt language like this: "You can enjoy ready access to firsthand information on the local level, plus the convenience of rapid transfer and communications a close-knit statewide banking system offers."

Mind you, these examples are not to deny that many magazine ads *do* what the successful magazines do—that many *are* interesting, informative, original, non-ady, and that they perform a service. Competition for attention has been the same inspiration for the advertisers as for the publishers. And more so for magazine ads than for TV commercials.

For television, the newer medium, proved so powerful that even distasteful, ady commercials seemed to produce results and TV advertisers were smug and less eager to improve their approaches than magazine advertisers have been.

Another catalyst for better ads has been copy research, which has been around longer for magazines—long enough to have acquired a track record and a pile of benchmarks.

Yes, magazine ads have improved mightily and the reading and noting scores attest to it. Here is an ad for a new G.E. toaster that can vie respectably with the editorial interest surrounding it:

It toasts:
Big slices, little slices, thick slices, thin slices, French bread,
buttered bread, garlic bread. Even top-browns muffins!
It bakes:
Cookies, rolls, frozen waffles, frozen pastries, frozen meat pies,
potatoes, chicken, meat loaf. Even reheats cooked foods!
It's General Electric's Toast-R-Oven.
(The toaster with the picture window).

The Starch score for women noting that black-and-white ad was 55 and a whopping 22 percent of the readers read most of the ad. This, on a cost basis, was 450 percent above the norm.

Here is an extract from an ad for Chrysler Corporation that one might call "institutional" which garnered a 69 noting by men and a 25 percent read most score:

For water, mud, marsh, sludge, slosh, slough, bog, fen, morass, quagmire, snow, slush, sand, silt, muck & mire.
This is called a marsh screw amphibian.
A new vehicle designed and built for adverse terrain by Chrysler Corporation under contract to U.S. Navy's Bureau of Ships for Advanced Research Projects Agency, Department of Defense.
It is 13 feet long, 8 feet wide, made of aluminum. It weighs approximately 2300 pounds and it's most at home where other vehicles are decidedly not.
Note the unusual pontoons, one on each side. Don't they look just like two giant screws? They act accordingly.

Considering that most people read only four or five in an issue chockablock full of ads, scores like those are truly impressive.

And the food ads: When they are good, they are very, very good. They follow all the guides that good communicators follow. They do "impart knowledge, make a connection, give to the reader as a partaker." They are operational; the reader can *do* something to translate them fully. They are different and interesting, for they show new ways to use food, and they use new ways to show it. Long experience has taught skillful copywriters of food ads to write recipes that are simple and explicit.

Campbell Soup advertising has offered consistently interesting ideas for serving—like "soup 'n sandwich," "soup on the rocks," "soup for breakfast." A strikingly simple ad shows hot tomato soup in blue cups with brightly contrasted pats of butter in the middle of each: "What a welcome —hot buttered soup and crackers."

A two-page spread for Minute Rice features fourteen unique recipes, each with a luscious picture and specific directions enclosed in a dotted line—encouraging the reader to clip out the recipes and store them, just the right size, in her recipe card file. That recipe ad won a 19 read most score.

And here, for the cognoscenti, was the kind of sparkling food copy that stood out from the clichés (selections of body copy, written by Stan Jones, in a Gourmet Food ad for General Foods):

> France, Sauce Bigarrade. A gourmet once said: "A duck served without Sauce Bigarrade is merely a small canoe with legs." This sweet, delicious sauce, redolent of currant jelly and oranges, will help your duck attain his destiny—with full military honors.
>
> France, Sauce Chasseur. French call it "The Hunter's Sauce." Based on a demi-glace, it is flavorsome, rich enough to be taxed out of existence. In its depths swim mushrooms, burgundy and fledgling shallots. Spoon it on the mallards Papa brings down . . . at the butcher's.
>
> Angleterre, Sauce Provencale. Contrived of mangoes and other rarities by our own Head Chef, who was awarded a higher hat for achievement. Rich. Reddish-brown. Hot. Thick. Broiled meats and poultry sizzle with delight on being basted and barbecues become civilized things under its benign influence.
>
> France, Sauce aux Fines Herbes. Featuring the shy truffle and cayenne, this delicate creamy sauce sheds a perceptible halo over your fish fillets, poultry roasts, and egg dishes. It is as typical of France as a shrugged shoulder.

What, when it comes to magazine writing, is that elusive state of mind we copywriters should cultivate? How is this for a definition?—Whenever we start to write and to conceive ideas with our partners, the art directors, why not simply say, "This ad must compete favorably, not only with the other ads in the book, but *with all of its editorial content"?* Assuming that the magazine is a successful competitor in its field, an ad that competes well with the magazine must communicate successfully.

Of Headlines, Subheads, Captions and Body Copy

Writing a magazine ad is really quite easy. All you have to do, first, is to get the big idea. That one, big startling thought. Then, simply express it.

"Try to state your one big thought," says Harry Hartwick, "in a memorable sentence, so you *package* it for the reader to carry away."

In some ads, that one big thought might be expressed visually, rather than verbally. But, supposing it is in words, that one memorable sentence usually is the headline.

The headline—a thing of beauty and a joy forever when it is born, like Venus rising from the sea, pure and shining and right. "If the headline doesn't stop people," says John Caples, "the copy might as well be written in Greek."

In writing a headline you should select the right audience for your message—yet not exclude any audience. Stop the most possible readers by telling them the most interesting news, but do not tell them so much that they need not read the rest of your ad. Leave enough unsaid and intrigue them so adroitly that they *will* read on—but say enough so that those who *are* only noters, who *refuse* to read your body copy, will carry away a memorable message. "Avoid *blind* headlines," says David Ogilvy, "the kind which mean nothing unless you read the body copy underneath them; most people don't." When you study your Starch scores, you will usually see that only 3, 4, or 5 percent of the people read most of the body copy. Ads with blind headlines can be a tremendous waste.

Good and bad headlines are quite recognizable, when you come to think of them. Here is an ad for Tender Leaf tea with a picture of a loving wife feeding her husband a cup of tea. The headline: *"It's all in the family!"* Could that possibly be a good headline? Does it fulfill any of our definitions of "communication"? Does it "impart knowledge," "give to someone as a partaker"; does it further "an interchange of thoughts"?

Here, on the other hand, are headlines that do express one big thought, that impart knowledge, that select their audience, that promise benefit, that involve the reader—that do all those magic things that add up to communication, to making a connection:

> World's only dog food that
> *makes its own gravy.*

> Now! Color only the gray
> without changing your natural hair color!

General Electric introduces P-7,
the oven that cleans itself.

Now a beer bottle you can open with your bare hands!

Those headlines make you want to read more. You want to know how
those benefits are possible. You find the promise worth reading about. But
even if you do not read more, you have the gist of the message. In the
case of the oven, the advertiser's name is propitiously in the headline;
but in the other three cases the logos were equally prominent for the
noter (Loving Care Hair Color Lotion by Clairol, Gravy Train by Gaines,
and Schlitz Beer).

No wonder headlines like those were read and noted and the one for
Tender Leaf tea was missed by most of the readers.

But, you say, all four of those products had important product news to
impart. How do we write headlines for benefits that are not new?

We cudgel our brains harder. Instead of writing about a perfume in the
same old way, one writer says, "Wear Crepe de Chine at 80 throbs a minute"—the headline for a picture showing a girl applying the heady stuff
to the pulse of her wrist. Instead of the usual clichés about beer, another
writer comes up with this inspired snobbery: "If they run out of Löwenbräu . . . order champagne."

"How long should a headline be?" That is a constant controversy. But
this writer, for one, could not care less—so long as it communicates. One
of the most memorable was two words long—"Think Small" for Volkswagen. The famous headline for Rolls-Royce was eighteen words long—
"At 60 miles an hour the loudest noise in this new Rolls-Royce comes from
the electric clock." And Chevron service stations ran a campaign with a
30-pt. headline more than fifty words long—and sold hundreds of thousands of seat belts:

> Today, you can get this auto seat belt for $5.95 each at most Chevron
> Stations, installed *free*.
> Why? Simply because Chevron believes that seat belts belong in your
> car and in every car.
> Is this a good deal? Yes, it is. Many have paid $12.95 for this same
> belt, *plus* installation.

What about subheads? Surely, we ought to write subheads as we write
headlines—only a little more so. They should, as Mr. Ogilvy puts it,
"heighten the reader's appetite for the feast to come." The best training
for writing subheads, this writer has found, is constantly studying those
that appear in *The Reader's Digest*. See how they develop the ideas in
the headlines, yet lead the reader on into the body copy:

Headline

THE POWER MEN HAVE OVER WOMEN

Subhead

The right glance, the right touch, the right word—these are the things that count.

(That subhead practically impels you to read on and discover what the right glance, touch, and word may be.)

Headline

Look at the New Flying Machines

Subhead

You may not have seen them, but they're here—and you may be flying in them in a few years.

(This is not science fiction, says the subhead; these planes are here. But they are still a mystery to you, the reader, so read on and find out what they are.)

Headline

The Wondrous "Inner Space" of Living Cells

Subhead

Scientists are learning that the miniature world of the single living cell is as astonishing as man himself.

(There is a provocative choice of an adjective; the word "astonishing" has a fine power of propulsion.)

Captions under pictures are too seldom and too lazily used. Research has shown that they can pull twice the readership of body copy; but, even more important, they can be used to pull the reader into the body copy. Again, we can draw inspiration from magazine caption writers, who know how to inform, yet further intrigue with captions. Browse through *Time* and see how titillating the captions can be. Often the caption is less informative than the headline, but is like a clue in advance to solutions buried in the body copy.

As for the body copy, here is the meat for our bones, the proof of our pudding; and yet too often, by the time we get to writing it, we are too bored to care. We write short copy because "people won't read long copy"; we write long copy "so the ad will have a look of authority." Instead, we must communicate *what needs to be said*.

Here is an example of body copy—just one of a long series of ads for

Sears, Roebuck which have been happily effective. It is, relatively speaking, a "long copy ad." It is not about a subject of high intrinsic interest, yet it is as easy to read as a primer. According to Julian L. Watkins, who cites this ad in his book of selections from *The Reader's Digest*, the "buried offer" in the last paragraph pulled thousands of write-ins.

The ad illustrates the credit card of Ted Williams, the famous baseball player. The headline and subhead read:

> HOW TO OPEN A CHARGE
> ACCOUNT AT SEARS
> You can open a charge account at Sears, Roebuck and Co. in person, by mail or by telephone. Their credit terms are so fair that more than ten million American families now have an active credit account at Sears.

Now read the body copy.

> More than ten million American families now have an active credit account at Sears. More than 75 per cent of all Sears appliances are sold on a credit basis.
> What makes this possible?
> First, the American consumer has learned a lot about handling credit. An overwhelming majority of customers now keep their debts at a level they can afford.
> Second, every time Sears has extended its credit policy, it has learned the same pleasant lesson: people are honest.
> Today, every item sold by Sears can be bought on credit. Tools. Furniture. Washing machines. A new kitchen. A mink stole.
> There is no minimum purchase necessary with a Sears revolving charge acount. No down payment, either. And you can leave the mathematics to Sears.
> You can open your account by telephone—and place your first order with the same call. Or you can open your account at any one of the 740 Sears department stores, or 944 catalog sales offices. Or, if you choose, you can do it by mail.
> Your revolving credit card gives you charge privileges at any Sears store, and on any merchandise in the Sears catalog.
> If you would like the latest catalog, free of charge, write to Sears, Dept. 139–21, Chicago 7, Illinois.

> This is the credit card of Ted Williams
> who was recently traded to Sears by Boston.
> (*Picture of Ted Williams' card*)

What is unique about the quiet, matter-of-fact copy in that ad? It has 275 words, and of those, 175 are single syllables. It has 41 verbs, 91 nouns, and only 15 adjectives and adverbs. It is copy that would be praised by Flesch, Strunk, and all the other good teachers of communication. Why? Because it is simple.

Simplicity is difficult. They used to call Walter ·Lippmann "The Great Simplifier"; he had to be wise to be so. In a creative advertising symposium of the 4A's, Charles Brower, of BBD&O, expressed it this way:

> I think that we perhaps have underestimated the average brow, but I think the problem is not so much that. I think that all great messages that have been received by humanity, and read, were of such ultimate simplicity that a child could understand them and an adult would be moved by them. . . . If we do our job right, and keep it simple enough and convincing enough, we will get them all at once.

Down the street from Mr. Brower worked George Gribbin, another successful copywriter, former chairman of the board of Young & Rubicam, Inc. He gave this simple formula for writing magazine copy, and while we avoid formulas, it is hard to quarrel with this one:

> 1. With the help of your art-director create a picture that will make a prospect look at the headline.
> 2. Write a headline that you are sure will make the prospect read the first sentence of copy.
> 3. Write a first sentence of copy that you are sure will make the prospect read the second sentence.
> 4. Continue this process until you are sure that the prospect will read the final word of the ad.
> 5. Make sure that the picture and all these words add up to a story that will make the prospect's mouth water for the product.

Of Layouts, Graphics, Color, and Type

In all the world of advertising, there is nothing so pure, so right, so enduring as the marriage between an imaginative copywriter and a brilliant art director.

An ad is the execution of an idea. And the idea is *one* thing. It is not a headline, not a picture, not type or space or color or texture—though it might, on occasion, be any one of those and no others. For the perfect execution of an idea, so that it comes out one thing, and not a catchall for a group of disconnected elements, we must have close, irresistibly close, collaboration.

The proof of that statement is in the best ads we see today. More and more often they are executed by agencies which enforce the law of holy wedlock between art director and copywriter. Many encourage their constant living together. "How do we work?" says the head of a vibrant young agency (Papert, Koenig & Lois). "A snarling copywriter is locked in a room with an egomaniacal art director and we don't let them out until they are purring."

This would seem logical, but for years, in perhaps the majority of cases, it has been otherwise. The copywriter has bashed off his brainstorm—so long a headline, so many words of body copy, a suggestion for an illustration—and often as not a traffic man has delivered it to the art director, in his cubicle on another floor, to be grumpily executed. The art director, who thought in pictures only, may have given short shrift to the copy and blown up the illustration. Somewhere along the line, a battle probably ensued. The copywriter, fire in his eye, may have screamed "How can you possibly cram 500 words of copy into a space made for 50?" The art director may have replied, "Nobody reads copy anyway. Why do you have to write so many words?" By that time, the deadline for the ad passed, the magazine was asked for an extension, and a careless compromise was made. Finally the ad appeared, all out of whack, unbalanced, unnoticed, and unread.

The marriage of art and copy is precisely like that of words and music. The first question people ask a professional lyricist or composer is, "Which comes first, the words or the music?" It does not really matter, the professional will tell you, and often he cannot even remember. There is a *rightness* to the combination, and when there is a true collaboration, both partners know it. They have respect for each other's ability and a feel for each other's craft. In a true collaboration, the art director may often originate the headline and the copywriter suggest the layout. More and more, these days, with the competition for the reader's time and attention increasing, graphics have become more important than words. Successful art directors are "admen" who create the ideal visual and layout, not just because they are aesthetically satisfying, but also because they are strategically right for the product.

If it were possible for a "Renaissance man"—skilled in both words and pictures—to conceive the entire ad, it might, in the long run, be better for the result, since it would bear the stamp of one person and the harmony of his single-minded direction.

This sometimes happens, as in the case of Onofrio Paccione, an art director. Riding to work one morning on the train, Paccione sketched a simple picture on the back of an envelope—a glass of champagne, beside a mug of Löwenbräu beer. The headline, he thought, was obvious: "If they run out of Löwenbräu . . . order champagne."

How did Paccione conceive this idea? Here is how he outlines its background:

> After a somewhat late start in the post-World War II boom in imported beers, Löwenbräu, the famous Munich brew, began a drive in the early Fifties which was to vault the brand into its present position as Number One among all imports, unseating Heineken's, the erstwhile leader, along the way.
>
> Given the assignment of further broadening Löwenbräu's share of a

dynamic market which had increased 400% since 1947, the Leber Katz Paccione agency had to come up with an advertising approach to convince the consumer that the most expensive beer available was actually worth its price and more. Based on a detailed research of the beer market, the agency was convinced that, because of a shift in consumer attitudes towards beer, Americans would respond to a "snob appeal" and that Löwenbräu with its price, its romance and its Munich origins was the one brand above all others to capitalize on such an approach.

Operating on a creative platform which stated, "there is a domestic beer, there is an imported beer and, in a class by itself, there is Löwenbräu," we set about developing the words and pictures to express the unique superiority of the product.

The problem was stated and the solution, like all inspirations, was strikingly simple: a beautifully assumptive statement, which capitalized on the already-accepted image of champagne as the nonpareil of drinks. In this case, the success of Paccione's ad depended on its understatement and on the participation of the reader. Agency and client had the temerity to run the idea, exactly as he had sketched it on the train, without extraneous additions, repeatedly for two years in a list of seven magazines.

In that case, the entire idea originated with one man, who happened to be the art director. It might just as well have come from the copywriter, or from a collaboration of the two. The important point is that it was a superb solution for the problem.

And that is the nub of our story. What kind of layout should an art director draw? What kind of pictures, what colors, what type should he use? How many words should the ad contain, and how should they be arranged? It depends on the problem, and our collaborators should be steeped in the problem together. Together they should find the best solution. The art director is like the architect. He has a space to fill. He does not fill it with joists and pipes, wallboards and windows. He fills it with a concept, an idea, a whole. The whole is equal to the sum of its parts.

How do our collaborators combine the parts? Take, for example, that classic ad for Volkswagen—"Think Small." The idea *dictated* a silhouetted photograph of a small car in a large white area. The picture had to complement the headline. Given the space of a magazine page, the art director had to fill more than 75 percent of it with that white space and small car. What kind of type did he use for the headline? The family font that had been established for the entire Volkswagen campaign—Futura, a Germanic, modern face, once considered ugly, but eminently right for this utilitarian, admittedly ugly little car. How long was the copy? Long enough to explain the idea and, at the same time, to permit the large white area that was essential. How large was the body type, how wide the measures, how many points of leading were used between the lines?

All of these questions were answered, in collaboration, by the *need* of the ad. And the ad communicated.

But it might not have been so. Creative director Fred Manley, in a speech before the San Francisco Advertising Club, satirically gave his formula for "nine ways to improve an ad," and showed how that same Volkswagen ad might have been ruined. One must follow "the rules" of advertising, said Manley. The first rule is to *show the product*. So we must not hide that Volkswagen in a sea of white. He showed a layout of an enormous car over the headline "Think Small." That headline would not do, though, because rule 2 is "Don't use negative headlines." He changed the headline to "Think BIG!" Next, said Manley, one must, whenever possible, *mention your product name in the headline*. The new headline became "Think BIG and you'll choose *Volkswagen!*"

So he proceeded, through the various clichés of "the ad game" until the final "improved ad" became a hilarious hodgepodge.

That was a satire, but it was painfully close to the truth. With our committee-minded, machine approach to ad-making these days, many a fine, simple idea is seriously butchered. All the more reason for that close collaboration, thoughtful structuring of an ad, and solidarity in presenting it, by the copywriter and his partner, the art director.

Everyone works differently, but, by and large, the method by which an art director visualizes an idea, or by which he collaborates with a copywriter, is similar to the way a copywriter works alone. Usually, the art director draws tissues—lots of round-about "noodling" with the elements of the idea—just as the copywriter goes "all around the subject" to find the right words. The art director's layouts may be symmetrical or assymetrical—orderly and "coaxial" or disorderly on purpose. It takes daring to draw a layout which is unorthodox. But interest derives from originality.

Ads, which people do not *want* to look at, should seize the attention. Art directors plan their elements to do this, with the arrangement of pictures, words, color, and type. "Designers," writes typographer Aaron Burns, "prime little typographic explosions to go off with a flash and a visual noise at the turning of a page."

"The turning of a page"—this is the reader's action which the copywriter and his collaborator, the art director, must arrest. Sometimes they do it with graphic symbols which hook on to the reader's mind and leave a lasting memory. Such graphic symbols are those of the Green Giant, of Elsie the Cow, of a big swash "K" for Kellogg, of a photograph for Dial Soap which in every ad has a refreshing vigor that belongs distinctively to that one product. One ad used the graphic symbol of a baby's small hand in his father's large hand—an emotional tug to communicate about life insurance. Another used a tear in the corner of a wife's eye which, combined with a smile, told an eloquent story for the gift of a Hamilton

Watch. Another showed an old-fashioned pump splashing cold water on a pailful of berries, making the message about Kraft's Jellies uniquely fresh and delicious.

In the case of mentholated cigarettes, similar graphic symbols were used by all the brands—the green symbols of springtime; the cigarettes continued to rival each other to "own" that association so that no one brand stood out. But the association of Marlboro with the graphic symbol of the tattoo was uniquely its own and soon successfully altered that brand's previous weak image.

A layout, as we said before, should be functional and should contribute to the best possible execution of the idea. In the case of an ad for a Buxton wallet, the idea was, clearly and simply, to demonstrate the wallet's many features. This was done with "callouts" which catalogued the points. In the case of an ad for Crepe de Chine soap, the pictures "functionally" illustrated a curiosity-arousing headline: "This is a bottle of Crepe de Chine," said the headline, but the photograph, instead of showing a bottle of perfume, revealed a bar of soap. The soap, in ten steps, gradually dissolved into a fragment surrounded by suds. "This is a bottle of Crepe de Chine" said the first picture and headline, "To wash with," said the last.

Collaboration between the art director and copywriter is a combination of inspiration and practical discipline. "There is in all art," wrote Oscar Hammerstein, "a fine balance between the benefits of confinement and the benefits of freedom. An artist who is too fond of freedom is likely to be obscure in his expression. One who is too much a slave to form is likely to cripple his substance. Both extremes should be avoided, and no invariable laws or methods should be obeyed."

So it is with our collaborators. The copywriter should understand the art director's problems. For practical discipline, for example, he should understand the limitations of space. In order to cast type, a manuscript should be prepared with copy typed as close as possible to preset left and right margins. Some agencies have copy paper printed with vertical rules already in place. Such a manuscript enables the art director to count the total number of words in the body copy and determine the number of characters per line. He has to know this, when he selects his type styles and sizes. You cannot fit sixty characters of a certain style and size into a column width that will only take fifty. You cannot fit a 72-point headline, approximately an inch high, into a half-inch space.

The purpose of type, like all the other elements of the ad, is to make the message clear and interesting. To be clear, it must be readable. To be interesting, it should be unique. These two goals entail all kinds of delightful subtleties of the art director's craft which contribute to the effectiveness of the idea.

Here, for example, is how the typography for a story on "Allergic Swelling" was explained by Aaron Burns:

> The type for this page was first set normally, and then photographically curved to achieve the "SWELLING" effect that we see. The idea was to make the reader want to "flatten" the page The sensual experience that the reader received was exactly what the designer wanted. The purpose of the design was to cause the reader to pause for a moment, long enough, perhaps, to read the message or remember the name of the product and its function.
>
> Notice how close the letters are in the word "SWELLING." They actually touch in some instances. Notice also how other letters in the headline appear to be set much closer than is possible in typesetting. The designer of this page used a razor blade on the type proofs in order to bring the letters closer together and so achieve the "tight" feeling that he wanted.

The selection of type itself can affect the meaning and mood of a message almost as vitally as the words themselves. There are three general classes of type: Old Style, which includes type with thick, slanting serifs, such as Garamond and Caslon; Modern, which began with the thick-and-thin strokes and narrow serifs originated by Giambattista Bodoni; and Contemporary, which are mostly sans serif, like Stymie and Futura. Nowadays, we find art directors mixing their styles with less concern for history than for the compatibility of the type with the message. Thus, in a text on "overeating," two contrasting type styles—one "fat," bold, and old-fashioned (Cooper Black), the other light and modern (Lightline Gothic) combined to symbolize the message graphically as well as to state it.

The copywriter who is sensitive to the nuances of type—as to those of pictures, colors, shapes, and other graphic symbols—can collaborate with his art director in a spirit of delightful discovery. "Some of the most carefully chosen words are pictures," wrote art director Robert Pliskin in *Printer's Ink*. He went on to suggest: "Find the right symbol, then turn it around to make it surprising. There are more effective symbols, and more ways for collaborators to use them, then were ever dreamed of in our old philosophy."

Ideas and Breakthroughs

"Good work will always be derivative," said Henry Wolf, chairman of the 38th Annual Art Directors Show. "I guess it is just human to conform." But he did lay claim to "a few exciting departures which will become the precedents for the next several years."

The trouble is that we have so few departures. It is true that much art is derivative, and this is not to say that it should never be so. But in advertising, more than in other fields of communication, originality is most desirable and it *is* at a premium. Since people do not wish voluntarily to read our magazine ads, and since the more original ads are, the more likely they are to attract attention, it is poor business to run copycat ads.

Yet they abound. Researchers like Gallup & Robinson highlight their prevalence when they run clinics pointing out trends. "In recent years," said one report, "rather dramatic improvement has been made in the technology of photography and reproduction which has provided the advertiser with greater opportunity to exploit the visual portion of the ad to communicate ideas. . . . The trend has been toward greater use of illustrations to communicate ideas."

The report then reviewed trends in illustrative techniques developed over a period of ten years, citing "Visualized Contrast," "People in Situations," "Editorial Formats," and the most recent use of "Close-Up Photography," "Giantism," and "Object in Isolation."

The awareness of such trends is of no use whatsoever when you consider that the idea is to stand out from all your neighbors and to use whatever technique is right for your subject. Trends may reveal that the use of one dominant illustration gets, on the average, greater attention. Yet an advertiser like Chun King runs a magazine ad in which nine small pictures —a Chinese grandmother topping a selection of exotic Chinese food—get more attention than almost every other ad in the book. The headline was an obvious phrase ("Just like Grandma used to make"), but it was seen in an unexpected light because it was associated with an incongruous picture (a *Chinese* grandmother).

We may be stimulated by studying trends—particularly in fields of communication outside our own—but the *ideal* is to be the trend *setter*. We want to reach "the greatest number of people at the lowest possible cost." The ad that attracts the most attention can cost the least, and it is likely to be the most original. The problem is to be original "with the best possible message."

Advertising breakthroughs in magazines have included the use of new space units, such as "checkerboard" ads and gatefolds, the use of inserts, popups, and of actual samples of the products. While some critics generalize that these are expensive "gimmicks," to the extent that they stood out *with* effective selling messages, they proved to be excellent strategy and even, in the long run, economical. The first ambitious insert of a booklet into a magazine—the thirty-six-page Ford ad in *The Reader's Digest*— dominated the magazine and more than paid for itself in goodwill, inquiries and tangible sales. Ford also used a six-page ad with a double gatefold to introduce its 1957 car; the size was not extravagant, for its purpose was to reveal a car, for the first time in its full sweep and detail, after Detroit had learned, through research, the obvious fact that people are interested in *the car itself*.

The use of the first comic-strip advertisement (in 1931 for General

Foods) won more attention than those that followed it. The same was true of the first insert of a product sample in a national magazine reaching millions (a Johnson & Johnson BANDAID in *The Saturday Evening Post*), of the first insert of a phonograph record (for Remington Shavers in *Look*, 1959), of the first ad printed in three dimensions (also in *Look*, in 1964, for the Kodel fiber division of Eastman Chemical).

The last-mentioned innovation, the process called Xography (patented by Visual Panographics, Inc.), is an example of the magazine medium's response to competition. It arrived at the precise time when color television was coming of age. Marvin C. Whatmore, president of Cowles Magazines and Broadcasting, Inc., spent some 13 years making his dream come true—the mass, high-speed printing of three-dimensional pictures which can be seen without the use of special glasses. The resultant process was developed through the collaboration of *Look* magazine, Eastman Kodak, and the Harris-Intertype printing firm. Once the process was perfected for magazine use, it also became available for packaging, labels, point-of-sale displays, books, direct mail pieces, etc. The momentum of this new art form is just beginning to be felt, as it triggers new ideas by copywriters and art directors.

All such breakthroughs have, of course, a strategic purpose—their merchandising possibilities with the trade. A company which advertises with imagination and excitement captures not only the consumer but also those all-important dealers who have to promote the product against its competition.

But the temptation, when searching for breakthroughs, is often to select a pyrotechnical technique at the *expense* of the product message. This is a danger, and nowhere was it more obvious than in the rash of gatefold ads when that new idea was first accepted by magazines. The reader had to wade through foldups, foldovers, Dutch-door folds, and what have you, many with no reason for being. The only reason for having a gatefold (or a color, a certain typeface, a picture, or a headline) is to execute the idea which is essential to communicate the subject. Such a gatefold was that used for a Father's Day gift ad for Remington shavers. With the gatefold closed, the reader saw a scowling father with a heavily bearded face. The headline read "Doubting Dad." The gatefold, opened, revealed half his face clean-shaven by a Remington and a beaming smile—together with the completion of the headline. "Not any more!"

That ad made the gatefold *functional*. It was, in effect, a moving demonstration in a normally motionless medium. Breakthroughs need not always be—and in fact, seldom are—unusual and expensive gimmicks. But they always require courage and conviction by all concerned, because they are original. To the extent that an idea has been used for another product, to that degree is it less fresh for yours. You might think such an idea, because it has proved successful, will be "safer" to use—but what good is "safety" if your idea is comparatively unnoticed? Plagiarism wins its own reward: a secondhand reputation.

One kind of breakthrough is to find and make a stronger product-benefit claim than anyone else is making. As Harry Hartwick pointed out, "People, usually, are already buying some product in your field, not yours. You have to *unsell* them before you can *sell* them. They are happy, most of the time, with what they are using." A product claim must be vital and different indeed to break through that apathy and satisfaction. Such was Crest's "23% fewer cavities" and the promise of a G.E. oven that cleans itself. Another way for a product to startle and persuade is to break out of the pattern of its own product category. For example, all vodkas were considered flavorless. So Wolfschmidt broke out of the mold ("If Vodka has no taste, how come I can tell which one is Wolfschmidt?").

Benefits vary widely according to the context and the audience. Magazine ads for the Peace Corps—whose appeal was to the idealist—promised "11 cents an hour" (showing a picture of a sweaty brow) and a chance to say "NO to being an organization man." An ad for Chock Full O' Nuts Instant Coffee was disarmingly honest: "We won't kid you! . . . It is not as good as *our* regular coffee, even though it is made of the world's first, most expensive coffee beans." The promise was effective because it appeared in the context of too many look-alike ads that made unbelievable claims for their instants.

Bantron and Robt. Burns Cigarillos, in context of the cigarette-smoking scare, had suddenly inflated consumer-benefits to offer. Robt. Burns ran a full-color magazine spread with only ten words of copy. The lefthand page showed the word "Question" and a pile of hundreds of cigarettes. The righthand page bore the word "Answer," a picture of a package of Robt. Burns Cigarillos and the words "Flavor you don't have to inhale to enjoy."

A black-and-white magazine page, for Bantron (smoking deterrent tablets) had some 1,000 words of copy. Headline: "It's hard for a writer to *Give Up Smoking.*" Subhead: "Here's how I cut from 4 packs to 0 in 5 days." Credit line: "by Quentin Reynolds." Main picture: Reynolds, smoking, with caption: " 'You'll never see me doing this again,' says Quentin Reynolds. This photograph was taken a few months before the author gave up smoking."

The body copy in the Bantron ad was as readable as Reynolds' own vivid reportorial writing. It was a narrative—absorbing, personal, and believable. It took the time, also, to be specific. These claims were operational—i.e., they could be verified, if one wished to do so:

The Bantron formula was discovered by doctors in the research department of [a great American university.] Its active ingredient is lobeline sulphate. Lobeline sulphate is extracted from the Lobelia plant, sometimes called Indian Tobacco. Hundreds of years ago the Indians used to smoke the leaves and flowers of this plant as a tobacco substitute. The extract is a first cousin to nicotine, mimicking its action without being habit forming. The lobeline acts by displacing the nicotine in the system and helps curb the desire for tobacco.

Which is better—long copy or short copy? In the case of the Bantron product—a pill, mind you, to inhibit smoking, not a pleasurable substitute —the long copy was justified, was in fact necessary. In the case of the Cigarillos, the contrasting pictures and the powerful promise needed no further gilding. Both ads, totally different from each other, were noticed, communicated, and helped to sell products.

Finally, involvement, as we emphasized in Chap. 3, is a massive weapon in the war to win magazine readers.

Here is an example of how one simple idea, executed in a black-and-white page without adornment, had the power to communicate beyond all the fancy gimmicks and color layouts of the other ads in the issue. It was a message for the Better Vision Institute and it simply featured a a reproduction of a letter in his own shaky handwriting, as shown on the opposite page.

Magazine ads, once they seize the attention of the reader, have the best leisurely setting in which to hold and heighten emotional response. Viewers can participate in the emotion of a TV commercial, but it wings by incredibly fast. A potent magazine ad may hold the reader for a long time and may linger with him long after.

Benefit, context, emotional involvement—all are elements that make for dynamic magazine ads. Try as we will to find formulas and to seek research that will back up judgment, usually we know when we have a good idea for a magazine ad. A good ad is startlingly simple, it "sells itself," it feels right. Such an ad was a little gem about Spalding golf balls. It told its story with a smile, with a twist, with an unexpected photograph that made "the familiar strange." Above all, it told its story—the promise of the greatest benefit a golfer wants from a ball. The picture: twelve golfballs, nestled in a cardboard carton where normally one would expect to see a dozen eggs. The headline: "Birdies-to-Be."

When I heard there's a campaign to get people to have their eyes examined regularly, I thought maybe I could drive this idea home by writing about it myself (with Mrs. Shearing's help).

Really. It should be a law, not just an idea. Seeing is one thing that shouldn't be left to chance. I know, I never had the chance.

But I have some idea of what I'm missed. My career as a pianist has taken me to many countries, judging from just the sounds and smells, it must be an unbelievably exciting world to see.

I'm not suggesting you'll go blind because you don't have your eyes examined. The chances are small. But why take the chance? But when a person like me would be grateful to see at all, a person like you has a choice. You can assume your eyesight is all right. Or you can become through examination that you might be seeing a lot better. I know what I'd do if I had the choice.

George Shearing

13

THE SEGMENTED MEDIUM

How Radio Survived

Radio reacted with brave ferocity when the seemingly overwhelming power of television attacked it. Here, at last, was a medium of communication which had practically everything—sight, sound, motion, and eventually the added dimension of color. Surely the medium of radio, with its single dimension of sound, was doomed and defeated. But radio refused to die.

Those of us who are old enough remember old-time radio with nostalgia. It was a huge Atwater-Kent console, placed prominently in the living room, surrounded by the alert ears of the family. Jack Benny, Amos and Andy, Fibber McGee and Molly, The Hit Parade, Inner Sanctum—half hours and hours, even two- and three-hour shows—were beamed to those attentive ears by giant radio networks.

Radio was the big medium, and when it came along, it too threatened to eliminate the need for other media—for newspapers, magazines, and direct mail. But they all survived and radio settled down to a long heyday of familiar voices, to the warm, shared pleasure of listening and imagining.

There was a deep empathy with the show biz of radio which television has yet to achieve (or achieved only briefly in its first years, when live dramatic shows so strongly involved the viewer). The family *knew* Amos and Andy, though they never saw them. In fact, they knew and loved them more for *not* having seen them, as was subsequently proved when those same characters became literal on TV and destroyed their own illusion.

But like all too-familiar fancies, radio, in the context of television, could never be the same and survive. It had to adapt to changing times. And the medium adapted in the most radical way. It did not change imperceptibly, as magazines and newspapers have been doing. It changed overnight. And it changed *completely*. Radio became the exact *opposite* of what it had been. As it had been stationary, it became mobile. As it had been large, it became small: one massive console became several small portable transistorized sets per family. And as radio had been centralized, with relatively few stations controlled by a few national networks, it now became segmented—many stations, more localized than national, and deliberately specialized in their programming appeals.

Today, at this writing, radio has more individual outlets than any other consumer medium. There are almost 5,000 radio stations, compared with about 1,700 newspapers, 500 TV stations, and less than 700 magazines. More families own more radio sets than they do any other means of communication—more than 225 million, an average of about four sets per home (almost triple the number per home as there were *before* TV came along). The numbers keep increasing. Over three times more radio sets than TV sets are sold each year.

One reason why there are so many radio sets is because this has become the most mobile medium. It started its move out of the living room. More radio sets are now in the bedroom than in any other room, but the new radio has also moved into the kitchen, the patio, and—importantly—into the car. Now we have become a nation on the go, often with two and three cars per family. And while TV, record-players, and tape-recorders are moving into the car too, they cannot begin to compete with more than 55 million car radios that go with us to work, to school, and away on vacation.

The nature of radio broadcasting completely changed. TV became the big medium, with the family glued to the set. Radio became lots of little media, providing something for everybody's taste, at any given time. And of all the tastes, music was the most popular.

Music as a background on radio took many forms. It filled an increasing need as America's population exploded, our wealth and leisure increased, and disposable income turned more and more to luxury items. The air became crowded with sounds, and we old ones, who could never study or work with distractions, were appalled to watch our youngsters doing their homework to the accompaniment of harsh tympani and the caterwauling of Beatles. Record sales soared. Hit Parades, which once featured the top ten, became the top thirty, forty, and fifty.

The story is told of one Todd Storz, who was sitting in his favorite bar, sipping a drink as the juke box was blaring. Why, he thought idly, as he heard tune after tune in the background, should these hundreds of tunes be limited only to these on-premise places? From that free association he founded a successful chain of radio stations and pioneered a new concept which became known as "The Formula."

The formula, according to Storz, was music-and-news. "But," says Miles David of the Radio Advertising Bureau, "there had been 'music-and-news' long before his time . . . What he did was to re-package radio so that it was as exciting and brisk as the popular music people liked." And according to David, what the new top tunes stations did was to recognize certain fundamentals:

1. That people who like music like music. Therefore all talk interruptions or other interruptions ought to be brief.

2. That people who like music with an exciting beat enjoy a similar pace in the news and talk that goes with it.

3. That listener involvement builds a station. Therefore, promotions and games and other techniques for bringing the listener and the station together were essential to build an audience.

4. That if people like the top tunes they like them over and over again. That's why there was a "formula"—the use of the top tunes frequently.

Another part of the nature of radio—and this was true even before TV was invented—is the fact that it is the fastest medium for news. Mechanically, one can communicate at the precise *instant* something is happening. Although videotape has made this instancy possible in TV, and will make it more so, at this writing its use is less widespread than the ever-present radio microphone. When Pearl Harbor was attacked, when President Kennedy was assassinated, radio was first with the news. It will continue to be a fast-breaking medium as our society continues to be on-the-run. Some stations, like WINS in New York, have responded to this advantage by eliminating music and broadcasting 100 percent news.

All in all, as we said earlier, radio has something for everyone. So when we approach it, as communicators, we should realize that it is segmented, that it is many media in one. The following are the principal current program trends (and among 5,000 stations, you may be sure that there are many permutations and combinations of these):

Contemporary music. Top forty best-selling records are the major programming feature. Songs played reflect young tastes and include rock and roll. News is in capsule form but covers all major developments. Occasional features are inserted into the schedule but most of the programming is music.

Modified contemporary. Less rigidly limited to best-selling records. Not quite as much emphasis on youth audience and the disc jockey. However, today's music remains the most important programming factor.

Talk-oriented. Much time devoted to the talk of personalities. Interview with interesting personalities, telephone chats with listeners. Music, while bright and popular, excludes most—often all—rock and roll. News is given in more depth.

Music with personalities. These stations feature contemporary music, standards, and some carefully selected rock and roll. Established person-alities have a strong voice. The news is emphasized at traffic hours, is usually mature, authoritative.

"Good Music" stations. Music may range from musical comedies to symphonies and operas. Unlike most other formats, which intersperse commercials throughout the hour, "good music" stations often cluster the commercials so that a listener may hear considerable uninterrupted music.

Ethnic. Music and personalities have ethnic origin and appeal. News, personalities, and community service programming all have strong ethnic direction.

A few stations have revived old drama (The Shadow, The Green Hornet) but audience appeal has been largely nostalgic, and any strong move toward radio drama will, in all likelihood, have to come out of to-day's problems and premises. (ABC Radio Network recently started a daily half-hour contemporary dramatic radio series.) Sports, music, news —all written and designed to appeal to the selective audience the station is seeking—are the basic factors which make up the successful new sounds of today's radio.

How does this new segmented radio affect advertising? With more than twice as many radio stations as there were before TV, the radio medium now has the most selective programming. Therefore, you can segment your audience and direct special commercials to people with special tastes and interests. New York City, for example, has thirty different stations, although ten cover most of the audience. You can pinpoint your audience, select the teenagers, the businessmen, the housewives, the geographical and ethnic groups. Radios reach into the suburbs more than do the daily newspapers, so you can supplant or supplement your local retail adver-tising to that vast middle-income group that has forsaken the cities. In the summer you can reach more adults with radio than you can with TV, for they are off and driving. People listen more to individual stations than to specific radio programs. So to reach the great masses with the complete impact of a major campaign, advertisers can buy at different times, on different stations, for saturation, frequency, tonnage, and repetition.

Of course, the best time-buying periods are now topsy-turvy too. Prime time for TV is in the evening; for radio, during the day—7 to 10 in the morning, 4 to 7 in the afternoon.

But the most important way the new radio affects advertising is in the nature of the commercials that support the stations. In this regard, the time lag in readjustment has been longer. Radio, in order to survive, changed itself completely in its programming. Radio commercials have changed less radically; and too often we write commercials as we did decades ago, when radio was still the center of attraction.

Adapting Commercials to the New Radio

Reiterating, as always, our concern with *attitude:* the copywriter's attitude about radio must be one of constant flexibility. We must be aware, as with all media, of our audience in its particular context of time and mood. A teenager, concentrating simultaneously on two different levels—on his studies in the foreground and "the beat" in the background—is a different audience from the all-night listener to "Music 'Til Dawn" or Barry Gray—and from the housewife, listening in the midmorning to "Make-believe Ballroom," as she does her ironing or gossips with a neighbor. The commuter in his car, during "drive time," tuned to the 7:55 morning news, is another kind of an audience, and the listener to Bartok on his favorite FM station is yet another breed of cat.

Jack Benny's integrated commercials on the Jell-O radio program many years ago were a joy to hear and boffo at the corner store. Remember Meredith Willson's "talking people" on the Tallulah program—how they would swing in and out of the program with aplomb so the commercial message was always pleasant and compatible? Without the advantage and continuity of a network program, the radio commercial today is often one of a pool of six or a dozen "reminders"—with a stet jingle and announcer over music, or with some kind of zany humor which may or may not be appropriate to its setting.

One of the favored ways to attract the right audience with the right message is to provide fact sheets for local radio personalities, to give them freedom to be their own copywriters and to express their commercial message in the same manner as they comment on noncommercial subjects. There are disadvantages in this system, to be sure, for the message will vary by personalities in length, pertinence, and intensity. But the biggest advantage is the ease and believability achieved.

The master of the person-to-person, conversational commercial has always been radio's strongest spokesman, Arthur Godfrey. Though he succeeded, for a while, on television, his greatest strength is in talking about products, in an informal and honest way, to radio listeners. He was the precursor of those hundreds of disc jockeys who now take their cue from him.

Can you call to mind the gravelly voice, the bemused expression? Just his manner of presentation spoke volumes. His tongue-in-cheek delivery seemed to say: "You and I know that selling products is relatively unimportant, in the scheme of things, but I do it for a living, and you can benefit from them in a small way, so let's not take ourselves too seriously about them. But you can take my word for it, that if I endorse them, they are pretty good. . . ."

A typical commercial might sound like this:

> Ah, boys, I'd like you to play a little music here for me. . . . No I wouldn't either. . . . (*Laughter*) Take it back. I would, but I forgot that this part of the program is sponsored by a very nice bunch of people who'd like me to mention—just *mention* the fact—that they make Bufferin. Bufferin, which is for your sufferin'. You don't ask for aspirin any more. It's old-fashioned. You ask for Bufferin. Bufferin, which contains a couple of "buffered ingredients." . . .

Despite the phenomenal success Arthur Godfrey had, when his flip manner of discussing products was a novelty, the power of other local radio personalities has never been fully exploited.

A recent plan, originated by media director Warren Bahr, proposes to take fullest advantage of the new radio, with its "frozen dial." This is the dial which certain groups of people, at specific times, keep frozen at their favorite wavelength. They are a loyal and constant audience. Whatever they may be doing at that particular time, it is usually a pursuit of habit. It is possible for a local personality, who has this audience's fealty, to speak at length, over a long period, about a particular product, and to communicate its story in depth.

This is the opposite theory from George Washington Hill's hypnotic approach, wherein one copy message—usually a single slogan, forever repeated in precisely the same way—is used to brainwash the audience.

According to the frozen dial theory, says Bahr, one can conceive his entire commercial strategy for a period of weeks, saying *all* that he needs and wishes to say, without concern for the confinements of such commercial time units as sixty and thirty seconds. If, for example, there is an educational story about the differences between detergents and soaps, about fluorescer levels, the fact that a detergent manufacturer has chemical differences in his product, this can be done at a leisurely pace by a local personality who has relatively the same audience every day. Copy can be written, in advance, to be 200 or 300 lines long—as much as thirty or forty minutes total time, if one wishes. It can then be divided into short episodes. The local personality can then deliver the whole story provocatively, in his own style. He has the advantages of time to communicate in depth, a hard-core audience to listen, and his own innate believability.

Whether this plan, which is both visionary and expensive, works out or not, it is deliberately calculated to take advantage of the nature of the new radio. Another approach to this local medium is to use it increasingly for retailing, with weekly specials and events like those which provide the greatest revenue for newspapers.

Even in the old days, radio was an active medium for local events. But prime time then—like time on TV today—was difficult to get on the networks.

Now, with the turnaround, radio is being used with sophistication by such local retail advertisers as supermarkets and department stores. A useful guide to the retail approach is the booklet issued by the Radio Advertising Bureau, "How to Use Radio to Sell Items." It tells the case history of the "Department Store Challenge," in which the Higbee Company of Cleveland, a store with 9,000 items to sell, ran a two-year concentrated test of radio commercials. According to the Bureau, radio proved 6 to 24 percent more effective than newspaper advertising during the first year and even more effective during the second. But more impressive than the statistics is the practical guide to retail radio writing and time-buying. The manual tells how to plan the radio budget and how to appoint and train radio coordinators and researchers. It tells how to obtain the best information for the radio messages from store buyers and division managers, how to plan events according to the seasonality of the merchandise in each department, how to support events like anniversary sales, January clearances, warehouse sales, etc.

The manual gives tips on "How to Write Selling Copy." And it tells the careful planning that went into the composition of a radio logo (or jingle) for the store. The following was the rationale:

> Higbee's is 100 years old. It's a Cleveland institution, but it is not feeble with age. Rather, in a quietly conservative way, it is aggressive, young, probably square foot for square foot the most exciting store in Cleveland due to a young management with a let's-do-it-best attitude.
>
> Higbee's had to convey that feeling in its Radio advertising—the feeling of a fine old store but of a young, aggressive store. That's the feeling we tried to convey in the jingle.
>
> To dissect the Higbee jingle for you: It begins with "Discover the wonderful world of Higbee's." This was designed to excite the shopping instincts of the female whose pulse quickens with the thought of going to see lots and lots of goods. The second line says, "Higbee's is a *nice* department store." Nice? Yes, nice—ask your wife to describe her favorite store—she won't call it exciting, she won't say it's delightful or vital. If she likes to shop there, it's a *nice* store. So that's what we decided was the key word in describing Higbee's. The claim that Higbee's is a nice department store is followed by a couplet, amusing and yet designed to convey our copy point—wide selections of merchandise. "We have escalators, elevators. Shoes that once were alligators." And there are other versions of this couplet:

We have full dress suits, cowboy boots,
Children's trains with built-in toots.

We have hi-fi tweeters, electric heaters,
Screens to keep out mean 'mosquiters.'

We have children's blocks, argyle socks,
And some very alarm-ing clocks.

We have street floor notions, beauty lotions,
Boats to float on bathtub oceans.

Note: The tempo of the music is a compromise between schmaltz and the big beat. The tempo is bright—one that most people 16 to 55 can identify themselves with.

Musical logos, while they are effective and have become traditional in both the old and new radio, are not the automatic cue for a radio copywriter. As in all media, we should make the form follow the function, and we can choose from millions of sounds. Most important, we must become aware of them. And this requires a special kind of discipline. For, in our accelerated, magnified world of sensual satisfactions, we are glutted with competing impressions and relatively deaf to sound.

The Sound State of Mind

Georges Simenon, in his sensitive novel, *The Bells of Bicetre*, tells of an important businessman, Maugras, who is totally incapacitated by a stroke. Lying in his hospital bed, unable to speak or move, his ears become acutely tuned to the small sounds of life around him:

> Cars drove into the courtyard and drew up at the foot of the central building, in which he was. Not far from his room there was a staircase with creaking treads. The church clock struck six and then the bells rang out for early Mass.
> The world was coming to life around him, still in slow motion. Garbage cans were being dragged across the pavement. An electric bell rang faintly in the distance, or it might have been an alarm clock, while down below, on the ground floor or in the basement, the clatter of enormous saucepans pounded from the kitchens. . . . He heard the sharp tap of rapid footsteps in the corridor, very different from the muffled gliding sounds that went on all day.

Maugras began to listen because he had nothing else to do. Can *we* cultivate his finely tuned state of mind without such a violent shutting off of the other senses? It takes some doing; but it's worth it. The world is a rich treasury of sounds. And every sound can evoke echoes in a listener's memory, pictures in his mind, even the association of taste and the imagined effect of a touch. (What else do we mean when we say that a sound "sends chills up and down my spine," when we describe the sounds of musical instruments as "sweet," "fruity" or "sour"?)

Let us consider a "catalogue" of some of the sounds which have come from a copywriter's awareness of the ideal form for the function. Logos in sound, for example, have been drawn from all kinds of instruments, effects, and voice manipulations. One of the most memorable radio jingles, for Ajax Cleanser, drew its "memory device" from a singer's bass voice mouthing sound-effect syllables:

GROUP: Use Ajax
BASS: Bum-bum
GROUP: the foaming cleanser
BASS: Ba-ba-ba-ba-ba-bum-bum
GROUP: Wipes off stains just like a whiz
BASS: Ba-ba-ba-ba-ba-ba-bum
GROUP: No hard rubbing—just relax
   There's a white, bright bleach in Ajax!
   So use Ajax
BASS: Bum-bum
GROUP: The foaming cleanser
BASS: Ba-ba-ba-ba-ba-bum-bum
GROUP: Floats grease and stains
   Right down the drain
BASS: Ba-ba-ba-ba-ba-ba-bum!

Looks silly on paper, doesn't it? But the sound of that bass singer was so pleasant and distinctive that it has reverberated in the minds of millions of people since it was first recorded.

Collecting and selecting sounds like that takes a special talent. Hayakawa likened advertising copywriters to poets, and of course we are more than just a likeness, but the actual thing. We use alliteration ("Brylcreem—a little dab'll do ya"), metaphor ("springtime mildness"), onomatopoeia (The Poptop Can) and rhyme ("Winston Tastes Good Like a Cigarette Should").

What is a poet? The dictionary says "One endowed with great imaginative, emotional, or intuitive power and capable of expressing his conceptions, passion, or intuitions in appropriate language." The word "appropriate" is the key. That open state of mind we acquire enables us to find sounds so appropriate to our message that the listener clearly comprehends them and they cling to his mind.

Why do certain phrases and sounds keep coming back to us? For one thing, because they seem so felicitous for their subject. Mark Twain, riding on the trolley car, composed his little doggerel,

Punch-punch-punch with care
Punch in the presence of the passeng-are

A blue-strip ticket for a five cent fare
A red-strip ticket for a ten cent fare
Punch-punch-punch with care
Punch in the presence of the passeng-are.

The poem is so perfect for the subject, so rhythmic that the reader "can't get it out of his head."

Since the beginning of time, the words and sounds poets and composers have conceived keep recurring—especially after we learn them fresh, when we are young, and they stick in our minds for the rest of our lives ("I wandered lonely as a cloud . . ." "Not with a bang, but a whimper." "'Twas brillig and the slithy toves . . .")

So, ideally, the best state of mind for a radio writer is to be so sensitive to sounds and aware of his subject that he discovers the perfect marriage of the two. He may not originate the music or select the instruments or develop the sound effect himself, but he can guide the conception and feel it is right and will work.

To get back to our catalogue . . . Some of the felicitous sound logos in radio included: The Bromo Seltzer "train" effect, using the Sonovox, a device that enables a musical instrument to talk (*"Bromo* Seltzer, *Bromo* Seltzer, *Bromo* Seltzer, *Bromo* Seltzer." *Fade out.*); a musical spot for Northwest Orient Airlines, in which singers, creating a mood of buoyancy in flight, were interrupted by one appropriate sound effect:

SINGERS: Give *wings* to your *heart,*
Your *spiiirit soars,*
With Northwest airman*ship*
You'll fly as you've never flown before!
Fly the best when you fly North*west*—
Northwest *Orient*
(*Sound effect: Oriental gong*)
Air*lines.*

That oriental gong made all the difference between an ordinary commercial jingle and one of the best remembered.

A music-and-sound-effect logo for Western Union featured an accelerated repetition of the name, mixed with a looped tape recording of dots-and-dashes and the clacking of a telegraph key—all appropriate to the urgency and excitement of the subject ("*Western* Union . . . Western Union . . . *Western* Union . . . *Western* Union . . . It's wise to wi-*er!*"). An appropriate sound trademark for Nestlé's chocolate—appealing to children with a twist on the familiar subject which made it "strange"—was the drawn-out pronunciation of the word: "Chaawclit."

A sound which seemed delightfully appropriate to its subject was the jingle for Goodman's soup. The musical accompaniment was a childlike sweet potato instrument, the girl singer had a bell-clear voice, and the nonsense rhyme (while it certainly *does* look nonsensical here) stuck in your mind like a nursery rhyme:

Goodman's Soup
Make some soup
Goodily moodily noodle soup.
Make a pot
Nice and hottily hot
So easy to doodily do.

Lyrics, as anyone who has an ear for music knows, have a way of being so appropriate and easy to remember that we like to savor them over. "Speak the speech, I pray you," said Hamlet, "trippingly on the tongue." You must speak your lyrics aloud, when you conceive them, and polish them so well that they roll like a ball. Some lyrics come out just right for remembering—such as these selections from radio commercials:

Who is the Ale Man?
He could be you:
A *man* with a thirst for
A *man*lier brew.

*Pep*si-Cola hits the spot
Twelve full ounces, that's a lot
Twice as much for a nickel too
*Pep*si-Cola is the drink for you.

You get a lot to like
From a *Mar*lboro—
Filter . . . Flavor . . . Flip-top box!

Wouldn't you really rather have a Buick,
A Buick,
A Buick,
Wouldn't you really rather have a Buick
Than any other kind of car.

A lyrical tour de force was the commercial for Cadbury Biscuits, newly imported from England. The entire spot, preselecting a sophisticated audience, was based on an Elizabethan madrigal. It was satirically overplayed, with "veddy, veddy British accents." The musical accompaniment was, of course, a harpsichord:

(*Harpsichord Intro*)
SHE: Sing hey nonny nonny
        For the *Cad*bury *Bis*cuit
HE: Nonny nonny *hey*
        For the *choc*-olate coat.

SHE: For the *Cad*bury Biscuit
The *Cad*bury Biscuit
HE: The *Cad*bury Biscuit
With the choc-olate coat.
SHE: Sing *hey* for the flavor
HE: The flavor of the *bis*cuits
SHE: *Nonny* for the cream
HE: The *cream* in the *choc*-olate.
SHE: The *dairy* milk chocolate
The *Cad*bury chocolate
HE: The *Cad*bury Biscuit with the choc-olate coat!

In those lines, and the rest of the song and script which followed, the name "Cadbury" was heard about 15 times. Who says repetition of the client's product has to be repellent?

Included in our catalogue of sound sounds must be the use of "variations on a theme." One of the best ways to establish your message is to conceive an idea that can be infinitely varied. For example, the Beechnut Gum "I'm not talkin' while the flavor lasts" campaign had a basic format which allowed the copywriter to embroider an endless, amusing serial. But one element never changed—the basic copy strategy of the product.

An appropriate sound for a copy strategy was the radio campaign for Marlboro Cigarettes, when the strategy was to change the brand image from that of an effeminate product to a masculine one. Julie London, who has a sensuous voice, was chosen to sing the Marlboro song in such a way that male listeners soon associated the brand with virility.

The catalogue must also include commercials which are tailored to their program environment.

Tailored to one kind of audience was a commercial for Benson & Hedges cigarettes, on an FM radio station (of course, the quality of the sound on FM radio also enhances a quality message):

Music: Harpsichord, under
VOICE: Come live with me and be my love . . . and we will all the pleasures prove . . . that hills and valleys, dales and fields . . . woods or steepy mountain yields. . . . Among the pleasures of life, many people count the classic pleasure of Benson & Hedges cigarettes. Expect to find in Benson & Hedges the pleasure of costly tobaccos, luxurious in flavor. Benson & Hedges also offers you America's only filter of natural cellulose. . . .

"Imagery transfer" was a phrase used by Joe Culligan, then of NBC Radio, to describe how radio advertising ties in with visual advertising and calls up "latent images" in the mind. He illustrated the idea with the sound of the squealing brakes of a car, pointing out that a picture of a skidding car, triggered by the sound, leaps to the mind. Just so, the following commercial, using many sound effects, stimulated a mental picture of an entire city:

> *Sound effects: Foghorn, traffic noises, a street musician, under*
> NARRATOR (*over*): You're listening to the sounds of San Francisco. . . .
> A street musician improvises on the corner of Market and Montgomery, and behind, the great harbor makes a music of its own!
> *Sound: Ship's whistle*
> Moody, romantic San Francisco. An American city. An Astrojet city. . . .
> The way to get there? American Airlines. Any day that you wish, an American Airlines Astrojet will take you to San Francisco—
> *Sound of jet plane*
> at nearly the speed of sound.

Clever use of personalities on radio can make commercials stand out from their background. As in other media, the trick is to conceive the unexpected. Here, for example, is a message for the Peace Corps, one of a series by the comedy team Nichols and May:

> MAN: Miss, I'd like to join the Peace Corps.
> WOMAN: May I ask what you do?
> MAN: What do I do? Why, I'm an engineer, a fairly good carpenter, I've studied medicine, and I'm working on a PhD.
> WOMAN: Yes? Well, that's wonderful. Do you know any basic languages? Hindustani? Swahili?
> MAN: No.
> WOMAN: Well, that's not so bad. You can learn, I suppose. Where would you want the Peace Corps to send you?
> MAN: Why, I don't care. Some rotten place. Mud huts, snakes, pellagra, beri-beri, you know.
> WOMAN: Mm-hm. We do have some need for nutrition in Afghanistan.
> MAN: Nutrition! Listen—I want mud, filth, pests!
> WOMAN: Mm-hm. Well, we have a kind of dirty road to build in—
> MAN: Look—you don't seem to understand. I want to *suffer*.
> WOMAN: Well, there are long hours, low pay, frustrations . . .
> MAN: No, no, no! Rickets! Hostile people! Miserable food! Two years in hell!
> WOMAN: I'm sorry. Peace Corps regulations are to keep the Volunteers alive and to send them wherever the people have asked for help.
> MAN: I'll go over your head! I'll write to the Peace Corps—direct. . . .
> ANNOUNCER: That young man won't get a plague—or even suffer a little. The Peace Corps doesn't offer danger for thrill-seekers. But it does have jobs to be done. And if you've got the energy—and the will to use it —you could join. Write the Peace Corps, Washington, D.C.

Sounds are all around us. And there are trends in sounds which, when we keep alert and aware, can give us inspiration. We can anticipate and ride a trend in music, be it the swim, bossa nova, folk songs, Mitch Miller's "sing-along" style, or Montovani strings. We can use pop tunes and musical comedy hits with commercial lyrics, as did White Owl cigars with "The Most Happy Fella," Ford cars with the show tune "Watchin' All the Girls Go By," and Pepsi-Cola with its revival of "Whoopee." We can use P.D. (public domain) songs, reaching as far back as did Pepsi-Cola with "D'ya Ken John Peel?" We can write parodies of hit shows, as did Stan Freberg for Meadowgold dairy products in his takeoff on "My Fair Lady."

Browsing through record-album catalogues and music stores, watching for new ideas and talent in the world of entertainment, we can find directions for radio commercials which nobody has tried before. Is flamenco played by Sabicas the "in" thing? Could Pearl Bailey put across a message for Rainier Ale? Would the new rave star, Barbra Streisand, sing a commercial? Could she be persuaded?

This is the kind of alert state of mind we have to cultivate if we are to make new breakthroughs. We have to have our mental antennae well tuned to sound. We need to, because, the fact is, there are far too few innovations in this, as in all the other media.

New Directions in Radio Commercials

The fact that radio since its heyday has been relatively neglected by the creators of advertising (in favor of the more glamorous television medium) makes it a fertile field for the enterprising copywriter. Copywriters and artists have been eager to innovate in print and TV. But the artists of sound have been comparatively overlooked. True, there are packagers of advertising jingles, specialists who use electronic sounds, composers and arrangers the advertisers and their agencies can call upon. But the fact that the agencies and advertisers employ thousands of full-time artists and writers, yet scarcely a handful of sound-experts, proves that they are neglecting radio. How can they be sufficiently aware of advances in sound, the innovations in music and drama *outside* the advertising profession, if they are not attuned to the subject?

Recording companies have had their Mitch Millers and Goddard Lebersons who understood, developed, and successfully marketed musical talent. The radio stations themselves—changed, as we described, by their struggle for survival—were far in advance of their advertisers in sound techniques. It has already been a number of years since stations started to broadcast their call letters, weather, and news services with the most ingenious and entertaining musical productions. Innovators like Eric Siday and Ginger Johnson produced packages of lushly arranged material with sparkling ideas, symphony-large orchestras, and top-name singers.

The cost of such productions—if anything, even more elaborate than the music surrounding them—was partly amortized by syndication, so that stations whose territories did not overlap purchased the same material, but with different call letters. The important point was that these stations "thought big" enough to want their own advertising to equal or surpass the sounds which surrounded it.

Electronic treatment of sounds—now fairly commonplace—was pioneered by these radio broadcasters and by a relatively few advertisers. This entailed experiments in scientific directions which had been explored by people like Vladimir Ussachevsky of Columbia University, John Cage, and Siday. They composed avant-garde music on tape—such as the music originated in France and Germany—using the audio oscillator, without musical instruments. They used "tape reverberation," by which the sound expert can control the rapidity of the repetition of words or musical phrases. He can use different tape speeds for different effects. He can record at 7½ inches per second, rerecord at 15, specially mix the material, and have it come out without the kind of distortion one hears with the voice of Donald Duck.

Another device they used was the "tape loop," similar to the use of looped film in TV to repeat frames. A signal is recorded at one speed, rerecorded at another, made into a loop, and run continuously, while another signal is mixed with it.

The purpose of all such experiments with sound was to find the best ways to express a message. It is possible to create a sound effect of a washing machine that is more appealing and "washing machiney" than the thing itself. Siday, using electronic devices and doctored musical instruments, created the sound of a coffee percolator for Maxwell House (in that case, used on TV) which was pleasantly musical—yet conveyed the essence of the percolator itself!

With electronic sounds, you can take phrases like "ice cold" and "red hot" and make them sound the epitome of cold and hot. While originality is one of the advantages of such sound treatment, it should be used, of course, to heighten a selling message, not to distract from it.

Today, most colleges have their own electronic recording studios, and professional studios are equipped to experiment with infinite ideas in electronics. Yet only about 5 percent of the commercials on the new radio have used this technique.

Breakthroughs are achieved with awareness of all the mainstreams of music and sound, as well as through inventiveness. When creative director Bob Pritikin had a unique idea for selling Fuller Paint on radio, he was aware of the existence of one Ken Nordine, originator of the popular record "Word Jazz." Together, they partly wrote and partly extemporized a series of "visual" radio commercials. The idea was to concentrate on

Fuller Paint colors, rather than the quick-drying or fast-spreading or non-drip characteristics other paint companies were stressing. Most unusual was to describe color with the sounds of music and words, and to encourage the radio listener to participate in the commercials and to do the picturing himself.

The Fuller Paint idea took best advantage of the single-sense, concentrated drama of radio. It harked back to the days when radio programs like "I Love a Mystery," "Lights Out," and "Arch Oboler Productions" deeply involved the listener.

Here are some extracts from this unique campaign, which had a brief, but resultful appearance:

> (*Phone rings*) Yello. Yes, I'll take your order. Dandelions, a dozen; a pound of melted butter; lemon drops and a drop of lemon? And one canary who sings a yellow song. Is there anything else? Yello. Yello? Yellow! Well, if she really yearns for yellow she'll call back. And if you want yellow that's yellow yellow—remember to remember the Fuller Paint Company —a century of leadership in the chemistry of color. For the Fuller Color Center nearest you, check your phone directory—the yellow pages, of course!

> The Fuller Paint Co. invites you to stare with your ears at color. Black as there; red as here; yellow as when; brown as then; blue as high; green as low; grey as now; white as forever.

> Among purists, and you know how many purists there are, brown was having some difficulty. Some of the purists wanted brown to be more (*deep drum sound*) and others wanted it more (*medium drum sound*). Still others wanted it more (*light drum sound*). A lesser color might have fallen apart, but brown met the problem by becoming more and more subtle. Brown has become about as subtle as subtle can get. That's why today you hear people saying, "My, that's a subtle brown. . . ."

Another effective, but often overlooked, way to use radio is to buy a large block of minutes on a station which has a loyal following, and to use those minutes as the station does, for localized service as well as sell. For example, a number of Buick dealers in Chicago pooled their resources and sponsored the all-night "East of Midnight" program. It gave them thirty hours of broadcasting each week, about an hour for each of the dealers. Instead of limiting their announcements to the usual "schlock" car buys, they personalized their messages, allowing Don Phillips, the emcee, to talk in the usual confidential, intimate tone appropriate to night programs. He gave public service tips on nighttime driving, news about local events, and details about the dealers themselves—how many children they had, facts about their community activities, hobbies, etc. This was the next best thing to in-person conversations. The non-ady atmosphere of the commercials helped those dealers to win first place among Buick's national dealers, and a thirteen-week trial sponsorship resulted in year-round use of nighttime radio.

Another unique use of radio, in a totally different direction, was the scheduling of hundreds of radio station time-breaks for Johnson & Johnson Baby Powder.

The "announcers" were very young children, who spoke in their haltingly natural manner. While the scripts were written and read first to the children in the studio, the moppets, who were too young to read scripts, were encouraged to extemporize. Here is the kind of fresh fillip people heard saturating the airways:

> LITTLE BOY: Johnson's Baby Powder is what you put on babies when you change their diapers. If your baby doesn't wear diapers anymore, then get a new baby. It's 12 o'clock.

> LITTLE GIRL: If anybody in your family wears diapers, you better get lots of Johnson's Baby Powder. You better get lots of diapers too. It's 11 o'clock.

> LITTLE BOY: My baby brother likes lots of Johnson's Baby Powder on him. Mother says he tells her so. I never heard him say anything. It's four o'clock.

A somewhat similar idea was created by Chuck Blore Associates, for Laura Scudder Potato Chips and their agency, Doyle Dane Bernbach. The challenge was to make "The Noisiest Potato Chips in the World" come alive on radio as it had on TV. Blore assembled a group of nonprofessional children in a studio, fed them lots of copy (and potato chips) and a series of amusing situations. A half-dozen little gems were culled from hours of tape recording. The humor and naturalness of the kids (in contrast with the usual slick, rehearsed commercials) was worth all the effort of extemporizing and editing. The agency successfully used those radio spots to supplement their TV campaign in areas where they could not get enough TV saturation.

There are too few commercial innovations on the new, segmented radio. First, because we too frequently create radio commercials with traditional methods. Sometimes we are professional enough to follow the old rules—a provocative opening, to seize the attention; avoidance of hard-to-hear sibilants and nonaural words; concentration on as few copy points as possible; the repetition fore, aft, and in the middle of our selling proposition. Our first solution, usually, is to whip out a jingle. But too often we are distracted from the essence of our medium. We do not take full ad-

vantage of the specialized nature of the different radio stations and programming, to tailor-make our commercials to fit the audiences at specific
times. Nor do we steep ourselves in the sounds of our subject. We are not
totally aware of sound.

Sounds surround us every instant of the day—sounds from which we
can draw inspiration by free association. Try pausing right now, from your
reading, for only sixty seconds, and listen, really listen. Do you hear the
dripping of a faucet, the creaking of a chair, a footstep, voices far off,
traffic, and the sounds under and beyond all those? In order to hear them,
you have to concentrate, don't you? You have to postpone, for that minute,
the absorption of your other senses and become all ears. Then your mind's
eye begins to translate. The sound of the faucet becomes a picture of
gushing water, the creaking chair and footstep denote someone getting
up and walking toward you. Who is it? Your mind invents a picture before
you actually see the person. And those voices far off, the traffic, all the
other sounds—you can go on imagining for hours, if you wish.

This is the big power of radio over the other media. It can encourage
people to use their imagination to the greatest extent. It can *involve* its
audience as no other medium can (except, perhaps, for posters). Here is
how one radio expert, Dallas Williams, expressed the difference:

> The greatest producer in the world would reach his limits of sheer im-
> agination and budget without even beginning to construct the setting that
> the merest child can build up here (in his mind) in an instant.
>
> Do you think that you will ever in all your life hold in your hands a
> picture that will match the word picture that Don Quinn gave of Fibber
> McGee's closet? Does anyone have an 8 by 10 glossy of Jack Benny's vault
> —or a film strip that follows the twists and the turns of Allen's Alley? I've
> seen pictures of Normandy Beach on D Day, but never one that got to me
> quite like radio announcer George Hicks did when he talked about it that
> morning. And the shots of the Hindenburg disaster were a fabulous pic-
> ture. But the thing that really tears your insides out is to hear that an-
> nouncer break up and cry like a baby. . . .
>
> But the classic example is Orson Welles and "The Men from Mars."
> About 11 minutes into that historic broadcast and a sizeable chunk of this
> country had gone plumb out of its nut. Out in the sticks a lot of people actu-
> ally took to the hills. In the more sophisticated big cities there were guys
> who got up on the roof and hollered down to the crowds in the street that
> they could see the monsters, moving around amidst the factory barges on
> the Jersey shore. They believed it—they actually believed it!
>
> But even if it had never happened, can you conceive of anyone produc-
> ing that same effect today, with TV? The viewer simply would not believe
> you. He would not believe you because, instead of letting his imagination
> run away with him, you're trying to give it all to him in a picture and
> you're limited by your budget and your set design and the raw credibility

of your visual evidence. You might entertain him but you'd never convince him.

The fact is that radio's greatest competitive weakness can be turned into its major strength. In TV, as we have pointed out, we are finding that we can win the involvement of the viewer by what we leave out. Nonverbal TV commercials encourage the viewer to fill in the words. Use of the montage—uncompleted scenes, juxtaposed—encourage him to elaborate on the story. Radio, with its whole-hearted concentration on its one sense of sound, already has the involvement built in. What we must do, as writers, is to find the sounds which will most vividly stimulate the listener's imagination.

14

THE IMMEDIATE-ACTION MEDIUM

The Anatomy of Newspapers

It is Sunday, June 7, 1964, and the *New York Times* has been delivered to almost a million and a half homes. The front page features stories on the hot news: Eisenhower acts to keep Scranton in the Republican race against Goldwater for the nomination for President. The Senate is about to vote on the attempt to invoke cloture of the debate on Civil Rights. There is a story about the commemoration of D Day, twenty years before. And one about the Secretary-General of the United Nations planning to confer with Russia's Khrushchev about seating Red China.

In this Sunday edition of the *Times*, hundreds of pages of type, most of it small, tell the major events of the day—sections on drama, screen, music, gardens, finance, sports, books, real estate, travel, and employment assail the reader with millions of words of news. The board of education has asked Mayor Wagner to approve a request for $5 million to implement its experimental plan for better education in slum areas. The three Roman Catholic dioceses in the metropolitan area are planning to blanket their vast school systems with closed-circuit educational television. Leigh Brenizer, a 1963 debutante who works in the society department of the *Boston Herald*, is to be married to William Calvin Chestnut Barnes, a student at Harvard Law School. At the Mark Hellinger Theater, Carol Burnett "breaks them up," in "Fade Out—Fade In," as she bares her teeth and sings "Call Me Savage." The public stock offer in Comsat, the Communications Satellite Corporation, has been a $200 million sellout. And the Dodgers have vanquished the Mets, with a 14-hit attack.

Meanwhile, amid the news of life and death, marriage and birth, vanity and violence, the advertisers hawk their wares. It is two Sundays before Father's Day, and the first section is chock full of gifts for dad. Van Cleef & Arpels offers three styles of cuff links, in onyx and gold, for $175. Mark Cross "Goes to Blazers in Terry Cloth." Stern's Store for Men features line-and-wash drawings with clothing "For Father, The Man of The Hour": knit shirts of Puritan Ban-Lon, robes of wash-wear Grand Vino, pajamas made of cool nylon tricot, and dress shirts of Dura-Wite Kodal. Cheek-to-cheek are ads for household goods and women's wear: Rare quality mink at the Tailored Woman, for $927. A "Smart Shift Dress" at Abraham & Strauss, for $5.00. Gimbels offers *double* value in a Hollywood bed" for only $59.

In all, that first section has 96 pages, 225 news stories, 250 display advertisements. There are hundreds of more news stories and features in the other sections, and, counting the classified ads for jobs and homes and cars, there are thousands of advertisements. All in this one Sunday issue of the *Times.*

Staggering? But this is the Sunday issue, you say, of the largest circulation newspaper. A smaller, weekday paper will not print so much. True, but there is still plenty to read in an ordinary daily and the successful ones are also loaded with ads. Take the *San Francisco Chronicle* of a month later—Wednesday, July 1, 1964. This issue has 64 pages, with more than a hundred display ads and many hundreds of classified ads. Tuesday, the day before, the *Chronicle* had 50 pages, Thursday 58 and Friday, July 3, it had 46. The stores were anticipating the Fourth of July holiday on Saturday, so Wednesday got the bulk of the advertising.

Let's see what the *Chronicle* was saying. The front page told about a big setback for Scranton in Illinois. Henry Cabot Lodge talked politics with President Eisenhower and gave a hint of big news. Teachers were told not to join unions. And a millionaire was murdered in his locked room. In the inside pages, there were stories about the Civil Rights Bill clearing its next-to-last hurdle, with anticipation of the President's signature in time for Independence Day. A local sculptor's group of nude statues was described as too candid for exhibition in the city's two top museums. And the Giants shut out the Mets, 5–0.

The ads in the *Chronicle* that week were declaring sales in honor of the Fourth and the '64 summer. Ransohoff's had an annual storewide clearance. I. Magnin's had a semiannual storewide clearance. Roos/Atkins announced that they were lighting a firecracker to prices. Macy's featured a "White Flower One Day Sale," with "Prices so low we can offer them

Thursday only." Sears ran eight pages for their holiday vacation sale. Gala Food stores said "Celebrate the 4th with BANG-UP BUYS." Between the food and department store ads, Seagram's ran a 1,000-line ad, saying "The Great Entertainer is the fifth for the 4th."

A review of those two papers—the Sunday *New York Times* and a weekday issue of the *San Francisco Chronicle*—gives you an instant analysis of the daily newspaper everywhere. It is the *now* medium. It is the medium that changes daily and is influenced hour by hour, minute by minute. On June 7 Eisenhower is reported to be urging Scranton to stay in the race. On July 1 it is reported that he may declare for Scranton against Goldwater. Two weeks later at the convention, the news has changed completely and the daily paper reports Ike's neutrality. On June 7, the Senate votes for cloture. On July 1 the paper reports an imminent Civil Rights Bill. Two days later it is passed. The newspapers report the stories the moment they break.

The daily paper is the people's diary and nowhere is the influence of context, on which we commented in Chap. 5, so pronounced. On June 7, the context of Father's Day influences the nature of the advertising. The stores plot their advertising for the July 1 issue to coincide with the context of an upcoming Fourth. Summer holidays, the state of the weather, the geography in which the paper appears, all affect the amount and nature of the advertising. New products are most compatible with the context of the newspaper. Those miracle fibers, with their odd-sounding names, in the Stern's ad for father, would have been out of context yesterday, and they may be obsolete tomorrow. The newspaper advertiser, like the paper's reporter, is constantly rushing into print with product news. The Bureau of Advertising, service organization for newspapers, issues guides to retailers about seasonal markets. When a store advertises skis or swimsuits the daily newspaper can reach the right audience in the right context of the season. "Back to school" sales, Christmas sales, sales of Easter bonnets all appear in the daily paper at the precise moment.

So to cultivate that state of mind the copywriter needs to write for a medium, we start at the heart of the matter: the newspaper is the now medium, and we, just like the newspaper's own legmen, are daily reporters.

How does the nature of the newspaper affect our audience, the newspaper reader? Nowhere does he read more deliberately. The paper is filled with facts—who got killed and who got married, what is happening in politics, what is playing at the movies—the who, what, why, when, and where of living. These are, as we cited in Chap. 4, the kinds of operational, explicit reports that make a connection. People are *naturally* interested when they read a newspaper. The function of a newspaper is to inform, completely and objectively. It is not, basically, a medium for entertainment. Newspaper readers want to *know*—they want to know what is happening to themselves and their neighbors. They are greedy for gossip.

This makes the daily newspaper not only nationally aware but intensely local. (Readership studies have shown that the number one interest of the female reader is the local news.) It makes the newspaper also, you might say, a community-owned property, for it reflects its time and place. And the newspaper not only reflects, it influences. The militant newspaper can bring about changes, or prevent them, probably more than any other communication medium. "Nothing moves Chicago like the *Tribune*" boasts that paper, and it tells how it issues career folders for youngsters, runs golf and ski schools, floods the city with flags. Meanwhile, brags the *Chicago American*, teenage interest in Shakespeare and fear of drug addiction have soared, thanks to that paper's crusading features.

Features, by the way, are the lifeblood of the circulation figures. They are why, claims the *Philadelphia Daily News*, "we are the fastest growing daily in the country." "News sells the paper," says the *News*, "but features keep the reader." What are the popular features? The same kind of *now* material. Columnists commenting on the news. Gossipers further spreading the gossip. Food editors talking up tomorrow's dinner. Critics guiding us to the play we will see tonight.

The wonder of the daily newspaper is that millions of readers—many of them mediocre and reluctant students at school—voluntarily devour it. Seventy-one percent of all newspaper readers, we are told, go through their daily paper thoroughly, page by page. We have become skillful at scanning the papers with swift-reading eyes which, exposed to other literature, might take hours longer to absorb half as much. The newspaper is probably our most powerful informational medium, because we read it by choice and we read it, not for escape, but for facts.

So this, boiling it all down, is the anatomy of the newspaper: It is the people's encyclopedia, their daily fact book, a medium of communication which is functional, one which the reader habitually uses to keep in touch with the real world.

Advantages and Disadvantages of Newspapers for the Advertiser

Immediacy, of course, is the biggest advantage of advertising in the newspaper. The food and department stores can advertise reduced prices on merchandise today and have it all sold tomorrow. We said, in Chap. 1, that people do not voluntarily seek out advertising and read it; but here, in the newspaper, is the one exception to that rule. Display advertising, after general news, is the second highest read part of the newspaper for women, third highest for men. On Thursday or Friday, the housewife thumbs through the paper to find the food store specials for her weekend shopping. She tears out the ads and uses them to make her shopping list.

The pulling power of the classified ad needs little elaboration. The reader who wants an apartment, a job, or a used car, tears out the classified section, ticks off his requirements, and answers the ads. It is important that the facts listed in those ads be precise and complete enough to be functional. Take, for example, a classified ad for the sale of a home. To the degree that the ad tells the particular reader exactly what he wants to know—the number of rooms, the selling price, the kind of heat and plumbing, the location, the aesthetics—to that degree is he narrowed down as an immediate prospect who may take action.

Immediacy makes the newspaper by far the favorite medium for the retail store. This is why, at this writing, more than four times the volume of local advertising is placed in newspapers than in all the other major media combined. Another advantage of advertising in newspapers is the attitude of the reader. He feels closer to the newspaper than to other media. After all, this is *his* newspaper. It is not like an impersonal TV network. He often knows where its office is, sometimes goes there, often calls the newspaper for information. If he gets het up enough, he writes a letter to the editor.

That being the case, the reader may believe the advertising in his newspaper more than in other media; and he may act on it so fast and frequently that he can quickly verify its truthfulness. (E.g., a supermarket which advertises frozen foods at a bargain, or a department store which features a loss leader, had better have the merchandise at those prices, *or else.*) The mood of the reader, relative to the advertising, may be more decisive than with other media. He has no time "to fool around." If he is in the market for a specific item, and he sees it in *his* personal newspaper at the moment he wants it, he is likely to take action that very day.

Other advantages of newspapers for advertisers include, of course, their local character and their flexibility. Hundreds of newspapers offer advertisers specific markets and accurate information about them. "What's different about San Diego?" asks the *San Diego Union,* and explains that there are no weather problems there—an important fact for certain types of advertisers. A group of New England newspapers offers intermedia comparative studies about that area, while the *Milwaukee Journal* offers its "41st Annual Consumer Analysis" of who's buying what, by product category. Advertisers can use newspapers singly, or in combination. For example, 25 percent of the nation's population buys 60 percent of the antifreeze car products; the media buyer can select only the papers in the cold belt to sell them.

Newspapers cover almost 90 percent of the population. Their space rates vary by circulation and can be twice as high for national as for local advertisers. But they can reach many people, efficiently, at one of the lowest costs per thousand. *Advertising Age,* giving an example of cost, showed how a fifty-line two-column ad in every daily in the nation would wind up costing only 1/20¢ per reading family.

All of the advantages of newspapers—immediacy, flexibility, high interest to the reader, relatively low cost to the advertiser—are considerations for the copywriter. But we should also be aware of the newspapers' disadvantages if we want to write effectively for them.

One disadvantage, at this writing, is that newspapers, compared with magazines, have relatively poor quality of ad reproduction. Uncoated newsprint does not allow for the fine screens and sparkling pictures we see in magazines. Ink spreads out and fills in the porous paper. Right now, full-color preprints on coated stock considerably raise the rates. Of course, as with all media, technological advances will solve these problems, but for now we do well to design ads that can look great even if they are blurred.

Newspapers do not have sound and motion, and are therefore less effective than TV as a demonstration medium.

Another current disadvantage—which, through the pressures of media competition, is bound to be alleviated—is the rate structure, by which national advertisers are charged more for their ads than are local advertisers. The reasons are deep rooted in the history of the medium, and some papers are pioneering a single rate. Meanwhile, the double standard makes for a vast network of "co-op advertising," whereby the national advertiser shares the cost of local advertising in order to have his products featured in newspapers by local merchants. Co-op advertising can be a bane as well as a blessing, for it can have the stereotyped quality of anything which is mass-manufactured. It may also be used more as a bargaining tool for local dealers than as a deliberately pinpointed message to the consumer audience.

Finally, the very immediacy which makes newspapers so forceful can also be a disadvantage. For the now medium has a short life. And you have to advertise frequently if you want to keep reaching the newspaper reader.

But for all these disadvantages, the newspaper has a vigor and muscle all its own. And there are many ways that a copywriter can accentuate the positives and turn the negatives to his profit. In no other medium have we such obvious lessons and inspirations for "how to write copy that communicates."

Special Characteristics of Newspaper Copy

The best way to learn how to write newspaper ads that communicate is to study the newspaper columns themselves. We can begin with the classified ads, for they are the smallest units. People who use the classified regularly—such as the real estate and used-car businesses—learn how to compress the strongest and fastest appeals into a brief text. These appeals are tightly disciplined by all the contexts of time, place, and audience. In San Francisco, for example, the word "view" has such a powerful pull that prospects know that when it is omitted, there is no view. "No Cash, $19.90 Per Month" is the headline for a used-car ad, and with the number and variety of used cars offered, that cost consideration can be the major factor.

Notice how many facts are packed into a seven-line "business opportunity" ad: "Estate compels sale of resort hotel at half price, 65 rms., 5 bldgs., 17 acres, falls, stream, pool. Also good for apts., factory or partnership on Rt. 52. Sull Co., N.Y. $25,000 terms; 15 unit Bung Col optional, 201 HE 4-8333 Jersey City or Jeffersonville 65 R-1—NY."

An interesting characteristic of the classified ads is how strongly they encourage reader participation. The reader pictures "17 acres, falls, stream, pool." He imagines himself the Boniface of a magnificent resort hotel, in a sylvan retreat. Wealth flows into his coffers, as he rents out his "15 Unit Bung Col" (even the abbreviations, in classified ads, require involvement). And that $25,000, with terms, is the clincher. Without that price, the ad would be worthless. Of course, it would be worthless, too, without the address and telephone number of the advertiser, and a great deal weaker without the word "terms."

All of this factual copy impresses us with the pragmatic atmosphere of a daily newspaper. In most newspaper ads, we cannot err by being too specific. The trick, in the larger display ads, is to find the way to arrange our elements so that too many facts will not discourage reading. But, for the retailer, facts, plenty of them, are still the stock-in-trade. One retail ad director—Grant Stone, formerly of the *Cleveland Press*—offered a "Checklist for Copywriters," to help writers on newspaper retail desks and in advertising departments of stores. The checklist covers scores of product categories. A typical list is this one for "Household Textiles, Sheets, Linen, Towels" (note how doggedly thorough it is):

- *Brand name:* Well-known trademark or descriptive trade name.
- *Materials:* Type of weave, stitching, finish, thickness, texture grade, blend.
- *Colors:* Patterns, designs, motif-matching and/or decorative possibilities.
- Initials or other type of identification available.
- *Sizes:* Lengths, widths, shapes, special fitting characteristics, custom-sized.
- Wearing qualities, facility of use. Special backing or lining?
- Complementary possibilities (other pieces or accessories).
- *Features:* Preshrunk, Sanforized, wrinkle-resistant, specially absorbent, ruffles, fringes.
- Number of pieces to the set as priced.

- *Cleanability:* Washable, drip-dry, dry clean? Color-fast? Shrink-resistant?
- *Prices:* Each, per pair, per set; prices for complementary pieces.
- Payment plan.
- Name and location of store or department. At branches, too?
- Hours store is open.
- Phone number.
- Phone and mail orders accepted?

This insistence on thoroughness is echoed by the Bureau of Advertising's booklet on "How to Check Your Ads for More Sell." Their guide to writing newspaper retail ads includes these rules:

1. Choose an Item that is *Wanted*
2. Pick an Item that is *Timely*
3. Select an Item that is *Stocked in Depth*
4. Advertise an Item that is *Newsworthy*
5. Feature Items that are *Typical* of your Store
6. Select Items which are your *Best Values*
7. Coordinate *Price Lines*
8. Don't go overboard on *Clearance Items*

Realizing the immediacy of the medium, the booklet goes on to spell out the how-to's that make for fast understanding:

1. Make Your Ads *Easily Recognizable*
2. Use a *Simple Layout*
3. Use *Dominant Illustrations*
4. Get the *Main Benefits* to the Reader in a *Prominent Headline*
5. Make Copy *Complete*
6. State *Price or Range of Prices*
7. Specify if *Branded Merchandise*
8. Include *Related Items*
9. Ask for the *Order Now*

All such guides, while they may seem obvious or picayune are peculiarly pertinent to newspaper ads, because these ads call for immediate action. Suppose, for example, that a store advertises a dress and omits the fact that it comes in sizes 8 to 12 only. A woman who wears a size 14 goes all the way to the store, only to be disappointed. One minor omission may have alienated that customer for good.

"All I want are the facts, Ma'am." The newspaper attitude is quite hardboiled, as, for that matter, are most newspaper reporters. Therefore, it is good practice for us copywriters to be hardboiled first, then daring and original afterwards.

We spoke about taking lessons from the classified ads. The news, features, and photographs also have inspiration for the copywriter. An ad for Land O' Lakes butter, using a cartoon-and-caption technique was remembered thirty-one times more than a conventional display ad. Ads featuring real news photos far outpulled those with photos of posed models. Food ads resembling the paper's own food service features do exceptionally well.

Continuity panel ads which have an amusing plot and are still germane to the product story, can get tremendous attention. Obviously, as the Bureau of Advertising stresses, "The mere art form of a humor panel, without the essential ingredient of humor, fails to produce high reading."

Comic-strip ads vary widely in overall reader performance. Above-average ones all convey the idea of a lot of activity.

One does not have to make rules, though, for writing these ads. We have only to study the comics themselves to see what manner of story and style succeeds.

The now medium, with its short life and flexibility, points up the importance of timeliness—the kind mentioned in Chap. 5, when White Owl and Kaiser Steel took advantage of current issues. The smart merchandiser constantly anticipates the newsbreaks of tomorrow and finds ways to tie in with them. The smartest newspaper advertiser is the one who has his hand on the pulse of local activities.

What is the best-read part of the newspaper? The news, of course. And so here is the ideal medium for introducing new products, for telling genuine news. Bond Clothes, then the largest chain selling suits for men, broke the big news of "The Two Pants Suit." Wanamaker's was the first to offer "Double Your Money Back" if you were not satisfied. Reynolds Aluminum broke their news story of the Aluminum Foil that produced "1,001 Kitchen Miracles." They used newspaper ads to sell dealers on stocking the foil. They moved from market to market, introducing the product in newspapers, until, in nine months, they had 60 to 80 percent distribution in sixteen major markets. Within twenty-four months, this unique product was a household staple with most American families.

Use of small-space ads is probably more effective in newspapers than in any other medium. That is, if they *are* small-space ads and not large ads, rescaled. A great small-space ad, with plenty of white space, with real "stopper" headlines and art, one that concentrates on one single, simple idea, can often dominate a whole newspaper page. You can add to this the cumulative power many advertisers achieve by constant repetition of a small-space campaign, as well as by a number of small-space ads throughout the sections of one issue of a newspaper. "With a small-space campaign," says the Bureau of Advertising, "you get Broad Coverage—because if one ad doesn't catch the reader's eye, maybe the next will. And the high frequency of insertions gives you Repeated Impact."

An example of a small-space success was the introduction of Smirnoff Vodka to the Los Angeles market in 1950. Hardly anyone drank Vodka then. Smirnoff came up with one compelling reason to drink it—"it leaves you breathless!" They then ran hundreds of small ads in newspapers, introducing numerous ways to mix the drink. Often five and six ads were scattered in the same edition of selected newspapers, several days during a week.

The result: Within six years, this advertiser helped create a $250 billion vodka market, virtually a new industry within the liquor field, and, starting with a limited budget, built overwhelming consumer preference for Smirnoff within this market.

Another example of frequent small-space ads was the campaign by Chicken of the Sea tuna. Each ad featured a "Tuna Tip" with a simple service idea for housewives. On one occasion, four ads, featuring Tuna Tips 11, 14, 17, and 19 ran in the same issue on general news, food, and feature pages. A readership check showed that the individual ads were seen by from 14 to 34 percent of the women who read the paper. But taking the series as a whole, 52 percent of the women remembered seeing one ad or more.

Plenty of facts, techniques borrowed from the newspaper sections, timeliness, news about products, repeated use of small space: these are characteristics especially right for newspaper ads. Another specialty of the medium is the art of selectivity.

Next to direct mail, the daily newspaper is probably the most convenient and inexpensive way to select your audience. We are all familiar with the small-space ads which flag their readers with selective headlines, like "Sufferers from Gout" and "Now, Relief from Psoriasis." An ad by one George Kaplin, in the *New York Times,* was about the ultimate in selectivity. It offered a fur coat for $18,750—plus a fashion stylist, a master fitter, and a bonded messenger to fly anywhere in the United States with a selection of skins from which the coat would be made.

At this writing, there has been an upsurge in the use of new-product introductory incentives in newspapers. Everywhere she looks, the housewife is offered such blandishments as: "We'll pay you 50¢ to try both—or 25¢ to try either one—McCormick Meat Loaf Seasoning, McCormick Tuna Casserole Sauce Mix" . . . "For Dogs? Yes, Burgers 'n Gravy . . . get 2 cans Free!" . . . "Save 15¢ when you try any 2 of these New Salad Bowl Dressing Mixes from Kraft." A housewife can hardly resist such generosity. When *every* advertiser, on every page, shouts his inducements, however, they may all be drowned in the din. So far, this does not seem to be happening and housewives are happily clipping coupons and reaping the rewards.

Innovations to Increase the Power of Newspaper Advertising

Just as you can be effective with ads which cleverly follow the newspaper's editorial techniques, by the same token ads which are completely in *contrast* with the newspaper can increase noting and reading.

This is not a contradiction. In the first place, we have already said there are no rules for advertising, and one product's editorial-type medicine can be another's poison. In the second place, creativity in newspapers is the same as in any other medium—the art, as we mentioned in Chap. 7, of "making the strange familiar and the familiar strange." People are used to seeing "ady ads." When they see an ad in the newspaper which has a familiar news-type photo, it is an original device. By the same token, when they see an ad in a newspaper full of coarse newsprint which is in sparkling full-color on coated stock, this too can stand out by reason of its strangeness in a familiar setting.

Of course, we must not be original just for the *sake* of originality, but always to pursue the best ends of our subject. Full-color preprints for newspapers (Hi-Fi and Spectacolor ads) are more expensive than ROP (run-of-paper) color and still costlier than black-and-white ads. There has to be good justification for spending the extra money. One justification, naturally, is that the advertising strategy calls for newspapers and the communication cries for color. Full-color preprinted inserts, for example, are used to demonstrate the appeal of colorful foods—to make the reader's mouth water for them. The first Hi-Fi ad ever run in newspapers was for Jell-O pudding, and its appearance—for such an appetizing subject—had enormous impact.

When Hi-Fi was developed, it required the invention of a new kind of layout. Because such printed messages tended to "crawl"—i.e., to vary in register—it was necessary to write and design ads which repeated themselves, like the patterns of wallpaper, and could be cut off at any point and still look and read right.

Later the newspapers developed Spectacolor which made possible full-color inserts with conventional, nonwallpaper layouts.

There are now hundreds of examples of successful uses of full-color preprints, but in every case they were successful because they had a sound *reason* for being. RCA's Jack M. Williams described his company's early use of Hi-Fi to introduce color TV sets as "the most successful promotion we have ever had." Their dealers and distributors were so enthusiastic about the idea that they, in turn, ran almost 4.5 million lines, using their own cooperative advertising funds to tie in with "RCA Victor Week."

During that promotion period RCA's share of the home entertainment market increased 26 percent and their total dollar sales to distributors were up 49.9 percent—all because they were the first big TV set company to use Hi-Fi and because they used it well. But what better *logic* to run such a campaign than to illustrate *color* TV.

The same logic applied to Wunda Weve carpets, a product which obviously requires color for demonstration. An additional tactic for its use was to get cooperative funds from the manufacturer of Wunda Weve's fibers (Chemstrand) and from the many local dealers who could "look big" by contributing to the campaign.

Of course, Hi-Fi and Spectacolor diminish in power as they appear in newspapers more often. When everybody uses full color in newspapers, the strange becomes too familiar and we have to dream up another totally out-of-context idea. Such an idea, for example, was the use of Day-Glo inks, which managed to outshout Hi-Fi. Another was the development, by the *Peoria Sun-Times,* of the newspaper gatefold.

A Word of Warning

We have spoken, in this chapter, about the value of being explicit, of giving complete information, of being selective of our audience, of anticipating the news breaks, of using small space. We have talked about some few innovations in newspaper advertising. And all of these avenues are bound to work somewhat, because of the innate power of the medium.

But, let us face it, newspapers have not been an exciting medium for copywriters.

The reason was frankly explained by Norman H. McMillan, an executive of N. W. Ayer & Son, in a speech to the Northwest Daily Press Association. Newspapers, he said, have an introverted tradition. He defined the ailment "as a tendency to be guided by the past, a state of mind anchored to what has been."

A case in point, said Mr. McMillan, is the annoying newspaper practice of charging national advertisers higher rates than local advertisers.

He then summed up the emotional climate of newspapers, as compared with other media, with these words: "If we look at broadcast media as the sexy divorcee who moves in next door, and magazines as the wealthy young society dame, newspapers would have to be likened to your mother-in-law sitting at the breakfast table in an old brown bathrobe, with her hair in curlers."

One of the main reasons for this rather blowzy image is the fact that newspaper advertising has been subservient to what we might term "the retail mentality." The retail mentality can contribute much to better copywriting in other media. It calls for facts more than fancy. It is more tactical than it is strategic. The merchant down the street lowers his prices and the retailer up the street reacts immediately with a special.

In the day-by-day battle for sales, the hard facts of price and inventory, traffic and location, all dictate the content of the ads.

But the important innovations in newspaper advertising will only come through a healthy awareness of the pitfalls in the retail mentality. Some retail-minded men may claim that they understand the need for "consumer benefit," dominant illustrations, simplicity, white space, etc., but they will usually insist, for tactical reasons, on cramming each ad with too many major elements, so that no one idea stands out. When the copywriter protests, they will call him impractical and fuzzy-minded. "You can't quarrel with success," they tell him. Retail ads work. Sure, they may look "schlock." But they pull in the business.

The fact that "schlock" newspaper ads work does not prove that fresh, original ads might not work better. As newspapers and magazines attempt to overcome their disadvantages, they are borrowing each other's best copy methods. Magazines, with more and more regional editions, faster closings, increased emphasis on nonfiction features and news, are approaching newspapers. The more localized they become, the more possible it will be for the ads to feature local dealer names, prices, and all the explicit details so typical of the newspaper ad.

On the other hand, newspapers, with their coated preprints, gatefolds, supplements, and entertainment features, are coming closer to being like magazines. The trend setters in newspaper advertising, sensing the change long ago, broke through with "image-building" retail ads—like those by the New York department store, Ohrbach's.

The double-rate structure of newspapers has tended to inhibit breakthroughs more than they have been discouraged in other media. Most merchants, we find, fancy themselves to be copywriters. Local-rate ads are prepared or influenced by a great variety of these experts. The worst villain in the plot to disparage fresh thinking is the system of co-op advertising, for it tends to encourage ads by committee, influenced by local stores, dealers, distributors, district and division managers, all translating their needs and prejudices to the copywriter, often through the extra strainer of a complex sales department.

It is necessary to understand the retail mentality and to take advantage of all it has to teach. But the innovator, in newspapers, will be the copywriter who—like Picasso, moving from objective to nonobjective painting —becomes thoroughly expert in the rules in order to break them.

15

THE STRAIGHT-LINE MEDIUM

The Aim and the Aimer

A New Jersey retailer—Gordon's Youth & Prep Shops—spent $100 on a direct-mail flier announcing a private sale for the regular customers on their mailing list. It was called the "Annual Old-Fashioned Sale" and the mailer pulled more customers in three hours than the store had seen on any day for the previous five years.

An airline in Europe—Air France—made a series of three mailings to a carefully selected list—the *beatispossedentes* ("blessed ones") who happened to be millionaires. The purpose: to sell round-the-world tours. The mailing pulled two sales and was considered successful.

The Slant/Fin Radiator Corporation selected 90 wholesaler firms to handle their heating equipment. This would be a tough sale, for wholesalers do not switch lines lightly. Slant/Fin spent $7,500 on five mailings on five consecutive days—all building up to a personal telephone call from the Slant/Fin sales manager to each prospect. The mailings were "spectaculars"—i.e., three-dimensional objects that had some value and were tied with the mailer's message. They included a 10-lb bag of peanuts, a football with an imprint, and a fancy pen-and-calendar set. When the prospect picked up the pen, a memo from the sales manager automatically popped out making an appointment for his phone call. This 3-D mailing, with its concentrated buildup, resulted in thirty-six converts out of ninety

—a 40 percent response "representing an annual sales volume of well over a million dollars."

Consider the case of Purolator Oil Filters. They had a highly successful commercial on TV—the one known as "the world's dirtiest commercial," in which a beautiful girl wriggles under a car in lover's lane to remove a sludge-filled oil filter. Purolator used direct mail to merchandise the commercial to some 60,000 service station operators. Their mailings included a sales-incentive program, with prizes for the operators' wives. At the end of three months, sales were up 64 percent in areas covered by the mailings, in contrast to only 18 percent in those areas which had no direct-mail coverage.

The point of these widely dissimilar examples is to show that the aimer of every kind of mailing has unique problems. And it is to emphasize, as well, that his aims are specific and the results are traceable and concrete.

The shortest distance between two points is a straight line; and of all the media—except for word of mouth—direct mail is potentially the straightest line to your target. We say "potentially" because plenty of dollars are wasted on the wrong message or the wrong mailing list.

But practiced mailers are sensible men. In the majority of the cases, direct mail is intended to get "direct response," and that calls for a steady bead on the target. The mailing list for that New Jersey retailer was a gold mine, because every name was a qualified, previous customer. Obviously, millionaires would be prime prospects for the time and cost of that world tour; and the sale of just two tickets would more than justify the expense of the mailing. Slant/Fin had such a small, personalized list to influence that they could well afford to zero in on their prospects with their five-day blitz. Purolator's aim was to magnify the power of their TV campaign. All of those users had a straight-line purpose for using direct mail. And it paid off, in measurable ways.

The use of direct mail—though it has the highest cost per thousand of any of the large media—is growing tremendously because it *is* paying off. Direct mail is a big medium—more than $2 billion worth—second only to newspaper advertising.

Why is it so popular if the cost is so high? Because, as every devout direct mailer will tell you (and this is Henry Hoke, one of the most devout, speaking), "There would not be so much petty competitive nonsense written or spoken against direct mail if media salesmen recognized the differences between cost per shot and cost per hit." In mail-order direct mail, for example, there is absolutely nothing vague about success or failure. You know exactly how much you spend on postage, envelopes, enclosures, and your mailing list. You know how many replies you get and what their worth is. Those direct mailers have break-even formulas like the following:

$$\text{Percent of return} = \frac{\text{number of orders or inquiries received multiplied by 100}}{\text{total number of pieces mailed}}$$

$$\text{Cost per order} \quad = \frac{\text{cost of mailings}}{\text{number of orders received}}$$

As you can see, you could get a very high percentage of returns and still have so high a cost of order that you could go out of business. For example, *Advertising Age* quoted a hypothetical case given by direct-mail expert Robert Stone, of a desk stamp-dispenser which cost $1.50 to manufacture. Shipping and billing cost was 33¢ (i.e., total cost $1.83 per unit). The selling price arrived at was $4.95 and a mailing piece was developed which cost $60 per thousand to mail. The seller sent out a test mailing of 5,000 pieces, and received 62 orders. Thus, using the formula above,

$$\text{Cost per order} = \frac{\text{cost of mailings}}{\text{number of orders}} = \frac{\$300}{62}$$

—the cost per order was $4.84. That was much too high. "It costs us $4.84 to get an order," the article continued. "The customer pays us $4.95. And it costs us $1.83 to deliver the item. On that basis, we lost $1.72 on each order."

The remedy, in that case, would either have been to develop a mailing piece that would pull a higher percentage of returns or to find a cheaper way of producing the product. The beauty of the method was that the direct mailer knew exactly where he stood. He could test his advertising in a small way before going all out with a big campaign.

From this way of thinking, we can see that the cost of direct mail cannot be compared with the cost of other media simply on a per-thousand basis. When we are after a direct response, the "coming-out cost" is more important than the "cost mailed."

Obviously, with that point of view, there is no rule for the percentage of responses a mailing should bring you. Bell & Howell, mail-ordering a high-ticket item like a home movie outfit, is often satisfied with 0.4% response, while a garden seed company in England boasts an average of 90 percent response. Robert W. Williams, a banker, quoted in *The Reporter of Direct Mail*, said "I know a banker who sent 50 letters to the new school teachers coming into his town, and got 49 new checking accounts in a couple of weeks!" "On the other hand," say direct-mail experts Yeck and Maguire, "if a dealer in large-sized yachts sent out 10,000 letters, got one return, and sold one yacht, his mailing would be a huge success . . . on a return percentage of 1/100 of 1 percent."

Of course, not all direct mail is designed to get a return order. Much of it is to win goodwill and to locate prospects for other kinds of selling.

(It should not be necessary, at this late date, to distinguish between "mail order" and "direct mail" . . . but just in case there is any confusion, "mail order" has to do with "ordering by mail," while "direct mail" is the broadest possible term for all kinds of advertising which use the medium of the postal system. You can advertise your mail-order wares in broadcast and publication media, as well as by direct mail.)

One of the most important purposes of direct mail is simply to get inquiries. These can be followed up by more letters or by direct selling. Direct mail can prepare prospects for a salesman's call and qualify prospects in advance to save on a salesman's shoe leather. The average cost per salesman's call, without any advance qualification through advertising, was $10.72 in 1945, $22.23 in 1958, and $30.35 in 1963. Direct mail can be an assistant salesman for many dollars less per call. Imagine the leverage an insurance salesman has, for example, if every prospect he calls was previously "qualified" by having responded to some kind of persuasive direct mail.

Another valuable kind of response from direct mail can be the gleaning of information—everything from a respondent's correct name and address (for "cleaning" mailing lists) to market-research information. Many authorities claim that research is better through direct mail than by personal interviews because the mail can reach more people selectively and anonymous responses are liable to be more truthful than those given in person.

But even direct mail which does not have to get a response (such as image-building mail, newsletters, stockholders' reports, etc.) is still considered a worthwhile medium. Among other advantages, well-planned and creative direct mail gets higher readership than most other ads. Magazine ads average 10 percent readership, while effective direct mail gets from 40 to 90 percent attention. It is the only form of advertising that is its own carrier, without anybody else's editorial climate surrounding it. This is one reason why there is so much more hue and cry against "junk mail" than against "junk ads." Is there more tasteless advertising by direct mail than by other media? Probably not. But it is a compliment to the notice people take of direct mail that they complain more about it than about ads and commercials. It is also a good reason why we must make our direct mail, if anything, *more* tasteful and interesting than our other copywriting.

Just consider the possible power of a letter—and the atmosphere in which it is read. Don't most of us, when we come home at night, ask, "Was there any mail?" Don't most executives look, first, at their daily mail? Isn't the mail, potentially, the most important person-to-person medium?

Yet direct mail, even though it is the second largest medium, and has such an attentive audience, is still a giant that has not quite realized its own strength. *Printer's Ink,* reporting on its new growth and stature, quoted a veteran as saying that "direct mail is currently going through the same metamorphosis that all advertising went through 50 or 60 years ago. It is emerging from its medicine man stage."

One reason for this time lag is that the big advertising agencies, which control so much of the wealth and talent, have traditionally turned their backs on direct mail. It has been handled by default, by mailing houses, sales promotion agencies, the smallest ad agencies, printers, and members of companies' internal advertising departments. Says *Advertising Age:* "Very little of direct mail volume passes through the hands of advertising agencies. Direct mail is, more than any other medium, a 'do-it-yourself' operation, a factor often cited by advertising professionals who complain about the quality of direct mail."

The quality is certainly varied and there is plenty of "schlock" direct mail. This results in constant cries for legislation against "junk mail" and for postal rate hikes. The answer? More creativity. But, say such experts as Leonard J. Raymond, president of the direct-mail firm, Dickie-Raymond, there is "a shortage of capable direct mail-minded, direct mail-oriented people . . . particularly creative personnel. . . . The advertising business in recent years hasn't been attracting its share of young people. . . . Those college graduates who *do* choose advertising as a career tend to be drawn by the glamour of television or full-color spreads in the national magazines."

The direct mailers, who are a special breed of copywriters, trained in the hard school of "cost-per-hit," speak disparagingly of the glamour boys. Typical comments: "Agencies are scared of a medium with measurable results." . . . "A neurosis affects ad agencies. All they want to do is get an ad they can repeat and repeat—that's how they make a buck."

Ad agencies, on the other hand, criticize the direct-mail experts for failing to promote and improve their medium. "In general," said John Crichton, president of the 4A's, "direct mail representatives from list compilers and mailing houses don't call on advertising agencies as frequently as representatives of other media do, and they come nowhere near to covering agency personnel in the depth other representatives do. This is particularly evident in creative areas."

"Compared with other media," wrote Thomas A. Tucker, director of Campbell-Ewald's mail department, "direct mail is confusing to buy. Price concessions confuse the buyer; there are too many variables, no standard rates. Much direct mail selling seems to relate direct mail more closely to the printing business than to its characteristics as an advertising medium."

Whoever is to blame for direct mail's tardiness, the fact is that it is catching up fast. By the time these words appear, most of the ad agencies will undoubtedly be moving into the medium. "Agencies that avoid direct mail miss major opportunity," bullets *The Gallagher Report:* "Second-largest medium after newspapers. More attractive as 1) agencies switch to fee compensation, 2) clients require coordinated ad campaigns including direct mail."

Other reasons why the medium is becoming more sophisticated are: the increasing evidence of superior results (e.g., average rate of coupon redemption from direct mail was shown by the A. C. Nielsen Company to be 17 to 24 percent, much higher than that from any other medium, and two to three times the rate of a coupon on or in the product itself); the swift arrival of computerization, which makes scientific, better targeted mailing possible; and the discovery by national advertisers of how to use direct mail to strengthen the pull of other advertising media.

One of the most telling pieces of evidence for the power of direct mail is that its major users include the very media which are most in competition with it—the magazines and newspapers which build their lists of subscribers and advertisers through intensively aimed letter-writing. Newspapers, according to a Department of Commerce survey, spend a fourth of their total advertising budgets on bulk third-class mail, and magazines spend more than a third. Other advertisers who are primary users of direct mail include fund raisers, politicians, book publishers and book clubs, recording companies, manufacturers of drugs and chemicals, and, of course, thousands of small retailers who can easily pinpoint prospects in their local neighborhoods.

Recently there also has been a trend toward direct mail by the huge mass marketers. The food and detergent industries are using multimillion coupon mailings. Big automobile advertisers catalogue car owners by mail. Gasoline companies rival one another with credit cards, premiums, and gift purchasing through stamps. Advertisers of common but nonconflicting products participate in gigantic cooperative mailings.

The medium is on the move and it is exciting. Most of all, since there is so much room for improvement and for education, it is exciting for the copywriter who is vitally interested in his craft.

The Arrow You Aim

If the direct-mail medium is to be straight and direct, then the arrow you aim—the message you send—must be sharp and true.

We said that experienced mailers are sensible men. They are more than sensible; they are among the keenest communicators in the world. Why? Because their wits and their words are sharpened by the incessant tests they are put to. The ability of the copywriter of magazine ads cannot be so accurately gauged as that of the direct-mail writer. The print writer can more often indulge his whims. Except for such measures as "reading" and "noting," it is often difficult to assess the success or failure of a magazine ad. But most of the direct-mail writer's actions are pragmatically judged. You can count the returns. Either a piece of direct mail pulled or it did not. What did he do wrong? He has a constant teacher in the day-by-day results of his work.

What does he learn? He learns, the hard way, all those principles we preached in the first part of this book: the imperatives of clarity, consideration for the reader, being explicit, proving your claim, making it believable, winning the reader's conviction sufficiently to incite him to action—to impel the reader to pick up the return card, fill it out, often to make out a check, sign, seal, go to the mailbox, and send his reply. That's a lot of action to win with one inanimate letter. Yet we have records of results like those of our seedsman in England, who got 90 percent returns, of our sellers of cameras and electronic organs, who not only get action but get it with checks in three and four figures.

How does the successful direct mailer do it? Well, for one thing, he does have a medium which is intrinsically high in its power to involve its audience. Remember, the principle of participation is the greatest truth in all forms of communication. Direct mail is a natural involver. "Essentially," says expert Laurence G. Chait, "people like to receive mail. . . . Prospect involvement will relate not simply to the direct offer made—but will be guaranteed by the visual and tactile 'feel' employed. . . . Mail recipients today are encouraged to, and expected to, remove and affix coins; select from perforated sheets of stamps; enter contests; study elaborate checklists to make a choice; fill out credit application forms; designate time and place where a salesman will call . . . in a word—to act, to become interested, to become involved."

Added to the natural involvement power of the medium is the fact that successful direct mailers are ideally endowed with common sense. Deciding what kind of a format to use, how to write and produce the message, what it should look like, and how much it should cost, are really quite simple decisions when you use common sense and give consideration to your audience. Take the format of the mailing, for example. Should it be a cheap, mimeographed letter, without a fill in, or an expensive three-dimensional piece, with some intrinsic value for the receiver? It depends on the impression your common sense tells you that you want to make. Fund raisers for nonprofit charities, for example, seldom use expensive pieces; obviously, they would imply to the receiver that his donation is more liable to be used extravagantly than for a worthy cause. Kaiser Aluminum, on the other hand, spent $5 apiece for a mailing of aluminum rulers to executives. The investment was warranted, considering the high-profit stakes and the fact that the rulers would remain on the executives' desks as constant reminders.

By the golden rule, direct-mail advertising which asks for an order begins with the offer. The more generous the offer, says our common sense, the more likely the response. In addition to using "loss leaders" or "introductory offers" which are exceedingly generous, successful direct mailers find ways to explain how even moderate offers are beneficial. They do that by breaking down the price (e.g., installment payments or measuring the cost per day, week, or month); by making a favorable comparison (e.g., citing how much less the cost is than other things); by spelling out the actual financial breakdown of the offer, including their own markup; and by making acceptance of the offer a privilege. In this last regard, a good example is the private sale, which stores offer to valued customers, before they open their doors to the crowds.

This last method feeds directly to what *Business Week* called a "desired self-concept." In other words, the reader is flattered. He likes the concept of himself as a "private sale" person—one who gets the inside track on a bargain before the common herd.

Direct mail is the best possible school for the art of consideration. Again and again, direct-mail teachers emphasize the need for putting ourselves in the other fellow's shoes. Writes Paul Bringe: "When we send a sales letter to 1,000 people and that letter takes perhaps two minutes to read, we have used more than 33 hours of valuable, never-to-be-replaced human time. . . . Don't we have the obligation, then, to write in terms of the reader's interests, to entertain him, or at least show him benefits he can gain from reading our letter?" Said Fred Ziegler, of McCann-Erickson, who had used an entertaining approach in a direct-mail campaign for Standard Oil: "We strongly believe in paying for what we get—*we never ask for something for nothing* from our audience."

Another kind of consideration is not just to offer benefits but to offer validation for them. "Since your direct mail's primary function," writes Orville Reed, "is to create prospect feedback in the form of an order, inquiry, or request for more information, your job is much more difficult than writing advertising which is read or heard by the masses. . . . To get the greatest results from your direct mail yc ¬ must prove every statement, every claim, every promise, by presenting conclusive evidence that your product or service will deliver what you claim."

Consideration and common sense dictate every direct-mail decision, whether it be the offer, the format, the opening line of a letter, or the composition of the reply card. If a letter should be as personalized and direct as possible, it should warrant the added expense of automatically typed fill-in names; it should have no resemblance to a form letter. Assuming that most people are lazy, busy, or both, consideration calls for designing your method of reply to be easy and convenient. On the other hand, if you wanted to reduce the number of respondents, and only to have the best qualified people reply, your common sense might dictate a less convenient, a more detailed reply form.

Consideration, of course, determines the essence of our copy, starting with "the opener." The first line of a letter is like the headline of an ad. It has to get the rest of the letter read. If it is a clever line that pleases the writer but does not involve the reader, it is a failure. "The best proof that a copywriter has failed," writes Reed, "is when he shows a letter he has written to someone and it triggers the remark 'that's clever.' Those two words, translated in my language, are 'Your words call attention to themselves, not to the benefit of the product they are supposed to be selling.' "

One of the most successful direct-mail letters—simply an offset, black-and-white letter with a reply card enclosed—was used by the Alexander Hamilton Institute without change for seven years. The opening sentence was as flat-footed and unclever as one could imagine: "Dear Sir. Nearly fifty years ago, we published an extraordinary little book called 'FORG-ING AHEAD IN BUSINESS.' " The letter went on, for two pages, to describe the booklet and to offer a complimentary copy.

Another successful letter, used to promote the Kiplinger Washington newsletter service for businessmen, opened with the question: *"Will you be ready for the boom years ahead?"*

Now, both of those letters were constantly tested against other appeals and consistently won out. The Kiplinger "boom years" statement pulled 50 to 100 percent more orders on test mailings than many other appeals that may at first have sounded more interesting to their writers.

They may find it hard to do, but direct mailers who religiously test their appeals, are the best trained writers in the discipline of divorcing *themselves* from their copy.

Sincerity is another hallmark of the direct-mail writer. The person-to-person atmosphere in which a letter is read makes the receiver peculiarly sensitive to phoniness. He is constantly getting letters which are obviously form letters yet claim to invite him into a select group. He will receive third-class mail with an airmail reply envelope urging quick action because the supply is limited. He receives letters that suffer from we-itis—loaded with "I," "We," and "Us," instead of "You." He receives an "Absolutely Free" offer, in the first sentence, which is linked with a trial-order stipulation in the last. So, of all our audiences, he is liable to be the most suspicious.

How do you "write sincere"? You can't unless you are. And you have to know your subject, study your mailing list, and, finally, talk aloud to each individual at the other end. You have to be natural. "Eliminate advertising jargon from your copy," says Reed. "If you wouldn't say something in person, don't put it in your letter. Can you imagine a good salesman completing his sales pitch with 'Act now'? Can you imagine a salesman calling on a new prospect beginning with 'Dear Friend'?"

One effective way to guarantee sincerity—cited in the *Reporter*—was used by an insurance agent of Bankers Life. He wrote a letter to his own family—to his wife and children—outlining his own insurance audit for them. He used this intensely personal letter in his meetings with prospects. "This letter is the heart of my Audit presentation," said the agent, Will Kuni. "It contains, in a conversational manner, the spirit and the specifics of what I have done for my family and myself."

We would all be better copywriters if we could write what we formally call "direct mail" as informally as we write personal letters to our intimate friends. And it would make business letters a pleasure too.

But the pleasures of creating direct mail these days are more varied than in merely writing informal letters. It is curious that anyone would consider the other media more glamorous. Direct mail, after all, is the only medium where you create your *own* vehicle. Someone else edits the magazine in which your ad appears. Someone else creates the TV programs. In direct mail, *you* are the showman. And your choices of format are infinite. Direct mail alone has no specifications—no time or space or material requirements (except for quite minor postal regulations). You can create booklets, circulars, house magazines, newsletters, diecuts, jumbo mailers, popups, three-dimensionals. You have an infinite choice of papers and envelopes, of colors, artwork, and type. A store featuring a new bath and body perfume sends, as an envelope stuffer, an order form impregnated with that perfume. A car dealer, selling Cadillacs, sends a "solid gold Cadillac letter"—the message offset on gold gift-wrapping paper. An instrument company, to dramatize the metal used in its cables, mails a letter made of stainless steel. A newspaper, mailing to a select list of media-buyers, sends live homing pigeons as its "reply envelope." *The Wall Street Journal,* to show "how well *The Journal* fits the consumer advertiser" mails out 400 Oxford cloth shirts to a list of valued prospects, each shirt with a WSJ label in the collar (neck and sleeve sizes are obtained through an earlier mailing to executives' secretaries).

Product samples have been sent through the mails with startling effect —not just periodicals, but such items as a filter-tip cigarette, razor blades, a Japanese cocoon, and a piece of bacon.

Here are a few examples of "spectaculars," or three-dimensional pieces, including those which have won awards from the D.M.A.A. (Direct Mail Advertising Association) for originality and effectiveness (note that most of these ideas are designed to remain with the recipient long after the day the mail arrives as a constant reminder of his correspondent):

* A series of eight mailings called "The Fisherman's Clinic," sent by an

automotive equipment company (Clark) to a blue-chip list of engineers. Goodwill-building items, from a creel, to line, rod, reel, and book of instructions on trout fishing. Each made a copy point, and the whole added up to a memorable lure.

• Membership in a paperback book club, sent by the salesmen of the Shipping Container Division of The Weyerhaeuser Company to their selected customers and prospects. Every six weeks members of the list received a selection from the Weyerhaeuser Little Library Book Club, including a dictionary, an atlas, thesaurus, legal encyclopedia, Bartlett's Familiar Quotations, etc.

• An attractive paper-folding campaign for Kimberly-Clark papers, which dramatized the product and took advantage of the interest at that time in Japanese origami.

• A complete chess set, made of aluminum, with a striking contemporary design, mailed by Alcoa (four pieces at a time) to a list of buyers and purchasing agents of aluminum foil printing. Supplementing the sales message that went with each mailing, the richness of the extruded pieces helped to enhance the company's image.

• A plastic eyeglass lens, mailed without a container by Univis to a list of eye specialists to dramatize its scratchproof quality. Covering letter: "This Univis plastic lens has traveled unprotected over 3,000 miles through the world's most famous and rugged mixmaster . . . the United States mail."

• A series of mailings by Du Pont to a list of extruders and wholesalers of plastic pipe. The purpose: to dramatize "The Big I.D."—the invisible difference in the resin Du Pont supplied for pipe from its indistinguishable resin competitors. The solution: mailings of Indian heads, some of which were 10¢ replicas, some $20 Folsom points; of nuggets of fool's gold and real gold; of Indian-head pennies with varying values. The dealers and extruders had to call the Du Pont salesmen, whose business cards were attached, to identify whether they had received the real thing or the imitation. Mailings garnered an 80 percent response, helped 37 percent of the wholesalers to increase their sales and, above all, involved the respondents in the copy point Du Pont wanted to make.

• A promotion by the *Boston Record-American,* delivered by Western Union to advertising prospects. The message: "We'd like a bigger piece of the pie." The dimensional: a freshly baked pie, nested in a large, permanent ashtray, plus a plastic knife-and-fork set for immediate eating.

The possibilities of three-dimensional pieces have barely been tapped, and direct mailers can borrow scores of ideas from the advertising specialties business, a somewhat neglected field which has endless resources. Advertising specialties are often personally delivered by salesmen as permanent reminders of their companies. But they can be ideal for direct mail, which someone described as "a thin salesman."

There are about 100 major firms which concentrate on making specialty items (the largest, currently, is Brown & Bigelow in St. Paul, Minn.). Through these firms you can obtain just about any three-dimensional concept your mind can conceive to express your message. Or you can browse by the counters of a five-and-ten, playing the game of association with your mailing problem on your mind. One's attitude, in this area of copywriting, is not to be thinking of words but of ideas.

And this, for that matter, is true of our approach to most direct-mail problems. Says Jack Shelton, direct-mail consultant, "If you are hiring a man to create direct mail, put him in a room with a typewriter, a stack of paper stock, and an assignment. If he starts by putting paper in the typewriter, don't hire him. He's an ad copywriter. If he starts folding paper and scribbling words and picture areas on it, hire him—he's a direct mail creator."

The point behind that description of a direct-mail writer is not that he is a "cut-paste-and-folder" versus a wordsmith, but that his attitude is unlimited. Because direct mail has practically no restrictions on space, time, or material, he can think in terms of the best solution, bar none, for his creative objective. While the most common direct mail often consists of an envelope, a letter, and one or more attachments—including a circular, for a longer spellout than the letter can give—your ideal solution can be anything at all that is acceptable to the U.S. Post Office.

What kind of envelope or container best fits the idea? That outer wrapping is your first entrée to the receiver, so, in effect, it may be your headline rather than the first line of the letter inside. Envelopes have been effectively used to involve an executive's secretary as she opens the mail (e.g., a message in shorthand, asking her cooperation), to be decorative themselves (e.g., a homespun company printed their bulk rate permit in Early American style), to protect and yet reveal the message inside (e.g., imprinted polyethylene bags), to be functionally convenient for the receiver (e.g., a "knockout" name and address section which has an order form or a coupon on the reverse side).

One piece of direct mail, from the Darling Envelope Corporation, consisted of the envelope only. It was a sample of that company's product, and the entire selling message was a cartoon and caption on the back side of the envelope, with no contents inside.

After the envelope, the letterhead, opening sentence, physical layout, and production method all contribute to the personality of the message we want to convey. For example, says the *Reporter,*

A mailer selling tractor tires to an audience of farmers may use a letter to tell his story. A famous jewel merchant may *also* use a letter to promote the sale of a single gem to a handful of prospective buyers. In each case, the format would appear to be the same. But are they? Without question, the jeweler would use an engraved letterhead, fine quality paper, and each letter would probably be personally or automatically typed and personally signed. . . . Can the jeweler afford to send out a less prestigious mailing package? . . . On the other hand, can the tire merchant afford to send out a better mailing piece? This too is hardly advisable. Our rural citizens . . . still recognize a kinship with simplicity. They recognize value and honesty, and they are understandably suspicious of frills and frippery that may exist only to lure the unwary.

The *attitude* of the mailer, says the *Reporter,* determines the format. And this determines everything we do with our copy. Experienced direct mailers tell us to break up the paragraphs of our letter, to use the layout and the punctuation to make it look open and inviting. But the very beginning of the letter is the most crucial, because it must either interrupt or coincide with the state of mind of the receiver at the moment of impact. Openings like these three (which proved successful) were so designed:

> Dear Customer:
>   It doesn't show on your balance sheet . . . but a good percentage of your profits are traceable to one basic fact—*your customers like you.*
> > —The National Research Bureau, Inc., Chicago, cited in *Planning and Creating Better Direct Mail,* by Yeck and Maguire.

> What do you say to a kid who can't walk?
>   You've seen her, haven't you? She lives down the street, or around the corner on the way to the mailbox.
> > From "Writing the Fund Raising Letter," *The Reporter of Direct Mail Advertising,* October, 1964.

> Lasor, Transister, Sybernetics. Three new words in business language of the Sixties. And all three misspelled, as I'm sure you noticed.
> > From an "introductory offer" letter from *Fortune* magazine.

Wouldn't you agree that all three of those openings involved their readers, the targets at which these arrows were aimed? The reader might quarrel with the first one, but it certainly flatters him and gives him food for thought. The second example would find few people so hard-hearted as not to be moved. And the third example—aimed at a list of business-men—discusses three subjects which are broad enough to be in some way interesting to every man on the list; yet they are explicit enough to focus each reader's attention quickly. The twist—that trick of making the familiar strange—is the ·misspelling of those new words. Some of the businessmen receiving that letter might not have noticed that all three words were misspelled, but chances were good they would catch one or two. And the third sentence complimented their perception.

There are any number of good points about the *Fortune* letter, all harking back to our discussion in Part 1. The writer was keenly aware of the contexts in which his audience would be reading his letter, including concern about the changing world this new language reflected and busy-ness which had to be interrupted fast. The writer had also researched his subject and had chosen perhaps the three hottest "hot buttons" in his audience's minds.

So much for the openings of our letters. As for the "body copy," it is very simple—every paragraph should be written in such a way as to march its reader into the next paragraph.

The reason we are dwelling here on letter copy, rather than on the copy for brochures, broadsides, house magazines, and other forms of direct mail, is because every successful direct mailer emphasizes the importance of the letter and few major direct-mail campaigns go out without one. Says Hoke, "In outlining a study program for direct mail, I usually emphasize and re-emphasize the importance of letters. Because letters constitute the basic format for direct mail. *The letter is the closest approach to the personal call.*" (Italics ours.)

Hoke then tells the story of one Louis Victor Eytinge, a prisoner who took up letter writing in jail, to mail-order curios made by his fellow-prisoners. Eytinge, limited for a while by the prison authorities to only two letters a week, learned "the tension of restriction."

> He learned that a letter with an obvious misstatement or an apparent exaggeration wounded itself. He learned that he had to write the simple truth about his goods. He learned that when he undertook to write nothing but the truth, he could do it with a force he had never felt before. . . . His letters, sometimes sophomorically fervent, bristled with personality. Every word was like the grip of a hand, to draw in a helper, a buyer, a friend. . . . Louis Victor Eytinge taught me to think in terms of one letter; to suppose that I had only one chance to make the sale; that I was appealing to only one prospect. . . . Even today, when I compose a multiple sales letter . . . I start out by writing Jack, or Paul, or Gene . . . some actual person I know and can see mentally.

The straight-line medium is the most practical instructor in the massive mistake of advertising as a whole—the mistake of thinking that we are talking to masses. We speak of "mailing lists," but these are names and addresses of individuals, and the moment a communication goes directly to a man or woman with a name (as opposed to those nameless people who read our newspapers and watch TV), we have a special obligation to think of the individual. There is activity, lately, to computerize the writing of letters in addition to their processing. The following is a letter which was actually composed by a computer:

Dear Mrs. _____:
    Your credit card account presently reflects an unpaid balance of $5.00.
If you have not forwarded your check to bring the account up to date,
we would appreciate your doing so at this time.
    Thank you for your cooperation.

> Yours very truly,
> Credit Department

Contrast that mechanical communique with this kind of breezy note
from the owner of a hardware store to the people on his inactive
account list:

    You don't owe us a cent—but we wish you did! Your account is always
open—won't you use it soon?

> Cordially,
> E. O. Rea

P.S. Just in case you've misplaced your old credit card, we are enclosing
a new one. It's good at all three stores.

We don't know how well the computer letter worked, but the latter, Rea
reported, reopened 50 accounts in two weeks and pulled $1,000 in busi-
ness. Can a computer have the imagination to sound human?

The Target You Hope to Hit

"I've got a little list," sang Koko, in *The Mikado,* "and they'd none of
them be missed . . . they'd none of them be missed."

To a copywriter, it isn't only Koko's list that wouldn't be missed—it's
almost any list you can imagine. We have a built-in prejudice against
lists. We associate the word "list" with statistics, and those are dull and
impersonal.

Yet lists are what direct mail is all about. "Boring or not," writes Hoke,
"the list emerges in almost every mail effort as the key to success or
failure. Brilliant copy, splashy four-color art and a dramatic format mean
just so many creative dollars down the drain when the effort has been sent
to the wrong audience. Conversely, a very modest and unpretentious
effort—even badly done—has half a chance to succeed *when the list is
right.*"

We have to deal with lists all the time because direct mailers, unlike
advertisers in other media, create their own circulation. There is no point
in spending time with anything boring, so how can we make mailing lists
interesting?

Again, it depends on attitude. We cannot do away with the term
"mailing list," but every time we think of it, we can substitute the more
personal word "people." At the same time, in our imagination, we can

visualize each person on our list, reading our mail. Suppose we are sending a letter to 5,000 doctors. We do not know them singly, but we can select any one and think of him as alive and breathing, busy or trying to relax, surrounded by the infinite burdens and interests of his profession. Now, all we have to do is get through to him, with the best possible message for *him*. Discovering what that is may not be easy, but at least we have started with a human frame of reference.

There are no people in the whole world served by the postal system that we cannot, in some way, locate for a mailing list. Sometimes it will take a lot of detective work to find our special target, but that is part of the thrill of the hunt. If it is retail direct mail, we can get lists of charge customers. We can get lists from inquiries pulled by advertising in other media. Valuable lists for manufacturers are the names on the warranty cards sent in by actual customers. Salesmen, of course, help compile lists of people they know—or want to know. News stories are about people. State and city records—of births and taxes and licenses and voting—give us more grist. There are hundreds of directories compiled about people— people who are sellers, buyers, legislators, students, club members, hobbyists, professionals, car owners, homeowners, and telephone owners. And there are lists about lists, like the "Guide to American Directories" (Prentice-Hall), the "Directory of Mailing List Sources" (Dartnell Corp.), the McGraw-Hill catalog of lists, etc.

Then, of course, there are professional list compilers, like O. E. McIntyre, Reuben H. Donnelly, and R. L. Polk. From them we can get: lists of car owners, by state, make, and year; lists of homeowners, divided into census "microunits," that stratify the nation demographically; lists of suburban families, broken down into age, income, education, etc. And we can have those compilers custom-make lists to our order.

Finally, there are the list brokers who can arrange rental or exchange of lists with people who have lists compatible with our needs. A good list broker, says copy chief Ken Johnson, "will earn his keep a thousand times over. The list broker does not make money on tests; he makes money on long runs. He does not make money on one-shot customers; he makes money on steady, repeating clients, whose efforts are succeeding. It is to the list broker's own interest to help you find as many good mailing lists —and to save as much of your time and your budget—as he can."

Brokers can find us lists, for rent or exchange, which already are proven to be people attracted to our kind of product or service. Take the subscription lists of magazines. There are 2,400 business publications alone, each with its own kind of audience. There are hundreds of scientific and hobby and homemaking magazines. From security analysts to spelunkers to hot-rod enthusiasts, "they've got a little list."

Now, as we said, direct mail is the personal medium, so we want to try to know the people on our list. That is relatively easy when they *are* people we know. So why don't we act as though they are? Why don't we arbitrarily decide that we will not concentrate on any mailing list unless we have made the names on it come alive?

Making a rule like that sets up certain stipulations. For example: when we know people, we know how to spell their names correctly, we usually know their current address, and we don't annoy them by sending them the same message over and over again. Yet mailing lists which are not "clean" may have a large percentage of the names misspelled and sent to wrong addresses. They say that 20 percent of all Americans move every year, so you can see how easily an old list can have errors. As for duplication of names, this has been one of the worst plagues of the industry. Said Boyce Morgan, executive of Kiplinger, one of the biggest mailers in the country:

> I think it is our weaknesses in this general area, rather than the area of copy or content, that are largely responsible for the increasingly bad public image which direct mail has suffered in recent years. . . .
>
> To be specific, I am becoming more and more concerned because, under our present methods of operations, it is perfectly possible for a prospect to receive a dozen identical Kiplinger solicitations within a few days of each other. . . .
>
> I am also deeply concerned because a company like ours, with five different products, naturally cross-solicits its own lists, at the same time we are making use of outside lists . . . and under our present method of operations we cannot even eliminate duplications between *our* own lists of active subscribers, let alone between those names we rent on the outside.

Since that statement, Kiplinger has no doubt partially solved its problem. For one of the cures for duplication, as well as for misinformation, is the increased use of electronic data processing. Companies are preparing computerized master lists which can be checked, at high speed, against rented lists, to eliminate duplication. The most revolutionary possibility will be one great computer clearing-house for all lists.

For the direct-mail copywriter, the increased sophistication of those "giant brains that think" can be, curiously enough, an important aid toward personalization. Each year, as data processing progresses, we can isolate and correlate facts about people in our mailing lists. Electronic tapes can then be scanned in such a way that you can call for special segments of your list to be selected and addressed automatically in a few minutes. Eventually, you will be able to isolate, for example, all the blue-eyed pregnant wives of brown-eyed husbands. Knowing your mailing list like that—and knowing your laws of genetics—you could make a mail offer of merchandise to match the eyes of those yet-to-be-born babies!

As for cleaning lists of wrong addresses, this is a little more difficult. Sending first-class mail won't clean a list because the post office will forward the mail to new addresses and you won't be informed of them. One way to clean a list is to pay 8¢ per letter, for third-class mail to be returned with the information "not at this address," but you will not always get the right new address that way or correct the misspelling of a name.

The very best way to clean a list is the way you *do* find out facts about the people you know: you keep in touch with them, and you *ask them about themselves*. People like to talk about themselves, don't they? When you write a personal letter to a friend, filled with news about *you* and no concern about him, you may not get much of an answer. But fill your note full of inquiries and concern, and watch the result—it's usually in the next mail! It is true, you may have to be more constant and persistent, to get all the familiarity you want from a mailing list. You may even have to offer incentives for eliciting information—as some research firms do when they make surveys by mail, often paying for the replies. But the more you get to know, the more you will be talking to *people* instead of to *lists*. You will learn not only correct facts about names and addresses, but about promotions, births, and weddings, what interests your people have in common, what they read, how they think, what they buy.

The best list any company has is the list of its current customers. These are the lists that the big, successful direct mailers cultivate—mailers like the catalog mail-order houses, Sears, Wards, Breck's of Boston; book and record clubs; the retailers with charge customers; the magazines which build their circulations by mail. They keep files on those customers, and the better the files, the more effective the mailings. They know which customers like and can afford which offers; they know about their credit and record of buying. They constantly broaden the profitability of each name on the list (if they are retailers, for example, they send enclosures with the monthly invoices, telling news of the store, of sales, and of special offers). Sometimes—as in the case of a handsome mailing by *Time* magazine to a list of charter subscribers—those intelligent mailers simply send "thank you" notes. Or, remembering that we are mailing to people, not lists, they will send a regular, month-in, month-out, series of "cordial contacts."

A "cordial contact" is what often-quoted copywriter Jack Carr called his reminder letters. According to his formula, a thousand such letters, sent out each month, could garner a 70 percent response at the end of five years. Be that as it may, the psychology makes sense. If someone you know only writes you self-seeking letters, you are less responsive than if you had often heard from him with cordial contacts.

Now, in addition to asking questions, keeping files, and keeping in touch, the way we get to know our lists is to test them. Most big mailers use "test control" batches of names from a larger list to measure the effectiveness of different letters, formats, timing, and offers. We can "qualify" the people on our lists, if we want responses for future selling, by narrowing our appeal. For example, say Yeck and Maguire, "If your message now reads, 'Please have a salesman call on __ at __ o'clock', you'll get a high-quality response, but you probably won't be overwhelmed with returns." You will, nevertheless, know the people on your list—i.e., that they are receptive to what you have to sell.

One way we can learn to personalize our lists is to use ourselves as guinea pigs and to analyze the mail we receive. For example, the author, who does considerable traveling by air to and from San Francisco, has been repeatedly impressed by the mailings sent to him by TWA: one a listing of movie programs for the following month; another a listing of radio programs, together with a reply card questionnaire "designed to round out information on our radio audience"; a third a "Quick-Way Timetable" from San Francisco; a fourth an attractive desk calendar. As a student of advertising, the author was also impressed by the "Strategic Advertising Casebooks" mailed by *Time*. As a car-owner, he was bowled over by the sixty-four-page lithographed magazine mailed by Buick to himself and to millions of other car owners. As an emotional creature, he was moved by the mailing piece, in braille, sent out by the *Ladies' Home Journal*, with the message that this is the only women's magazine in the world to be published in braille. But as a preoccupied businessman, the author was infuriated when he received from his secretary, among the open correspondence, a sealed envelope, marked "Personal" in red—only to find an advertisement inside, with the following first sentence: "Dear Sir: The reason that this letter is marked 'Personal' is because our boss doesn't believe in 'advertising.'" The letter proceeded, believe it or not, to solicit assignments for the creation and production of radio and TV commercials.

While the last-mentioned example is an extreme case of depersonalization—not to mention gall—it is not difficult to distinguish the thoughtful letters in your daily mail, in which you are considered as a *person,* from those in which you are treated as only a name on a mailing list. Study your daily mail for the next year or so, saying to yourself as you read each piece, "Does this person or company want to know *me?*" With such a common-sense system, you will have as good a guide to direct-mail practice as you can get from any expert or book.

THE CAPSULE MEDIUM

The Heart of the Matter

Every time Gulley Jimson saw a wall, he wanted to paint a picture on it. The bigger the wall, the better he liked it. You may remember that the movie made from Joyce Cary's novel, *The Horse's Mouth,* ended with Gulley drifting down the Thames and passing a battleship. A demonic gleam came into his eyes, as if he was thinking "acres and acres of blank space, and all mine!"

This is one of the two great pleasures of the outdoor medium: it's big. A 24-sheet poster is pasted on a panel 12 ft high and 25 ft wide. A 30-sheet poster gives you 25 percent more display area. And painted bulletins may be twice the length of the 24-sheet poster.

The other great pleasure of outdoor advertising is that it is brief. It is meant, mainly, to be seen from a car. People usually have only 5 to 15 seconds to see it, depending on how fast they drive.

Big and brief—what better combination to give a communicator pleasure. He can say it boldly, he can say it quickly; and the demands of people who want to complicate the message can be stubbornly met with "it won't work in outdoor."

Poster making is an artist's mecca. "I don't know any medium that has more kicks," said artist-agency president Julian Koenig. "After all, where else can you find hundreds of square feet in which to work your magic on the world?"

And it should be a copywriter's mecca too. For the poster gives form to the dreams we have—of cutting through all the undergrowth to the pure, simple heart of the matter. "Long ago," wrote Garrett P. Orr, eastern art director of Outdoor Advertising, Inc., "we learned the stern discipline of the 'inexorable rectangle.' We learned that it was a matter of creative life or death to pluck out the one compelling sales idea and to stick to that idea. We learned that copy must be so simple, so direct, so compact, that it can deliver its full meaning in a matter of seconds."

Outdoor posters flash by at about five times the rate of radio and TV commercials. Whether they use words or pictures, or a combination of both, they've got to be strong, simple, and fast. The outdoor poster, said art director Jack Anthony, "cannot afford the luxury of even one unemployed strawberry."

The Makeup of the Medium

Outdoor advertising, compared with the other media we have discussed, has had rough going. As of this writing, it is making a healthy comeback after more than a decade's decline.

One reason for the medium's unpopularity was its poor reputation with the government and public. The industry policed itself more sternly than any other medium has done, standardizing its panels (beginning with an attractive Raymond Loewy design), reducing the number of panels nationally to a quarter-million, and placing them only in areas zoned for business, away from freeways and natural scenery.

But outdoor was unpopular with advertisers too. One reason was the industry's vague and unscientific approach to media selling. There was no audit bureau of circulation, as magazines had. And there were fewer measures of the impact of its messages. Among the solutions to these problems was the setting up of the T.A.B. (Traffic Audit Bureau) and the continuing Starch study of readership. Now research of all kinds is being computerized and it is possible for media buyers to learn the reach and frequency of the different numbers of showings, the cost per thousand at different times and places, and the demographic makeup of every outdoor market.

Like other media, outdoor has a terminology peculiar to it, but its lingo is more peculiar than most. Says media director Charles T. Skelton, "Any medium which offers such contradictions as a No. 100 poster showing that doesn't contain 100 posters, a 24-sheet poster not made up of 24 sheets, and rotary bulletins that don't physically move, is bound to be baffling to the uninitiated." Actually, the term "#100 showing" is a good one, when we consider that its purpose is to offer as close as possible to 100 percent coverage of a market. The outdoor operator, who leases or owns locations for the poster panels, divides his market into posting zones (three miles of a heavily traveled street). A "#50" showing will have one panel in each zone, a "#100" showing will have two. In Aguila, Ariz., where there is a population of 400, only two posters are required for a #100 showing; in the San Francisco Bay area, with a population of almost three million, about 200 posters would be needed to reach almost every driver.

Another negative that held back the industry was the belief that posters do not communicate enough of a story to sell a product. One of the replies to this criticism has been the fact that outdoor costs less than other media (as little as 18 to 19¢ per thousand impressions), and can therefore be used with great saturation and repetition. Frequently cited was the Wilbur Smith study that showed that a #100 showing for thirty days reached 94 percent of the people twenty-one times at a cost of 36¢ per thousand—a bargain indeed. Summarized the report: "The market-wide reach of Outdoor Advertising . . . combined with its tremendous frequency adds up to persistence unequaled in any primary medium."

But in addition to the advantages of high exposure at low cost, many advertisers have found that a powerful poster can be far more than a reminder. Wrote a respondent to a *Printer's Ink* survey, "Outdoor should be presented as a primary medium for those products not requiring long copy and as a superb extender of advertising for products that do require long copy."

Which products require long copy may be highly debatable. Among those who have used outdoor extensively have been makers of products ranging from a 5¢ candy bar to a $10,000 car. Biggest single user of outdoor, at this writing, has been General Motors, second biggest Budweiser beer; and these are the leading sellers in their product categories. Industries which have favored outdoor have included those marketing foods, cars, petroleum, and beverages. Outdoor is a favorite medium for the launching of new products. Hotels, restaurants, banks, and retailers—especially anxious to communicate with motorists driving in and out of town—can use the medium locally for quick action as well as for repeated reminding. And all advertisers who do use outdoor agree on these advantages: low cost, a universal audience, and the ability to communicate with size and color and to penetrate a market with a fast message in a short time.

But of all its advantages, outdoor's greatest strength is its encouragement of audience participation. A cleverly conceived poster can "say more by saying less." This was discovered, for example, in a test of five different media, by the Florists' Telegraph Delivery Association. They found that the use of outdoor resulted in more sales volume than did any of the other media. Research director Dr. Jaye S. Niefeld, of the Association's advertising agency, explained the reasons like this:

> Television, with its literalness and the completeness of its presentation, perhaps spelled out the advertising appeal in too much detail. Newspapers, without the use of color, did not capture the essence of this creative approach. Outdoor on the other hand, provided the essence of the creative appeal and benefited from leaving much to the interpretation and imaginative involvement of the viewer.

The Search for the Essence

If we would not be accused of exploitation, we could do worse than to hire a staff of children to create our posters. As Rosten said, people who communicate are those who have retained their infantile *directness*, and in no medium is this a greater asset than in posters.

The ideal poster would be one which uses symbols that are so direct that everyone would instantly react to them. They would not only be quickly assimilated, but they would also evoke a response. And that response would go on—or at least remain implanted in the mind, to be called up when the occasion is right—after the person has read and run.

Such symbols are the word "Stop" and a red light; the military command "Halt, Who Goes There?"; the shout "Fore!" on a golf course; the red-and-white stripes of a barber pole; the symbol of a pointing finger.

Symbols like those, of course, are learned, and some of them have different meanings, according to the audience. For example, a policeman's palm, held up and forward, means "Stop" to an American; but to a French cab-driver, that is an insulting gesture, like thumbing the nose. Churchill's famous "V" for "Victory" sign would have been, in Italy, an insult to a man's virility.

But the child, in using symbols to express a poster message, is less likely to have his clarity crippled by education. So it was with an eleven-year-old, whose poster for Persil washing powder was reprinted in *Graphis*, the international yearbook of advertising art. The primitive drawing showed an impossibly tall and narrow apartment house with dazzling white wash hanging on the roof. Near the top story was an impossibly white cloud in the shape of a halo circling the building. Smaller, squat buildings, with grey wash and black smoke were at the foot of the picture. And at the very top were the words, "Persil alles uberragend" (which means, in German, that Persil exceeds everything—but the picture is so expressive we don't have to understand the language).

To the uninitiate, such graphic simplicity may seem easy to come by. But, as art director Ed Graham expressed it, "Outdoor copy and design, when well done, is so deceptively simple that few people realize how tough it is to achieve a good board. . . . But once you get involved in it, it's like graduating from simple crossword puzzles to double crostics."

Restraint is always difficult. The more you know about your product, your market, and the likes and dislikes of your client, the harder it is to restrain yourself. You have to work back, discarding layers and layers of possible copy, until you get to the essence.

Going backwards, for our inspiration, is especially apt for poster making. It is the oldest form of advertising. Stone Age hatchets cut posters in rocks and on trees—in the shape of arrows, pointing to the salt fields. One Queen Hatsheput's exploits were advertised in 3000 B.C., by an inscribed obelisk 100 feet tall, weighing 350 tons (her designers made today's 24-sheet artists appear small-minded). Pompeii, when excavated, was still covered by wall posters, the size of subway one-and-two sheets (for example, the picture of a boy being whipped advertised a tutoring school). Of course, the Greek and Roman empires were practically as busy with signs as we are today; the Dark Ages, however, were a setback for advertising. Then came the trade guilds with pictures to tell their story: a gilded arm and hammer, to say "gold-beater"; three nuns with embroidery, to say "draper"; and a striped pole to say "barber" (that gay symbol derived from the functional habit of wrapping cloths, wet from bloodletting, around a pole to dry).

The point of reciting this past history is to emphasize that our posters today have much the same purpose as their ancestors had—to read fast and true in the context of our time and of the people who are seeing them. Nothing has changed in thousands of years. We are still trying to communicate the essence.

The Prize-winning Posters

Through the years—by professionally judged contests, consumer research, and successful case histories—certain outdoor campaigns have emerged as classics of what good posters should be. Let's consider some of them, and discuss their more obvious attributes.

The Ford Motor Co. campaign has had a certain continuity, since Henry Ford was credited with inventing the line "Watch the Fords Go By." That was the reference to the Ford's performance in racing, but the line stuck; and the pictures of heads and eyes following a speeding "off-camera" car made for a strikingly active campaign. Someone has called the outdoor medium "television through the windshield." In most cases, the "movies" are the cars and not the boards. But as long ago as 1907, Ford managed to get action into a single-frame billboard, without benefit of animation or Tri-Vision.

The Ford campaign has, of course, had many other prize-winning entries. Probably the most famous is the board illustrating a baby carriage, with the line "Only Convertible that Outsells FORD." Close contender was the board illustrating a greyhound and a scottie dog, watching a car disappear in the distance—caption, "No use, Mac, it's a Ford V-8." A daringly assumptive idea, in 1949, was to show a father and son, peering excitedly through a dealer's window. The only copy on the entire board was the word "Ford" on the window, and that was spelled backwards!

That board, said Wallace W. Elton, officer of Ford's agency, the J. Walter Thompson Co., "could have been run only by an advertiser who had achieved a high level of familiarity with the viewers." He went on, in a speech given before the First Annual Outdoor Seminar, to describe the continuity in the entire Ford campaign as "self-assured simplicity . . . an appeal to what the viewer already knows, or believes, or has heard."

In other words, that advertising had the look and feel of a leader.

The most outstanding other poster campaign for cars has been the one for Volkswagen. It has the same honest, assumptive air as the Ford campaign, but with perhaps a stronger bite (which is understandable, because this foreign car maker has a need to be more competitive). The Volkswagen billboards are closely linked with the print campaign. Among the best: Two VW's parked in one side of a two-car garage, the other side empty—caption, "Two can live as cheaply as one." Two VW's, side by side, identical except that one is shiny and has no license plate, the other is dusty and has a plate—caption, "Cheap new. Expensive used." Picture of a VW, with driver, going off the left side of the board—caption, "Everyone's getting the bug."

What powers do the Volkswagen boards have to communicate, besides their simplicity? Most of those we discussed in Part 1. They have inherent drama, they are explicit, they have the feel of reality and a style all their own (note their down-to-earth language). Above all, they have the power to involve. The viewer can contribute much more to these open-ended statements. In the case of the first board, he could expound on the space-saving qualities of this compact car, on the advantages of owning two low-priced cars instead of one expensive one, etc. In the case of the second board, he could discuss the low depreciation on a Volkswagen—on which he has probably been well-grounded in advance by the print ads that expand on the story. And in the case of the third board—what friendly familiarity he can feel toward a company that dares to admit that their product is a funny-looking little "bug"!

The familiarity both the Ford and Volkswagen campaigns were designed to achieve is the main purpose of the famous Morton Salt series. Outdoor is the closest medium to the point of sale—both in the character of its copy, and in the fact that it is the last medium a driver is likely to see on the way to a store. Package identification, in full-color and giant size, is a big advantage of the medium. If it is possible, with strong "symbology," to implant a product, its trademark, its package, its use, and its desirability—all in the consumer's mind, so they trigger his response at the store, then we are using outdoor in its ideal capacity.

This is precisely what Morton Salt has done. And, of course, because they have done it, you probably need little reminding of what their campaign looks like. Every poster shows the most luscious food and the most prominent Morton Salt package possible. The lighting, art direction, and graphics are consistently fresh and inventive. The campaign began, years ago, with fairly long copy—i.e., "Any melon worth its salt . . . is worth Morton's," plus their regular slogan "When it rains it pours." For many more years, the posters have been totally nonverbal—except for the slogan on the package.

An enormous advantage of outdoor—especially for new and old products that are fighting to win or to hold shelf space—is that the medium is "self-merchandising." That is, as the Outdoor Advertising Association explains,

> It is the one medium that has the greatest exposure to the retailer. . . . For example: Daytime television and radio have proved effective in the food field. However, the retail food merchant works long and confining hours and his opportunity to hear, or see, daytime television is greatly limited. Yet the advertiser's poster waits for him until he closes the store and goes home. It is there to greet him on the way to work in the morning. He has tangible evidence of the support the manufacturer puts behind his product.

This is one of the motivations of such a campaign as the month-in, month-out billboards of Morton Salt. It is not only for the public but for the trade. Ordinarily salt is a commodity of the lowest interest. This kind of advertising support is life insurance for the product at the point of purchase.

And that kind of merchandising cannot be underestimated in these times of automated marketing. An advertising man experienced in the baking industry had this to say about it: "If you have to choose between two advertising campaigns—the first, one that you prefer, and the second, one that has the enthusiastic support of the plant managers and driver-salesmen—choose the second. If you don't have their support, all the great advertising in the world won't work—because your product won't be up there in front, on the shelf, when the customer comes to get it."

Among the consistent prize-winning posters are the ones for Mars, Inc., makers of various candy bars. Their potential market is everyone, so they use outdoor for its broad, repetitive reach. Their style—gay and happy, compatible with the nature of the product. Bright colors, cartoons, catchy copy: "Mars Milky Way—so rich in milk it almost *Moos*" . . . "Mars Snickers—It's a Milky Way *Gone Nutty*" . . . Cartoon of a Hallowe'en witch: "Best candy on Earth comes from *Mars.*"

Notice how those posters use plays on words. Visual and verbal puns are characteristic of prize-winning posters. It is fashionable these days to bewail the pun. But in posters, provided it's "on the subject," the pun is a principle. With good reason, for a pun, according to the dictionary, is "the humorous use of a word in such a manner as to bring out different meanings or applications"—and that is precisely what we want to evoke in the mind of the viewer. For example:

A Thurber-like cartoon of a dog, with a realistic halftone can of Ken-L-Ration in his middle: "Inside America's happiest dogs!"

A poster for Pacific Gas & Electric promoting appliances: "Don't be a Dishwasher—buy one!"

One of a long line of powerful Bank of America billboards—picture of a blank check: "People love to endorse our product."

A big closeup of a jar of Louis Sherry *Diet* Jams and Jellies. The "twist" is that the jar is wearing a cowboy hat. And the caption reads "meet slim."

A closeup of the gas gauge from the dashboard of a car. The letter E for "empty") . . . the arrow pointing to the letter F (for "full", but in this case, the word reads "Falcon").

Unexpected metaphors and combinations of words and pictures are the norm in well-remembered posters, not only because originality is needed in all advertising, but because posters have to reach out and grab you fast. The horse's mouth indeed is one Savignac, who brought his brand of European design to such contrasting commodities as *Life* magazine and Cheer detergent. The poster, he said, should be a "violent scandal, but subtle enough to reverberate in the memory like the refrain of a song." Savignac is childlike and irreverent. "The public is so bored by the monotony of its existence that advertising has the duty to amuse it," he says. He catches that passing motorist by shaking him up: "Only shock can distract his attention away from himself and offer him a certain altruism. The shocks in the street go from accidents to rape, and include fires and crimes. The poster is a visual shock."

The way Savignac applies shock is to show an elephant in a bathtub, with the caption "You get fun out of Life," a monkey with his hands blindfolding a man, with the caption, "You get surprise out of Life," a grey mouse gazing sadly at a white mouse on a box of Cheer, with the caption "Cheer Washes Whiter." In short, he uses phantasy and the pull of the unexpected. One of his French posters, for *"Machines a Laver,"* shows a happy little man tossing his clothes into a washing machine. On his head is a hat, on his face a smile, and the rest of him is stark naked except for an unexpected figleaf where his shorts used to be.

Every few years, American advertisers "discover" the school of the European poster artists. Then there is a debate, as to whether they are too sophisticated, too slyly "soft-selling," or too "way out." Now, with international marketing on the rise, the validity of what they have taught us is reconfirmed. From Toulouse-Lautrec on, their work has been typically audacious—in color, simplicity, gaiety, and charm. These artists, in turn, had grown up to a school where language barriers between countries were overcome by pictures that told stories and where the competition of fifteen or twenty different posters on one kiosk was overcome by originality. Thus, we see a light-hearted poster for Coca-Cola where the horse and the jockey, each with a straw, share a drink of Coke, from the same bottle. We see a travel poster for Finland, where an airplane fuselage and engines take the form of fish—to say, in a symbolic flash, that you should fly to Finland for the fishing. We see a French poster in which a man embraces a huge glass of Grutli beer and kisses the white foamy head—in the silhouetted shape of a pretty girl. These poster artists love anthropomorphism— just as did the creators of Greek mythology, hundreds of years before. And all because it is making the strange familiar and the familiar strange.

One more characteristic we find in prize-winning posters—more difficult in this than in most other media—is the technique of demonstration. It is well done in a board for Cannon towels. Two huge, coral-colored bath-towels hang side by side—one wrinkled, the other smooth. The word "Yours?" is embroidered on the wrinkled towel, the word "Ours!" on the smooth one . . . and below is the caption "Guaranteed never to pucker —Cannon Royal Family Towels." Among the international examples of demonstration is a board for the Olivetti Lexicon typewriter. No words, but a picture of the typewriter and a row of enlarged keys. A bouncing ball, leaving a buoyant dotted line in its wake, has just depressed one of the keys and has bounced high in the air, demonstrating, to those who run but cannot read, that the Olivetti Lexicon typewriter has a light touch.

Demonstration, phantasy, puns, appetite appeal, open-ended involvement—these are some of the attributes of the prize-winning posters. Common to all is their instancy—the ability to catch even the corner of the eye of their moving audience. "The outdoor advertisement," says the guidebook published by the Association of National Advertisers, "must be to advertising what the editorial cartoon is to journalism." That cartoon is the one dominant element in a mass of small type. It is pertinent and punchy and eye-catching. So should the poster stand out from a mass of distractions.

Ways and Means

In all of the preceding, we have been using the words "billboards," "outdoor boards," and "posters" interchangeably. The word "bill," in the early days, meant any written or printed public notice, as well as a bill of exchange and a bill for money owed. Bill posters banded together and went around posting notices on any wall, fence, or exposed object they could find (one is said to have created a unique billboard from the flank of a dead horse).

The commonest "outdoor boards," as we said earlier, are 24-sheets, 30-sheets, and painted bulletins. The word "24-sheet" derived from the number of individual sheets that had to be printed (by the lithograph process) and pasted together to give the huge size desired for the outdoor sign. When presses improved, less than half the number of sheets were needed to cover the same area, but the industry kept the familiar term "24-sheet."

There are also smaller boards for lease by the outdoor companies—including 3-sheet and 6-sheet posters. And there are the painted bulletins, which, to further confuse the picture, are not necessarily painted. Their main characteristic is that they are larger, more elaborate and custom-made than the others we have described. You can have cutouts, extensions, 3-D effects—all designed to fit your ideas with a painted bulletin.

The painted bulletin might be called a "spectacular," except that there are outdoor spectaculars in the form of illuminated electric signs, like those pioneered by the Douglas Leighs of Times Square. The painted bulletin is also sometimes referred to as a "rotary bulletin," when displays are rented on a rotary plan, changing locations every month or two, so that within a year an advertiser can blanket a whole city with his tailor-made, giant-size ads.

Still, we have more "billboards" to think about, if we consider the field known as transit advertising. This is a different industry from that of outdoor advertising. It is run by different companies and has its own trade association. Transit advertising consists of the ads run in subways, busses, taxes, and trains. They include 1-sheet, 2-sheets, 3-sheets, car cards, and the so-called "traveling display" you see on the outside of a bus or street car.

For our purposes, since we are concerned with the creative function, we would like to cut through the confusing terminology and think only in terms of *the poster*. And we would like to define the poster, for this chapter, as a brief message to be seen by a moving audience. A car card in these terms, would not be a poster—though it can be a brief message. That is because the average ride, by a commuter sitting down in a subway or bus, is 25 minutes, and he has ample time to read a longer message.

(Witness, for example, the car-card campaign which helped to give River Valley Frozen Foods a 600 percent sales rise; copy ran as high as a hundred words to a card.)

On the other hand, according to our definition, a big "traveling display" on the outside of a bus is a poster. It is seen and noted by people in the street, as the bus passes by, so lettering should never be less than 2 in. high and, like a 24-sheet, the display would seldom have more than five to eight words.

The ways of poster design are the province of the artist, but they are good for the copywriter to consider when he is mulling over ideas. The fewer the elements the better; and when we say "elements," a slogan would be one element, an illustration another, a package or logo would be a third. A one-element poster would be the famous one for Genesee Beer, which was an enormous full-color closeup photo of a beautiful girl —just her head and the fingers of one hand emerging from the sea—and in her hand a can of Genesee with the words "more refreshing," partly obscured, under one finger. A good example of a two-element poster could be the one we mentioned from the Bank of America—the picture of a check and the caption "People *love* to endorse our product." Some of the cleanest three-element posters have been those for the Atlantic Refining Company—breathtaking panoramic photographs of American outdoor scenes and historic sites, with the slogan "Keeps your car on the go" and the Atlantic logo mortised into one corner. These ads have convinced garden clubs and civic organizations that roadside posters can be beautiful. They are so attractively designed that the company receives an average of 100 requests a week for posters for home decorating use. There are more of their posters in rumpus rooms than in their entire outdoor schedule.

One to three elements would be right for the big, brief poster. Go beyond three, and you proceed at your own risk!

Another must in poster design is the use of a quickly recognized silhouette. Cars are approaching a billboard at different speeds from hundreds of feet away. People have different kinds of eyesight. We would like to have them spot a shape on the billboard with as quick recognition as a plane spotter can identify the silhouette of a moving plane or a typographer can spot the g's in various typefaces. One way companies have done that is to have silhouettes all their own—the shape of the Coca-Cola bottle and the unmistakable shape of their trademark lettering, the distinctive shape of the Heinz shield, the Wrigley spear, the Seagram seven-crown, the Shell shell, and the Chevrolet logo. If symbols are strong to begin with, and they are repeated, over and over without change, they can eventually become ingrained. Witness the outdoor symbols we react to, dozens of times a day, as we drive past traffic control devices.

A third guide to poster design is the use of strong contrasts. Clear color separation, contrast between the warm and cold colors, contrast in the arrangement of the elements.

Of course, the kind of lettering a poster designer uses is of extreme importance. The trend has been to sans-serif type and to lowercase only—all with an eye to removing clutter and furthering quick reading.

Then, too, as we said before, very few words. But this does not mean that pictures must replace words. Bert Stern, an artist-photographer, cited as one of his favorites the English poster "Drinka Pinta Milka Day." Stern said, "I don't think it was good because it was well designed. . . . It's like the ingredients you put in something. It's the recipe that counts . . . the thought . . . the idea."

Such an idea was the poster for Coldene, which you could neither identify as words or picture—but was, rather, the participating experience of the audience. It was a great big expanse of black paper. At the upper left, in white letters, were the words "John, is that Billy coughing?" At the lower right, in white letters, were the words "Get up and give him some Coldene." It was the viewer who painted the real picture—in his mind—the picture of a husband and wife in bed, of the wife groping for the medicine cabinet, of her opening a bottle of Coldene and ministering to her child. That was the kind of billboard that set up that kind of "reverberation" Savignac was talking about.

Yes, the ways and means are all there, just as they are in TV, magazines, and newspapers, to express the best possible message for your subject in this medium. What's more, in contrast to ads in other media (which have "noted" and "read most" scores), you can be certain that a well-designed poster will be totally observed.

The Outlook for Outdoor

Despite continuing attacks from some public and government groups, we suspect that the outdoor medium will survive and will probably continue to improve its position. A Federal Highway Act in 1958 offered states a bonus of 5 percent of the cost of interstate highway construction if they would control—i.e., ban—outdoor advertising along Federal highways. Twenty states signed up for the privilege but only a few qualified for bonuses. In the meantime, the outdoor industry policed its positioning of boards quite stringently. In 1965, when President Johnson proposed a beautification program which would regulate outdoor advertising, the Outdoor Advertising Association of America pledged its support. It is likely, therefore, that in general the *number* of boards in the future will continue to decrease.

But the increase in automobiles and the motoring habits of Americans seems bound to affect the growth of outdoor's use. This is especially noticeable in the eleven states of the West, particularly in California, where the people live outdoors more than anywhere in the country and where population and car ownership are rising fastest.

The West has been the bellwether for the industry. According to Hugh Smith, president of Western Outdoor Markets, every five Western families own two or more cars compared to one in seven elsewhere in the nation. Starch research, he maintains, has shown that 93.6 percent of all Westerners were outdoor readers compared with 81.6 percent in the rest of the country.

This is why outdoor budgets are by far the highest in the West and why most of the innovations in the industry have originated there. For example, the huge painted bulletins came into their own in California. These were, for years, painted individually, by gangs of muralists resembling the staffs of Michelangelo. An experimental development, through Metromedia's Foster & Kleiser Division in San Francisco, was an electrostatic printing process designed to replace painting by hand. The advent of Tri-Vision, pioneered by the Pacific Outdoor Advertising Co., gave us the possibility of using motion in our billboards. With Tri-Vision, we could have three parts to our message, each appearing every few seconds before a motorist drives by.

Now Gino Raffaeli, the enthusiastic chief art director of Pacific Outdoor, predicts a new kind of "lenticular device," which will allow four picture changes every few seconds, completely by electronic control, without the need of the mechanical louvers used in Tri-Vision. He anticipates that these changing pictures will be painted or printed with clear colors that will give the brilliance of a photographic transparency. Eventually, three-dimensional pictures will be possible, along with new movement and clarity.

The outlook for outdoor includes more imaginative and daring use of its immediacy and flexibility. Boards can be "sniped," or changed as often as once a day, with personalized, localized messages—for example, messages outside a supermarket pertinent to that location, with the name of the local manager, or a message about a special at that locality.

This flexibility will be especially important in the future when so much selling will be automated and the billboard will act as a kind of point-of-sale reminder for impulse buying.

A clothing store in Los Angeles (Dorman's) used the billboard on top of their own building, as a kind of weekly panel comic strip—telling a humorous story which progressed each week, for nineteen weeks—involving a feud between the store owner and a temperamental sign painter. This use of continuity involved thousands of motorists who passed by regularly and looked forward to the next episode.

The Frito-Lay potato chip company used a teaser campaign to introduce their New Era chips. A beautiful girl was shown, holding a telephone, with a caption, "What's the latest? Dial WE 7-3450." More than 40,000 phone calls resulted in ten days, and the callers were given commercials about "the latest in lightness"—the message for the new chips which was posted after the ten-day teaser period.

Another poster campaign run by Frito-Lay uses viewer involvement to the nth degree. It shows a scrappy, freckle-faced boy, holding a bag of Lay's potato chips, challenging the passerby, "Betcha can't eat only one!"

One of the best strategies for use of outdoor in the West are the welcoming signs used at the points of entry to California, where tourists and many of the more than a half-million immigrants arrive every year. Companies like Standard Oil, Union Oil, Bank of America, Olympia Beer, etc., introduce themselves in this way to the newcomer who may have used other brands in his former part of the country.

Probably the biggest use of outdoor in years to come will be as a balance with other media. "Meshing and matching is . . . a notable feature of outdoor," says Joseph T. Donovan, of D'Arcy Advertising Co. "It's important to include outdoor's flexibility in media plans that balance night and day, one season versus another, visual with audio, selected geographical areas with blanket coverage, men with women, indoor with outdoor, young with old, inexpensive with expensive, color with black and white, and 30-day exposure with less consistent issues and programs."

For copywriters and art directors, meshing the outdoor medium of the future with the rest of their media will be easier and more interesting. It will be easier because of faster and more inventive methods, more interesting because, if the medium is revitalized, they will be thinking, once again, in terms of the poster technique which was neglected for so many years. And that will mean cultivating an attitude of simplicity, the greatest art of all.

17

THE LAST-CHANCE MEDIUM

She has seen the TV commercial, read the magazine ad, skimmed through the newspaper, driven past the billboard, and now she walks into the store.

According to one study, she has probably forgotten, within twenty minutes, 40 percent of all the advertising she may have noticed. And she will have forgotten 60 percent within four hours.

Forgotten or not, there is plenty of likelihood that she will choose many of her products on impulse, right there in the store. In fact, another study claims that 75 percent of all supermarket selections are unplanned. The customers came with certain items in mind, but through inspiration, accident, special sales, point-of-sale influence, packaging, or what-have-you, they suddenly made up their minds, then and there, to buy other items than those they have listed.

So here is our last chance to communicate. Our "last-chance medium" includes the point-of-sale displays and packages that might flag her down in the store.

The last-chance medium has also been the last considered when it comes to advertising programs. That is why it has not, strictly, been in the domain of most copywriters.

But in the automated marketing of the future, the last may well prove to be first. And so this is an appropriate subject to conclude this media section, before discussing the total campaign.

The Advantages of P.O.P.

Point-of-purchase advertising should be important. After all, it is at the point of purchase. The customers, or potential customers, are there. Usually, they are not there by accident. They have come to buy or at least are looking.

This is the ideal for which the advertising man is always searching—a receptive target. When he places an ad in a mass-circulation magazine or on television, it is impossible to predict how many of his multimillion audience will be remotely in the mood for his message.

But at the point of sale, the audience is in the buying mood. Who could want a more receptive audience?

Here is another advantage point-of-sale has over other mass media: it has less waste circulation. W. Parlin Lillard, a former vice-president of General Foods, illustrated this tellingly in a speech to POPAI (the Point of Purchase Advertising Institute):

> I understand that there are 46 million out of 53 million families in the United States who have no interest in baby food . . . because they do not have a baby between 4 months and 23 months old and they do not expect to have a baby—so can these 46 million families be considered as real prospective customers for these baby food products?
>
> The same thing might be said of the advertising we see for parakeet and canary bird food. . . . Out of these 53 million homes in the United States . . . I am told . . . there are only 1½ million with a canary . . . yet we see this Reader's Digest magazine advertising and one company used the Tennessee Ernie Ford show on ABC network to sell their Bird Food . . . Couldn't this be considered waste "Canary Bird Food" advertising to the 51½ million homes out of the 53 million homes who do not have a canary?

Point-of-sale advertising has a more selected audience than those mass-media ads which want to appeal to parents of babies and owners of parakeets. The customer heading for the baby-food section is going there with a purpose; the family in the pet department is already interested in pets.

Of course, you say, the customers have to get there in the first place. National advertising helps to send them there. And it often sends them there predisposed toward a particular brand.

True, but today's marketing, with its super-stores, relies more and more on impulse buying. What's more, a well-planned point-of-sale piece can retrigger the message of previous advertising.

What about the cost of point-of-purchase display? Does it cost more per thousand than the major media? It all depends, of course, but with even the most bearish estimates, p.o.p. compares favorably. POPAI puts out a "Point-of-Purchase Exposure Cost Calculator" with which cost of reaching consumers can be reckoned. It has a table of "exposure factors" for different kinds of stores. Figuring how many displays are up, for how many days, how many checkouts the store has, and how much each display costs, the estimator can sometimes get down to pennies per thousand.

And, say the proponents of p.o.p., you can only get C.P.M. (cost per thousand) from other media. With this one you get C.P.B.M. (cost per *buying* thousand).

What do the displays themselves cost and what should they be? It all depends—on the budget, the message, the audience, the outlet, the laws (if they are for alcoholic beverages, etc.).

Displays of any quantity and importance vary in cost from, say, $3 apiece to $15 or $20. As you add to a lithographed picture a die cut, animation, lighting, etc., the cost, of course, rises. But you have a wide range to choose from. Categories for which awards in POPAI's "Hall of Fame" are given include:

> Animation, lighted and unlighted—cardboard and corrugated or plastic
> and permanent
> Audio and Audio-Video
> Clocks
> Cloth Banners and Drapes
> Decals and Flexible Films
> Paper Sculpture
> Photogelatine
> Thermometers
> Signs, indoor and outdoor, plastic and metal
> Silk Screen and Rubber Plate

Here is another reason why point-of-purchase advertising is important: In today's shopping, there are fewer clerks to communicate with the customer. Therefore, except for the package itself, the point-of-sale display takes the place of the salesman. It can tell the customer what the product is, how it will benefit him, and what it will cost. It can, as the POPAI slogan has it, "complete the cycle of the sale."

It can, that is, if it is there.

The Dismal Dilemma of Point-of-Sale

The big disadvantage of point-of-sale advertising is that you can seldom be certain it will be at the right place at the right time. Those lovely, expensive displays may be in their unopened mailing cartons in the store's back room. Or they may be piled in your wholesaler's warehouse, or in the district salesman's garage. This is one of the major problems of point-of-sale advertising. Magazines and newspapers have as much space for advertising as the traffic will bear. TV is crowded, to be sure, but you can locate positions if you have enough money to spend. But these big supermarkets, chain stores and drugstores are glutted with thousands of items. Every square foot of space is vital to the store's profit. In answer to a survey made by the Audit and Surveys Co., in cooperation with the U.S. Department of Agriculture, store officials gave space as their prime consideration in the use of point-of-sale advertising. The message, color, and design of a display were important to them, of course, but their first concern was "Will I have room for it?"

The other part of the dilemma is that point-of-sale displays are seldom created with the same state of mind and in the same stimulating atmosphere as are ads and commercials. For one thing, that very problem of space results in thousands of advertisers vying to induce store managers (or the supermarket "buying committees," which are all-powerful and even less accessible) to put their displays up. This, in many ways, can take their eyes off the main target, the customer. For another thing, the unorthodox manner in which this kind of advertising is placed often results in "wheeling and dealing"—the kind of practices which inhibit sincere creativity.

Finally, the "nature of the beast" has made it less attractive to the top creative men in advertising. This is partly because of its history. Like direct mail, advertising specialties, exhibits, etc., point-of-sale has not even been considered "advertising." It is called "sales promotion" by manufacturers and "collateral" by advertising agencies. The latter nomenclature was invented because charges for displays were noncommissionable. Only commissionable advertising (in broadcast media and publications) was called "advertising."

How short-sighted that semantic difference has been—and what inefficiencies have resulted! Something "collateral" means "situated at the side," "secondary," and "indirect." What could be less indirect than the point-of-sale display which the customer sees at the precise moment when he might reach for the product! Yet advertising agencies, because they could not make as convenient a profit on point-of-sale displays, relegated them to a secondary position, and some agencies have resisted having anything to do with them. As a result, the majority of point-of-sale advertising is created by advertisers, rather than by their advertising agencies, by "sales-promotion agencies" which have hastened to fill the gap, and by the display producers—lithographers, fabricators, companies that specialize in point-of-sale. It is possible, though, that the use by many advertising agencies of the fee system, instead of straight commissions, will increase their activity in this field.

Point-of-sale, relatively speaking, is the least of the major media. It accounts, at this writing, for an average of only 5 percent of the total advertising budget. Although point-of-sale is supposed to "complete the cycle of the sale," it is usually the last factor considered in a total campaign. Since most of it is prepared through the advertisers, directly, its planning often has to wait on the national media planning with the advertising agency. Then, of course, everything is on a crash basis. Time for creative thinking, estimating, and production is telescoped. Sometimes the actual results appear long after the national advertising with which they are supposed to be coordinated. Or, if the point-of-sale advertising is prepared without consideration of the national campaign, there is no attempt to coordinate at all.

Symptomatic of the atmosphere in which point-of-sale is prepared is the prevalence of "speculative" presentations by various p.o.p. houses. Point-of-sale producers are often expected to invest in copy, art, and construction dummies, in competition with one another. Any entrepreneur with an idea may drift in and out of the business. This is true in other fields of advertising, but probably most so in point-of-sale, because it is not so regulated and respected a medium.

This is not to say that the main producers of displays are not creative. They may, in fact, be even more creative than the fat cats in the more glamorous media. For the habit of turning on a dime, of doing the impossible, of constantly solving the practical problems of space and time, develops a hardy race. Just think, if this is so, how much more can be accomplished as point-of-sale becomes as respected a member of the marketing mix as the print and broadcast media.

And what has all this to do with the copywriter? To repeat, a copywriter these days does not deal with words only. He communicates with concepts and ideas. He may conceive a copy strategy for many different media. Now, as automated marketing improves, point-of-sale displays are increasingly important. We have to be aware of all the elements of the point-of-sale picture if we are to have the balanced point of view to improve it.

Advertising Displayland

Forgetting, for the moment, the ins and outs, the sacred cows, the neglected state of the medium, anyone with imagination can run wild with point-of-sale.

"It's all ingenuity," says Aaron Friedman, of Display Mart, Inc. "You can use any material known to man."

And display makers have done just that. They have used metal, wire, wood, cloth, and combinations. They have used building materials—from chicken wire and gypsum, to gravel, glass, and aluminum. The commonest display materials are paper and cardboard, which are cheap and expendable. But you can fit your designs and materials to every purpose. And in that regard, point-of-sale is a lot like television. *Any* display idea *can* be executed. The technicians will tell you whether your idea is affordable, but they can accomplish almost anything.

Do you want to bring a trademark to life—like the famous full-rigger of Cutty Sark Scotch? The display man, with his gears and gadgets, managed to produce two thousand of those within the cost budgeted (about $15 each). Now people stare, as the Cutty Sark rises and falls, plunging through a stormy sea, in its bottle on the backbar or in the liquor store window. The cost per thousand is small when you consider how long this display will be up.

Would you like the center of the stage for your story about Burgie beer, and how it is "balanced right"? Here is a moving, spectacular display of a seal, actually life-size, balancing a ball on his nose and turning round and round on his pedestal (this was a most costly piece, about $100, and it went from store to store, the way painted bulletins are rotated).

Illuminated shadow boxes with changing scenes; 3-D transparencies, which need no artificial light source; waterwheels that pump real water; lighthouses that throw real beams; marine displays where fish wiggle, ogling beer cans in a fishnet; and 8-mm color films, revolving perpetually when you press a button—these, and a million more ideas, can make an adventureland of point-of-sale advertising. If you can get the space.

Nor do intriguing displays have to be expensive. Polyethylene can be shaped and lithographed to sparkle as window stickers. Silk-screened counter cards can be more brilliant than litho (they used to have to be done by hand, in small quantities only; now, through a Swedish process, they can be printed at the rate of a thousand per hour).

Paper displays can be sculptured to be three dimensional. Cardboard can be die-cut. Plastic can be vacuum-formed into every shape you can imagine. Shelf-talkers that cost a few cents apiece move and waggle by means of a wire. Mobiles, hung from the ceiling, are rotated by the air currents. Bottle-toppers, printed in Day-Glo, snap at your eyes as you pass by. Cardboard displays can be animated by batteries that last up to a month. Other inexpensive displays, with holes in the top, are called "light thieves," get their illumination for transparent letters or pictures from the store's ceiling lights.

All is possible in the point-of-sale medium. Radio has sound, print has color, TV has sound and motion and color. But point-of-sale can have all of these, plus three dimensions, tangible texture, even fragrance. It can be the medium of all the senses—if you can get the space.

And here is where all your ingenuity comes to a head. How can you get the space for your display? Above all, by giving the retailer what he wants.

What does the retailer want? He wants more traffic in his store. He wants ideas that are flexible, compact, above all, that cause *him* no trouble

—no trouble to set up, no trouble to maintain. He wants goodwill from his customers. He wants ideas that will sell more of *your* product for him, but—better still—that will help him to sell other products in addition.

How do we give the dealer what he wants? Just as we appeal to the consumer—with something worthwhile. We help to get the traffic he wants with displays of "related premiums." (Such as the long-playing record issued by Schlitz, titled with the beer's slogan—"Real Gusto"—and featuring "The 12 hits that made the big bands famous," a $3.98 value for $1.00.) We give him the kind of "instant display" he likes—the kind that's *no trouble*. (Like the one for ReaLemon. A shipping carton turned into a display when the storekeeper ran his thumbnail over a perforated line, pulled a tab, and released a prestocked display bin filled with plastic squeeze lemons.)

How about goodwill? You can think of a lot of ideas that sell your product and, at the same time, provide his customers with a service. (Like the Gallo Wine Selector, that displayed each wine with the food it complemented; like the Old Charter "baseball expert" display, that challenged ball fans to a quiz game on the spot; like the hundreds of food displays tied in with recipes.)

As for ideas which will sell more products than your own—here is an area to tax your greatest ingenuity. For "unselfish displays" which give the dealer a storewide promotion can be weak for the sponsoring product and tie-ins with other products can be strained and unrealistic. Rather, like the "Fall Cheese Festival" of the American Dairy Association, in-store display material should be so natural and delicious that it triggers a whole chain reaction of impulse-buying.

Still, to compete for that precious space where this "last-chance medium" can work, we need irresistible arguments. And that is what broke the dam and released the flood of special incentives which at once placate and plague the industry.

How Premiums, Promotions, and Deals Influence Displays

Harrison F. Dunning, head of the Scott Paper Company and archenemy of "the gimmicks, the come-ons, the hokey-pokey," cites a cartoon he saw, of a lady taking inventory with her husband after a shopping trip. "Let's see," she said, "trading stamps, stamp book, premium catalog, contest entry blanks, list of next week's specials—good gracious—the groceries!"

It's no wonder she forgot the groceries when they were hidden behind a welter of special inducements to buy. And the reason Dunning decried such inducements is that they are "borrowed interest," extraneous to the merits of the product.

It may be that many marketing men, feeling an urgent need to attract attention from the consumers, and feeling that advertising was failing to do this job for them effectively, have turned to the gimmicks and the come-ons because they tell their story on the shelf in the market place, they get the attention of the consumer as she walks through the store, and they hope that getting this attention will result in larger business. I think this perhaps is the easy way out and I think the base is anything but solid, because I am sure that if one man can give 3 cents off the label, the next man can blunt his effort entirely with 4 cents off the label; if one man can give away bicycles, the next man can give away automobiles. If one man can offer a trip to Europe, the next man can have a trip around the world. This certainly isn't employing the marketing skills that I think companies expect from their marketing personnel. I'm darn sure that we don't need any high-priced executives to dream up the best give-away. It's simply a matter of economics and of dollars and cents, and I am sure that these things can never be an effective long-range substitute for effective selling and advertising of a product with value.

There is no question that premiums and contests and deals do stimulate sales. And they help to get the displays up. How can we, in response to Mr. Dunning, sell the product's value and still get the displays up?

The answer, as in all media, is to be creative *on the subject*. Incentives which do not in themselves promote consumption of the product cannot possibly be as profitable as incentives that do (assuming, that is, that both are equally ingenious). The former are simply a way to buy the customer instead of inducing the customer to buy. It is possible, through your imagination, to give the dealer and his customer a genuine extra incentive, which can have all the leverage of the borrowed-interest deals and, at the same time, give a healthy growth to the product.

First, there is the extra incentive when you have genuine news to tell— the introduction of a new or greatly improved product which deserves to be quickly sampled. The ad features a price-off coupon, or a free or self-liquidating premium, to induce people to go to the store and look for the display which ties in with the advertised offer. Because the ad has genuine news to tell, it is easier for the copywriter to stick to his subject, the product, instead of having it dragged in by the heels as an incidental in the sale of a premium or a coupon. Here, for example, is an original way of expressing a coupon promotion, which was germane to the intro-duction of the product and for which any salesman could enthusiastically justify a display:

> (*Two-color newspaper ad, illustrating a coupon surrounded by a hypnotic colored pattern of shapes and lines, similar, at that time, to what later turned out to be "op art."*)
> Headline:
> Please stare at this coupon and count to ten slowly.

Headline on coupon:
BIRDS EYE
SPECIAL INTRODUCTORY OFFER
Get 10 cents off your next can of Awake

You are now hypnotized.
You will cut out this coupon and take it to your grocer.
He will give you ten cents off on a can of Awake.
You will remember that Awake is neither an orange drink nor frozen
    orange juice, but an entirely new and different breakfast drink that
    tastes as good as frozen orange juice.
You will remember that one 9-oz. can of Awake makes as much beverage
    as two 6-oz. cans of frozen orange concentrate.
You will remember that Awake has more Vitamin C, B_1 and A than orange
    juice.
Now, at the count of ten, AWAKE.

The incentive to try that new product was easy to express in an ad or
display—simply a coupon offering a discount. But when it comes to premiums, it is hard to sell the premium well and still communicate about
the product. The first guide to writing copy for a premium ad is to concentrate on the premium—make the customer's mouth water for that
premium—and definitely diminish the mention of the product. If you are
offering a rosebush, for example, for a low price and a box top, you illustrate that rosebush, you romance it, you compare its value with other
comparable rosebushes. How can you possibly romance the dog food, or
the pie filling, or the aluminum foil it is calculated to promote—and still
do justice to that rosebush? You can't—but if it is *directly* tied in with the
product it is promoting—a fertilizer, for example—then purchase of the
rosebush can further sales of the fertilizer, and it is quite natural for the
copywriter to expound on the merits of both.

Just so with the promotion of free fruit with the purchase of Kellogg's
cereal. They just naturally went together. And the cheese festival we mentioned earlier. The point-of-sale displays showed luscious go-togethers:
"GOUDA CHEESE—a tasty snack with juicy pears" . . . "Franks stuffed
with cheddar and wrapped with bacon" . . . "BLUE CHEESE AND
BURGERS" . . . "PIZZA A LA PROVOLONE." Lithographed overwire
hangers were as rich as still lifes by a Dutch painter. Ads in magazines
offered a "cheese-barrow" premium—a fruitwood cheese server with slicer
and spreader, for $2 and a label from any brand of cheese. At the store,
the premium was displayed in all its glory, but it was not borrowed interest—the customer simply *had* to buy cheese if she was going to use
that spreader.

The same was true with a free premium offer of a Jell-O recipe book.

It was called "Joys of Jell-O" and it had ninety-six pages and 250 ideas for using Jell-O for desserts, salads, and parties. The book was featured in magazine ads and with p.o.p. displays and some were ordered by customers who had to enclose twelve box fronts for each. Think of the amount of Jell-O consumed through that offer! Equally successful was the Campbell self-liquidator "Cooking with Soup" (for "Only 50¢ and 3 different Campbell's Soup labels"). It was a genuine bargain, for it featured "608 skillet dishes, casseroles, stews, sauces, gravies, dips, soupmates and garnishes."

Another immensely successful premium at point-of-sale was the Maxwell House coffee in the carafe—a display formed by the package itself, when Instant Maxwell House came in a handsome Pyrex carafe made by Corning Glass. Maxwell House sold millions of these carafes, and how did the housewife use them? To make more coffee.

Contests, too, can be on the subject and can encourage use of the product. What could be more apt than the Dial soap "Instant Sweepstakes," in which the contestant could step into a shower or bath, wash with Dial, and see the magic number the water revealed on a piece of paper? Then he went to the store where the point-of-sale displays helped him arrange for his payoff.

Now, aren't these all obvious ways to push products with deals, premiums, and promotions—to justify and encourage the retailers featuring those products and their displays? Don't these rather simple ideas also live up to the principles we have been preaching about good communication—to be pertinent and explicit, to interest the consumer? Don't they also *involve* the audience, by encouraging her to serve coffee in glass, to follow the recipes, to eat fruit with cereal? Certainly ideas like these can answer both the advertiser's need to get his displays up and Dunning's plea for creatively selling the quality of the product. And they are the easiest kinds of ideas to come by, for you simply get them by that game of free-association we discussed in Chap. 7. You ask yourself, "What goes with cheese?" "What premium can I associate with coffee?" Browsing through the big premium shows, which feature thousands of enticing items, your power of association can also work in reverse. You can see an attractive premium and think of a relevant use. For example, at one show there was a "Dental Care Center" offered for $19.95. You could associate that with a toothpaste promotion. Then there was the "Family Travel Booklet," which told sixty ways to keep children happy in the car with games, puzzles, etc. That was a natural for a tire or gasoline manufacturer.

It is so obviously easy to make these associations that you wonder why advertisers keep going afield. They offer a manicure set when you buy a dog food, a free hostess tray for a demonstration of vinyl floor tile, a set of cutlery for seals from some coffee jars. Why do they do it? Because they feel that the premiums will pull. Often, they know that they will, because they have been carefully tested. The trouble is that while such offers will stimulate traffic and sales they *are* expeditious, they *are* shortsighted. It is up to the creative people—in our case, the copywriters—to use their imagination to encourage more point-of-sale, more traffic and sales, more service to the consumer, all *on the subject.*

The Package and Its Purposes

"The package is where good advertising should start," said Abe Plough, President of a multimillion-dollar complex of well-known products, who began his career selling Plough's Healing Oil from the back of a horse and wagon. Certainly the package is where good advertising now ends, on the shelf of the store, where it must compete with other packages, to catch the eye of the customer, who passes by at the rate of perhaps three seconds per facing. And it ends in the consumer's house, where the package is used and often reused.

Is the package an ad? There are those who say no. But with our definition of advertising as communication, it had better be. Also, unlike our billboards and magazine ads and commercials, the package is a *functioning* ad, so close to the product that it often inspires its manufacture and opens up profitable markets, employment, and satisfaction for the consumer.

Think of what the development of the aerosol package, the tin can, and frozen food packaging meant to marketing. Now we have the convenience of pop-top cans, of pull-open bottle tops, of twist-off spouts, and quick-opening zip tabs. We have a variety of pouches and boxes and closures and overwraps; a galaxy of designs and decorations, of gift wrapping and protective wrapping, of labels, seals, and tags, of directions, news, and services—all in the rich packages that festoon the supermarket, like the treasures of Aladdin. All were designed to be practical containers, to please the shipper and the storekeeper, and to benefit the consumer.

If ever an advertisement had to be on the subject, explicit, interesting, communicative, *this* is the payoff. Is the package of interest to the copywriter who is an idea man, who understands that all communication about the product is related? You bet it is. Yet packaging, for the most part, has been in the domain of the manufacturer and the package designer. Since it affects everything we do, it is about time we copywriters got into the act!

Package advertising is important. So much so that more money is spent on packages than on all other forms of advertising combined. Now, in the 1960's, some 400 billion products are consumed every year. That takes a lot of packages. The population is growing, and with it the number of families and homes. The consumers of abundance keep having more and more discretionary dollars to spend. The manufacturers, competing for those dollars, keep thinking up new ways to save work, worry, and time; new ways to make products more healthful, appetizing, inexpensive, and available. Self-service markets and vending machines have made packages doubly important; they must speak for themselves. National advertising identifies the package away from the store—its shape and color and main characteristics—and the tangible package dovetails with the advertising at the point-of-sale.

The beauty of the package, as an object lesson to us copywriters, is that it is totally pertinent. It is the essence of the personality of the product—an advertisement with all the fat removed. That is, it should be if it is to look well and stand out on the shelf. Thus, it becomes a functional thing. And all its functions are calculated for one purpose: to please the customer. So here is an advertisement that epitomizes the whole meaning of our work.

Just consider some of the examples of successful packaging and why they were conceived. The pop-top beer can saves customers the trouble of using openers. The new plastic cigarette package is sturdy, tactile, and keeps cigarettes fresher. The rigid foil container and the polyethylene and polyester pouch allow cooking in the package. Plastic tubes are easy to carry in a purse. Pop-up packages are self-dispensing. Closures seal themselves. Aerosols measure the spray. Transparent containers let you see what you are buying. Lightweight multipacks let you save repeated purchases. All of these ideas, and hundreds more, were conceived for one purpose: to benefit the buyer. *That* is communication.

And what about the aesthetics of packaging? This too, is for the benefit of the audience. The idea, says designer S. Neil Fujita, is to relate the design of the package to pleasurable human experiences. For a paper company promotion, he designed the label of a fictitious coffee which read "Instant Morning Coffee." The design had the typography and general feeling of a morning newspaper. A picture of clear brown coffee, in a white cup, on a light violet background, gave the label a cheerful identity. Here is how Fujita described the derivation of his design:

> Look around you. Design is everywhere in nature. In the shape of a seashell. In a bird's wing. In the form of a tree with its pattern of branches and veined leaves. Design, then, is fundamental in man's surroundings. In fact, man has become so accustomed to design as an integral part of everyday life that he reacts—almost without realizing he is reacting—to every new design. Man intuitively, subconsciously, relates these new forms to past experiences—other patterns.

It follows that in fashioning a package the designer works toward a design that triggers a recollection of something pleasurable in the customer's experience and associates it with the product being sold. In this instance, the product is coffee. The label must, in every way, convey the pleasant thoughts most people attach to coffee. Now, certainly one of the most pleasurable of daily human experiences is coffee at breakfast. This, above all, is the cup that clears the mind and braces the spirit against the trials of a new day. The design of this instant-coffee package, therefore, uses a group of familiar elements and concepts that help the viewer recall this "wake up" function.

The design of a package, while it is the visual work of artists, is essentially an idea and can well come from a collaboration between copywriter and designer. The designer does everything for a purpose. He has to be as aware of the nature of the product, its customers and competition as a copywriter is. Designer Walter Landor, asked for a definition of himself, first replied, not that he was an artist, but "an individual who is interested in people and sympathetic with their needs." He then defined himself as "an artist with a strong sense of technological and business needs and methods. In solving clients' problems, a designer has to take into account highly practical problems of economics, production, distribution, and sociological trends. He must be deeply concerned with those trends. He must have an awareness of what has gone before, what the consumer has been conditioned by in the past and he must build against that background."

This is a challenging kind of endeavor, for, as we emphasized in Chap. 2, all people have different collections of stuff, and in the abstract field of design, one person's favorite color or shape could be abhorrent to another. The designer has to find common denominators which can express the purpose of the package, compete for attention, appeal to the individual, and still be in the mainstream of American taste.

Packages have a psychological effect all their own. This has been dramatically proven in the case of wines and beers, when taste testers, given the exact same blend in packages with different labels, attributed wide differences of taste to the samples. Just so, packages which have had loyal users, can evoke hostile attitudes if they are radically changed without explanation or functional reason.

Some advertisers change their packages so adroitly that the consumer is hardly aware of the changes, yet they fit the contemporary environment or strategic purpose. Labels on Heinz cans, for example, were recently simplified, but the familiar keystone symbol, which had identified the product throughout the century, was even more emphasized.

Trademarks, logos, and brand images will undergo almost imperceptible changes to keep up with the decades. Sometimes, according to objectives, the designer goes backward in time. For example, Landor cites the designs for Sara Lee frozen baked goods, which drew inspiration from his museum of Early American packages—old-fashioned backgrounds of a country store, or apothecary jars, etc., surrounded by big, appetizing shots of the products, capped with the copy "From the Kitchens of Sara Lee—bakers of America's Best Loved Cakes." Here was a fast reminder which immediately contradicted the image of the streamlined impersonality of modern freezing. Sara Lee had found a way to freeze baked goods and retain their rich, butery, old-fashioned flavor. The name and reputation of Sara Lee, the character of the products, all demanded that unmodern kind of design.

The package has so many purposes and facets, we could go on for too many pages. Its first purpose, of course, is for identification, and here the copywriter and designer must consider, as with print ads, that all display is no display and that certain elements must come functionally first. We must tell the customer immediately what the product is and what it is for. The name of the maker should be relatively prominent if it is an asset to communication. The degree of emphasis between the brand identification (Sara Lee), the generic identification (Cakes), and the difference from other products (Made with Fresh Butter) depends on what is the best strategy. Four Roses whiskey, for example, was a blend that appealed to a certain kind of drinker, but had relatively poor sales and reputation with the straight bourbon drinkers in the West. Still, the brand name Four Roses had cachet with the trade and deserved some mention. When "Antique Bourbon" became a companion product, its label carried the name "Four Roses," but that was subordinated. "Campbell's Soup," on the other hand, is so valuable a brand name that it is the most prominent element on all packages.

It is essential for copywriters, who might have a great deal to say, to understand the problems of the package designer, and his expertise. He is working with both flat surface design and with three dimensions. The customer looks at the package from many different angles, not just as he reads an ad, head on. Sometimes he picks the package up, puts it down, turns it around; so all its sides must be related.

Robert I. Goldberg, in the *Modern Packaging Encyclopedia,* refers to the designer's "alphabet" and "vocabulary" as a "language of vision." He tells how the designer deals in shape or mass and in line.

Shapes, we know, can influence emotions. Triangles and rectangles look masculine, circles and ovals look feminine. Line, consisting of typography, dots, ruled directions, can make sharp differences in meanings. So much so that an improperly designed package could lead your eye directly to its competitor on the next shelf.

And of course, color strongly affects reactions. Designers want to attract attention, but colors that shout are not the only answer. (Landor, in redesigning a line of labels for Gallo wine, chose a deep maroon for a full-bodied red wine, pink for Vin Rosé, a muted olive green for a dry Sauterne, and brown for sweet Marsala.)

Color is a strong factor at the store, and can be multiplied in its effect in national advertising—like the quickly recognized Pall-Mall red and the Newport turquoise. But the mass and line of these packages had to be carefully designed to be equally memorable on black-and-white TV.

"A rule of thumb," says Goldberg, "in the use of the 'alphabet' of package designing is to let one communicative element dominate over all others and then to progressively emphasize . . . only two other elements. This can be referred to as the 'Big One,' 'Smaller Two' and 'Smallest Three.'"

That rule certainly seems to coincide with what we know of posters, print ads, and TV commercials. We can say just so much strongly, which is why we invented headlines and subheads, dominant illustrations, and commercial leads.

One elemental change Raymond Loewy made in a Lucky Strike package doubled its registration. Formerly, the bulls-eye had been on one side only. A billion packages were sold a year. People naturally throw a cigarette package down on a table. By placing the familiar bulls-eye on both sides, Loewy doubled its appearance as a billboard.

What about writing copy for package labeling? There are infinite variations. Take state and federal regulations, for example. Some nine federal agencies, working under various tariff, container, and labeling acts, make sure that packages carry the vital statistics. Currently, Senator Hart's "Truth in Packaging" Bill has focused on long-seething complaints by consumers against deceptive labeling. But it is often important to our communication to find space on the package to specify ingredients far beyond legal requirements. For example, take the case of Kellogg's Concentrate. This cereal was created as a nutrition food, so the more explicit the package is, the better chance it has to win the buyer's conviction. Read the long, fact-packed copy on the back panel of the package:

Kellogg's
Concentrate
Ready-to-serve Nutrition Booster
What it is:

Kellogg's Concentrate is an unusual new ready-to-serve cereal with concentrated nutrition—40% high-quality protein, 99% fat-free, with defatted wheat germ added.

Concentrate is also an excellent general-purpose food, especially helpful to weight watchers, children and adolescents with finicky appetites, women during pregnancy, and all people requiring a high-protein diet.

Reasonable in price because it's so concentrated.

One ounce (about ⅓ cup) contains:

PROTEIN 11.3 gm. More than an egg and 2 strips of bacon.

IRON 5.0 mg. As much as 2 ounces of beef liver.

VITAMIN B_1 (thiamine) 0.5 mg. As much as 3 oz. of pork.

RIBOFLAVIN 0.6 mg. More than 4 oz. of Cheddar Cheese.

NIACIN 5.0 mg. More than 3 ounces of beef steak.

VITAMIN C. 15.0 mg. About as much as a 4-ounce glass of tomato juice.

VITAMIN B_6 1.0 mg. More than 5 carrots.

VITAMIN B_{12} 2.5 mcg. As much as in one oz. of meat or fish.

VITAMIN D 200 USP units. As much as two full glasses of vitamin D milk.

NO COOKING—NO REFRIGERATION NEEDED

One side panel goes into even more detail, with a listing of the percentages of vitamins and nutrients and a listing of ingredients. The other side panel shows attractive color illustrations of various uses of the cereal, including casseroles and salads. The front panel, on the other hand, boils down the message to make room for an enormous initial "C" in the word "Concentrate."

Contrast with that long-copy package the copy on a bottle of 7-Up soft drink. On the front of the bottle and on the neck is the one big element "7-Up." The back label simply reads "Seven-Up, The 'Fresh Up' Drink," and lists the few ingredients in less than twenty words of small type. There is no need to labor the copy here, for 7-Up is not, like Kellogg's Concentrate, a health food. The designer works more with his vocabulary than with ours.

The designer's ideal, of course, would be to have the package communicate nonverbally, even at a distance. How many Coca-Cola bottles can you think of—unmistakably engraved in the public mind, even without words?

But in addition to quick identification, specifying contents, having distinction, and, of course, protecting the product, the package can have many other purposes. It can provide services, such as recipes and premium offers, which work after the package is in the home. Its function in the home can be a communication in itself. The design might whet the appetite in the store but be an eyesore in the kitchen. Many manufacturers are designing their packages to be used as "unselfish" decorations and utilities—such as bathroom tissue boxes in different decorator styles (the commercial overwrap is removed and thrown away), the Maxwell House Coffee decanter, etc.

Where Packaging Ideas Come from

Remember the nuisance of opening ice-cream cartons? how the ice cream would drip out, if you didn't use it all? Some thoughtful packager came up with a carton that opened with a zip-tab, then reclosed neatly, and one more consumer inconvenience was gone.

Remember the unsanitary inconvenience of the milk bottle top? Now milk opens and closes with a press of the fingers against the paper container.

Remember how quickly crackers became soggy and stale? Now they are wrapped in glassine inner liners that keep out the moisture, keep the cracker crisp, and give the copywriters another selling point.

Remember how fast bananas died on the shelf? A cellophane overwrap, with tiny holes that let the bananas breathe, extend their shelf life.

The point is, that every one of those packaging ideas answered a problem. And this is the easiest possible way to conceive good packaging ideas —find the consumer needs that still exist, then solve them.

For example, vaccines and antibiotics are wonderful, but they hurt when administered with a hypodermic needle. The packaging industry discovered that these medicines could enter the bloodstream just as well when administered with an aerosol spray: a new idea to relieve pain.

For example, modern bacon is attractively processed and packaged, but the grease will still spatter when you cook it. So one packager came up with the idea of a heat-conducting container which you could pop into the oven so your bacon would be toasted without mess.

For example, what problem remained in the matter of feeding your dog? Cleaning the dish, decided General Mills. So they marketed Speak, in a disposable dog food dish.

What is the problem in mixing a very dry martini? Getting just a whisper of Vermouth into that lethal potion of straight gin. Voilá—a sensational packaging idea: Whisp, the spray Vermouth in the aerosol package!

"How can I help the poor, overworked mother of a new baby?" thinks the inventive packager. The problem is mixing those complicated feeding formulas and cleaning up after them. He develops a whole new line of disposable formula packages, and he creates a bright new market.

All of these ways of thinking, in the search for better packages, come from a state of mind to which we copywriters are accustomed—a bent for *service,* for finding ways to interest the customer by benefiting him. And these packaging benefits can help win the competitive battle . . . while giving us a constant supply of copy news for the ads in all our other media.

What Lies Ahead for Packaging?

Is it always possible for problem-solving packaging ideas to become a reality? A few years ago we would think not. But each day, in this miracle age, the impossible becomes more rare. New materials seem unlimited.

They can be formed, shaped, cut, laminated, printed, and combined however you please. Paper, paperboard, films, foils, glass, and metal containers are chosen for what they can do best. High-temperature polyethylene film is ideal for vended hot foods. Vinyl-coated cellophane gives gloss, transparency, and protection. Polycarbonate sheet and film and molded break-resistant bottles are used for products that need extra strength in their packaging. Transparent vinyl sleeves, with their own built-in muscles, hold on to vegetables. Modified aluminum alloys can make rigid, heat-reflective containers and lighter, cold-holding cans. Polystyrene sheet can be thermoformed for the shape and intaglio designs you want. Vinyl-based foam can be sprayed on to the product, so it is protected and you can see it, yet it retains its *own* packaged shape.

Fiber-and-foil composite cans, which cost less to ship and store and discard, are popular today for motor oil, paint, and coffee. Aerosol cans have been perfected which need so little propellant that you can have 14 oz. of food in a 16-oz. can. Fluted glassine cups can be made in continuous sheets to hold candy. Polyethylene beverage cases, strong enough to ship, weigh 60 percent less than wood, cost less to distribute. Paper sleeves, strong enough to hold twenty-four beverage cans together, eliminate the need for cases altogether. The savings can be passed on to the retailer and the consumer, and there is an extra incentive to buy by the case, because now you can carry more beverages with less labor.

Yet many of these advantages and materials will soon be commonplace, even passé. Packaging advances are coming so fast that what we say here can be obsolete tomorrow.

Right now, folding paper cartons are the most prevalent containers, but glass, which is made from unlimited supplies of sand, is a strong contender.

Right now, metal containers are the biggest money-makers of packaging materials (over $2 billion), but plastics are coming up fast.

Right now, polyethylene, just a few years old, is the largest volume packaging film, but time-honored cellophane is still first of the films in dollar-volume. The materials keep jockeying for position, and they rise and fall in popularity according to the daily poll of consumer needs and our inventive ingenuity to meet those needs.

Whatever the packages and materials of tomorrow, we feel confident of one prediction: packaging is certain to increase in importance as an advertising medium. "Robot retailing," whether it be through closed-circuit TV, in-store cybernation or some form of mail order, is bound to become prevalent. As it does, the package, at the point-of-sale, will serve as its own major medium of communication.

PART 3

THE
FUTURE
CAMPAIGN

18

THE WHOLE EGG

In Search of Symmetry

The presentation, made by this writer to the management of a major corporation, began with a bit of showmanship. Reaching into his suitcoat pocket, and holding the exhibit gingerly so that it would not break, he revealed the white, spherical form of an egg.

"If I were to ask you what this object is," he said, "what would you answer?

"Would you say that it's albumen? Yoke? A paper-thin shell? Or would you say it is an *egg?*"

The point being made was that the advertising campaign about to be presented was supposed to be a unified, integrated whole. While it had many different aspects—just as the egg was composed of different elements, like albumen, yoke, and shell—the sum of the parts were supposed to add up to "the whole egg."

When the presentation was over, the chairman of the board wagged an admonitory finger under the presenter's nose. "I understand what you're driving at. But it can't stop here. It can't just be magazine ads and commercials. You've got to get everybody into the act."

The first person to understand the idea of an integrated campaign was the chairman of the board, because it was he who saw his vast corporation every day from the top and it was he who was constantly questioning,

"What are we? What do we add up to? How do we communicate it to our many publics?"

The problem of corporations today, as they grow larger, as they diversify, is to present some kind of unified message to the public. It is also the problem of any one product, which is presented in different media, by different people, and with widely ranging techniques. The solution has been variously called "brand image," "the integrated campaign," and "total marketing communication." The analogy of the whole egg was easier to grasp because it was a metaphor, and brought ·a high-level abstraction down to a specific object, in everyday experience. It became a convenient point of reference from then on—when television commercials, magazine ads, point-of-sale displays, words, pictures, and so forth, were being judged in relation to one another—to ask, "Do they add up to the whole egg?"

Few people in advertising have been wise enough—or sufficiently autonomous—to materialize a whole egg. It has been effected, to a degree, when the entire program is designed and dictated by one forceful personality or when a beautifully simple idea comes through so forcefully that it pervades and dominates all the facets of a campaign.

The reason the whole egg is so elusive, though, is because it is difficult for us all to communicate to one another what we are talking about. It comes down to a kind of philosopher's stone which each man knows, in his heart, exists, but which he cannot articulate or bring to life in a tangible form.

One method that is helpful, in trying to coordinate the campaign for a product or service, is to personify the subject. George Gribbin, in a speech presented at a meeting of the American Association of Advertising Agencies, once revealed this as his "unscientific, hitherto undisclosed method of ad assessment." He said, "I make it a point to compare ads to people. I say to myself, would I like a man or woman to act the way this ad does? Would I choose this ad—if it were alive—for a friend?"

"If it were alive" is an exciting way to look at our product—an inanimate thing—and to try to conceive our campaign, something so amorphous. It is appropriate these days, when advertising increasingly takes the place of a living salesman and has to perform the entire communication. And, when we consider it, this is what we have meant all along by "image." We want the product and the campaign to have a personality all their own—not the copywriter's personality, not the personality of the advertising manager, or of the chairman of the board—but of the thing itself. "In the process of reducing a concept to practice," wrote Gordon in *Synectics,* "the object that is being constructed begins to have a life of its own. . . . Successful invention depends on permitting the object to act with sufficient autonomy to guide the inventor."

The biggest trouble, in the complexity of modern marketing, is to identify the object in the first place. It may be an automobile, a breakfast
cereal, or a life insurance policy. But its personality may, also, be tied in
with the company that makes it (e.g., if it is to have an "old-fashioned"
personality, like the Sara Lee baked goods mentioned in Chap. 17, can
that be compatible with a "modern" personality which the company itself
might wish to have?) Also, if the object is just evolving, as in the case
of a new product, being pursued in research and development, will its
personality fulfill the wants of a waiting public? We may not be able to
divine the purposefulness of a living person; but in the case of these inventions of ours, we are being godlike and must therefore have a total
appreciation of what they are being created for. This, we feel, is the be-
all and end-all of so-called "marketing and advertising goals and strategies," which are forever debated in the councils of corporations. The
trouble is that there is such a large committee of gods involved in the
one creation.

The Many Cells of the Whole Egg

If the integrated campaign is, like a person, a living organism, then it
has a complex cellular structure. Each cell is part of a system which has
its own uniqueness, yet contributes to the operation of the whole.

Take the physical form of a product, for example. If a living person is
tall or short, fat or thin, male or female, these characteristics naturally
contribute to his or her whole personality. Just so, if the product is to
come to life, and communicate itself, all of the characteristics that go into
its design contribute to the whole egg. Suppose it is a cosmetic, for example. Let us make one up: an after-bath oil for women, designed to
restore the natural oils that soap and water wash away. The liquid itself,
of course, will be an emollient. It should be easily spreadable, so we
make it into an aerosol spray. The container should be holdable with wet
fingers, so we design it with a nubbly surface to give a good grip. On
the other hand, since it is a feminine product, the nubbly surface does
not have sharp edges, but curved surfaces, and the container is curved
also. The fragrance of our bath oil will, of course, influence its personality.
If it is heady and full, its mood may be passionate; if it is delicate and
springlike, its mood may be gay.

Now what's in a name? Everything! If we call our product "Chi-Chi,"
it evokes a French atmosphere. Perhaps the color of our package is pink;
perhaps it is illustrated with a Toulouse-Lautrec dancer. Or suppose, if
it has that passionate perfume, we name it "Intrigue." All of a sudden
we are carried into the Casbah, with agent 007 panting in pursuit.

While we are making up products, let us consider, in contrast, an after-shaving lotion for men. The liquid will not be emollient but bracing. It will not be a spray that could sting his eyes, it will be poured from the package into his palm. Since his hands, too, may be wet, we design the package for a good grip, but its form is masculine—with sharp edges, straight lines.

Certainly this product will not have a feminine fragrance or a name like "Chi-Chi." It could have a name like "Intrigue," but to give it instant recognition as a man's product, suppose we call it "Karate." Immediately, such a name evokes images of action and violence. Of course, as Chi-Chi sounds French, the name Karate sounds Oriental. So we might use Oriental symbolism on our package—a sunburst for example, the black belt of a karate expert.

All of these examples, obviously, contribute to the whole personality of our product. And we have not even begun to consider the cellular system which is normally called "advertising"—mass communication which tells the consumer, in words and pictures, who this personality is. What does the product stand for? Why was it conceived?

This calls for a "copy claim" or, as the textbooks say, a consumer benefit. Suppose the benefit of our after-bath oil was truly medicinal. Suppose it contained an ingredient which not only lubricated dry skin but also, by some synergistic action, caused it to secrete its own restorative oils. What do we say and how do we say it? Before we even consider the copy claim, were we wise, with this kind of a product, to design the package as we did, to use the fragrance we chose, and to name the product Chi-Chi? Is that not a frivolous kind of name and package for a medicinal product?

So it goes. Form and function affect the name and the package, they all affect the nature of the copy claim, and all together affect the total personality, or the whole egg.

Now, suppose our copy claim takes the form of a slogan. Constantly repeated slogans, like graphic symbols, are an effective way to synthesize a campaign. The slogan cannot be created in a vacuum either. Would it be wise to have a gay, frivolous slogan with a medicinal product—or a nuts-and-boltsy slogan like "Builds Body Oils 12 Ways Because It Has Synergistic Action" with a charming, Gallic product like Chi-Chi?

All this would be laboring the obvious, if it were not that so many products—created by a committee of gods—are made up of so many conflicting personalities.

Let us consider more cells in the whole egg. It has been decided, by a proliferating committee, to use the broadest possible media mix for the advertising campaign to introduce Chi-Chi. The campaign will include newspapers, magazines, radio, television, and outdoor. Because we have just so much to spend, we can only afford black and white in newspapers, small space in magazines, I.D.'s on radio and television, and a #50 showing in outdoor. It is true that this is a woman's product and there will be a lot of waste circulation in these media, but the committee has decided that they want to influence men to give Chi-Chi as a gift, hence the broad media plan. Unfortunately, without color in newspapers, we cannot do justice to the gay pink package; with only small space in magazines, we cannot tell a believable, long-copy story about the synergistic action. And that slogan, about building body-oils twelve ways because it has synergistic action, will have to be cut down to just three words ("builds body oils") in radio, television, and outdoor.

How is our product's personality emerging? Somewhat confused. And the cells we have been describing are still only part of the whole egg. What about the pricing of the product? its form of distribution? the so-called "sales promotion"? In the marketing terms of the past, these elements are as separate a part of the communication as product research and development is from packaging, and packaging from advertising. It is decided that, instead of marketing Chi-Chi as a premium product, it will have an extremely low price and will be distributed through high-volume outlets. Because it is costly to manufacture, it will be necessary to set top wholesale prices. To force distribution and high-volume sales, the product will have to be introduced with generous deals for the retailer and irresistible sales promotion to the consumer. The sales promotion will include a contest, offering free trips to Paris, a cents-off coupon which will be distributed by direct mail, and a self-liquidating premium consisting of an electric carving-knife. Point-of-sale displays will of course feature these promotions, rather than the story of the product.

All those decisions, having been made by a different committee of gods, causes the product's personality, through its channels of sales promotion, to be further obscured. In fact, if we try to assemble all the cells we have discussed, and to look at the "living" personality we have created, she looks something like this: A gay, feminine French creature (Chi-Chi), with a harsh, clinical way of speaking (builds body oils twelve ways), unintelligible because she says different things at different times ("7 cents off," "Win a trip to Paris"), but available at a low price if you are able to find her, and are willing to take her along with various other personalities who are not even related to her ("big bargain—an electric carving knife!").

We readily admit that this fictional example has been a *reductio ad absurdum,* but it is done to emphasize the desperate need for coordination in all the elements of the whole egg.

Ways to Coordinate

As ever, throughout this book, we are talking about *attitude.* And the attitude we must cultivate, to achieve the whole egg, is that *everything* pertaining to our subject—the product or service we are communicating —will be thoroughly, stubbornly, religiously integrated.

This will call for a kind of perpetual feedback to some coordinating person, or group of people, from those who are concerned with different aspects of the product. If marketing research reveals that what product research and development (R & D) is doing requires alteration to fulfill consumer wants, our attitude will dictate alteration. If marketing research and product R & D inspire a copy approach which affects the naming and packaging of the product, it will be so named and packaged. If new uses discovered for the product reveal the need for a new marketing strategy, the old strategy will be changed (e.g., the discovery of a new appeal for first aid cream, as relief from "detergent hands," took it out of the medicine chest and into the kitchen, suggesting a whole new advertising strategy).

In today's "era of radical change," which we will discuss later, new product categories continually come and go. Some of the most successful innovations of the past ten years were instant coffee, spray starches, all-purpose cleaners, stainless steel razor blades. At this writing, the latest ideas include wrinkle removers, complete frozen dinners, shampoo hair-colorings, spray-on bandages, intermediate-moist dog foods, and instant breakfasts.

Each of these new ideas, as they originate, must be introduced into a market already glutted with ideas, on to shelves already overcrowded. As each is introduced, it triggers a new competitive situation, and the requirement for counteractions by existing products.

For companies to survive and grow in such a constantly changing atmosphere, they need to multiply and magnify the effect of their communication. A product story which is thoroughly coordinated in all its communications is bound to be more successful than one which is fragmented.

Exactly what do we mean by "all its communications"? We advertising and marketing men have come to think narrowly in terms of our particular specialty. But to the consumer, who has never been behind the scenes, any aspect of the product is a communication. If he sees its name on a packing crate which is being loaded into a truck, that is a communication. If he reads publicity in his newspaper, which refers to the product, it is as much a communication as a television commercial. Word of mouth is, of course, a communication, and the tone of voice with which the person speaks of the subject (a sound of respect when he mentions "G.E.," a feeling of skepticism when he mentions some product's "secret ingredient"), is often as much a communication as a full-page newspaper ad.

The way salespeople reflect on the product is a crucial communication that must be coordinated. How can advertising claims possibly be made about a product which are not paid off at the place of purchase? How can a friendly, modern, enlightened atmosphere pervade the advertising while the dealership is unfriendly, ugly, and behind the times?

Finally, the product itself, in action when the consumer uses it, is a communication. If the advertising says "convenience," and the food wrapping will not roll out of the package easily, that communicates "inconvenience" and the whole egg has been cracked. If the advertising campaign says "The On-Time Airline," that company had better look to its schedules.

All of these generalities are an attempt to foster the attitude that nothing about a subject is not germane to its communication. Let us consider some specific examples of powerful associations which had their effect on the whole egg.

Products or services have been characterized, with the use of living creatures, such as Mr. Clean, The Green Giant, Elsie the Cow, and Smokey the Bear. The minute you create a live character to represent a product, the idea of a coordinated campaign is made more obvious. Mr. Clean endowed the product with his personality. The name was supposed to represent the strong, efficient cleaning power of the product. The graphic representation of the name went with its character. Even the bottle was shaped to look like Mr. Clean.

Sometimes an inspired copy theme can dictate the nature of the entire campaign and can make coordination relatively easy. Such was the slogan for Miss Clairol hair coloring. "Does She . . . or Doesn't She? So Natural Only Her Hairdresser Knows for Sure!" The idea was based on all the contexts prevalent at the time, which the copywriter, Shirley Polykoff, summed up as follows: "There's only one reason to use this stuff and that's so nobody will know you use it." Once that slogan was established, it dictated the execution of the ads. The models had to look natural, they had to have "class," they would be more believable if they were mothers shown with their children, etc. Merchandising of the campaign to the trade came naturally, since the slogan itself involved the expert, the hairdresser.

The case of Tang has become a classic of coordination in marketing history. Consumer research and creative execution helped the technical research people to know what kind of product to develop *before* they started to work on it. The new products department of General Foods began simply with the notion of a "powdered instant orange juice." During a period of some four years, before test marketing, it was determined that the drink should be a synthetic, that it should contain important vitamins and minerals. Questions to determine its whole personality included the following:

1. How should Tang be positioned in the Market?
   a. A nutritious all-day beverage?

  b. A breakfast drink?
  c. A soft drink—fortified?
2. What color should the product be dry and in solution?
  a. Orange?
  b. Pink?
  c. Ambrosia, etc.?
  (Powder was white colored—which would have given it a sugary image)
3. What flavor should it be?
  a. Orange, pineapple, grapefruit?
  b. Fruit blend, etc.?
  c. Sweet or tart?
4. What nutrition should it contain?
  a. Vitamins A, C, B, D, etc.?
  b. Minerals?
5. How should it be packaged?
  a. Glass? (This would be costly—would affect freight charges, etc.)
  b. Tin?
  c. Paper or board?
6. Size of package and number of sizes?
7. What should its name be?
  a. Breakfast image? (We cannot say "orange juice.")
8. Where should it be shelved in the store?
  a. New food category?
9. Who and where would our prime market be?
  a. Children—families with children?
  b. Younger families—instant coffee families?
  c. Should it follow orange juice? Single strength and concentrate market?
  d. Urban, more than rural?
10. What should its price be? Wholesale and retail.
  a. Give trade 20% mark-up—better than single strength and concentrate orange juice?
  b. Retail between premium priced nationally advertised brands and price brands, on equivalent ounce basis?
  c. 7-ounce—39¢, 14-ounce—65¢?

Concurrent with this questioning, creative ideas were being conceived and evaluated—including ideas for naming the product. Through a process of the kind of feedback we have referred to, there emerged a new, nutritional breakfast drink called Tang, one that would be in powdered form with an orange color and an orange flavor, sweet rather than tart. It was to be packaged in glass similar to instant coffee—to help its breakfast connotation. And it should be available in two sizes, 7- and 14-ounce, immediately. It should contain more vitamin C per serving than orange juice and more vitamin A per serving than tomato juice. Other vitamins and minerals were unimportant to the consumer and should be eliminated from the product.

Many more decisions were made through test marketing, with and without sampling. When the product went fully on the market, it was a complete personality, its name contributing to its taste and breakfast use, its color to its competition with orange juice, its price and packaging to its position at the stores (in the juice section), its merchandising to the trade coordinated with advertising to the consumer, its copy and graphic appeals compatible with all other elements of the campaign. And the sales success of the product was phenomenal.

We have spoken about characterizations, themes, and consumer research, all contributing to coordination. Often a product which is obviously an improvement over previous products can start a copywriter on a whole chain of coordinated ideas. For example, a new conduit was developed by Kaiser Aluminum for use in the electric wiring systems of buildings. This new conduit was lined with silicone to enable electricians to thread the wire through the conduit twice as fast as they had done before. This threading process was called, in the technicians' terms, "fishing." By the association process, the copywriter, John Trimble, conceived the idea of naming the conduit "Kingfisher." A kingfisher is a bird which catches fish. The technical term for the process is "fishing." A king is a royal person. The color for royalty is purple. When all these associations were put together, an integrated campaign emerged. The silicone lining of the pipe was colored purple, which gave it a distinctive trademark in the supply room, in transit, and on the job. A little kingfisher bird became the emblem which appeared on the product, on packaging, on point-of-sale pieces, and in the industrial ads. The copy claim, which dovetailed with the name, the graphic symbol, and the purpose of the product, was "Cuts Fishing Time in Half."

The whole egg is a tenuous thing. What people want dictates it; the kind of people they are dictates it; the nature and function of the product or service dictates it; the shape of the product, the color of the product, the name of the product, its packaging, distribution, and price dictate it; the nature of the company, its goals and aspirations dictate it; the words and pictures and what they are going to cost dictate it; and, of course, all the media through which the consumer gets the communication dictate it.

There are many, many people involved in bringing together all those elements. All those people have their own points of view, tastes and judgments. To continue the analogy we have been using, we want the product to appear like "the whole man" described in Overstreet's *The Mature Mind.* How is this possible, when there are so many people involved in its birth and upbringing?

For the answer to that question, enter: the compleat copywriter.

19

THE COMPLEAT COPYWRITER

A New Breed

We have maintained that the role of the copywriter is to communicate. And we have claimed that communication for a product or service over the long run, is the same as for a human being during his lifetime: a whole act, which cannot be separated into emotional versus rational, graphic versus verbal, one technique or medium versus another.

If there is anything to what we say, then someone is going to have to synthesize the whole communication of the product. There will always be specialists—in product research, industrial design, packaging, merchandising, and the many different media that require so much expertise. But who is going to be the hub of the wheel, to bind all the spokes together?

The marketing director, for many advertisers, is supposed to be the focal point of the marketing concept, of sales and advertising, of total "corporate identity," and the integrated campaign. In many organizations, his main role is to set goals and objectives and to administer a continuing series of measurements to see that they are achieved.

The advertising director is an administrator of all the facets of the advertising campaign.

Many marketing and advertising directors are imaginative people.

Many are pragmatic. In either case, their job is not to conceive the idea for the campaign but to set its goals and superintend its activities.

The people who conceive the concept, the essence of the communication, must be the innovators. And those who coordinate the idea, who can see its creative application in *all* areas, from name and package to ad and billboard, must be broad-gauged and imaginative (not just the administrators, but the artists, too).

The world, wrote James Webb Young, in *The Technique of Producing Ideas,* is divided into two main types of people. He cited the Pareto theory, which identified them, in the French, as the *speculator* and the *rentier.* The *rentier,* translated into English as the stockholder, is the steady-going, pragmatic type of person. The *speculator* is speculative— "constantly preoccupied with the possibilities of new combinations." He is among the reconstructors of the world.

"I think we all recognize that these two types of human beings do exist," wrote Young. "Whether they were born that way, or whether their environment and training made them that way, is beside the point. They *are.*"

Of the two types, the reconstructive kind of person must be the hub of our wheel. How he will be adapted to the present structure of corporations and advertising agencies remains to be seen. Some advertising agencies have "creative directors" who are approaching the ideal. But, at this writing, most of them have only to do with national advertising media rather than with the whole egg. The ideal "compleat copywriter" will be a new breed who, by temperament and experience, by deliberate training and assignment to the tables of organization, will be qualified to coordinate *all* communication—whether it be name, shape, color, design, or packaging of the product; television commercials; direct mail; publicity; dealer shows; or sky projection. After all, the consumer neither knows nor cares how the communication gets there. All he knows is what he sees and hears, and that can be anything and everything.

Why do we call our coordinator the compleat copywriter? The term might just as well be the compleat art director or the compleat advertiser, or, better still, the compleat communicator. The point is that the new breed we are describing are generalists, broad thinkers, conceptualizers.

Charles Mortimer, former head of General Foods, was quoted in *Advertising Age* as saying, "One of the biggest advertising and marketing problems facing large corporations is finding resourceful young men who can think conceptually and can develop a new idea from already established ones."

This difficulty is understandable, because the most exceptional new ideas or concepts are those which break with the past, and that means taking a chance. This does not square with the more common attitude of management, that all concepts must be pretested within a gnat's eye. The compleat copywriter is the kind of person who loves taking chances—who knows that only from great risk comes great accomplishment. A most compleat copywriter, Bill Bernbach, says, "One of the disadvantages of doing everything mathematically, by research, is that after a while, everybody does it the same way. . . . If you take the attitude that once you have found out what to say, your job is done, then what you're doing is saying it the same way as everybody is saying it, and you've lost your impact completely."

This is the reason why the compleat copywriter must be a reconstructor: the concept has to be different. Bernbach points out that 85 percent of all advertising does not get looked at.

> So the most important thing as far as I'm concerned is to be fresh, to be original—to be able to compete with all the shocking news events in the world today, with all the violence. Because you can have all the right things in an ad, and if nobody is made to stop and listen to you, you've wasted it. And we in America are spending so damn much money for efficiency, to measure things, that we're achieving boredom like we've never achieved before. We're *right* about everything, but nobody looks.

Curiously enough, the increased use of research in advertising and the advent of the computer have been accompanied by increasing importance for copywriters. Martin Mayer, author of *Madison Avenue, U.S.A.,* in an article in the *Saturday Evening Post,* wrote:

> The annual outlay for advertising in the U.S. has jumped from $8 billion to almost $14 billion since 1954. In the process, the agencies which write and place most of the ads have tended to confer more and more power (and pay) upon their copywriters, art directors, and other "creative" employees. . . .
>
> "As recently as five years ago," says President Rosser Reeves, head of the Ted Bates agency, . . . "the boys were selling research, services, personality. Now everybody says, 'There's no substitute for copy.' The clients have found out that if you've got appendicitis, all the machines in the Mayo Clinic won't help you; you need a surgeon."

The surgeon, in this case, is the reconstructor who can cut through all the entanglements and come up with one pure, multimillion-dollar concept like, "Does she . . . or doesn't she?," "You'll wonder where the yellow went," "It's such a pleasure to take the bus and leave the driving to us."

As computers become more prevalent in advertising, media, and marketing research, we predict that creativity will be even more at a premium. Infinite facts and figures will be at everyone's command, which will equalize the pragmatic part of the business, and the unexpected creative use of those facts will give advertisers the competitive edge.

Involved with the Product

"I think the most important element in success in ad writing is the product itself. And I can't say that often enough. Or emphasize it enough." So says compleat copywriter Bernbach. "That's why we, as an agency, work so closely with the client on his product—looking for improvements, looking for ways to make people want it, looking for additions to the product, looking for changes in the product. . . . We never kid ourselves about the magic of advertising. The magic is in the product."

And that is why this new breed of advertising man has to be thoroughly involved with all the aspects of the product. Which also calls for a new atmosphere between the manufacturers and the advertising men. The atmosphere will have to be less structured and channelized. The compleat communicator will be constantly collaborating with the R & D, sales, marketing, advertising, and publicity people, as a kind of quality control officer of communications, to make sure that the whole egg is intact. If there is to be a new package design, for example, it might affect the advertising theme, the execution and the use of media. As it is now, some companies have departments or outside designers who remake packages without even consulting advertising. The same may apply to new product names, which might now be suggested by anyone from the president to the mail-room boy and chosen on whim or by research outside the context of advertising. Our compleat communicator, because he is on the side of the consumer, and has the consumer's overall view, would make sure that all systems would harmonize.

Keeping the Whole Egg Fresh

Fred Papert, head of one of those upstart agencies that made news because they dared to be different, said this about advertising: "There is no one right way to do things. But the right way is the way that everybody is enthusiastic and exuberant about."

Everyone who is really *in* advertising, who is really "with it" knows this to be true. You can do all the pretesting and posttesting you want. You can analyze, rationalize, and computerize. You can set up a "mathematical model" for decision making; but when it comes to an advertising concept, all those methods will be only useful to reduce the risk of a mediocre campaign.

Those pragmatic methods cannot help with the most exciting advertising because that kind of advertising is unprecedented. Mayer reports that when Bernbach had researchers test the Avis "We're Only No. 2" campaign on a panel of consumers, the testers came back with a thumbs-down recommendation on the grounds that Americans like to think of themselves as No. 1 people and do business with No. 1 companies. "Bern-bach brushed aside the advice and proceeded, and the resulting campaign is credited with turning Avis from a money-loser into a profitable busi-ness." The same kind of negative response, according to Fairfax Cone, was the consumer panel verdict for "Does She? . . . Or Doesn't She?"

The trouble with talking to consumer panels about unprecedented ideas is that they cannot express a valid opinion about how they are going to react to an idea when they have not yet experienced it.

But to get back to Fred Papert's point, the big ideas, the concepts that really take off, are the ones that make all of us who are professionals in the business feel exuberant. Our instincts, as Whit Hobbs put it, go "boiing!" We feel, according to this writer's method of recognition, a bristling of the hackles. We *know.*

Until caution sets in.

And there is where the compleat copywriter enters—with fire in his eyes. If he has learned the lessons we discussed earlier, on "communicating about the communication," he is enthusiastic. Like the screwball character in *Arsenic and Old Lace,* he whips out his sword and cries, *"Charge!"*

Who wants a screwball leading the charge? "Don't Fire the Screwballs," reads a headline on the business page of a newspaper. And the story goes on to quote Paul Pigors, industrial relations professor at the Massachusetts Institute of Technology: "Every company should have a few dissenters, nonconformists, screwballs and generally unreasonable employees, . . . business needs nonconformists because *almost all progress is due to the thoughts and actions of unreasonable men."* (Italics ours.)

Beethoven, an irascible genius, was a screwball. The Wright Brothers were screwballs. And incidentally, according to a fascinating article in *Fortune,* Charles Babbage was one of the greatest screwballs of them all, and he first conceived the pragmatist's friend, the computer (*vide,* "The Cranky Grandfather of the Computer," *Fortune,* March, 1964).

But nobody is going to follow that screwball if their minds have not gone "boiing!" They are not going to follow him if they do not understand that conceiving an exciting concept for advertising is, essentially, an art. An art in the sense that it creates for people—who, remember, are bored and anxious and eager for change—a fresh experience.

The reconstructer is, by nature and habit, a lover of change. He thrives on it. This does not make him, at all times, an admirable person, or one who is easy to get along with. Ask the wives of the most successful copy-writers, and we will wager that the majority will describe their husbands as restless doers, who have too many projects going at once to permit a normal everyday kind of placidity or an extended vacation.

Trying as this disposition may be to wives, it is made to order for what Max Ways, in *Fortune,* called the times we are now living in—"The Era of Radical Change." If, as we maintain, every advertising idea should be fresh and original, and if all the parts of the whole egg should be unique, and if new products, new packaging, new uses for old products, new media, new ideas, and new markets are the wave of the future, who is better prepared to ride the crest of that wave than Mr. Change himself?

The Care and Feeding of the Compleat Copywriter

Complete copywriters (or complete communicators) have existed, and do exist today. But they have not been that way by design so much as by accident of circumstance and of personality. As the famous house ad for Lennen & Mitchell advertising agency said back in 1924, "There is only one solution to an advertising problem: *Find the man!*"

Through the years, plenty of advertising problems have found the man, and vice versa. He has been a man who, as that ad put it, was "an artist in advertising." Some of those men are the heads of multimillion-dollar ad agencies today. "In 1954," reported Martin Mayer, "the nation's seven largest agencies were all run by 'businessmen'; 10 years later, four of them had copywriters at the helm, and two of the others had moved 'creative' men into the heir-apparent positions." Associate Prof. Richard Thain, of Roosevelt University, in an article analyzing the advertising man, wrote: "If a serious study of the sociology of the advertising agency field were ever undertaken, it would undoubtedly make it clear that almost all the towering figures past and present in the agency arena are copywriters who have never completely deserted their muse."

This is not to say that the days of the businessmen in advertising are numbered and that the dreamy-eyed visionaries are about to take over. On the contrary, the most successful advertising is through a close and understanding collaboration of the two—of the pragmatist and the reconstructor.

But the importance of copywriters in the past, and their increasing importance in the era of radical change, underscores the need for a deliberate, intensive cultivation of the compleat copywriter. He should be indoctrinated in the colleges, sought for in recruiting by the advertising agencies, and given continuous, on- and off-the-job training. What do we mean by "off-the-job training"? The more this renaissance man absorbs of the world around, the more "open" he is encouraged by his employers to become, the more broad-gauged and ready he will be for his exciting profession. He should be sent to some of the stimulating seminars now being conducted by colleges and foundations—seminars on far-ranging subjects outside the narrow fields of advertising. He should be a traveled person, getting out constantly to absorb the real-life atmosphere of the individuals who are the "markets" in this country and around the world. He should be encouraged to be broad-gauged in his tastes too.

On-the-job training for the compleat copywriter would include practical exposure to *every* facet of communication involved in the whole egg. He should be as familiar in the ateliers of Raymond Loewy, Eliot Noyes, and Charles Eames as he is in the studios of Richard Avedon and Bert Stern. He should be as concerned with the recommendations of a corporate symbol by Lippincott & Margulies as he is with the editing of a film sequence by V.P.I. or M.P.O. He should study with R. L. Polk and Reuben Donnelly, as well as with the Bureau of Advertising and the R.A.B. He should be keenly aware of all the current media, their shortcomings and improvements, and with technical developments that can change their status and create new media. He should get into government activities, for they affect everything he does. And he should start being involved in the activities of IBM, Sperry Rand, RCA and Control Data, for these companies are making breathtaking discoveries with the computers that will be his servants. In short, if he is to become a generalist, he should study communications in general.

But, one might ask, who, while this super-dilettante is being developed, is going to be "minding the store"? Who will be doing the punctilious work, day by day, of writing scores of scripts and grinding out scads of ads? Do not misunderstand our intentions in painting this broad vista. There will always be specialists, and our compleat copywriter, at the beginning, will be a specialist too. The wisest men who are doing the recruiting and training will find that some writers have a dominant aptitude for print copy, while others can conceive excellent television commercials but feel confined by space advertising. They will find that certain creative people will always get their greatest satisfaction from concentrating on one medium and fine-tooling that well. Many writers, in fact, will scorn the generalist as too shallow and superficial in his knowledge. To them will go the continuing rewards of one craft, which they do eminently well, and which is coordinated into the whole egg.

What the trainers will find, as they proceed in the care and feeding of the compleat copywriter, is that each creative person should be used according to his fullest capacity. Over the years, copywriters will be assigned to specialties, but enabled, with part of their time, to delve into other areas that interest them. Gradually, those who are by nature more versatile will emerge and graduate into the broader ranges of general training and assignment.

But there is one more vital contribution to the care and feeding of the compleat copywriter, and it is certainly the most important one. That is the attitude of the companies that make and market the products—the advertisers. They will have to agree, wholeheartedly, that there is a desperate need for the whole egg, and that the best qualified person to effect it would be the compleat copywriter. They will have to make him a partner of all their research, development, and marketing. And they will have to—as John Kelley, advertising director of the Goodyear Tire & Rubber Company put it—"write excitement into the strategy statement." The essential part of persuasion these days, said Kelley, is excitement. "We advertising people often forget that we're not just competing among ourselves—but with a dazzling, sad, sexy, funny, ghoulish welter of news and information. . . . You sometimes wonder how advertising ever gets through. . . . But it does—that advertising which is exciting, different, charming, alive, romantic, energetic, vital."

The compleat copywriter will be the one who will make certain that every part of the communication comes to life.

OUR TOTAL ENVIRONMENT

The Marketing Marathon

In the race to win the consumer, everything, as we said in Chap. 18, is a communication.

Years ago, before there was a glut of consumer products, manufacturers would make a product and then go out and *induce* people to buy—in other words, *sell* them. Now the manufacturer has to communicate with the consumer, in our best definition of the word; that is, he has to have an interchange of thought. He has to listen and respond. He has to find out what the people want, then make it, and market it. Or—because the people cannot always express what they want—he has to be so sensitive that he can anticipate their desires. This is what "the marketing concept" is all about.

"Selling focuses on the needs of the seller, marketing on the needs of the buyer." So wrote Theodore Levitt, of the Harvard Business School, in his polemic, *Innovation in Marketing*. He attacked the buggy-whip mentality of many companies (i.e., the buggy-whip makers had gone out of business because they could not see how fantastically the internal combustion engine would answer the wants of the people and change the state of the nation.)

Levitt recited many examples of "management myopia," which was based on the old notion that the product was the thing and the public be damned. He told how the railroaders lost out to the car, bus, and plane because they believed that they were in the railroad business rather than in the business of giving the customer what he wanted—better *transportation*. He told how the petroleum companies refused to recognize any fuel possibilities but their own—pouring millions into petroleum research and development, but failing to realize that they were in the *energy* business and that other sources of energy would be worth exploring. Hence, while they themselves owned the natural gas, they left it to someone else—the pipeline companies—to start the industry.

Frozen orange juice had to be started by a company which was not in the frozen food business. The monolithic movie companies fought TV instead of realizing the customer might want it. The food chains who resisted the idea of self-service supermarkets "kept their pride but lost their shirts."

Levitt's book was not written fifty years ago, when the marketing concept was conceived, but at the beginning of the 1960's. At the same time, like-minded men were preaching the gospel of the marketing concept with increasing fervor. Marketing consultant Russell H. Colley, pleading for marketing objectives and measurements, pointed out that the whole idea began, not with the manufacturer, but with the communicators who worked for them: "The cornerstone of modern marketing . . . was largely the insight of early advertising men. It has taken several generations for this philosophy to sink in among the staunch producer-oriented companies." Bernard Trujillo, whose firm, the National Cash Register Company, gives courses in modern merchandising methods, stressed the fact that an election is going on in retailing every day, that the consumer by his presence and absence expresses his preferences, lets his vote be known by the vote on the cash register.

The validity of the marketing concept is constantly being proven, but the reason it took so long to become a way of life with top management was, again, a simple matter of attitude. The advertising man could conceive the idea because, in trying to communicate every day of his life, he was conditioned to appealing to the reader's self-interest, rather than to his own. The manufacturer, on the other hand, was so imbued with the problems of production that he had an entirely different ingrained attitude. Just as a copywriter falls in love with his brainchildren, the manufacturer's products were near and dear to him. He was sincerely concerned if a competitor made a better product in the same category, and would spend huge sums on product R & D while he begrudged investments in marketing R & D.

It is hard to turn your mind inside out and to break the attitudes of a lifetime. Many corporations would change the title of sales manager to marketing director and claim that they were in the marketing business.

But the newly titled men would still have the old orientation, of selling the needs of the product rather than being attuned to the wants of the customer.

The 1950's were the turning point. Technical advances, during World War II, in electronics, plastics, and textiles were being exploited to the public. A great backlog of customer wants was being filled. Television, the magnificent communications tool, arrived. And the car makers in Detroit started to roll. The Korean conflict forced industry to expand to answer military as well as civilian needs. And as we entered the sixties, the proliferation of new products and industries and inventions out-distanced all our technology since the country began.

The reason: consumer wants. Wants much deeper and broader than just necessities. From 1950 to 1963, our total disposable income had doubled—from $207 billion to $400 billion. Whereas, in 1950, we spent 58 percent of that income on basic living costs (food, clothing, and shelter), in 1963 we spent more on discretionary goods and services (52 percent). One projection, for 1974, showed a disposable income of $640 billion, of which only 33 percent would be spent on basic needs, the rest on "things we don't need."

What do we mean by "things we don't need"? A major criticism of advertising is that it promotes a wasteful way of life. The following was one advertising agency's answer—copy from an ad which won the *Saturday Review of Literature* award for advertising in the public interest:

> There is no chestnut more overworked than the critical whinny: "Advertising sells people things they don't need." We, as one agency, plead guilty. Advertising does sell people things they don't need. Things like television sets, automobiles, catsup, mattresses, cosmetics, ranges, refrigerators, and so on and on. People really don't need these things. People don't really need art, music, literature, newspapers, historians, wheels, calendars, philosophy, or, for that matter, critics of advertising, either. All people really need is a cave, a piece of meat and, possibly, a fire. The complex thing we call civilization is made up of luxuries. An eminent philosopher of our time has written that great art is superior to lesser art in the degree that it is "life-enhancing." Perhaps something of the same thing can be claimed for the products that are sold through advertising. They enhance life, to whatever degree they can. Indeed, that is the purpose of our unique and restless economy. It is fundamentally devoted to the production and distribution of things people don't need. Among them are toothpaste, electricity, outboard motors, artificial satellites and education. Without advertising, that economy cannot exist. . . .

The economy that the marketing concept is now trying to serve has infinite levels of want, depending on the markets. To people in the still-underdeveloped countries, the wants are more like those our ancestors had when the Industrial Revolution began. To the consumers of The Common Market and the booming economies of such countries as Japan and Sweden, they are wants inspired by American methods, plus a new, lustily competitive spirit all their own. To Americans, they are wants of the Negro, of the Appalachian poor, of the working housewife, of millions of teenagers needing jobs and education.

American companies, with their communicators, the advertising men, are now committed to the marketing concept—to the quandary and excitement of knowing, anticipating and satisfying consumer wants. And the one thing we can be sure of is that these wants will swiftly and constantly change. Max Ways, writing for *Fortune,* called our times "the era of radical change." The acceleration is so swift, he said, "that trying to 'make sense' of change will come to be our basic industry."

This is why the copywriter we have been describing throughout this book will be so important. He will be one of the key people who will have to make sense of change. For example, until now we have been accustomed to thinking of America's major industries as chemicals, machinery, public utilities, automobiles, construction, petroleum, lumber and paper, food and beverages. In terms of the changes that lie ahead—the changes, for example, that cybernation will bring—the balance could radically alter and our major industries could become education, culture, and social service.

"The real crux of the matter," writes British economist Walter Taplin, "is that, in a modern society, most of the wants of consumers lie above the level of subsistence and are part of the desire of individuals to make interesting use of their lives. We are dealing with something subtle, complex, and shifting—with the devious aspirations of the human spirit."

The fact that those aspirations are devious, and that they are constantly in flux, infinitely affected by the total environment around us, is fully recognized by the marketing concept. And the only way that we will know what those wants are, and how to respond to them, is through better communication.

New Products and Services

Finding and filling the consumer's wants follows the very same process as communicating them. As we have discussed throughout these pages, that begins with an attitude—an awareness of the total environment. Wrote Levitt: "The questions that constantly need to be asked about the outside environment are as follows: How will the changes affect our company's survival power? How will they affect our opportunities? . . . But to be able to ask yourselves these questions you have to sensitize yourselves first to seeing the facts in the world, so that you can be in a position to evaluate their possible impact on you. *The first step to becoming sensitive is to recognize the importance of being sensitive."*

This recognition, by a company, results in the same kind of open receptivity with which the copywriter gets his best ideas. Company management, concerned with profit and loss statements, is often looking for pragmatic assurances of making the right marketing moves. "Foolproof method for predicting fate of new products?" asks a *Printers' Ink* headline, and the story discusses a mathematical model being devised to take the risk out of new-product marketing. "Can science take out the guesswork?" asks another feature, and it discusses the "Bayesian decision theory," "Adaptive Planning and Control Sequence," and other computer-age methods for decision-making.

Any or all of these methods, like the copywriter's fact-finding and free association, can contribute to the final judgment to market a new product or to improve an old one. Researchers dig into every aspect of the current environment and how the consumer is affected by it to try to figure out what he wants next. The hopes and anxieties raised by automation; the population explosion; the passage of a Medicare, housing, or education bill; the reduction of income and excise taxes; the pressures of a war in Asia; and the pleasures of being a two-car family with a mortgage-free home—all of these contexts which affect the consumer come together in the minds of the managers as they weigh their marketing moves.

But then, mulling over all of these facts and associations, the manager finally has to make a decision. And that decision is based on a combination of pragmatic knowledge and intuitive judgment.

Copywriters, who love the heat and humanity of intuition, worry about the advent of the computer age. They fear that everything, including the creation of advertising, will be done "by the numbers." It is encouraging, in fact inspiring, to see how creative are the marketing decisions made by the management of successful companies.

Consider the case of General Foods, a company with all the scientific and statistical resources one could imagine. This company dares to innovate and to make mistakes. They are more often right than wrong because they are imbued with a simple, common-sense goal—constantly to make the housewife's life more convenient. "In addition to selling food," says a *Fortune* article, "G. F. is selling convenience. . . . The housewife is buying time when she buys food that has been pre-washed, pre-cooked, pre-mixed, or pre-peeled. . . . Of course, everybody in the food industry today sells convenience. . . . But General Foods . . . was the first food outfit to make a conscious strategy of convenience."

Another factor in General Foods' success was the matter of momentum. Starting with a surefire philosophy, they kept going. It was that same kind of drive that made the swift growth of the Alberto-Culver Company such a phenomenon. Its founder, Leonard Lavin, explained his four-part formula in an address before the New York Society of Security Analysts: "(1) A philosophy—to which we adhere (i.e., to make a better product —sold at mass-premium prices, and distributed through all possible outlets); (2) the guts to back it up; (3) the knowledge and the grip to make it count; and (4) the desire to make it grow."

It was this formula that enabled Alberto-Culver to get up a head of steam and keep going. They started with an aerosol hairspray that answered a need (until then, hairsprays had been sticky—this one was crystal-clear "to hold hair in place and let the beauty shine through"). They invested the highest advertising-to-sales-dollar ratio of all the 100 largest national advertisers. "We create an aura of excitement and adventure about our product. If we don't spring loose the dollars to match the advertising of our strongest competitors, then we try to out-promote and out-merchandise them."

The attitude that pervades both the long-established General Foods and the relatively new Alberto-Culver, matches the analysis made by the Stanford Research Institute on companies that have outstanding growth records. The reasons, it was found, were that "they systematically seek out, find, and reach for growth products and growth markets" and "their top management slots are staffed by uniquely courageous, adventurous, high-spirited executives who bubble with dissatisfaction and are driven by an energetic zeal to lead rather than to follow."

Every day, with the increased acceleration of change, it becomes more evident that innovation, rather than being foolhardy, is the practical route to growth. This is the reason why, since the acceleration began in 1950, new products and services have become *a way of life* for successful companies. Of the major companies studied by the Stanford Research Institute, "almost one-third realize 50 percent of their current sales from products introduced within the past decade."

The proliferation of new products and services, as we look around us at any given moment, is at once a reflection of the world as we see it and a view of what it is going to be like. That is why advertisers who are looking for market research to make their decisions for them are living in a dream world. We can ask the people what they want, but we can only get a feeling for their needs. "I have learned," wrote Leo Burnett, "that the public does not know what it wants, and that there is really no sure way of finding out until the idea is exposed under normal conditions of sale. I believe it was David Belasco who said, 'The art of showmanship is to give the public what it wants just before it knows what it wants.' . . . If people could tell you in advance what they want, there would never have been a wheel, a lever, much less an automobile, an airplane, an electric refrigerator, or a TV set. There would never have been a Barnum and

Bailey circus. a South Pacific, or a modern magazine. Somebody with the urge, the inspiration, and the drive had to think it up and push it through."

That kind of drive is what motivates advertisers who are attuned to change. Of course, they do not take risks for risk's sake and just to keep innovating. Matching the increased speed of change is the increased efficiency of fact-finding. In addition is the facility to reduce risk by such methods as test marketing and of faster "feedback" from the points of distribution. Thus, companies can cut and fit, feel and probe, adjusting their intuitive judgments with that kind of "thermostatic control" that is the heart of modern marketing.

But innovation in marketing follows the same law as the creative idea in advertising—i.e., the effectiveness of an idea is in inverse ratio to how many times it has been used.

We can find lots of precedents for that truism. For example, in the bellwether automotive industry, the big success stories of recent times were the cases of American Motors and the marketing of the Ford Mustang. In the first instance, the marketers of the Rambler sensed that what people *really* wanted, at that precise moment, was an economy compact car, although all the marketing research resources of the big companies failed to recognize that want. By the time Ford marketed the Mustang, it had a wealth of research and rationale for the move. The spirit of the times, sensitivity to the youth market (and to those adults who would think young), a carefully prepared position in the racing world, the impetus of a hot-selling car year, all these factors gave Ford the ideal climate in which to launch an economical, everyman's sports car. The capper to that right strategy was that the Mustang campaign was mounted with utmost vigor, boldness, coordination, and flair. One of the main clues to success is the "self-fulfilling prophecy," by which a company, once it decides to launch a new product, does it with the confidence of a winner.

Another example of an innovation-minded company, almost in spite of itself, was AT&T. Criticized though it might be for monopoly and conservatism, the Bell System began in the early fifties to become marketing-oriented. "In 1954," wrote *Business Week*, Bell "decided to do more than take orders for telephones and started to sell." No company, in our environment, could be in a better position to innovate. "First came extension phones and promotion of long-distance calling. . . . Then color telephones were introduced on a mass basis. . . . The proliferation of new products and services turned into a flood. . . . Color phones were followed by wall phones, speakerphones, the call director, the Princess, home intercom, recessed panel phones, pushbutton phones, and this year the Trimline, with dial built into the handset. . . . One guess is that

Picturephones may be in some offices by 1968, homes by the early 1970's."

The experience of the airlines called for the most daring and resourceful innovation. Each year they have had to anticipate the needs of the age of acceleration, and this meant almost unbearable investments in the future. They had to mortgage themselves for fleets of jet planes before the runways were ready for them and then for the supersonic jets while they were still paying for today's ordinary jets. It is tough enough for General Foods to have to obsolete a new packaged product. But just consider the headaches preparing for new jets that will cost about $25 million each, compared with $7 million for the present giants. Then, too, the airlines had a divided audience—the businessmen who flew regularly and the vast majority who had never flown. The airlines' answers, though, have not been so dissimilar from those for Jell-O and Minute Rice: pleasure and convenience. Pleasure from inflight banquets and entertainment, convenience from instant reservations made, for example, by Sabre, the country's first sophisticated computer system, which cost $30 million. And the seats have been filled by the fast-growing credit card business, by the packaged sale of the airplane and the rental car, and by the irresistible urge to vacation in romantic foreign lands on the go now, pay later plan.

All around us, every moment, we see new products and services that answer "the devious aspirations of the human spirit"—some in a minor way, some more importantly: Micro-wave ovens that cook a typical meal in four minutes instead of the normal 20. Instamatic cameras that focus and load film automatically. Electronic "building blocks" that enable even a clumsy do-it-yourselfer to assemble his own walkie-talkie or AM/FM radio. Boats for the whole family, with all kinds of electronic gadgets to play with. Time-shared computers for small companies to have big-company data processing. Home kegs of draft beer that fit neatly into the refrigerator. Hot lather shave cream. Stretch pants that mold to a girl's shape, yet keep *their* shape. Color TV, at a low price. "Tummy TV" battery portables. Custom-designed refrigerators. Oral contraceptives for men.

At the moment we are listing those "new developments," we feel frustrated. For by the time these words are published, those ideas will *not* be news. Within a matter of months, many of them may either have failed, been superseded, or surpassed. "The very moment you put a new product on the supermarket shelf," said Charles Mortimer of General Foods, "it is out of date."

The point of mentioning those particular "innovations" is to illustrate their diversity and how, at their point in time, they may serve specific wants, affect the response to other products, and, in some way, alter people's lives.

How did these new ideas come about? Whoever conceived, developed, and distributed them followed the same path we copywriters go along. "To communicate is to be *interesting*." To be interested is "to recapture that fresh variety, the firsthand experience of childhood." What can be more interesting than innovation? The marketing concept is, in every way, a creative function.

The Changes Ahead

When Jules Verne and H. G. Wells made predictions, many of their readers were skeptical. But if we predict far more startling changes, no matter how outlandish they might once have seemed, they would not warrant a raised eyebrow today.

Anything is possible in the era of radical change. "In the late-nineteenth century or early-twentieth century," wrote Max Ways, "to be 'up to date' was a boast. In 1964 the very phrase sounds dated, for everyone knows that to be up to date means to be on the verge of becoming out of date."

How does this era of radical change affect people in general and the marketers in particular? There is a whole chain reaction, but the main affect is an accelerated need for education. If we are to be aware of the total environment that will affect the consumer, we have to start learning. We have to learn without graduating, learn without letup, learn, learn, learn.

We have to learn about transportation. If the predictions come true—that trains will run in underground tubes, at 300 or 400 mph; that cars will cruise at more than 100 mph, driven automatically on freeways by electronic controls; that fast planes will take off and land vertically on small airfields and supersonic planes will enable us to commute daily to work across the country and around the world—what will all this mean to marketing? What new changes in products, in pleasure, in construction, in world trade?

We have to learn about communication. Will UHF TV and/or CATV (community antenna television) make television outlets as numerous as the radio stations? Will pay TV compete with commercial? What are the illimitable possibilities of Comsat—with worldwide satellite television translated into all languages? What new problems and opportunities can we foresee from the Picturephone? And what about the Touch-Tone telephone, which is already in use? Not only will it cut calling time in half, but, reports *Business Week,* "Bills could be paid . . . by dialing your bank's computer and then using the Touch-Tone buttons to give it coded instructions for debiting your own account and crediting that of the store."

But telephone communication might also be rivaled by miniaturized, electronic walkie-talkies that resemble Dick Tracy's two-way television wrist radio. What's more, computerized telephone marketing may be hooked up with closed-circuit TV, so you can browse through your "catalogue" on the screen. How will this affect the marketing of products? Will today's big shopping centers and supermarkets be obsolete? Will new products actually be developed, researched, and distributed by pushbutton voting from the home? How will all this affect the traditional media we discussed earlier and the way we communicate our story? Will newspapers, magazines, and letters be reproduced in our homes by facsimile transmission?

What is the future of videotape? Says *Time* magazine, "The greatest market potential—the U.S. home—is still untapped. Inexpensive portable video outfits could take much of the fuss out of making home movies. . . . Videotape recorders can be adjusted to turn on tv sets and record favorite programs while people are away from home, enabling them to play back the programs later. Eventually, video-taped news and sports events, plays and educational shows could be sold or rented for replay on home tv sets." Even now, Sony and Ampex are marketing Portable Home Videotape Recorders. Is it also possible that American marketing will be able to bring the cost of videotape cartridges down so low that they will rival the volume of the current sale of books and records? Will libraries as we now know them be changed into audio-visual centers?

We have to learn about scientific advances in the fields of medicine, natural resources, space exploration. Already, most of the drugs that are prescribed by doctors were not available when those doctors were in medical school. Antibiotics, tranquilizers, steroids, hypotensive agents, antihistamines—much of the doctors' information about those wonder drugs has come from the promotional programs of the pharmaceutical manufacturers. And how about the success of low-caloric foods and those low in cholesterol and polyunsaturates? What discoveries in foods and drugs are in the making that will affect marketing communications as those advances did?

Consider the field of oceanography. Is this the great new frontier, before the conquest of space? Seventy percent of the earth is covered with water. "Aquaculture"—the science of cultivating and conserving the resources of the sea, as farmers and foresters have used the land—may give the world the answer to food and water shortages, to infinite sources of fuel and minerals. What work is now being done underwater by the Institutes at La Jolla, Woods Hole, and Miami, by the oil companies, by the food companies, by diamond and gold miners? We have to learn, currently and continually, because all these activities are part of the feedback of change.

We have to learn about foreign markets and their heady, breakneck surge for our kind of abundance. Not only because some of us will be directly involved, but because they will affect our way of life here. There is a give and take that makes for great problems and opportunities. "To American businessmen," reports *Newsweek*, "this adds up to the greatest opportunity since America itself. In a short fifteen years, they have poured nearly $10 billion into Europe—building factories and refineries, buying companies, setting up sales organizations, and changing the face of the Continent . . . The French have a word for it: 'Coca-colonization.'"

We have to learn how the resentment which coined such a word is mixed with grudging admiration for our methods. Now, in many ways, Europeans are going through our pioneer stage of marketing and advertising, but in other ways they are more sophisticated than we. Restrictions on advertising include rules that inhibit the hard sell. They can teach us a lot about graphics. The idea of corporate-image building through excellence of design—a relatively new American discovery—has flourished in European business for years. A prime example was that of the Olivetti Corporation, which started the principle of integrated design. Olivetti, doing business in 106 countries, long ago devised "a universal symbology" —physical elements of form and color which bypassed the barrier of language difference.

What will be the effects of other countries coming closer to our economy and our coming closer to their cultures? The so-called "advanced countries" (Canada, the United Kingdom, France, West Germany, Italy, Japan, and the United States) have certainly demonstrated the vitality of the enterprise system. They added more to their gross national product in the past twenty years than they had in the preceding fifty. What will they add in the next twenty and how will we react with our marketing concept?

Finally, we have to learn about automation, cybernation, and the computer. We are living in "the boundless age of the computer" and we will be hearing more and more of its lingo. We will also be hearing, for a long time, the debate between the prophets of doom and of glory through automation. "The electronic computer has a more beneficial potential for the human race than any other invention in history," *Time* quoted one authority. Wrote Gerard Piel, publisher of *Scientific American*, about cybernation, "If a fraction of the labor force is capable of supplying an abundance of everything the population needs and wants, then why should the rest of the population have to work for a living? The liberation of people from tasks unworthy of human capacity should free that capacity for a host of activities now neglected in our civilization: teaching and learning, fundamental scientific investigation, the performing arts and the graphic arts, letters, the crafts, politics, and social service."

On the other hand, the *Ad Hoc Committee on the Triple Revolution,* of which Piel was a member, sent a memorandum to the President, predicting grave consequences of automation if fundamental changes in the

American approach to employment were not made. They called for massive government programs of education, public works, low-cost housing, etc., to offset the possible "physical and psychological misery and perhaps political chaos" that could accompany the transition to cybernation.

The more optimistic champions of automation predicted that it would make for constantly more jobs and more productivity. Said John Diebold, the man who invented the word *automation,* "Ninety percent of the productivity gains of the past fifty years have come from improved technology, and the technology of today is automation." So far, at this writing, Diebold has been proved right and the country's gross national product, income, and employment are all at a healthy high.

Whatever happens during the transition, there is no question that automation and the computer *could* make possible the swift assembly of all the knowledge of man and could eventually eliminate most of his drudgery.

The Challenge to Communicators

George Orwell's *1984* and Huxley's *Brave New World* were fiction. But now the realities of the era of radical change make their predictions seem terribly near. Thinking of what can happen could scare us out of our wits. "I'm not at all sure we're going to make it," said automation expert Michael Harrington, as he was being interviewed in a trenchant British film, *On the Edge of Abundance.* "The change is so extremely fast that the thought is going to have to run very fast to catch up with it and we've hardly begun. I don't see the motive for our thinking so radically. Abundance seems to create a certain kind of complacency rather than an ability for candid thought. . . . Perhaps we will be—and it will be one of the greatest paradoxes in history—perhaps we will be victimized by our creation of abundance."

But those of us who welcome change see a thrilling challenge in this new abundance. We react as Winston Churchill is said to have done at the time of the fall of Dunkirk. He called an emergency meeting of his cabinet and, after reviewing all the difficult events, he said, "This, gentlemen, is the situation. For myself, I find it very stimulating."

The parallel is not perfect because the era of radical change has not been let loose by forces of evil but by man's brilliant and positive accomplishments. Nevertheless, for us, as communicators, it can be stimulating beyond description.

In our primary function—the creation of advertising for products and services—we can be stimulated by the tools we are being given. Some copywriters fear that the machines will attempt to take over their functions. They will, in fact, increase our creativity. As we discussed in Chaps.

6 and 7, the creative mind seeks infinite facts and ranges far and wide for ideas. Computers will be able to range farther, deeper, and faster than our minds. But our minds will always be of a higher order, because they can ask the questions. We will still have to dig for facts, in the ways described in Chap. 6, because facts do not interpret themselves. But computers will be able to assemble and codify whatever we need, at tremendous speed. We will not have to be technically oriented ourselves to use the computers, any more than we now need to know the technical aspects of film and engraving. There will be specialists to work the machines for us, and we will be able to summon all kinds of knowledge, at will. Facts about people, about media, about competing products, about sales flow, about readership, that now take months to compile, may then take minutes. With these new tools, we can become more intimate with our audiences than we ever dreamed possible. And this is bound to result in more meaningful messages.

But even beyond the interpretation of products and services, the copywriter may now come into his own as an interpreter of ideas. If our basic industry is to be "making sense out of change," then the communicator will be the most important person in our society. Computers will assemble knowledge and work machines. They may even, "heuristically," learn by trial and error, as they now play checkers and war games, and use a kind of judgment in making decisions. But computers, as one agency's house ad put it, "don't cry." They do not have imagination. And, above all, they do not have empathy, which is the heart of communication.

What do you tell the young girl who, answering a magazine survey about the future, replied, "What concerns us is a fear of becoming anonymous. We look at the complexity and hugeness of life and wonder how we'll keep our individuality"? How can you thrill her with her own inexhaustible potential?

What do you tell a worker who does have the problem of readjustment? How can you excite him with the adventure of learning a new trade?

If, as John Diebold maintains, automation can multiply jobs instead of reducing them, and swiftly raise our standard of living, who can communicate the fact, to help make it come true?

If, as Gerard Piel maintains, automation can free men from work for the pursuits of the mind and spirit, who will be the communicator of culture?

Advertising man Arthur Meyerhoff, in *The Strategy of Persuasion*, has pleaded for the government to use the unique talents of advertising men in the war for human minds and hearts. He has shown how the Russians, though far behind us in advertising, have been far ahead of us in propaganda. If, as we have illustrated, the copywriter, by training and temperament, is one of the keenest of communicators, then he should be in the forefront of the interpretation of the era of radical change.

This era can see great feats of urban renewal—intelligent, tasteful master planning for the land, which is still only slightly urbanized; growing accomplishment by the Job Corps and the Peace Corps and other contributors to The Great Society; the spread of abundance throughout the world and the breakdown of the barriers of language and custom; the conquest of physical and mental disease; the end of mind-sapping labor and the spread of universal, perpetual adult education.

But for all these feats to be accomplished, they will, at the same time, have to be communicated.

What an exciting future for the compleat copywriter!

ACKNOWLEDGMENTS AND CREDITS

All advertising copy is the result of a collaboration, and so is this book. I have many people to thank for help, advice, and cooperation.

First, my wife Marcy, for putting up with more than a thousand days and nights of discomfort while the book was written, and for reading every chapter aloud and keenly commenting.

Then Steuart Henderson Britt, my mentor and consulting editor for McGraw-Hill, who started me on the idea eight years ago, and kept taking my original outline out of his tickler file, to write, "How about now?" He finally sent me an urgent letter: "Joe Dooher, of McGraw-Hill, says he must have a book called *The Compleat Copywriter*. You've got to write it now or never."

I did not know at the time that Joseph Dooher, sponsoring editor, had never heard of my original title and outline, and had conceived the idea of *The Compleat Copywriter* on his own. Since that happy conjunction three years ago, Joe and Steuart have spent endless hours and have dictated dozens of letters nursing this opus along—so if you like the book, you can give them joint credit, and if you do not, I guess they must share part of the blame.

Next, I want to thank Mary Beth Baker, my secretary, who has typed and typed and researched and researched—manuscript, letters of inquiry, releases—all in between times doing her regular job as girl friday to a hyperthyroid creative director.

Hazel Conway, in charge of the Young & Rubicam library, deserves singling out for research and patience above and beyond the call of duty. Also J. E. D. Falby, film-maker par excellence, who turned his hand to jacket-designing; and J. Toto, for the jacket photo. And Liz Collins, my secretary *pro tem* in London, who helped me read proof and index.

The following were some of the individuals who gave me general encouragement and advice, or specific information: Allan Gardner of Anheuser-Busch; Minor (Toby) Raymond of Procter & Gamble; John Kelley, George Lenox, and Hank Cook of the Goodyear Tire & Rubber Co.; John Aberle of San Jose State College; TV expert Harry Wayne McMahan; Ted Gillette of *This Week;* David Reider of Doyle Dane Bernbach; Aaron Friedman of Display Mart, Inc.; Carl Rosenfeld of Walter Cribbins Co.; Dr. S. I. Hayakawa of San Francisco State College; Leonard Lavin of Alberto-Culver Co.; Herb Breckheimer, Ed Shaw, Harry Butler, Sid Marshall, George Kohlmann, Lou Heckmann, Walt Chamberlain, Pete Forsch, Joe Wilkerson, Mike Slosberg, Milton Monroe, Karl Vollmer, Charley Feldman, Hanno Fuchs, Steve Frankfurt, Jerry Darrow, Virginia Miles, Pat Steel, Jack Worth, Jack Morris, Fran Healy, Terry Pellegrino, Warren Bahr, Dick Baznik, Art Burdge, Wes Shaw, and Ed Bond—all of Young & Rubicam.

There were scores of other manuscript advisers, typists, editors, and aides: Mik Kitagawa and Pat Byrne, for advice on design; Jan Maakestad, Carolyn Carlton, Marilyn Ginoux, Doris Hara, my daughter Wendy, and Pat Black, for typing. And for reading and commenting on individual chapters: Bob Mayer, Norm Toback, Maison Clarke, Mike Robbins, Jim Molica, all of Young & Rubicam; Dalton Bishop and Gino Raffaelli of Pacific Outdoor; Hugh Smith of Western Outdoor Markets; Bob Stovell of Walter Landor Associates; George Hooper of the Bureau of Advertising; Henry Hoke, Jr., of *The Reporter of Direct Mail;* and Miles David of the Radio Advertising Bureau.

For specific material used in each chapter, I have had so many aides and accomplices that it would be more efficient to list them chapter by chapter:

Preface

Quotations from Dave Cleary, Sally Guthrie, Tom Lapham of Young & Rubicam, Inc.

Chapter 1

Permission to quote in this and later chapters from *Lyrics* by Oscar Hammerstein II, Simon and Schuster, Inc., New York, 1949.

Permission to quote from *Creative Advertising* by Charles L. Whittier, Holt, Rinehart & Winston, Inc., New York, 1955.

Permission to quote in this and later chapters from *The Art of Clear Thinking* by Rudolph Flesch, Harper & Row, Publishers, Incorporated, New York, 1951.

Permission to quote from an article in *Changing Times,* July 1963, The Kiplinger Washington Editors, Inc.

Permission to quote in this and succeeding chapters from letters to the author: Harry Hartwick, Copy Supervisor (retired), Young & Rubicam, Inc.

Permission to quote in this and other chapters from *Applied Imagination* by Alex F. Osborn, Charles Scribner's Sons, New York, 1963.

Permission to quote from a letter to the author: Dave Cleary, Vice-President and Account Supervisor, Young & Rubicam, Inc.

Permission to quote Prof. Wendell Johnson, from *Language, Meaning and Maturity* by S. I. Hayakawa, Harper & Row, Publishers, Incorporated, New York, 1954.

Chapter 2

Permission to quote from "The Language of Advertising" by William H. Whyte, Jr., *Fortune* magazine, September 1952.

Permission to use example of cliché campaigns: Sylvia Simmons, Vice-President, Young & Rubicam, Inc.

Permission to quote Leslie A. White, from *Language, Meaning and Maturity* by S. I. Hayakawa, Harper & Row, Publishers, Incorporated, New York, 1954.

Permission to quote from *Adventures of the Mind* 17, "How Words Change Our Lives" by S. I. Hayakawa, *Saturday Evening Post.*

Permission to quote from "Logic & Psycho-logics" by J. Samuel Bois, *ETC.,* September 1963: S. I. Hayakawa, Editor, *ETC.,* International Society for General Semantics.

Permission to quote in this and later chapters from *The Tyranny of Words* by Stuart Chase, Harcourt, Brace & World, Inc., New York, 1938.

Permission to quote from a letter to the author: John Blumenthal, Copy Group Head, McCann-Erickson, Inc.

Permission to quote in this and later chapters from letters to the author: Dick Lord, Vice-President and Creative Director, Warwick & Legler.

Permission to quote from a speech he gave: Leo Burnett, head of the agency bearing his name.

Permission to quote in this and succeeding chapters from *Synectics* by William J. J. Gordon, Harper & Row, Publishers, Incorporated, New York, 1961.

Chapter 3

Permission to quote from "Talkies" by Peter Bogdanovich, *Esquire* magazine, August 1962.

Permission to quote from a speech entitled "Changing Men's Minds": Prof. John T. Lanzetta, University of Delaware.

Permission to quote from a letter to the author: Prof. John Aberle, Marketing Department, San Jose State College.

Permission to quote from *Language in Thought and Action* by S. I. Hayakawa, Harcourt, Brace & World, Inc., New York, 1939.

Permission to quote from an ad about Jamaica: Jamaica Tourist Board and Doyle Dane Bernbach, Inc. (Ron Rosenfeld, Copywriter; Bob Gage, Art Director).

Permission to quote from a tape-recorded conversation: Robert Drew, Drew Associates, Inc.

Permission to quote from Cheer "Eye Witness" and "Supermarket" commercials: Procter & Gamble, Inc.

Chapter 4

Permission to quote from an ad about a portable television set: H. Unoki, Sony, Inc.

Permission to quote from an Underwood typewriter magazine ad: E. G. Zern, Geyer, Morey & Ballard, Inc.

Permission to quote from an ad for IBM Selectric Typewriter: Robert H. Hutchings, Advertising Manager, IBM Office Products Division and Benton & Bowles, Inc. (Paul Podgus, Copywriter; Thomas Ruriani, Art Director).

Permission to quote from a 4A's speech by Dave Garroway: Richard L. Scheidker, Sr., Vice-President, American Association of Advertising Agencies.

Permission to quote from a report of S. I. Hayakawa's and Rosser Reeves's debate about *Reality in Advertising, Advertising Age,* December 25, 1961.

Permission to quote from *My Life In Advertising* by Claude Hopkins, Harper & Row, Publishers, Incorporated, New York, 1927.

Permission to quote from a series of Zippo cigarette lighter ads: Jack Mc-Cutcheon, Advertising Manager, Zippo Manufacturing Co.

Permission to quote from a Volkswagen ad about torsion bars: Robert Fine, Doyle Dane Bernbach, Inc. (Bob Levenson, Copywriter; Helmut Krone, Art Director).

Permission to quote from a speech, "My Son, the Creative Director": James C. Nelson, Creative Director, Hoefer, Dieterich & Brown, Inc.

Permission to quote from a letter to the author: Stanley T. Burkoff, Vice-President and Creative Director, W. B. Doner and Company.

Permission to quote the caption from a cartoon by R. Weber, *The New Yorker* magazine, September 14, 1963.

Permission to quote from a Campbell's soup ad: BBD&O.

Permission to quote from a Lees Carpet ad: Doyle Dane Bernbach, Inc.

Permission to quote in this and later chapters from *How to Write a Good Advertisement* by Victor O. Schwab, Harper & Row, Publishers, Incorporated, 1962.

Permission to quote from an ad for Comet cleanser: Compton Advertising, Inc. (Jack Duern, Copywriter; Ben Quinn, Art Director).

Permission to quote from an ad for Scripto pencil: McCann-Marschalk Co.

Permission to quote from an ad for Betty Crocker Noodles Almondine: General Mills Inc. and Doyle Dane Bernbach, Inc.

Permission to quote from a letter to the author: Ed Reich, Copy Supervisor, Young & Rubicam, Inc.

Permission to quote from an ad, "The Extravagance of Rita Puotila": Dansk Designs, Inc. (Adrienne Clairborne, Copywriter; Louis Dorfsman, Art Director).

Permission to quote in this and later chapters from *Confessions of an Advertising Man* by David Ogilvy, Atheneum Publishers, New York, 1963.

Permission to quote from an essay by Prof. John R. Kirk in *Language, Meaning and Maturity* by S. I. Hayakawa, Harper & Row, Publishers, Incorporated, New York, 1954.

Chapter 5

Permission to quote in this and later chapters from a presentation to General Foods: Dermott McCarthy, Creative Director, Young & Rubicam, Inc.

Permission to quote from a White Owl ad: Joseph H. Vaamonde, Account Supervisor, Young & Rubicam, Inc.

Permission to quote from a letter to the author about the White Owl ad: Jack Reynolds, Copywriter, Young & Rubicam, Inc.

Permission to quote in this and later chapters from *Communications of an Advertising Man* by Leo Burnett, privately printed, Chicago, 1961.

Chapter 6

Permission to discuss the Candid Camera art of questioning: Allen Funt.

Permission to quote master brewer: Alvin Griesedieck, Falstaff Brewing Corporation.

Permission to quote from a G.E. portable TV ad: General Electric Company.

Permission to quote from a letter to the author about G.E. TV ad: Bob Higbee, Copy Group Head, J. Walter Thompson Co.

Permission to quote from a fashion interview about paint: Mrs. Frances Healy Geyelin, Chief Stylist, Young & Rubicam, Inc.

Permission to quote from *"Where Did You Go?" "Out." "What Did You Do?" "Nothing."* by Robert Paul Smith, W. W. Norton & Company, Inc., New York, 1957.

Chapter 7

Permission to quote from *Imagination* by Harold Rugg, Harper & Row, Publishers, Incorporated, New York, 1963.

Permission to quote in this and later chapters from letters to the author: Charles Sweeney, Associate Creative Director, Young & Rubicam, Inc.

Permission to quote from a letter to the author: Bill Lacey, McCann-Erickson, Inc.

Permission to quote from a letter to the author: Maury Flantzman, Copy Supervisor, Honig-Cooper & Harrington.

Permission to reproduce "doodles" cartoon: Jack Sidebotham, Creative Director, C. J. LaRoche & Co., Inc.

Permission to quote from a letter to the author: Judy Blumenthal.

Permission to quote from a tape-recorded discussion about Wine Advisory Board: Mike Slosberg, Copy Supervisor, and James McManus, Vice President and Account Supervisor, Young & Rubicam, Inc.

Permission to quote from a tape-recorded "brainstorming" about lamb: Dinalda McCrea Mansfield, J. E. D. Falby, Lou Heckmann, Helen Ennis Koreneff, Roberta Baily, Jane Worthington, all of Young & Rubicam, Inc.

Permission to quote from a letter to the author: Alexander (Pete) Peabody, Associate Creative Director, Young & Rubicam, Inc.

Chapter 8

Permission to quote from *The Elements of Style* by William Strunk, Jr., and E. B. White, The Macmillan Company, New York, 1959

Permission to quote from an ad about British Rail: J. H. Nunneley, British Railways Board (Toni Bird, Copywriter).

Permission to quote from an ad about Wolsey Vanity Fair: R. Bray, Wolsey Limited (Toni Bird, Copywriter).

Permission to quote from an ad for Oroweat Bread: Oroweat Baking Company.

Permission to quote from "How Language Shapes Our Thoughts," *Harper's Magazine*, April 1954.

Permission to quote from an article by Irving A. Taylor, *Advertising Age*, December 10, 1962.

Permission to quote comments by Hooper White, Film Director, reprinted in *Advertising Age*, September 30, 1963.

Permission to quote in this and later chapters from Crepe de Chine advertising and from a letter to the author about it: Delehanty, Kurnit & Geller, Inc. and Herb Green, Associate Creative Director, McCann-Erickson, Inc.

Chapter 9

Permission to quote from *On the Writing of Advertising* by Walter Weir, McGraw-Hill Book Company, New York, 1960.

Permission to quote from *Measuring Advertising Effectiveness* by Darrell Blaine Lucas and Steuart Henderson Britt, McGraw-Hill Book Company, New York, 1963.

Permission to quote from "Defining Advertising Goals for Measured Advertising Results" by Russell H. Colley, in *Evaluating Advertising Effectiveness*, vol. VII, The Association of National Advertisers, Inc., New York, 1961.

Permission to quote verbatims from Gallup & Robinson *Impact* magazine research: Goodyear Tire & Rubber Company (per Donn M. Tee).

Permission to quote from *The Spenders* by Steuart Henderson Britt, McGraw-Hill Book Company, New York, 1960.

Permission to cite in this and later chapters research and marketing methods of Alberto-Culver Company: Leonard Lavin, President, Alberto-Culver Company, Inc.

Permission to quote from a talk entitled "Into the Forest of Copy Research": Bob Mayer, Associate Research Director, Young & Rubicam, Inc.

Chapter 10

Presentation re Woman's Market cited: Mrs. DeNalda McCrea Mansfield.

Chapter 11

Permission to quote from an article about television by Arnold Toynbee, *The New York Times Magazine*, August 12, 1962.

Permission to quote from a Rubbermaid TV commercial, "Sound of Safety": Ketchum, MacLeod & Grove, Inc. (Art Ross, Copywriter and Art Director).

Permission to quote from a letter to the author about Chevrolet commercials: Kensinger Jones, Senior Vice-President and Creative Director, Campbell-Ewald Company.

Permission to quote from a letter to the author about sound track for Goodyear commercial: Norman Toback, TV Production Supervisor, Young & Rubicam, Inc.

Permission to quote a tape-recorded description of Kaiser Aluminum commercial: Paul Frahm, TV Art Director, Young & Rubicam, Inc.

Permission to quote from a baby powder TV commercial: Johnson & Johnson Company (Bill Schnurr, Copywriter; Steve Frankfurt, Art Director).

Permission to quote from complimentary letters reprinted in *The Triangle* about TV commercials: John P. Kelley, Advertising Director, Goodyear Tire & Rubber Company.

Chapter 12

Permission to quote from "The Crisis in American Magazines," *Barron's National Business & Financial Weekly*, February 4, 1963.

Permission to quote from a column, "Century of the Uncommon Man," by John Crosby, *New York Herald Tribune*, January 10, 1962.

Permission to quote in this and later chapters from articles in *The Reader's Digest:* The Reader's Digest Association, Inc.

Permission to quote from "Cutting Calories," *Time* magazine, May 15, 1964.

Permission to quote from "He Keeps an Eye on 2,300 Girls!" by Thomas Corwin Mendenhall II, *Look* magazine, June 2, 1964.

Permission to quote a G.E. toaster ad: General Electric Company.

Permission to quote from an ad about a Chrysler vehicle: Chrysler Corporation.

Permission to quote from ads about Gourmet Foods: General Foods Corporation (Stan Jones, Copywriter).

Permission to quote from an ad about Chevron Stations: BBD&O.

Permission to quote from *Best Advertisements from Reader's Digest* by Julian L. Watkins, Random House, Inc., New York, 1962.

Permission to quote from a 4A's speech by Charles Brower: Richard L. Scheidker, Sr., Vice-President, American Association of Advertising Agencies.

Permission to quote from a letter to the author about copywriting: George Gribbin, former Chairman of the Board, Young & Rubicam, Inc.

Permission to quote from a letter to the author about Löwenbräu beer: Onofrio Paccione, Vice-President & Creative Director, Leber Katz Paccione, Inc.

Permission to quote from a speech, "Nine Ways to Improve an Ad": Fred Manley, Vice-President and Creative Director, Carson, Roberts, Inc.

Permission to quote from *Typography* by Aaron Burns, Reinhold Publishing Corp., New York, 1961.

Permission to quote from Robert Pliskin, in *Printer's Ink*, June 14, 1963.

Permission to cite information on Xograph: Visual Panographics, Inc.

Permission to quote from an ad about Bantron: Wade Advertising.

Permission to reproduce part of the George Shearing ad for the Better Vision Institute: Doyle Dane Bernbach, Inc. (Leon Meadow, Copywriter).

Chapter 13

Permission to quote from commercial about Bufferin: Bristol-Myers Co. and Grey Advertising.

Permission to quote from *How to Use Radio to Sell Items:* Radio Advertising Bureau.

Permission to quote from *The Bells of Bicetre* by Georges Simenon, trans. by Jean Stewart, Harcourt, Brace & World, Inc., New York, 1964.

Permission to quote from a radio commercial about Ajax Cleanser: Colgate-Palmolive Co. and Norman Craig & Kummel, Inc.

Permission to quote from a radio commercial about Northwest Orient Airlines: Northwest Airlines, Inc. and Campbell-Mithun, Inc.

Permission to quote from a radio commercial about Goodman's soup: Doyle Dane Bernbach, Inc. (Paula Green, Copywriter; Jerry Kreeger, Production; Mitch Leigh, Music).

Permission to quote commercial about Cadbury Biscuits: Cadbury-Fry, Ltd.

Permission to quote from a radio commercial about Benson & Hedges cigarettes: Benson & Hedges and Benton & Bowles, Inc.

Permission to quote from a radio commercial about American Airlines: Doyle Dane Bernbach, Inc. (George Rike, Copywriter; Jack Hubler, Producer).

Permission to quote commercial about Peace Corps: Young & Rubicam, Inc.

Permission to quote Fuller Paint commercials: Campbell-Ewald, Inc. (Bob Pritikin, Creative Director).

Permission to quote baby powder commercials: Johnson & Johnson Company, Inc. (Jane Taylor, Copywriter).

Permission to quote from a speech about radio: Dallas Williams.

Chapter 14

Permission to quote from *Checklist for Copywriters:* Grant Stone, formerly Ad Director, *The Cleveland Press,* now Newspaper Advertising Consultant, Cleveland, Ohio.

Permission to quote from *How to Check Your Ads for More Sell:* Bureau of Advertising of the American Newspaper Publishers Association.

Permission to quote speech: Norman H. McMillan, N. W. Ayer & Son, Inc.

Chapter 15

Permission to quote from articles and cite numerous examples of direct mail case histories: *The Reporter of Direct Mail.*

Permission to quote from a talk about direct mail: Jack Shelton.

Permission to quote from *Planning and Creating Better Direct Mail* by John D. Yeck and John T. Maguire, McGraw-Hill Book Company, New York, 1961.

Chapter 16

Permission to quote from Garrett P. Orr, in *Printer's Ink,* July 22, 1960.

Permission to quote: Dr. Jaye S. Niefeld, Research Director, Campbell-Ewald Company.

Permission to quote from "Outdoor Advertising—the Modern Marketing Force": Outdoor Advertising Association.

Permission to quote from an article by Joseph T. Donovan, *Printer's Ink,* May 29, 1964.

Chapter 17

Permission to quote from articles and cite examples of point-of-sale case histories: Point of Purchase Advertising Institute.

Permission to quote from a speech about promotions: Harrison F. Dunning, President, Scott Paper Company.

Permission to quote from an ad about Awake: Birds Eye Division, General Foods Corporation (Gilbert Ziff, Copywriter; Sam Cooperstein, Art Director).

Permission to quote comments about label design: S. Neil Fujita, Creative Director, Ruder, Finn & Fujita.

Permission to quote comments: Walter Landor, Walter Landor & Associates.

Permission to quote package copy: Kellogg Company.

Chapter 18

Permission to quote from questions used in marketing research for Tang: General Foods Corporation.

Chapter 19

Permission to quote from *A Technique for Producing Ideas* by James Webb Young, Advertising Publications, Inc., Chicago, 1949.

Permission to quote from "Madison Avenue: The Big Invisible Sell" by Martin Mayer, *The Saturday Evening Post,* March 13, 1965.

Permission to quote comments by Bill Bernbach about copywriting, *Advertising Age,* April 5, 1965.

Permission to quote from a letter to the author about advertising: Fred Papert, President, Papert, Lois & Koenig.

Permission to quote from and cite in this and succeeding chapter "The Era of Radical Change," by Max Ways, *Fortune* magazine, May 1964.

Chapter 20

Permission to quote from *Innovation in Marketing* by Theodore Levitt, McGraw-Hill Book Company, New York, 1962.

Permission to quote from an agency house ad: Young & Rubicam, Inc. (Pat Steel, Copywriter).

Permission to quote from "For the Bell System, All Phones Are Ringing," *Business Week* magazine, January 9, 1965.

Permission to quote from "Taping Untapped Markets," *Time* magazine, February 19, 1965.

Permission to quote from "The U.S. Business Stake in Europe," *Newsweek* magazine, March 8, 1965.

Permission to quote: Gerard Piel, Publisher, *Scientific American.*

Permission to quote from the film, "On the Edge of Abundance": Rediffusion Ltd.

A SELECTIVE BIBLIOGRAPHY
FOR THE COMPLEAT COPYWRITER

Association of National Advertisers, Inc., *Essentials of Outdoor Advertising*, 1952.

Baker, Stephen, *Visual Persuasion*, McGraw-Hill Book Company, New York, 1961.

Berrien, F. K., and Wendell H. Bash, *Human Relations: Comments and Cases*, Harper & Row, Publishers, Incorporated, New York, 1951.

Britt, Steuart Henderson, *The Spenders*, McGraw-Hill Book Company, New York, 1960.

Britt, Steuart Henderson, and Darrell Blaine Lucas, *Measuring Advertising Effectiveness*, McGraw-Hill Book Company, New York, 1963.

Chase, Stuart, *The Tyranny of Words*, Harcourt, Brace & World, Inc., New York, 1938.

Diebold, John, *Beyond Automation*, McGraw-Hill Book Company, New York, 1964.

Flesch, Rudolph, *The Art of Clear Thinking*, Harper & Row, Publishers, Incorporated, New York, 1951.

Gordon, William J. J., *Synectics*, Harper & Row, Publishers, Incorporated, New York, 1961.

Hammerstein, Oscar, II, *Lyrics*, Simon and Schuster, Inc., New York, 1949.

Hayakawa, S. I. (ed.), *Language, Meaning and Maturity*, Harper & Row, Publishers, Incorporated, New York, 1954.

Hayakawa, S. I., *Language in Thought and Action*, Harcourt, Brace & World, Inc., New York, 1939.

Hopkins, Claude, *My Life in Advertising*, Harper & Row, Publishers, Incorporated, New York, 1927.

Hopkins, Claude, *Scientific Advertising*, Moore Publishing Company, New York, 1952.

Levitt, Theodore, *Innovation in Marketing*, McGraw-Hill Book Company, New York, 1962.

McLuhan, Marshall, *Understanding Media*, McGraw-Hill Book Company, New York, 1965.

Meyerhoff, Arthur E., *The Strategy of Persuasion*, Coward-McCann, Inc., New York, 1965.

Ogilvy, David, *Confessions of an Advertising Man*, Atheneum Publishers, New York, 1963.

Osborn, Alex, *Applied Imagination*, Charles Scribner's Sons, New York, 1963.

Rugg, Harold, *Imagination*, Harper & Row, Publishers, Incorporated, New York, 1963.

Samstag, Nicholas, *Persuasion for Profit*, University of Oklahoma Press, Norman, Oklahoma, 1957.

Schwab, Victor O., *How to Write a Good Advertisement*, Harper & Row, Publishers, Incorporated, New York, 1962.

Strunk, William, Jr., and E. B. White, *The Elements of Style*, The Macmillan Company, New York, 1959.

Weiss, E. B., *The Vanishing Salesman*, McGraw-Hill Book Company, New York, 1962.

Whittier, Charles L., *Creative Advertising*, Holt, Rinehart & Winston, Inc., New York, 1955.

Yeck, John D., and John T. Maguire, *Planning and Creating Better Direct Mail*, McGraw-Hill Book Company, New York, 1961.

Young, James Webb, *A Technique for Producing Ideas*, 6th ed., Advertising Publications, Inc., Chicago, 1949.

INDEX